# CURRENT PERSPECTIVES
## *in the*
# PSYCHOLOGY OF RELIGION

# CURRENT PERSPECTIVES
## *in the*
# PSYCHOLOGY OF RELIGION

*Edited by*

## H. Newton Malony

### WILLIAM B. EERDMANS PUBLISHING COMPANY

*Second printing, August 1979*

**Library of Congress Cataloging in Publication Data**

Main entry under title:
Current perspectives in the psychology of religion.

Bibliography: *passim*
Includes indexes.
1. Psychology, Religious—Addresses, essays, lectures.
I. Malony, H. Newton.
BL53.C79          200'.1'9          76-44493
ISBN 0-8028-1660-6

To
**LEE EDWARD TRAVIS**
Mentor, colleague, friend
Psychologist of religion—religious psychologist

# Contents

## THE RELIGION OF PSYCHOLOGISTS

# Preface

I have several goals in mind for this book. The first is to provide a current survey of various issues and approaches in the psychology of religion; the second to gather together and pay attention to the broadest range of contemporary viewpoints in the field; the third to show interrelationships between the psychology of religion and psychology in general.

All of the articles included in this collection have been published or presented within the last fifteen years. Therefore, while several authors review the history of the psychology of religion, in all cases the content is up to date and reflects present thinking. My intent was to be both comprehensive and current and, as such, I hope that the student will find this book a useful introduction to the field. Additionally, I believe that this collection will serve to complement other introductory texts, such as the ones listed at the end of this volume.

Perhaps the most unique contribution this book makes is in the section "The Religion of Psychologists." Here the objective was to set out in detail the relationship between choice of religion as a subject of study and the faith of the psychologist. It is well known that personal interest is a factor in scientific endeavor, and this is no less true when the subject is religion. As a Christian, I am convinced not only that my faith provokes my interest in the psychological study of religion, but also that it provides the basis for asking important questions. I hope this section will produce among students a concern for the issues that relate faith and scientific practice.

The material in this collection has been organized in such a way as to make it a useful foundation for undergraduate and graduate course work. The introduction to each section provides the student with a synoptic overview of the material presented. The author and subject indexes facilitate cross reference between sections. References, which are included at the end of each article, will lead the reader to additional material for study. An annotated bibliography of important studies is included at the end of the book.

Throughout this endeavor, I have benefited from the cooperation of the contributors to this volume. They are among those who are making the psychology of religion come alive again. Although most articles are printed *in toto,* some minor abbreviations have been made with the permission of the authors.

It is a pleasure to take this occasion again to publicly record my thanks to the publishers whose names appear in the acknowledgements at the beginning of each selection and whose help was indispensable to this venture.

I also wish to thank my secretary, Marsha Lucas, for her long-suffering assistance and Dean Neil C. Warren of the Fuller School of Psychology for his encouragement and support. May this volume stimulate interest and excitement in many future students of the psychology of religion.

H. Newton Malony, Ph.D.
Fuller Theological Seminary
Graduate School of Psychology
Pasadena, California

# Contributors

Gordon W. Allport, Ph.D., Harvard University (deceased)
Paul F. Barkman, Ph.D., Private practice in clinical psychology, Pasadena, California
Glen D. Baskett, Ph.D., Tuskegee Institute, Tuskegee, Alabama
Benjamin Beit-Hallahmi, Ph.D., University of Haifa, Israel
Peter L. Benson, Ph.D., Earlham College, Richmond, Indiana
David C. Bock, Ph.D., Associated Psychological Services, Pasadena, California
Donn Byrne, Ph.D., Purdue University, Lafayette, Indiana
Donald E. Capps, Ph.D., University of North Carolina, Charlotte, North Carolina
Walter Houston Clark, Ed.D., Andover Newton Theological School, Newton Centre, Massachusetts (retired)
John A. Clippinger, Ph.D., Baker University, Baldwin City, Kansas
James E. Dittes, Ph.D., Yale University, New Haven, Connecticut
William G. T. Douglas, Ph.D., Cape Cod Community College, West Barnstable, Massachusetts
David Elkind, Ph.D., University of Rochester, Rochester, New York
Craig W. Ellison, Ph.D., Westmont College, Santa Barbara, California
Robert A. Embree, Ph.D., Westmar College, LeMars, Iowa
Kenneth A. Feldman, Ph.D., State University of New York, Stony Brook, New York
David A. Flakoll, Ph.D., Rafa Counseling Associates, Pleasant Hill, California
Richard L. Gorsuch, Ph.D., University of Texas, Arlington, Texas
Joseph Havens, Ph.D., Shuttsbury, Massachusetts
Ralph W. Hood, Jr., Ph.D., University of Tennessee, Chattanooga, Tennessee
Richard A. Hunt, Ph.D., Southern Methodist University, Dallas, Texas
John P. Kildahl, Ph.D., Consulting Psychologist, New York, New York
Morton B. King, Ph.D., Southern Methodist University, Dallas, Texas
H. Newton Malony, Ph.D., Fuller Theological Seminary, Pasadena, California
Sam G. McFarland, Ph.D., Western Kentucky University, Bowling Green, Kentucky
Robert L. Pavelsky, Ph.D., Pacific Christian College, Fullerton, California
Paul W. Pruyser, Ph.D., The Menninger Foundation, Topeka, Kansas
J. Michael Ross, Ph.D., Associate Professor of Sociology, Boston University, Boston, Massachusetts
Victor D. Sanua, Ph.D., Professor, Department of Social and Psychological Foundations, City College of the City University of New York, New York

## Current Perspectives in the Psychology of Religion

James R. Scroggs, Ph.D., Bridgewater State College, Bridgewater, Massachusetts
Charles M. Spellman, Ph.D., Woods County Guidance Clinic, Alva, Oklahoma
Bernard P. Spilka, Ph.D., University of Denver, Denver, Colorado
John A. Stoudenmire, Ph.D., Mental Health Complex, Tupelo, Mississippi
Orlo Strunk, Jr., Ph.D., Boston University School of Theology, Boston, Massachusetts
Neil C. Warren, Ph.D., Fuller Theological Seminary, Pasadena, California

# HISTORY AND TRENDS
# IN THE PSYCHOLOGY OF RELIGION

# Introduction

H. NEWTON MALONY

Whence has the psychology of religion come? Where is it going? These questions lie behind a study of the past, an analysis of the present, and an anticipation of the future. The articles in this section consider all three issues.

Beit-Hallahmi not only describes the rise of the study of religion by psychologists but also explains its decline in the 1920's. He suggests that the time was ripe for a new scientific study of religion at the turn of the century but that interest faded toward the end of the second decade when, in fact, religion became one of psychology's taboo topics.

Strunk, likewise, surveys the central figures in the history of the movement and notes significant contributors during the 1930's and 1940's—a period which Beit-Hallahmi calls a "decline." In regard to the future, Strunk proposes a humanistic model which would emphasize the experiencing person. He suggests that this model is more in accord with the uniqueness of religion as a subject of study.

In the article by Capps, two of the central figures in the history of the psychology of religion, Freud and James, are compared. Freud was inclined to study the origins of religious behavior while James tended to investigate present religious experience. Capps points out the need for a unifying format which would study many dimensions of religion, ranging from beliefs to behaviors.

Pruyser concludes this section with a call for a reconsideration of the task of the psychology of religion. He uses the term "object relation" to describe persons' relationships to God. Thus religious behavior is similar in terms of psychological processes to all human efforts to make sense of reality. Therefore the psychology of religion must be concerned with validity issues, i.e., Is there a God? Is religion good or bad?

This portion of the book will give the student a sense of the place of the psychology of religion within the development of American psychology and will also provide a foundation for understanding many of the basic approaches and issues in the field today.

# Psychology of Religion 1880-1930: The Rise and Fall of a Psychological Movement

BENJAMIN BEIT-HALLAHMI

Allport (1950) pointed out the interesting change in the status of religion and sex as appropriate subjects of study among psychologists since 1930. Sex became a very fashionable area of research, while religion became a taboo subject. The relative lack of attention to religion as a subject of study did not always characterize mainline American psychology. During the last two decades of the 19th century and the first quarter of this one, American psychologists were the pioneers and the leaders of the "psychology of religion" movement (Pratt, 1908; Schaub, 1922; Schaub, 1924; Schaub, 1926a; Schaub, 1926b; Page, 1951). This article analyzes the rise and fall of the study of religion as a popular topic in American academic psychology, and suggests possible explanations and implications.

## THE MOVEMENT

Beginning in the middle 1890's books and articles dealing with religious behavior became a frequent and welcome sight on the American psychological scene. *The American Journal of Psychology,* and later *The Psychological Bulletin,* which started in 1904 (and since the first volume had regular annual reviews of the psychology of religion) published most of the articles and served as the mouthpieces of the new movement. The first empirical study of conversion was published by J. H. Leuba in 1896 (Leuba, 1896) and three years later the first book entitled *The Psychology of Religion* (Starbuck, 1899) was published. This title was to become very popular in the ensuing 30 years. In 1902 W. James published his epoch-making *The Varieties of Religious Experience* which gave another impetus to the movement.

Reprinted with permission of author and publisher from:

*Journal of the History of the Behavioral Sciences* 10 (January 1974): 84-90. Clinical Psychology Publishing Co., Inc., 4 Conant Square, Brandon, Vermont 05733.

Mormonism, and to some degree revival movements, became popular topics for application attempts, some of which were influenced by the growing psychoanalytic movement (e.g. Prince, 1917). Titles of articles dealing with religion became more and more ambitious, reflecting the confidence of their writers. Woolston (1902) dealt with "religious emotion"; Calvin (1902) tried to prove the "psychological necessity of religion" and Morton Prince took issue with the mainstream of opinions on conversion (Prince, 1906). E. S. Ames (1910), G. Betts (1929), G. A. Coe (1916) and J. C. Flower (1927) contributed one book each to the growing literature.

Schaub (1924), describing the movement, wrote: "In the psychology of religion American scholars were the pioneers; and they have throughout remained in the vanguard of progress" (p. 115). "When we consider such problems as conversion, revival phenomena, normal religious growth, or the influence of adolescence upon religious life, the American primacy is indisputable" (p. 117).

## THE LEADERS

As we study the literature of this era, four names stand out. Two of them are those who gave the theoretical impetus and practical encouragement: G. S. Hall and W. James. Two others did most of the empirical work and took over the leadership from the first generation: J. H. Leuba and E. D. Starbuck. William James is usually credited with most of the influence on the psychological study of religion in the U.S., following his *Varieties* in 1902. A closer scrutiny of the historical facts reveals that G. S. Hall was more instrumental in bringing about psychological studies of religion. Hall encouraged empirical studies, and his students J. H. Leuba and E. D. Starbuck were the real pioneers, publishing their studies in the 1890's before the "revival" caused by the publication of the *Varieties* in 1902.

J. B. Pratt, in an article published in the heyday of the psychology of religion, describes the development of "this growing branch of psychology" (Pratt, 1908). According to him, G. S. Hall is the guiding influence in this area, being the founder of the "Clark school of religious psychology." Early in the 1880's G. S. Hall began lecturing and writing on the "moral and religious training of children and adolescents" as part of his general interest in developmental problems. The publication of his article on the above subject in 1882 marked the beginning of the new movement.

Hall provided both encouragement for empirical studies as a teacher and testable hypotheses as a scholar. His interest in adolescence

18

brought about empirical studies of religious conversion, which became the most popular subject for such studies. Conversion was studied, among others, by Leuba (1896), Starbuck (1899), Coe (1916), Clark (1929) and Hall himself (1904). The pioneering journal established by G. S. Hall in 1904 under the title *American Journal of Religious Psychology and Education* appeared in four volumes from May 1904 until July 1911. It was then continued as the *Journal of Religious Psychology, Including its Anthropological and Sociological Aspects,* which was issued for three years, beginning with 1912, as a quarterly, but then only irregularly till 1915.

J. H. Leuba (1868-1946), the most active among Hall's students, was born in Switzerland and his European background affected his interests (e.g. Leuba, 1893). Studying under G. S. Hall, he graduated in 1895 from Clark University and then became a fellow there. Later he moved to Bryn Mawr College where he was the head of the psychology department. His numerous publications, most of them in the *Psychological Bulletin* (Leuba 1896, 1912, 1917, 1921, 1926a, 1926b, 1934), gave him the leadership position in the movement as long as it existed. At the international congress of psychology held at Grönigen, Germany in September, 1926, a session devoted to the psychology of religion was addressed by P. Janet, Ernest Jones, J. H. Leuba and R. H. Thouless (Leuba, 1926c).

E. D. Starbuck (1866-1947) was a student of W. James at Harvard, before moving to Clark University and studying under G. S. Hall. In 1890 he was stirred by Max Muller's *Introduction to the Science of Religion* and similar works and decided to start studying the area systematically. In the same year he presented a paper to the Indiana College Association, dealing with the study of religion. In 1893, at Harvard, he put out two questionnaires (or "circulars," as they were called then), one on conversion and the other on "gradual growth." According to James (1899) Starbuck's basic aim in starting his studies was to bring conciliation into the feud between science and religion. In 1894 and 1895 he presented papers to the Harvard Religious Union. After graduating from Clark, under G. S. Hall, he was a fellow there during the late 90's, together with Leuba.

Both Leuba (1896) and Starbuck (1897) published studies of conversion while at Clark, but Starbuck's study is better known. Starbuck's 1899 book *The Psychology of Religion* was based on the studies started at Harvard under James and continued at Clark, under Hall. Starbuck had the guidance and encouragement of both James and Hall in his work. E. S. Conklin was another member of the Clark school of religious psychology, graduating from Clark, under Hall, in

1911, and later becoming head of the psychology department of the University of Oregon. His book on *The Psychology of Religious Adjustment* (1929) was the swan song of the group's activity, together with the books by E. T. Clark (Clark 1929) and G. Betts (1929). J. B. Pratt (1907, 1920) can be regarded as one of W. James' followers in the study of religion. Most of the other writers in the area (Ames, Coe, etc.) may be regarded as "independent," since no other "school" can be described, in addition to the "Clark school of religious psychology."

## THE ZEITGEIST

In an article published in 1924 (Schaub, 1924), the rise of the movement was described in a way that gives us some insight into the *Zeitgeist* that produced it: "The dawn of the twentieth century witnessed the rise of a new approach to the study of religion . . . psychological investigations along strictly empirical and scientific lines" (p. 113). As we go back to Starbuck (1899) in the first book dedicated exclusively to the psychology of religion, this positivistic approach becomes even clearer: "Science has conquered one field after another, until it is now entering the most complex, the most inaccessible and, of all, the most sacred domain—that of religion" (p. 1).

Philosophy has always dealt with questions of belief and religion. Psychology as a legitimate heir and descendant of philosophy, took upon itself the chore of objectively studying subjects that formerly belonged to philosophy. The pioneers of the empirical-experimental approach to human behavior saw religion as a subject fit to study, and eagerly wanted to prove that even this area of study can be studied "scientifically." Great advances were being made in the sociology of religion and in anthropology. Studies of primitive religion by Frazer and Tyler aroused much interest and theorizing. Given this background, the pioneers in the movement felt that the time was right for a positivistic approach to religion in psychology. Another important factor was the basic positive attitude to religion, as reflected in the above quotation. Together with the faith in the scientific spirit, there was also a profound respect for religion as a human and social enterprise.

Following the traditional view of religion as something necessary to human society the references to religion itself in the writings of W. James, G. S. Hall, J. H. Leuba and E. D. Starbuck show this attitude of deference and reverence to basic religious dogmas. Publication of psychological articles in religious and theological journals shows the spirit of cooperation and contribution to religion that prevailed in the movement. Schaub (1924) claims that to the influence of the psychology of religion "may be traced much of what is most distinctive in the religious thought, as well as most fruitful and promising in the religious aspiration and procedure, of the past generation" (p. 114). The Hartford school of religious education of the Hartford Seminary Foundation held in October, 1926, a conference on "The possible contributions of modern psychology to the theory and practice of religion." J. H. Leuba read a paper at this conference (Leuba, 1926c) presenting his view of the contribution to the "progress" of religion.

Schaub (1924) discusses ten contemporary definitions of religion, which can best be described as "naive," e.g. Pratt's definition: "... an experience the form of which is determined by the inborn nature of the individual, but the matter, or particular content, of which is derived from his social milieu" (Schaub, 1924, p. 122). As late as 1907, as Schaub testifies, religion was described by E. D. Starbuck as a "regulative" and "governing" instinct, or a blending of a "cosmo-aesthetic" with a "teleo-aesthetic" sense.

## THE DECLINE

The rapid decline and final demise of the movement were reflected in the disappearance of the annual reviews of the psychology of religion field, published in the *Psychological Bulletin*. Since 1904, though more particularly beginning with its issue of June, 1909, the *Psychological Bulletin* had carried reviews of publications in the psychology of religion. The area of "the psychology of belief" was also covered in some volumes. The decline in the area was reflected in the fact that no reviews were published between the years 1928 and 1933. The last review (Cronbach, 1933) contained mostly material taken from German and French sources, showing the loss of interest in the area in the U.S. Since 1933 the term "the psychology of religion" has been rarely mentioned in the pages of the *Psychological Bulletin*, which once was the mouthpiece of the movement.

A survey on courses in psychology offered by undergraduate colleges, published in 1938 (Henry, 1938), showed the decline of interest in this area, compared with the previous decade (cf. Schaub, 1924). Out of 154 colleges surveyed, only 24 offered psychology of religion courses. Thus, a little over three decades after its birth, the psychology of religion movement was dead.

Douglas (1963) offered the following reasons for the decline:

1. The psychology of religion failed to separate itself from

theology, philosophy of religion, and the general dogmatic and evangelistic tasks of religious institutions.

2. In the desperate effort to be recognized as "scientific," there was an emphasis on collecting discrete facts, without integrating them into a comprehensive theory.

3. The use of data-collection methods and explanations was often uncritical and incompetent.

4. The climate of public opinion was changing, away from religion and towards a behavioristic and positivistic world view.

5. The study of religion was conflictual for both researcher and subject, because of their own personal investment in religion.

6. "Subjective" phenomena were avoided by developing social science, which tried to be "empirical" and "objective."

Strunk (1957) regarded the following factors as crucial:

1. Theological interest in the field introduced speculative and apologetic tendencies, which hampered advancement.

2. Psychoanalytic approaches to the study of religion attracted more attention and efforts, since they seemed more promising.

3. The influence of behaviorism led to the neglect of complex human behaviors as the focus of attention in academic psychology.

As illustrated above, the philosophical-mystical approach could not have gained much respect for the psychology of religion area among younger, and more critical, scholars. Despite the publication of several impressive empirical studies (Starbuck 1897; Leuba 1896, 1921; Coe 1916; and others), such a naive theoretical approach limited the impact of the movement on general psychology and separated it from the mainstream of academic research. Inside academic psychology in the 20's and the 30's, interest in religious behavior began to be perceived as evidence of unscientific orientation. The theoretical and ideological basis of the movement showed that the psychology of religion was basically a residue of the philosophical tradition in psychology. This was probably the most severe limitation of the movement, which ultimately caused its decline.

The contribution of psychoanalysis was a two-edged blessing to psychology of religion. On the one hand, it created interest and controversy. On the other hand, it never generated systematic research, nor did it penetrate academic departments. One of the reasons was Freud's historical-hypothetical approach (Freud 1913, 1939), which was followed by others. Another typical psychoanalytic approach to research was the use of anecdotal evidence and case studies. Psychoanalysis did not contribute to the acceptance of religion as a topic in American academic psychology, and it even added to the state of stagnation.

In addition to the reasons suggested above, some other factors can be identified. One is the growth and development of other areas of academic psychology that introduced new "fads" which won interest, energy and students. Another may be social pressure, or lack of support from the outside. The book by Thurstone and Chave (1929) signified a new stage in the development of social psychology and coincided with the decline in the psychology of religion area. Objective methods of attitude measurement gave a new boost to the area of studying social and political behavior. We would expect social psychology to incorporate the study of religious attitudes into its realm, and thus transfer the study of religion into a new stage. This did not happen.

The issue of social pressure is rarely discussed in connection with the psychology of religion. However, as Glock and Stark (1965) show, any serious systematic study of religion must be a threat to religious institutions. The threat posed by the psychology of religion movement was responded to by taking it over. The second generation of workers in the movement (such as Pratt, Coe, Ames and Johnson), as Strunk (1957) points out, were theologians first and psychologists second.

In giving a theological interpretation of the decline of the movement, Homans (1970) claims that this decline "coincided with the beginnings of both theological existentialism and psychoanalysis" (p. 99). These beginnings brought about a "shift in cultural modes of self-understanding" (p. 99). It is, of course, hard to determine whether the impact of the beginnings of both psychoanalysis and "theological existentialism" caused a culture-wide change in self-understanding. Another coincidence pointed to by Homans (1970), which is easier to prove empirically, is the one between the appearance of pastoral psychology and the decline of the movement. Homans also suggests that the pastoral counseling process is the heir to the conversion experience described by the psychologists of religion around the turn of the century.

It is suggested here that neutralizing the threat of the movement by taking it under the wings of religious institutions had a significant role in its decline and stagnation. No sinister, deliberate conspiracy is implied. The movement was not an unwilling victim, since its friendliness to religion was widely proclaimed. The whole takeover process was a rather natural one, a combination of inherent weakness and external pressure. Pastoral counseling is thus the natural successor to the psychology of religion movement.

Another important social factor that seems to influence psychologists is what is called here "the ivory tower effect." As early as 1921 (Leuba 1921, 1934) it was shown that scientists, and especially psychologists, are less religious than most of the American population. Recent studies show the same phenomenon (Stark, 1963). Since academic communities in general are less religious than most of the population, social scientists acquire the impression that religion is "neutralized" (Adorno et al., 1950). This misconception may have contributed to the declining interest in religion. Scientists in the 30's might have felt that the long war between science and religion was won by science, and there was not much left to study in religion.

## CONCLUSION

As the discussion above indicates, it was a combination of inherent, internal weaknesses, and the existence of outside pressures, which caused the decline in acceptability of religion as a focus for psychological inquiry. One possible inference is that the internal weaknesses, mainly the lack of a non-religious, non-philosophical theoretical bias, doomed the movement from its inception and caused its early death. At the same time, outside pressures, both within and without academic psychology, were considerable. The movement was obviously an easy prey, and its demise was quick and total.

Attempts to revive the field of psychology of religion are constantly being made, and gained some success in the sixties. An important lesson from the past movement may consist of asking the same questions in regard to present efforts. Any serious revival of the field will have to face similar internal weaknesses and similar outside pressures.

## REFERENCES

ALLPORT, G. W. *The Individual and His Religion*. New York: Macmillan, 1950.
AMES, E. S. *The Psychology of Religious Experience*. Boston: Houghton Mifflin, 1910.
BETTS, G. *The Beliefs of 500 Ministers*. New York: Abingdon, 1929.
CALVIN, S. S. The psychological necessity of religion. *American Journal of Psychology*, 1902, *13*, 80-88.
CLARK, E. T. *The Psychology of Religious Awakening*. New York: Macmillan, 1929.
COE, G. A. *The Psychology of Religion*. Chicago: University of Chicago, 1916.
CONKLIN, E. S. *The Psychology of Religious Adjustment*. New York: Macmillan, 1929.
CRONBACH, A. The psychology of religion. *Psychological Bulletin*, 1933, *30*, 377-384.
DOUGLAS, W. *Religion*. In N.L. Farberow (Ed.). *Taboo Topics*. New York: Atherton Press, 1966, 80-95.
FLOWER, J. C. *An Approach to the Psychology of Religion*. New York: Harcourt, 1927.
FREUD, S. *Totem and Taboo*. New York: Norton, 1950 (1913).
FREUD, S. *Moses and Monotheism*. New York: Knopf, 1947 (1939).
GLOCK, C. Y. and STARK, R. *Religion and Society in Tension*. Chicago: Rand McNally, 1965.
HALL, G. S. The moral and religious training of children. *Princeton Review*, 1882, *9*, 26-45.
HALL, G. S. *Adolescence*. New York: Appleton, 1904.
HENRY, E. R. A survey of courses in psychology offered by undergraduate colleges of liberal arts. *Psychological Bulletin*, 1938, *35*, 430-435.
HOMANS, P. *Theology After Freud: An Interpretive Inquiry*. Indianapolis: Bobbs-Merrill, 1970.
JAMES, W. Preface. In Starbuck, E.D. *The Psychology of Religion*. New York: Scribner's, 1899.
JAMES, W. *The Varieties of Religious Experience*. New York: Longmans, 1902.
LEUBA, J. H. National destruction and construction in France as seen in modern literature and in the neo-Christian movement. *American Journal of Psychology*, 1893, *5*, 496-539.
LEUBA, J. H. A study in the psychology of religious phenomena. *American Journal of Psychology*, 1896, *5*, 309-385.
LEUBA, J. H. *A Psychological Study of Religion*. New York: Macmillan, 1912.
LEUBA, J. H. Extatic intoxication in religion. *American Journal of Psychology*, 1917, *28*, 578-584.
LEUBA, J. H. *The Belief in God and Immortality*. Chicago: Open Court, 1921.
LEUBA, J. H. Psychology of religion. *Psychological Bulletin*, 1926, *23*, 714-722. (a)
LEUBA, J. H. *The Psychology of Religious Mysticism*. New York: Harcourt, 1926. (b)
LEUBA, J. H. Note on meetings and conferences for the discussion of the psychology of religion. *Psychological Bulletin*, 1926, *23*, 729. (c)
LEUBA, J. H. *Religious Beliefs of American Scientists*. Harper's, 1934, *169*, 297.
PAGE, F. H. The psychology of religion after fifty years. *Canadian Journal of Psychology*, 1951, *5*, 60-67.
PRATT, J. B. *The Psychology of Religious Belief*. New York: Macmillan, 1907.
PRATT, J. B. Psychology of religion. *Harvard Theological Review*, 1908, *1*, 435-454.
PRATT, J. B. *The Religious Consciousness*. New York: Macmillan, 1920.
PRINCE, M. The psychology of sudden conversion. *Journal of Abnormal Psychology*, 1906, *1*, 42-54.
PRINCE, W. F. Psychological tests for the authorship of the book of Mormon. *American Journal of Psychology*, 1917, *28*, 373-389.
SCHAUB, E. L. The present status of the psychology of religion. *Journal of Religion*, 1922, *2*, 362-379.
SCHAUB, E. L. The psychology of religion in America during the past quarter century. *Journal of Religion*, 1924, *4*, 113-134.
SCHAUB, E. L. Psychology of religion. *Psychological Bulletin*, 1926, *23*, 681-700.
SCHAUB, E. L. The psychology of religion in America. *Symposium*, 1926, *1*, 292-314.
STARBUCK, E. D. A study of conversion. *American Journal of Psychology*, 1897, *8*, 268-309.
STARBUCK, E. D. *Psychology of Religion*. New York: Scribner's, 1899.

## B. Beit-Hallahmi

STARK, R. On the incompatibility of religion and science; a survey of American graduate students. *Journal for the Scientific Study of Religion,* 1963, 3, 3-21.

STRUNK, O. The present status of the psychology of religion. *The Journal of Bible and Religion,* 1957, 25, 287-292.

THURSTONE, L. L. and CHAVE, E. J. *The Measurement of Attitude.* Chicago: University of Chicago, 1929.

WOOLSTON, H. B. Religious emotion. *American Journal of Psychology,* 1902, 13, 62-80.

# Humanistic Religious Psychology: A New Chapter in the Psychology of Religion

ORLO STRUNK, JR.

Despite arid times and periods of near eclipse, the psychology of religion has manifested a fascinating and strangely persistent style of survival. When William James elected to speak on what he called "man's religious constitution" as his Gifford Lectures at the University of Edinburgh in 1902, he could not have guessed that his subject matter would launch a discipline capable of attracting some of the keenest minds in Europe and America. Even recognizing the fact that there were several eminent scholars in the field before James's excursion— he himself acknowledged some of them in the Preface to *The Varieties of Religious Experience*[1]—it was undoubtedly James who set the stage and established part of the future pattern of the discipline. More important still, it was James who promoted the humanistic spirit which has tended to reassert itself whenever the field has been in danger of annihilation via insipid scientism.

## HISTORIC ASPECTS OF RELIGIOUS PSYCHOLOGY

Though this is not the place to offer a history of the psychology of religion—a feat not yet consummated by any contemporary scholar, although several prolegomena to a history are now available,[2] an historic sensitivity of a sort is needed if one is to see how contemporary humanistic psychology is both an innovational propulsion for the psychology of religion and at the same time a catalytic reminder to the discipline of some of its original intentions as established by its founder, William James.

When psychological science first glimpsed the possibility that

Reprinted with permission of author and publisher from:

*Journal of Pastoral Care*, 1970, 24(2), 90-97, published by the ASSOCIATION FOR CLINICAL PASTORAL EDUCATION, INC., in cooperation with the American Association of Pastoral Counselors, Inc.

religion, as the British anthropologist Sir James Frazer put it, could be approached "as phenomena of consciousness to be studied like any other aspect of human nature,"[3] an idea and a principle came forth which would mold a new discipline, potentially second only in boldness to Freudian psychoanalysis, which from its inception did not hesitate to examine religions and religious behavior. And like psychoanalysis, the psychology of religion's reception into the halls of the behavioral sciences was stormy, partial, and highly complex.

In the United States, where behaviorism already was beginning to get a throat hold on the psychological profession, the psychology of religion could be entertained only by a handful of eminent psychologists—G. Stanley Hall,[4] James H. Leuba,[5] E. D. Starbuck,[6] and, of course, William James.[7]

Hall was able to promote the field under the authority of not only his stature as the founder and first president of the American Psychological Association, but because he was also the chief administrative officer of an American university. Besides, he was not the kind of man to have an interest thwarted by the sniffings of scientific purists. Undoubtedly his personal interest in the field motivated him to pursue it with some vigor, although he himself recognized that his professional life was "a series of fads or crazes," and his interest in the psychology of religion was but one of many such excursions.

The case was different with James H. Leuba, who brought to the field an empirical zeal comparable to any contemporary behaviorist. Hiltner's evaluation of Leuba's contributions now appears a bit severe: ". . . unlike James, his general attitude to religion has been anti- rather than pro-. Indeed, Leuba was the earliest and most obvious reductionist among the psychologists of religion. Because of his scholarship, his works had to be taken seriously. But no one liked them except those whose attitudes also demanded a dethronement of all gods. Since this was the clear, and eventually the stated, purpose of Leuba's work, it is doubtful how much he may be considered interested in a psychological understanding of religion."[8] Despite Leuba's intentions, he represents another of the pioneers whose approach was severely conditioned by the *Zeitgeist,* in this instance reductionism.

E. D. Starbuck, on the other hand, felt the same pressures from all his colleagues as did Leuba, but he approached the phenomena with sympathy and insisted that the psychological study of religion was as legitimate a topic for psychologists as any other. The exact contributions of Starbuck have not yet been fully identified and appreciated, but there are reasons to believe that he was the first psychologist to use the term "psychology of religion," and this over the objections of his psychological colleagues who at the time felt that such an association could only lead to no good end.

In a real sense, these early pioneers stuck their intellectual necks out by expressing interest in religion. They became fair game for psychologists and theologians alike. But there was no stopping the interest that had been uncovered by these early workers, and in the early nineteen hundreds a moderately impressive line of psychologists and theologians began to do research and to write books. The movement took a firm hold in New England—especially at Boston University under the leadership of F. L. Strickland[9] and later Paul E. Johnson;[10] and it found further extensions on the other side of the Charles River in the text by Walter H. Clark[11] at Andover-Newton Theological School, and the important excursion at Harvard University of the late Gordon W. Allport.[12]

Since James, literally thousands of books and articles have appeared which legitimately might fall under the rubric "psychology of religion." One of the most recent bibliographies identifies nearly six thousand items in social scientific studies of religion,[13] many directly oriented in terms of traditional religious psychology. Add to this the excellent annotated bibliography of W. W. Meissner[14] with its nearly three thousand items and we see that the psychology of religion has produced a relatively impressive body of literature. Even acknowledging the fact that the applied areas of pastoral counseling and religion and mental health have greatly overshadowed the field, empirical and religio-psychological research in the area of religious phenomena continues at a rapid pace. Two very recent volumes, Joseph Havens' *Psychology and Religion*[15] and Paul W. Pruyser's *A Dynamic Psychology of Religion,*[16] demonstrate the current interests, the latter presenting approaches to religious behavior and experience consistent with much in contemporary clinical psychology and at the same time in keeping with the humanistic spirit of James.

## RESISTANCE TO PSYCHOLOGY

But throughout this somewhat fascinating development there has been a strange dynamic at work. André Godin has aptly characterized it as "eagerness for and resistance to the scientific psychology of religion."[17] Within organized religion there has been a vigorous interest in psychological insights and what they might reveal as to the nature of the religious sentiment. At the same time, there has been a cautious resistance to the field, especially to that type of "nothing but" psychology which tended to blanket the American scene during the behavioristic eclipse. And within psychology proper there has been an eagerness on the part of a surprising number of psychologists to study religion, especially by those comprehensive theorists who were convinced that psychology, if it is to be anything worthwhile, cannot neglect any aspect of man's behavior and experience. At the same time, psychology has resisted concerted attempts to treat the religious sentiment intensely and seriously, feeling, as Starbuck's colleagues did at the turn of the century, that such an association might taint the objective purity so cherished by much of the psychological community.

These historic and contemporary propensities are illustrated remarkably well in the phrase "psychology of religion" as contrasted with the term "religious psychology." In Germany the term *Religionspsychologie* is used extensively to describe the field known in America as the psychology of religion. Americans invariably and rightly translate the term *Religionspsychologie* as "psychology of religion," but their reason is not simply a linguistic predilection; the phrase psychology of religion suggests an objective commitment lost in the term religious psychology which seems to imply a religious stance of the psychologist. It is an interesting but telling artifact that we do not assume an industrial psychologist to be necessarily an industrialist or that a child psychologist is a child, but we are prone to think that a religious psychologist must surely be religious!

It has been argued that this seemingly irrational sensitivity has served to discourage irresponsible speculation on the part of workers interested in studying religious behavior. But it has also tended to delimit the subject matter tackled by the psychologist of religion, and most obviously it has devastatingly curtailed the methodological perspective and interdisciplinary mood of the religious psychologist. It is here where contemporary humanistic psychology holds forth hope for a deeper and more significant religious psychology of the future, one more in keeping with the earliest projections of men like James and Starbuck.

## HUMANISTIC PSYCHOLOGY AND THE PSYCHOLOGY OF RELIGION

The contemporary humanistic movement in psychology stresses an orientation which provides greater conceptual and methodological freedom than has been generally true in the history of American psychology. One of the leaders of the movement has suggested that the humanistic psychologist tends to be characterized by the following traits or tendencies:

—Disavows as inadequate and even misleading descriptions of human functioning and experience based wholly or in large part on sub-human species.
—Insists that meaning is more important than method in choosing problems for study, in designing and executing the studies, and in interpreting their results.
—Gives primary concern to man's subjective experience and secondary concern to his actions, insisting that this primacy of the subjective is fundamental in any human endeavor. . . .
—Sees a constant interaction between "science" and "application" such that each constantly contributes to the other and the attempt rigidly to separate them is recognized as handicapping to both.
—Is concerned with the individual, the exceptional, and the un-predicted rather than seeking only to study the regular, the universal, and the conforming. . . .
—Seeks that which may expand or enrich man's experience and rejects the paralyzing perspective of nothing-but thinking.[18]

Similar, but with even a broader scope, are the four characteristics espoused by the American Association for Humanistic Psychology, the professional organization which attempts to give identity to the new movement:

—A centering of attention on the experiencing *person,* and thus on experience as the primary phenomenon in the study of man. Both theoretical explanations and overt behavior are considered secondary to experience itself and to its meaning to the person.
—An emphasis on such distinctively human qualities as choice, creativity, valuation, and self-realization, as opposed to thinking about human beings in mechanistic and reductionistic terms.
—An allegiance to meaningfulness in the selection of problems for study and of research procedures, and an opposition to a primary emphasis on objectivity at the expense of significance.
—An ultimate concern with and valuing of the dignity and worth of man and an interest in the development of the potential inherent in every person. Central to this view is the person as he discovers his own being and relates to other persons and to social groups.[19]

Such intentions and sets—even recognizing the splinter-like nature of the movement—hold many potentially fruitful implications for the psychology of religion and for research in religion generally. For one thing, as has been noted, the psychology of religion has always been influenced directly by the *Zeitgeist* of the greater psychological community. As humanistic orientations become more and more a part of the climate of psychology proper, they, too, will influence the selection of research problems and the theoretical propensities of psychologists. Already, for example, one of the members of the humanistic group has recognized and critically prescribed the need for a new thrust in the psychological study of religion:

> A humanistic psychology of religion would not lose Tillich's depth dimension; it would not lose the heart of that which is religious in the name of ease of observation and measurement. In short, contrary to the present dominant positivistic *Zeitgeist,* the humanistic psychological study of religion would deal in whatever way it could with the subjective meaning of life—with that which is existentially valid. ... The traditional scientific approach to the psychological study of religion, one of the most important and ubiquitous characteristics of mankind, has not yet penetrated very deeply. It seems to me that the humanistic approach is more likely to probe the "inner man" because of its greater willingness to deal with the fullness of subjective experience via an all-encompassing phenomenology as opposed to a narrow, albeit more rigorous, empiricism.[20]

A second possible contribution to the enrichment of the psychology of religion, and one particularly relevant to scholars outside the psychological field itself, may be found in the promise of greater interdisciplinary involvement under the distended canopy of the humanistic orientation. In the past, the religious psychologist has tended to work exclusively within his own framework, drawing very little from the other sciences of religion and practically nothing from the humanistic disciplines. With the founding of the *Journal for the Scientific Study of Religion* in 1962, a bit more interdisciplinary sharing began; but the interdisciplinary activity of this movement has so far centered pretty much around the research of psychologists, sociologists, and anthropologists. The humanistic workers, the biblical scholars, religious educators, and the theologians have not generally been represented in any significant way.

One of the major reasons for the severe paucity of interdisciplinary research in the psychology of religion has been the tight conceptual framework of the psychologist of religion. Often controlled by a behavioristic bias, frequently motivated by a reductionistic wish, and sometimes intoxicated by a crass positivism, he has found it impossible to communicate with those disciplines which move outside the constellation of such assumptions — especially theology proper. Theology, including practical theology, has often recognized the potential contributions the behavioral sciences, including religious psychology, could make to its endeavors. But the conversations have been difficult and infrequent. The two communities have their own vocabularies and their own sets of assumptions. Even the psychology of religion itself, although frequently housed in the theological schools, has found it difficult to contribute significantly to the theological dialogue because its conceptual scheme and its research activities have seemed irrelevant or superficial or too far removed from the deeper meanings of the religious quest.

A few current tendencies, however, demonstrate that the interdisciplinary approach is possible and productive. The explorations at recent American Psychological Association meetings where psychologists and theologians have entered into dialogue;[21] the Gallahue Conference on Religion and Psychiatry where psychologists, philosophers, and theologians have considered the nature of the will;[22] the recognition of the contents of the journal *Archiv für Religionspsychologie* by a German theological journal;[23] and the very recent attempt of the Secretariat of the National Conference of Catholic Bishops to elicit information from non-theological disciplines, including psychology, in the study of Catholic liturgy — all signs that open conversations can fruitfully take place and may well be on the way.

A third result of the humanistic thrust may be the complete restructuring of the discipline itself. Traditionally, religious psychology has tended to walk a tight rope, carefully avoiding references to ontological questions and cautiously assuring everyone that it was descriptive only. Equally conservative was its preoccupation with religious experience, evading both the more "mundane" aspects of religion and also the more complex ones such as theological beliefs and systems.

Paul W. Pruyser makes this last point well when he writes that "the psychology of religion cannot confine itself to the private side of religious experience such as solitary prayer or mystical episodes, but must also come to grips with such public phenomena as theological treatises and liturgical processes."[24] He would have the psychology of religion attend to these objects using essentially *psychological* categories. With a similar motive at work, but within the framework of the history of religion, Erwin R. Goodenough makes an opposite sort of observation:

> To appraise the great body of religious data will demand that one rethink much of psychology, as one would have to do if faced with any other large body of unconsidered data. The business of the "psychology of religion" is not to fit religious experiences into the pigeonholes of Freud or Jung or into the categories of *Gestalt* or stimulus-response or any other, but rather to see what the data of religious experiences themselves suggest....[25]

At first glance, these two prescriptions may appear at odds, but both are making a plea for a reconsideration of perspective for the psychology of religion. And I would suggest that their claims be extended even further by insisting that religious psychology might also relate recent cosmological arguments to its concerns. For example, the brilliant statements of Pierre Teilhard de Chardin[26] and Sir Alistir Hardy[27] in regard to evolutionary patterns of understanding, the stimulating insights of M. Polanyi on the nature of the scientific enterprise,[28] the whole range of research being done in the discipline of world religions,[29] the recent tantalizing suggestions of Edward D. Vogt for what he calls "religionics,"[30] and the suggestion of Bernard Spilka that we consider the formulation of a "theological psychology,"[31] will need to be included in future work in the psychology of religion.

Undoubtedly, William James would be elated over the new possibilities for the future development of religious psychology, thanks partly at least to the humanistic stress beginning to be felt in psychology proper — a mood so characteristic of James himself. Just how influential this new liberalization in conceptualization and methodology will be in religious research remains to be seen. But certainly humanistic psychology has set ajar just a bit more the interdisciplinary doors and it now appears that a new chapter in the history of the psychology of religion is beginning to be written.

## NOTES

[1]William James, *The Varieties of Religious Experience* (New York, Longmans, Green, 1902).
[2]Cf. Orlo Strunk, Jr., *Readings in the Psychology of Religion* (New York and Nashville, Abingdon, 1959); and Chapter II of G. Stephens Spinks' *Psychology and Religion: An Introduction to Contemporary Views* (Boston, Beacon Press, 1963).
[3]James Frazer, *The Gorgon's Head* (London, Macmillan, 1927).
[4]G. Stanley Hall, *Adolescence* (New York, Appleton, 1904, 2 vols.).
[5]J. H. Leuba, *A Psychological Study of Religion* (New York, Macmillan, 1912).
[6]E. D. Starbuck, *The Psychology of Religion* (New York, Scribner's, 1899).
[7]William James, *op. cit.*
[8]Seward Hiltner, "The Psychological Understanding of Religion," in Orlo Strunk, Jr. (Ed.), *Readings in the Psychology of Religion* (New York and Nashville, Abingdon, 1959), pp. 74-104.
[9]F. L. Strickland, *Psychology of Religious Experience* (New York, Abingdon, 1924).
[10]Paul E. Johnson, *Psychology of Religion* (New York and Nashville, Abingdon, 1945, 1959).
[11]Walter H. Clark, *The Psychology of Religion: An Introduction to Religious Experience and Behavior* (New York, Macmillan, 1958).
[12]Gordon W. Allport, *The Individual and His Religion: A Psychological Interpretation* (New York, Macmillan, 1950).
[13]Morris T. Berkowitz and J. Edmund Johnson, *Social Scientific Studies of Religion: A Bibliography* (Pittsburgh, University of Pittsburgh Press, 1967).

[14]W. W. Meissner, *Annotated Bibliography in Religion and Psychology* (New York, Academy of Religion and Mental Health, 1961).

[15]Joseph Havens (Ed.), *Psychology and Religion: A Contemporary Dialogue* (Princeton, Van Nostrand, 1968).

[16]Paul W. Pruyser, *A Dynamic Psychology of Religion* (New York, Harper and Row, 1968).

[17]A. Godin, *From Religious Experience to a Religious Attitude* (Brussels, Belgium, Lumen Vitae Press, 1964).

[18]James F. T. Bugental (Ed.), *Challenges of Humanistic Psychology* (New York, McGraw-Hill, 1967).

[19]Charlotte Buhler and James F. T. Bugental, *American Association of Humanistic Psychology* (brochure) (San Francisco, American Association for Humanistic Psychology, 1965-66).

[20]Joseph R. Royce, "Metaphoric Knowledge and Humanistic Psychology," in James F. T. Bugental (Ed.), *Challenges of Humanistic Psychology* (New York, McGraw-Hill, 1967), pp. 21-28.

[21]Joseph Havens (Ed.), *op. cit.*

[22]James N. Lapsley (Ed.), *The Concept of Willing* (New York and Nashville, Abingdon, 1967).

[23]Wilhelm Arnold, "Die Religionspsychologie auf neuen Wegen," *Münchener Theologische Zeitschrift*, 1968, 19, 46-49.

[24]Paul W. Pruyser, *op. cit.*, p. 333.

[25]Erwin R. Goodenough, *The Psychology of Religious Experience* (New York, Basic Books, 1965) p. xi.

[26]Pierre Teilhard de Chardin, *The Phenomenon of Man* (New York, Harper and Brothers, 1959); *The Future of Man* (New York, Harper and Brothers, 1964).

[27]Alistir C. Hardy, *The Living Stream* (New York, Collins, 1965).

[28]M. Polanyi, *Personal Knowledge* (Chicago, University of Chicago Press, 1958); *Science, Faith and Society* (Chicago, University of Chicago Press, 1964).

[29]See, for example, Wilfred C. Smith, *The Meaning and End of Religion* (New York, Macmillan, 1963); and Erwin R. Goodenough, *op. cit.*

[30]Edward D. Vogt, "Religionics: A Neglected Approach to the Study of Religion," paper read at the 1968 meeting of the Society for the Scientific Study of Religion, Montreal, Canada, October 25, 1968.

[31]Bernard Spilka, "Conceptions of Man and Dimensions of Personal Religion," paper read at the Institute on the Psychology of Religion, Catholic University, Washington, D.C., June 17, 1969.

# Contemporary Psychology of Religion: The Task of Theoretical Reconstruction

## DONALD E. CAPPS

The psychology of religion has come to a fundamental impasse in its development as a science of religion. Most psychologists of religion consider the *theoretical constructions* of traditional psychology of religion to be too limited. On the other hand, the same psychologists tend to accept the validity of the philosophical assumptions which have undergirded the preferred *research methods* of the discipline. Indeed, a strong argument against the theoretical constructs of traditional psychologists of religion is that they are incompatible with the assumptions implicit in accepted methods of research. More precisely, the research assumptions manifest an expansive understanding of the psychology of religion while the traditional theoretical constructions reflect a restrictive view. Thus, the task now confronting the psychology of religion is to formulate a new theoretical stance more congruent with the philosophical assumptions which undergird its preferred research methods. I shall develop this general argument in the discussion which follows, focusing specifically on the psychologies of religion identified with Sigmund Freud and William James.

## FREUD AND JAMES: THEIR THEORETICAL CONSTRUCTIONS

The theoretical premises of both Jamesian and Freudian psychologies *as general psychologies* have been discussed in great depth. There have been numerous discussions of the broadly phenomenological perspective of James, the neopositivistic philosophy of Freud, and even one or two significant comparative studies of the two psychologies. However, as we address their psychologies of religion specifically, it is

Reprinted with permission of the author and publisher from:

*Social Research*, 1974, 41(2), 362-383, published by THE NEW SCHOOL FOR SOCIAL RESEARCH, 66 West 12th Street, New York, N.Y. 10011.

useful to talk in terms less broadly philosophical. The theoretical constructs of these psychologies of religion can best be discerned by posing the question: What, precisely, is the phenomenon which these psychologies of religion seek to explain? What is the focal object of their investigations? In general, the Freudian tradition in the psychology of religion takes the position that the examination of religion or religious experiences must begin at the point of their origins. The focal object of Freudian psychology of religion is the *origin* of religion, whether its origin in the individual life or in the prehistory of mankind. On the basis of their examination of these origins of religion, Freudians move to consideration of its development and its functions, but not before first attempting to establish the point of origin.

Freud's own considerations of the origin of religion centered on the Oedipus complex, on its emergence both as an infantile conflict (that is, the need to appease a potentially wrathful deity) and as a social phenomenon (that is, the totem meal instituted in response to the act of parricide committed by the primal horde). There has been much debate concerning this proposal that religion originates in the Oedipus complex. Even within psychoanalytic circles the possibility of a more fundamental point of origin than the Oedipus complex was being debated long before Freud's death. Indeed, Freud himself invited the debate when he entertained an argument, only to reject it, that there may be a more primordial origin of religion than the Oedipus complex. This argument was proposed to Freud by his patient and friend, the biographer Romain Rolland, who argued for "a sensation of 'eternity,' a feeling as of something limitless, unbounded—as it were, 'oceanic.'" In commenting on this proposal, Freud claims that it assumes the sensation to be "the source of the religious energy which is seized upon by the various Churches and religious systems. . . ." Freud acknowledges that he cannot convince himself of the "primary nature" of this oceanic sensation and, while he does not presume to deny its effect on other people, "The only question is whether it is being correctly interpreted and whether it ought to be regarded as the *fons et origo* of the whole need for religion."[1]

Here, Freud demonstrates his primary concern to understand religion by ascertaining its point of origin. Freudians may disagree with Freud concerning the precise nature of the origin of religion in human history and in the development of individuals, and these disagreements may have an enormous effect on the resulting view of religion, but they recognize the discernment of religion's point of origin as the foundation of the psychology of religion. Some have recommended that the origin of religion be traced to the mother instead of the father relationship. Erik

## D. E. Capps

H. Erikson, in his discussion of the ontogeny of ritualization, has suggested this on the individual level, while Erich Fromm, employing the *mutterrecht* theory of J. J. Bachofen, has made the same argument on the level of human history.[2] Hence, if origins are the focal object of Freudian psychology of religion, this reflects the theoretical premise that, without knowledge of the origins of a phenomenon, discussion of its development and functions lacks foundation.

As we shift attention to the Jamesian tradition, we find it considerably less inclined than the Freudian to investigate religion *qua* religion. The Jamesian is not particularly interested in religion as such, but in the "religious" as a property of other objects. This very preference leads to a certain blurring of the distinction between the "religious" and the "nonreligious." For example, as James E. Dittes points out, the so-called religious experience is not clearly differentiated from other experiences: "I can find no counterpart in James's thinking and certainly no warrant in his spirit for such notions as a distinctive religious sentiment or the idea that the 'peak experiences' are removed from other psychological functions and somehow of a different order."[3] As James himself expressed it, "As there just seems to be no one elementary religious emotion, but only a common storehouse of emotions upon which religious objects may draw, so there might conceivably also prove to be no one specific and mutual kind of religious object, and no one specific and essential kind of religious act."[4] Thus, the religious is no more (but no less) *sui generis* than any other property of phenomena. On the other hand, James is more interested in certain phenomena to which the adjective "religious" is attached than in others. Thus, while he resists distinguishing religious from nonreligious experiences, he recognizes experience at the individual level to be more fundamental than collective forms of experience. He writes:

> In one sense at least the personal religion will prove itself more fundamental than either theology or ecclesiasticism. Churches, when once established, live at second-hand upon tradition; but the *founders* of every church owed their power originally to the fact of their direct personal communion with the divine. . . . So personal religion should still seem the primordial thing, even to those who continue to esteem it incomplete.[5]

To be sure, the view that personal religion is primordial may be arbitrary, perhaps reflecting the psychologist's tendency to exaggerate the importance of the personal, solitary experience. James recognizes this: "Religion, therefore, as I now ask you arbitrarily to take it, shall mean for us *the feelings, acts, and experiences of individual men in their solitude, so far as they apprehend themselves to stand in relation to whatever they may consider the divine.''*[6] Nonetheless, to recognize this bias in favor of experience, such that the solitary experience becomes the focal object of psychology of religion, is not the same as drawing a firm line between religious and nonreligious experiences. Rather, it distinguishes between individual and communal forms of the religious. In short, the primary concern of Jamesian psychology of religion is not, as with Freud, the origin of religion. Its object of investigation is the solitary experience as the *sine qua non* of religion. And, if the solitary experience is the focal object of investigation, this reflects the theoretical premise that social expressions of the religious are derivative from individual experience.

However, if James and Freud adopt differing focal objects for their respective psychologies of religion, their theoretical constructs also manifest a certain degree of common agreement. In some respects, their objects of investigation are complementary. As Freud concerns himself with the *origins* of religion, and James recognizes the solitary experience as its *sine qua non,* it does not require a major departure for either perspective to incorporate into its theoretical construct the conceptual framework of the other. For example, James believes that the solitary experience constitutes the origin of religion as we understand it. Thus, he first traces the religious impulse in history to the solitary experiences of religious founders—Buddha, Jesus, Muhammed—then he considers the possibility that their solitary experiences point back to even more original sources of the religious sentiment. In so doing, he unwittingly takes up Freud's argument that religion originates in the "superstitions" of primitive tribes. He writes: "There are, it is true, other things in religion chronologically more primordial than personal devoutness in the moral sense. Fetishism and magic seem to have preceded inward piety historically—at least our records of inward piety do not reach back so far." However, James then defends his stress on solitary experience rather than fetishism and magic on the grounds that many anthropologists want to distinguish religion from magic, with fetishism and magic being construed as "primitive science" and personal religion marking the real beginnings of religion. He lets the matter rest at this point, noting that the "question thus becomes a verbal one again; and our knowledge of all these early stages of thought and feeling is in any case so conjectural and imperfect that further discussion would not be worth while."[7] In short, James's view of the solitary experience as the *sine qua non* of religion lends itself quite naturally to the *origin* view which Freud promoted.

With tacit approval from James, many Jamesians have taken a similar position when investigating the place of religion in individual lives. As even the most cursory reading of the works of Leuba, Starbuck, Coe, and other early Jamesians reveals, this tradition takes special interest in adolescent conversion experiences. Such experiences mark the awakening of individual religious consciousness. Prior to these experiences, the individual's religiosity was determined primarily by his social milieu. But, with the adolescent conversion experience, religion becomes "personal" and hence this experience marks the *origin* of authentic religion in individual lives. Thus, if Jamesians consider the grave danger in human history to be that man will revert to purely social understandings of religion (for example, Gordon Allport's "extrinsic" mode), the spiritual danger confronting the recent convert is that of reverting to his preconversion sentiments, which were socially determined.[8] In short, the move from understanding the solitary experience as the *sine qua non* of religion to the recognition of its role in the origination of religion is relatively modest.

Conversely, the Freudian interest in the *origin* of religion lends itself to the *sine qua non* view. If the Oedipus complex stands at the beginning of all religion, individual and historical, then the conclusion that it is also the *sine qua non* of religion is virtually inescapable. Indeed, there is no other logical reason for Freud's rejection of the "oceanic feeling" as a source of religion even while acknowledging that something of the sort has been experienced by many people. In his view, religion cannot have more than one source:

> I cannot think of any need in childhood as strong as the need for a father's protection. Thus the part played by the oceanic feeling, which might seek something like the restoration of limitless narcissism, is ousted from a place in the foreground. The origin of the religious attitude can be traced back in clear outlines as far as the feeling of infantile helplessness. There may be something further behind that, but for the present it is wrapped in obscurity. *I can imagine that the oceanic feeling became connected with religion later on.* The "oneness with the universe" which constitutes its ideational content sounds like a first attempt at a religious consolation. . . .[9]

In other words, the oceanic feeling must either have preceded or succeeded the feeling of infantile helplessness; it could not have paralleled it because there can be only one source of religion. Hence, the oceanic feeling must be derivative. And, if the Oedipus complex is understood as the sole origin of religion, it must also be its *sine qua non*, for how can it possibly be said that there was a time when religion lacked its *sine qua non*? The *sine qua non* must have been part of religion from its inception.

In short, the Jamesian and Freudian theories have much in

common. Significant parallels exist between the *origin* and *sine qua non* theories of religion. Both tend toward a unidimensional view of religion inasmuch as both attempt to isolate its essential element. That they isolate different elements—the Oedipal event and the solitary experience of the divine—militates against efforts to finally harmonize the two positions. But the fundamental theoretical difficulty is their common assumption that the object of inquiry is a singular phenomenon. This difficulty lies at the heart of any effort toward theoretical reconstruction in the psychology of religion.

## FREUD AND JAMES: THEIR METHODS OF RESEARCH

The second major issue in contemporary appraisals of traditional psychology of religion is research methodology. In addressing this issue, I should like to center attention on the philosophical assumptions which undergird the research methodologies of the two traditions. These philosophical assumptions lend themselves to discussion under two general headings: (1) the idiographic mode and the question of importance; and (2) the development of an empiricism appropriate to the multidimensionality of religion.

*The Idiographic Mode and the Question of Importance.* Gordon W. Allport, a major representative of the Jamesian tradition, popularized the distinction made by the German philosopher Wilhelm Windelband between *nomothetic* and *idiographic* forms of knowledge. These terms refer to the fact that, as Allport expresses it, "the human mind is capable of two modes of interest and attention, either or both of which it may employ in relation to the complex universe of surrounding events. The mind may classify its experience and contemplate the general principles that emerge, or it may be concerned with the individual happening or single event confronting it."[10] Allport acknowledges that the prevailing bias in psychological science is the former, nomothetic mode, but he argues that the idiographic mode deserves priority in psychological research, and this for the simple reason that:

> In psychology, the font and origin of our curiosity in, and knowledge of, human nature, lies in our acquaintance with concrete individuals. To know them in their natural complexity is an essential first step. Starting too soon with analysis and clarification, we run the risk of tearing mental life into fragments and beginning with false cleavages that misrepresent the salient organizations and natural integrations in personal life.[11]

Thus, the idiographic mode is a necessary first step not only in the obvious sense that it provides acquaintance with the concrete before the general, but also because it initiates the integrative process which the

**41**

nomothetic mode then takes up and expands. The idiographic mode is not limited to the study of discrete entities wrenched from their environmental setting; on the contrary, it examines these objects in their situational complexities.

In a passage in *The Varieties of Religious Experience* from which Allport quotes, James makes somewhat the same distinction between idiographic and nomothetic modes of investigation. However, he distinguishes the two modes not in terms of logical or temporal priority (that is, that one must be familiar with the concrete before one makes generalizations) but in terms of their "importance" to the researcher. Objects which are important to us lend themselves more naturally to the idiographic mode. As James illustrates this notion of importance:

> The first thing the intellect does with an object is to class it along with something else. But any object that is infinitely important to us and awakens our devotion feels to us also as if it must be *sui generis* and unique. Probably a crab would be filled with a case of personal outrage if he could hear us class it without ado or apology as a crustacean and thus dispose of it. "I am no such thing," it would say; "I am myself, myself alone."[12]

Hence, if the focal object of our research is important to us, even awakens our devotion, we are liable to carry out our investigations in the idiographic mode.

James's own psychology of religion was firmly established in the idiographic mode. If he allowed himself to generalize, especially as illustrated in his penchant for typologies, these generalizations were modest extrapolations from scores of concrete cases. And, as evidence that "importance" was a major determinant in his choice of the idiographic mode (he did not use the idiographic mode in his philosophical works), it is frequently observed that he included his own case history in his discussion of "the sick soul." His account of a state "of the worst kind of melancholy" purportedly reported to him by a young Frenchman is undoubtedly autobiographical.[13] In a footnote to the account by this "French" sufferer, James makes reference to a similar case of sudden fear experienced by his own father, Henry James, Sr. Hence, this case of the "sick soul" had importance to James not only because it concerned his own experience of spiritual panic but also because his father had earlier reported a very similar experience. In short, James's psychology of religion exemplifies the researcher's investment in the focal object of research. The difference between this philosophy of research and most psychological research which emphasizes the neutrality of the researcher is quite apparent.

As we turn to Freud's use of the idiographic mode in his psychology of religion, we encounter a difficulty. Paul W. Pruyser puts the problem well when he notes the discrepancy between Freud's practice of basing his general psychology on case materials and his reluctance to follow the same procedure in his psychology of religion:

> It has always impressed me that Freud in his published work seems to have shirked the individual approach in seeking answers to his questions about religion. He never published a full-fledged case study that focused on the dynamics of religion in the life of a person. . . . Though he said much about the cognitive process in religion in *The Future of an Illusion,* he did not make individual applications but spoke only globally of "believers" or "the faithful." Even if some of the clinical case studies he published contain remarks and observations about the patients' religious behavior, they are at best secondary to his purpose of presenting syndromes, symptoms, and dynamics.[14]

Pruyser notes the fact that Freud's comments on Schreber's autobiography may come close to what we have described as the idiographic mode. But, while "Freud noted many odd religious ideas and showed an interest in tracing their psychodynamic reasons and origins . . . this is still far from coming to grips with the origins of belief in God and the dynamics of faith in Schreber's life."[15]

That Freud neglected the idiographic mode in much of his psychology of religion is true. However, an important qualification of this judgment must be made, and this precisely in terms of the matter of importance. As David Bakan has shown in his controversial book *Sigmund Freud and the Jewish Mystical Tradition,* the biblical Moses played a role in Freud's life commensurate with James's description of an object of intimate importance to the researcher.[16] Among his four book-length studies of religion, *Moses and Monotheism* stands out as Freud's most idiographic treatment of the subject of religion. That it was also the last book he wrote lends weight to the argument for Moses's importance to him. Most significantly, however, the biblical story of Moses concerns the origin of personal religion among the Jews. Hence, in turning to the figure of Moses, Freud was addressing the origin of his own cultural tradition and, as Bruno Bettelheim argues, the figure of Moses loomed large in Freud's argument that religion in general is traceable to the father image.[17]

In short, interpreters of Freud agree that his interest in Moses carried well beyond scientific curiosity. But even if this were not the case, the element of importance has figured prominently in Freudian psychology of religion since Freud. Recognizing Erik H. Erikson's considerable influence on psychoanalytic psychology of religion, Pruyser enumerates the more important aspects of Erikson's approach as exemplified in his classic study of Luther. Interestingly enough, Erikson's use of the idiographic mode, followed immediately by the matter of importance, stands at the head of Pruyser's eight-point enumeration. Thus: "1. The case study method is superb in showing how religion 'fits' into the rest of life. 2. Any writer's personal equation on religion, being a unique perspective, is a powerful determinant in the discovery and selection of relevant data."[18] Notice that Pruyser's first point emphasizes not only the "single case" method but also the object's embeddedness in its situational complexity. And, as to his second point, the importance of the subject to the researcher, Erikson's own comment concerning his decision to write about Luther is especially apropos: "My choice of subject forces me to deal with problems of faith and problems of Germany, two enigmas which I could have avoided by writing about some other great man. But it seems that I did not wish to avoid them."[19]

In short, the psychology of religion, unlike much psychology in general, manifests a decided preference for the idiographic mode of investigation. This preference has been influenced in no small degree by the fact that individual psychologists of religion have identified the focal objects of their research according to their importance to the researcher. Whatever the theoretical weaknesses of Freud's psychology of religion, there is little doubt that "origins" held unique attraction for him. And, whatever the theoretical limitations of James's psychology of religion, it is evident that the "solitary experience" was of great undergirding interest. Thus, one major philosophical assumption undergirding the research methods of the psychology of religion is its preference for the idiographic mode, a mode selected in large part because the discipline was shaped from its inception by research problems having profound importance in the lives of its own founders.

*The Development of an Empiricism Appropriate to the Multidimensionality of Religion.* A second major philosophical assumption undergirding the research methods in the psychology of religion has been its broadly conceived empirical base. This broadly construed empiricism has been evident in two important ways: in the willingness of psychologists of religion to employ an array of research methods and in their reluctance to draw a firm line between "religious" and nonreligious" phenomena. Regarding the former, it is significant that, while the objects of investigation have been quite narrowly conceived, the research methods employed in examining these objects have been extremely wide ranging. Data have been derived from a great variety of sources, from literary documents, historical texts, dream materials, autobiographical writings, case-study materials, myths and folklore, and various philosophical works. This very range of materials has given the psychology of religion a rather chaotic appearance in comparison to other disciplines within psychology. There is, however, a significant reason for the wide variety of research methods employed in the psychology of religion. The questions which psychologists of religion raise rarely admit of easily accessible answers. This may be due to their importance to the researcher; perhaps the elusiveness of answers is directly proportional to their importance to the researcher. Whatever the explanation, it is a simple fact that the origin of religion and the solitary experience are extremely elusive objects of investigation. By nature, origins are neither immediately visible nor self-evident. As Freud points out, they need to be reconstructed from surviving evidence, and such reconstructive work is necessarily risky. That the search for the origins of religion in the human psyche is promised any success at all is due to the fact that, as Freud contends, "in mental life nothing which has once been formed can perish . . . everything is somehow preserved and . . . in suitable circumstances (when, for instance, regression goes back far enough) it can once more be brought to light."[20]

Similarly, the investigation of solitary experience in the effort to elucidate the "religious" requires the researcher to attend to phenomena which, virtually by definition, resist direct observation. Consider James's description of his own solitary experience:

> Whilst in this state of philosophic pessimism and general depression of spirits about my prospects, *I went one evening into a dressing-room in the twilight,* to procure some article that was there; when suddenly there fell upon me without any warning, just as if it came out of the darkness, a horrible fear of my own existence. . . . It was like a revelation; and although the immediate feelings passed away, the experience has made me sympathetic with the morbid feelings of others ever since. . . .[21]

The elusiveness of this experience is also apparent in Henry James, Sr.'s account of his experience:

> One day . . . towards the close of May, having eaten a comfortable dinner, *I remained sitting at the table after the family had disappeared,* idly gazing at the embers in the grate, thinking of nothing, and feeling only the exhilaration incident to a good digestion, when suddenly—in a lightning flash as it were—fear came upon me and trembling, which made all my bones to shake.[22]

In both cases, we have an experience observed by no one but the sufferer himself, and in neither case does the sufferer attest to any outward behavioral manifestation accompanying his "inner" torment.

On the other hand, the real problem facing the investigator here (as in the case of Freud's "survivals") is not primarily the fact that the experience is unobservable. For, in another sense, these experiences are observable inasmuch as both sufferers were capable of articulating their experiences. Rather, it would seem that the deeper problem the investigator faces is that of identifying the "religious" quality of these experiences. Is the religious element in the momentary sense of terror, in the sympathy for others which the experience evokes, in the unhappy reflections which preceded and perhaps triggered the episode, or in the sense that the "fear" came from outside oneself? If we answer this question by saying that the religious element cannot be so readily isolated from other aspects of the experience, then we are confronted with the next logical question: In what sense is there any meaning in the distinction between religious and nonreligious phenomena? This raises the second implication of the broadly conceived empirical base of the psychology of religion, namely, its reluctance to draw a firm line between the religious and nonreligious.

That the Freudian and Jamesian traditions resist firm distinctions between the religious and nonreligious may seem, at first glance, incongruous. Freud's attacks on religion would appear to indicate that he had no hesitation in recognizing a clear distinction between religion and other cultural forms. There is no denying the fact that Freud makes formal distinctions between religion, art, and science, and that these distinctions do not admit of much blurring of lines separating these three cultural phenomena. However, when we look closely at his actual statements concerning religion, we discover a reluctance to make any hard and fast differentiation between religion and other products of culture. The reason for this reluctance is his underlying conviction that all achievements of culture can be traced to the same point of origin: "I have tried to show that religious ideas have arisen from the same need as have all the other achievements of civilization: from the necessity of defending oneself against the crushingly superior force of nature."[23] And, if these achievements of civilization finally originate from the same need, they continue to remain interrelated even as they develop their own peculiar forms:

> No feature, however, seems better to characterize civilization than its esteem and encouragement of man's higher mental activities—his intellectual, scientific and artistic achievements—and the leading role that it assigns to ideas in human life. Foremost among these ideas are the religious systems, on whose complicated structure I have endeavored to throw light elsewhere. Next come the speculations of philosophy; and finally what might be called man's "ideals"—his ideas of a possible perfection of individuals, or of peoples or of the whole of humanity, and the demands he sets up on the basis of such ideas. *The fact that these creations of his are not independent of one another, but are on the contrary*

*closely interwoven, increases the difficulty not only of describing them but of tracing their psychological derivation.* [24]

Here, Freud rejects the notion that religious ideas and systems are *sui generis;* they have the same motivating force as all other cultural achievements.

Now, it could be argued that these statements are merely evidence of Freud's "reductionistic" view of religion—that is, that religion can be reduced to its motivating forces. However, this argument does not obviate the fact that, even in its fully developed manifestations, religion is difficult to distinguish from other cultural forms. The reason for this is, quite simply, that these modes of thought and action are not independent of one another but are closely interwoven. Thus, the fact that they are closely interwoven leads Freud to prefer to investigate the general "process of civilization," to identify the task of the psychologist as that of demonstrating the continuities between the libidinal development of the individual and the total process of civilization, and thus relieving the psychologist of the task of relating individual development to constituent parts of the civilization process.

We have already noted James's theoretical position on this issue. Dittes expresses this position quite succinctly when he observes that James "sets up no boundaries marking religion off from other experience." [25] But, in addition to his theoretical views concerning the *sui generis* argument, there is another basis for his reluctance to make clear distinctions between the "religious" and "nonreligious" in his research. As Dittes also notes, James resisted the distinction between religious experiences and their presumably nonreligious determinants. To be sure, James was considerably more interested in the "outcome" of a solitary experience than in its determinants; what mattered to James was whether an experience led to the release of creative industry, acts of sympathy, cognitive clarity, and the like. On the other hand, James had no interest in disparaging determinants and motivating forces. That "higher experiences" may have their roots in ordinary needs, even pathological temperaments, does not in the least invalidate the experiences. James's own experience in the dressing room was triggered by a general depression concerning his professional prospects. On the basis of his own experience, therefore, he found little reason to distinguish the "religious" experience from its "nonreligious" determinants. There is no such gap between the "higher experiences" and the experiences which precipitate them. It is more accurate to talk in terms of a complex of meanings in which the experience in the dressing room is part of a close interweaving of experiences, sentiments, anticipations, outward events, and the like.

In the final analysis, therefore, there is a congruence between the broadly construed empiricism of the psychology of religion and its resistance to the narrow compartmentalization of religion or the religious. The very elusiveness of its object of investigation requires a flexibility and openness concerning the nature and scope of the religious. However, more important than the mere fact of this expansive understanding of religion and the religious, is the further implication that religion must be approached as a constituent in a total complex of meaning. The religious is not elusive because it lurks behind ordinary phenomena but because it is woven into these phenomena. This interwovenness suggests that no ordinary phenomenon can necessarily be ruled out as the bearer of religious meaning, nor can it automatically be relegated to derivative status. Origins and solitary experiences may have impressed Freud and James as especially vital forms of the religious, but the assumptions underlying their research methods suggest that religion or the religious is multidimensional, feeding into all aspects of human existence.

This leads us to the final point in the argument being developed in this paper. If we take seriously the philosophical assumptions undergirding its research methods, the psychology of religion cannot limit its object of inquiry to origins and solitary experiences—events which have special psychological salience. Rather, its object of investigation is the very multidimensionality of religion which its research methods assume but which its traditional theoretical constructs undermine. If it is appropriate to talk about limitations on the range and scope of research in the psychology of religion, this limitation comes not at the level of theoretical construction but at the level of research methodology. Thus, on the one hand, the philosophical assumptions undergirding research in the psychology of religion point toward a broadly construed empiricism commensurate with the multidimensionality of the object of research. On the other hand, the psychologist of religion prefers the idiographic mode, and this suggests that the questions he chooses to address within these larger dimensions will be determined both by their importance to the researcher and by their accessibility to research centered on the individual case. The necessary limitations placed on the discipline are therefore determined by the idiographic mode, not by the object of investigation.

## THE MULTIDIMENSIONALITY OF RELIGION: TOWARD A NEW THEORETICAL CONSTRUCT

But how are we to understand the multidimensionality of religion? How is it to be understood as the object of inquiry? As an object of investigation, the multidimensionality of religion establishes certain boundaries around the discipline, not for the purpose of limiting its range of inquiry but in order to shape this inquiry. The expansiveness of the inquiry is assumed; the intention of recognizing an object of inquiry, even one as inclusive as the multidimensionality of religion, is to provide this expansiveness a certain formal cohesion. Thus, Clifford Geertz proposes that religion now be construed in terms of "socially available 'systems of significance'—beliefs, rites, meaningful objects— in terms of which subjective life is ordered and outward behavior guided." But how does one begin to identify these systems of significance? Geertz suggests that one does not begin with the task of defining religion, sorting out religion from superstition, magic, philosophy, custom, folklore, myth, ceremony, etc. Rather, the task is more akin to beginning in a fog and trying to clear it.

> One can begin with an assortment of phenomena almost everyone but the professionally contrary will regard as having something vaguely to do with "religion" and seek for what it is that leads us to think so, what it is that leads us to think that these rather singular things certain people do, believe, feel, or say somehow belong together with sufficient intimacy to submit to a common name. . . . We look not for a universal property—"sacredness" or "belief in the supernatural," for example—that divides religious phenomena off from nonreligious ones with Cartesian sharpness, but for a system of concepts that can sum up a set of inexact similarities, which are yet genuine similarities, we sense to inhere in a given body of material. We are attempting to articulate a way of looking at the world, not to describe an unusual object.[26]

Here, Geertz proposes that we think about and perceive religion as a system or structure of meaning which is based not on the dichotomization of religion and nonreligion but on the pattern which religion, in spite of its diffuseness, its multiplicity, presents to the observer as he begins to clear away the fog. Some distinctions must of course be made as one begins to discern the system of significance. The various dimensions of the system come into focus, and these dimensions begin to constitute the shape of the total configuration. These dimensions are not exclusive but inclusive; they give texture to an otherwise undifferentiated though related mass of experiences, sensations, thoughts, attitudes, activities, etc. As the clearing of the fog proceeds, it may be possible to isolate and actually name various dimensions of religion.

**49**

Attempts of this sort have been made by sociologists, anthropologists, and historians of religion. The psychologist of religion might contribute to such efforts. For example, extrapolating on the efforts of the historian of religions, Ninian Smart, I have found useful a six-dimensional schema which, taken *in toto,* addresses virtually all of the current research concerns of both Freudian and Jamesian psychologists of religion.[27] These dimensions include: *the mythological dimension* (including both the study of mythical consciousness and specific types of myths); *the ritual dimension* (including both the problem of the ritualization of everyday life and specific religious rituals); *the dispositional dimension* (the formal systems of meaning which dispose men to cognize, perceive, and value their lives and the world in consistent ways); *the social dimension* (encompassing the larger social context of which religious organizations are part but whose religious aspect is not exhausted by such organizations); *the experiential dimension* (personal religion as exemplified by experiences, moods, emotions, and aspirations having religious salience); *the directional dimension* (foil to the dispositional dimension, with the dispositional capturing the element of arranging and structuring systems of meaning and the directional centering on the process of individual and group realization in terms of these systems).

In proposing this six-dimensional schema, I am merely drawing attention to dimensions which have relevance to the psychology of religion. I have not attempted to describe how psychologists have addressed specific topics. However, any development of this or similar schemas would undoubtedly need to center on some of the following issues: (1) What psychologists of religion have to contribute to our understanding of each dimension in the generic sense. (2) How psychologists' studies of specific topics illuminate our understanding of the dimension as such. (3) How psychologists identify and evaluate current manifestations of the dimension. (4) How psychologists attempt to relate two or more dimensions, both generically and topically. Taken together, these issues reflect a concern for an appropriate balance between past and present contributions to the discipline, for contributions both generic and topical, and for attention to current forms of religion and the religious, thus counterbalancing the traditional tendency of the discipline (especially in its Freudian expressions) toward the discovery of primitive forms of religion. However, the most profound implications of the multidimensional approach center around the fourth issue, the relation of two or more dimensions to one another. It is this systemic thrust which is most lacking in the Freudian and Jamesian traditions.

This leads to a final concluding comment: The dimensions of religion are more than mere categories. Taken together, they constitute a configuration which is itself the object of investigation. However, systems or configurations require a vitalizing element, some aspect of the system which effects the coherence of the whole. Gestalt psychologists have recognized this requirement in their law of *pragnanz,* that is, that structures when allowed to develop without undue interference are guided by an inherent tendency toward good continuation, even completion. Significantly, Smart unwittingly employs this very notion when he suggests that it is the experiential dimension of religion which "animates" the whole. Personal religion is not the *sine qua non* of religion, it has no logical or temporal priority, but it is that dimension which vitalizes the total system. We can accept this proposal, acknowledging that it has special appeal to the psychologist of religion, because it fits especially well with the emphasis of the psychology of religion on the idiographic mode which, as we saw earlier, has an integrative function.[28] At the very least, this proposal serves as a cautionary note that, in its current mood of expansiveness, the psychology of religion must not lose sight of what has been its creative exaggeration in the scientific study of religion: its traditional focus on the individual and his religion.

## NOTES

[1] Sigmund Freud, *Civilization and Its Discontents,* translated and edited by James Strachey (New York: W. W. Norton, 1962), p. 12.

[2] Erik H. Erikson, "The Ontogeny of Ritualization in Man," in Rudolph M. M. Loewenstein and others, eds., *Psychoanalysis—A General Psychology: Essays in Honor of Heinz Hartmann* (New York: International Universities Press, 1966). See also Erikson's *Young Man Luther: A Study in Psychoanalysis and History* (New York: W. W. Norton, 1958), pp. 263-264. Erich Fromm, *The Forgotten Language: An Introduction to the Understanding of Dreams, Fairy Tales, and Myths* (New York: Grove Press, 1957), pp. 205 ff.

[3] James E. Dittes, "Beyond William James," in Charles Y. Glock and Phillip E. Hammond, eds., *Beyond the Classics: Essays in the Scientific Study of Religion* (New York: Harper & Row, 1973), p. 313.

[4] William James, *The Varieties of Religious Experience* (New York: New American Library, 1958), p. 40.

[5] *Ibid.,* p. 42.

[6] *Ibid.;* author's italics.

[7] *Ibid.*

[8] The early psychologist of religion, Edwin Diller Starbuck, was especially concerned with this problem of lapsing. See his *The Psychology of Religion: An Empirical Study of the Growth of Religious Consciousness* (London: Walter Scott, 1914).

[9] Freud, *Civilization and Its Discontents,* p. 19; my italics.

[10] Gordon W. Allport, *The Use of Personal Documents in Psychological Science* (New York: Social Science Research Council, 1942), p. 53.

[11] *Ibid.,* p. 56.

[12]James, *The Varieties of Religious Experience*, p. 26.

[13]See Erik H. Erikson, *Identity, Youth and Crisis* (New York: W. W. Norton, 1968), pp. 152-153.

[14]Paul W. Pruyser, "Sigmund Freud and His Legacy: Psychoanalytic Psychology of Religion," in Glock and Hammond, *Beyond the Classics*, p. 252.

[15]*Ibid.*

[16]David Bakan, *Sigmund Freud and the Jewish Mystical Tradition* (New York: Schocken Books, 1965). Erich Fromm has a briefer statement of this argument in his *Sigmund Freud's Mission: An Analysis of His Personality and Influence* (New York: Grove Press, 1963), pp. 80-84.

[17]Bruno Bettelheim, *Symbolic Wounds: Puberty Rites and the Envious Male*, rev. ed. (New York: Collier Books, 1962), p. 154.

[18]Pruyser, "Sigmund Freud and His Legacy," p. 282.

[19]Erikson, *Young Man Luther*, p. 9.

[20]Freud, *Civilization and Its Discontents*, p. 16.

[21]James, *The Varieties of Religious Experience*, pp. 135-136; my italics.

[22]Quoted in F. O. Matthiessen, *The James Family* (New York: Alfred A. Knopf, 1948), p. 161; my italics. Erikson discusses this experience in *Identity, Youth and Crisis*, p. 153.

[23]Sigmund Freud, *The Future of an Illusion*, edited by James Strachey, translated by W. D. Robson-Scott (Garden City, N.Y.: Doubleday, 1964), p. 30.

[24]Freud, *Civilization and Its Discontents*, p. 41; my italics.

[25]Dittes, "Beyond William James," p. 313.

[26]Clifford Geertz, *Islam Observed* (New Haven: Yale University Press, 1968), pp. 95-96.

[27]Smart's schema includes the following dimensions: ritual, mythological, doctrinal, ethical, social, and experiential. See his *The Religious Experience of Mankind* (New York: Charles Scribner's Sons, 1969), pp. 6-12.

[28]Allport has more recently replaced the terms "idiographic" and "nomothetic" with the "morphogenic" and "dimensional." His view of morphogenic science as the study of *patterned structures* supports the argument that personal religion is no mere anomaly in the scientific investigation of the multidimensionality of religion but is itself a dimension which vitalizes and thus works toward the integration of the total system. This vitalizing function is attributable to the fact that, as Allport points out, "The challenge of morphogenesis (accounting for pattern) grows more rather than less acute as we discover the commonalities of life." See his "The General and the Unique in Psychological Science," *Journal of Personality*, XXX (1962), 405-422.

# Some Trends in the Psychology of Religion

## PAUL W. PRUYSER

Speaking before a Society for the Scientific Study of Religion, one is tempted to start with apologetics, particularly of the *pro vita sua* kind. My first impulse, on being asked to appear before you, was to pull all my punches and tell you various details about my professional and ideological life in the hope that this might enable you to "understand me better." On second thought, I suppressed this impulse and am content now to preface my presentation with one personal statement, namely, that I am a clinical psychologist and that my only claim for professional competence lies within the field of psychology. That field is broad enough and holds considerable fascination for me. It comprises all the phenomena of life in its psychic and holistic aspects.

Let me therefore open with a quotation from a fellow psychologist, Gordon Allport: "A narrowly conceived science can never do business with a narrowly conceived religion. Only when both parties broaden their perspective will the way to understanding and cooperation open" (1). This is a very interesting statement in several ways. It tells us that, for the writer, science is not one thing but many and that religion is also not one thing but many. It says that we can have various attitudes toward science as well as toward religion. Such a critique can be possible only from a viewpoint well above science and religion, but whether there is any such vantage point, and what its name is, I cannot tell. Allport speaks further of science and religion "doing business with each other," and it strikes me that this does not quite fit with the cool and splendid detachment which my teachers told me was the attitude of scientists. And then he mentions this "broadening of perspective." Why should any discipline broaden its perspective? Is not psychology broad enough, and is it no longer true that religion deals with the whole

Reprinted with permission of author and publisher from:

*Journal of Religion,* 1960, 40, 113-129, copyright 1960 by the UNIVERSITY OF CHICAGO, 5801 Ellis Avenue, Chicago, Illinois 60637. All rights reserved.

universe, "while it groaneth and travaileth in pain"? And what about the "working together" of science and religion—is it merely because "togetherness" and "groupiness" are the catchwords of our time, or is there a scholarly interest in mutual learning and edification? If not, which other purpose could be served by such working together?

Despite their ring, these are not rhetorical questions. Consequently, they will not receive a rhetorical answer from me. Instead I shall try to give some comments on what I think has happened during the last fifty or sixty years in psychology and religion as these two have been brought into relation with each other. And I shall show in due time that Allport's statement makes eminent sense. I do so in the hope that an awareness of trends and developments may help us to find some sturdy footholds for further study. This will not be comprehensive but, for limitations of time and libido, only an elaborate sketch. I shall content myself with a few typical phases.

Let us first look at that rather specialized part of psychology which is called "psychology of religion." More than fifty years ago the leading academic psychologist in America at that time was asked to give the Gifford Lectures in Edinburgh. What William James said on that occasion constitutes probably still the most important single psychological work on religion (14). He made some excellent propositions: (a) that religious phenomena are continuous with other psychic phenomena; (b) that in religion, as everywhere else, the sublime and the ridiculous are two poles of a continuum, with a lot of ordinary, drab, and hackneyed happenings in between; (c) that in religion, as in other human endeavors, feelings tend to be more important than thoughts; (d) that there is not one single psychic wellspring for religion in the form of a special instinct, sentiment, or disposition; (e) that religion has a human and a divine side and that psychology can study only the former; and (f) that people do not simply *have* a God but that they *use* their God and that religion is known by its fruits in behavior. A little later, psychoanalytic investigators would repeat this last statement with more vigor and with a more precise knowledge of the kind of use people make of their God. James added a simple typology and had a keen interest in the medical side of religion, not only diagnostically, but also in terms of mental hygiene. That later interest is again rearing its ugly head in our day (27, 37).

I believe that James's fourth point—that religion cannot be delegated to one special psychic function—is of major scientific importance. Before and after him many people have asked whether the essence of religious experience is to be found in a feeling, act, attitude, value, cognitive state, drive, or whatever. They sought an element, a *prima materia,* of religious experience. James's answer is the parallel in religion to the debunking of the old and outworn phlogiston theory in chemistry. *All* the psychological part processes may participate in religious experience, and *none* of them is specific to religion. Instead of raising the wrong question about specificity, let us inquire what the preponderant part processes are in the religious experience of certain people or in certain systems of religion; in other words, let us set forth the *varieties* of religious experience.

But, as soon as that inquiry has been made, one must raise the next question: whether the gist of religion really lies in part processes or whether it has to be sought elsewhere. If religion claims the whole man, as some of its spokesmen say, by what sort of process does it achieve its holistic, integrative character—if it ever does? James answered tentatively that this would involve a shift in the center of energy, but he could not pursue the matter in further detail.

There is some reason to wonder whether James's most lasting legacy, which led to the phenomenon known as the "James tradition," was not at bottom a political as well as a scientific contribution. After James the term "religious experience" has become an expression for a somewhat cagey way of dealing with certain aspects of the psychology of religion. Its premises seem to be: (*a*) some people have subjective experiences called "religious" of one sort or another; (*b*) psychology, as an empirical science, deals with experiences of people; therefore, (*c*) the psychology of religion, if it is to be empirical, deals with the subjective experiences of people called "religious."

There is nothing wrong with this conclusion, except that it is based upon too narrow a premise. For James, subjective experience meant feelings, and the best empirical data were to be found in the feelingful expressions of feelings. This emphasis on feelings and utter subjectivity cuts down on the importance of cognitive states, decisions, and acts—on the very things that systematic and moral theology is interested in. Hence the work of James and his followers needed not to be taken too seriously by the theological disciplines. After all, *this* psychology of religion dealt only with the very subjective, all-too-human side of religion—it dealt neither with God, with doctrine, nor with the nature of the redemptive community. It did not even deal with the nature of faith. To be sure, it touched upon the nature of man, but only so lightly and so humanly that it necessitated no change in churchmen's thoughts about God and his relation to man. Moreover, even James's pragmatism was sufficiently palatable to the prevailing theological climate of the time to prevent all too vigorous skirmishes.

My thesis is that James set up narrow boundaries to the field of the psychology of religion and that many of his successors held to those limits without giving the matter much thought. Perhaps they found the limitation tactically useful. Some exceptions must be noted, but they had little influence. The Wiemans (45), for instance, deplored the fact. A few of James's contemporaries, notably Coe (5) and Leuba (24), were more daring on this point, but most students take no recourse to their original works. Leuba must be credited with having faced the question of the existence and the nature of God; he took the viewpoint that religion deals with an illusory reality. Freud would have more to say about that later.

Religious life involves images, intuitions, concepts, and the human history of all these about God. But, above all, it involves an object relation with God, and psychology must be interested in all these aspects. I am not sure whether psychology can or should waive the ontological question, as, by the way, some theological systems also do, but I am sure that it cannot stop short of man's thinking about God and the forming and obtaining of his image. Beside the feelingful renditions of religious feelings stand the thoughtful renditions of religious thinking. Diary pages, such as James used, may be excellent sources to get at feelings; it would seem to me that theological treatises are the appropriate sources for religious thoughts in an articulate form. Psychology is interested in what psychoanalysts call the primary as well as the secondary processes of religion, in the latent dream thoughts as well as in the dream work and the manifest dream content, including the secondary elaborations.

The method of the James tradition consists chiefly, if not exclusively, in non-experimental fact finding and description. Use is made of biographical materials, questionnaires, and simple or complex (but mostly simple) correlation techniques. Much work has gone into correlating incidence of conversion, frequency of prayer, loyalty to parental beliefs, etc., with global personality traits.

There were others of course. An interesting psychologist of religion is R. Mueller-Freienfels, who published in 1920 two little volumes in German (30). His work is broad and helpfully systematic but not always deep. Of particular importance is his description of the field: individual forms and institutional forms of religion are put side by side, and much attention is paid to myths, liturgy, and such religious acts as prayer and sacrifice. He uses no special methods of investigation but works, as many students of religion do, from his desk, using a simple Kantian scheme which emphasizes feeling, willing, and thinking.

Under "thinking" are included all possible cognitive aspects of religion: the acquisition of knowledge, contemplation, and the use of symbols. I believe that this latter emphasis is of importance.

Mueller-Freienfels' contribution also contains a helpful schematization of historical trends in the psychology of religion. He considers the following five tendencies or schools of thought:

1. Theological schools of thought which try to give psychological underpinnings for a given theological system. An example is Schleiermacher, who defined religion in its subjective aspects as the feeling of utter dependence.
2. The ethnopsychological school produced by French and English positivism, exemplified in Wundt's work.
3. A school of differential psychology particularly strong in America, with its traditional interest in individual differences. Examples: Leuba, James, Starbuck.
4. A psychopathological school, particularly strong in France. Examples: Delacroix, Flournoy.
5. An analytic school aiming at an independent analysis of traditional religion, knowing that its psychological roots are often purposely hidden from scrutiny. Examples: Feuerbach and perhaps Nietzsche.
6. The psychoanalytic school, which emphasizes the role of unconscious motivation, of drives, and of the function of the superego.

We will come back to some of these schools later and consider psychoanalysis first.

Psychoanalytic studies of religion started early in this century. One of Freud's first case studies, that of the wolf man (7), contained some interesting notes on the role of religion in psychopathology. In addition to Freud's *Totem and Taboo* (10) and *The Future of an Illusion* (8), the works of Pfister (33, 34) and of Jones (17, 18, 19) must be mentioned here. Because of the general hostility to psychoanalysis in the early decades of our century there was at first very little carry-over of the analysts' observations and theories into the main body of religious studies. Why it failed to be taken seriously by the official body of the psychology of religion is a more complex riddle. A 1958 textbook (4), under the somewhat presumptuous title *"The" Psychology of Religion*, contents itself with some meaningless eulogies on Freud but fails to make use of the main propositions of psychoanalysis. Even the work of Pfister, the Swiss pastor and one of Freud's earliest and most sincere colleagues, is not mentioned!

Psychoanalytic studies of religion have, of course, a special character, conceptually as well as methodologically. They are basically studies of motivation for religion, and the person's set of beliefs and practices are approached from the point of view of wish fulfilment,

**57**

drive control, primary- and secondary-process thinking, object relations, the genesis of conscience and the ego ideal, and the economics of libidinal and aggressive urges. Because the word "symptom" in psychoanalysis covers an almost infinite range of possibilities, religion can be approached as a symptom. Psychoanalysis said more forcefully what James had said earlier, namely, that people *use* their God.

The mechanics of the psychic household, the defense processes of the ego, and the fundamental psychosocial constellations, such as the oedipal conflict, were all brought to bear upon religion, phylogenetically as well as ontogenetically, individually and collectively, within a genetic-dynamic formula. This formula added an entirely new dimension to the methodology of the psychology of religion in that it demanded longitudinal assessment of the individual in the network of his object relationships. It also holds that personal documents, which were the mainstay of James's studies, cannot be taken at face value but must be approached with analytic sophistication. And, since for practical reasons such studies nearly always coincide with the process of psychotherapy, an excellent opportunity is here provided for evaluating the significance of religion in relation to other pursuits, preoccupations, values, and needs of the individual. In other words, here is one place where one can study how religion "fits" into life.

An interesting feature of psychoanalytic study of religion is its shortening of the psychological distance between God and man. Note that I speak here of psychological, not of ontological, distance. God's names, as Jones has remarked, such as Father, Maker, Sustainer, and Provider, are relevant to the family drama. To me, the statement that God is a father figure may also imply its complement—that biological fathers have numinous qualities. In other words, psychoanalysis has established a new affinity (not identity) between God and man which cuts across the technical distinction between God's transcendence and his immanence.

As to the old dispute on psychology's relation to the ontological question about God, I would like to make a second comment. It seems to me a perfectly psychological question to ask why and on what grounds some people answer the ontological question about God vigorously in the affirmative, why some deny it, and why a third group of people say that they do not know. Particularly since the matter cannot be decided logically, as even some theologians admit, the psychology of knowledge, like the sociology of knowledge, may have some important contributions to make. The ontological question with capital letters is one thing; but every individual's way of coming to grips with it is quite a different thing.

Freud's term "illusion," denoting the formal psychological status of religious belief, has given rise to bitter opposition, particularly from those who have only read the title of his book. The book itself (8) clarifies the meaning of the term: religious beliefs are illusions in the sense that they are not pure products of experience or end results of thinking but fulfilments of the oldest, strongest, and most urgent wishes of mankind. An illusion is not a mistake. Rather it is like Columbus thinking he had discovered a new seaway to India, while he had actually discovered America! An illusion is not necessarily false, that is, incapable of realization or contradictory to reality. The great question is: If illusions are needed, how can we have those that are capable of correction; how can we have those that will not deteriorate into delusions?

I can find little fault with these definitions. They bring to my mind Paul's admonition to the Corinthians: "For now we see in a mirror dimly, but then we will see face to face." Knowledge of God is always approximate and always full of distortions; it needs correction at any stage in life. Of this, the sincere Christian should be more convinced than anyone else. Our psychic organization, our perceptions, our thoughts, our wishes, our moods participate in the shaping of our beliefs. We knew this before the "New Look" in perception and before the concept of perceptual defense. As the theologian Tillich (43) points out, our doubts codetermine the dynamics of our faith. The divine purpose is never completely known by mortals, and, because of this, we find ourselves making guesses about it. The guesses may not be unaided; they may be wise and inspired; but they remain *our* guesses. Moreover, as Jones has remarked, "what one wants to know about the divine purpose is its intention towards oneself" (17). It is exactly because religion deals not with abstractions but with realities by which to live that psychoanalytic formulations must be taken seriously.

But perhaps the most significant contribution of psychoanalysis to the psychology of religion is its insistence upon the role of conflict in religion, and of religion in conflict, personal as well as social. Religion is now no longer an item or parcel of experience but a quality of an individual's experiencing the world and himself; it can be defined as a way of problem-solving. This point had already been made in 1911 by a non-analytic psychologist, George M. Stratton (41), who saw the source of religion in man's being entangled in all kinds of conflicts, stemming from inner and outer polarities. I believe that this position is heuristically of great importance to the psychology of religion. Several questions come to mind right away:

1. Which problems have been solved or can be solved by religion?
2. What kind of religion can solve a given problem?
3. To what extent are problems really solved by religion or which problems are refractory to religious solutions?
4. Can a man fall back on traditional religious thoughts and beliefs, or must he look for religious innovations?
5. Which new problems are in turn posed by attempts at problem-solving through religion?
6. Does religion, as it is used in problem-solving, remain itself problem-free or does it become conflict-laden?

Some of these latter questions seem particularly relevant to certain developments within Protestant theology and to recent thinking on the problem of mental health. Both Christianity and mental health seem to require some degree of tension and of "considered non-conformity" (40), to use Shoben's beautiful phrase.

At any rate, within such a framework the concept of religious experience as a state has to give way to the concept of religion as a process. Problem-solving takes time, and it always involves a future, that is, the unknown. Phenomenologically, it may even mean a preoccupation with the unknown (35, 36). The person who is engaged in problem-solving proceeds by hypotheses—one after another. How are his hypotheses corrected under the impact of experience? How does he draw, and modify, his cognitive maps?

With psychoanalysis the psychology of religion should have undergone a change in concepts, in orientation, and in attitude toward the material studied. Instead, it underwent a change in personnel. For psychoanalysis is also a branch of psychiatry and, through it, of medicine. Within psychology, its impact was felt mostly in the specialization of clinical psychology, which has had relatively little contact with the psychology of religion—the latter has remained more closely in the fold of academic psychology and educational psychology. The psychoanalytic impact on psychiatry is great. Its impact is also felt keenly in pastoral education, even in pastoral theology. I believe that this selective spread of the influence of psychoanalysis is altering the status of scientific concern with religion in a major way.

First of all, it has meant a shift from pure science to applied science. Second, it has meant a shift from the traditional academic department to the professional training program. Third, much, if not most, of the activity in psychology and religion has moved from the university campus to the psychiatric clinic, the hospital, and the parish. Indeed, the combination "religion and psychiatry" is now more popular than the psychology of religion, and pastoral theology is rapidly becoming also a pastoral psychology.

# Some Trends in the Psychology of Religion

Many of these changes seem to depend on the emergence of a new professional specialty, that of the psychotherapist, and on the uncertainty about the prerequisites for his training. But whoever he may be, and whatever his academic background, it is important to note for our purposes that his role implies both a marvelous opportunity and a profound ambiguity in relation to the possibility of an advancing psychology of religion. The psychotherapist admittedly combines science and art, and he combines them in unsteady proportions. On the one hand, he is in a unique position of nearness to deep and subtle processes, just at that level of depth which many of us have surmised is the level at which religion may be significant in a person's life. Certainly, he reaches a stratum of personality functioning by which the psychology of religion could be immensely enriched. But the deeper he goes with his patient, the more difficult it becomes for him to maintain the cool, objective, and detached attitude of the curious scientist. Moreover, the psychotherapist's endeavor to help (and "helping" is one of the foremost definitions of his profession) is matched by his patient's desire to obtain health, and this may place the observational data about the patient's religion, if any, in a distorted, or at least very limited, perspective. For, despite the intriguingly deep level at which observations about an individual's religion may be obtained in such a setting, the purpose of "helping" and "being helped" tends to give rise to cheap superficialities about religion as a mode of, a vehicle for, or a criterion of adjustment or to the tedious attempts at establishing correlations or even equations between religion and mental health.

This perhaps is as good a place as any to mention the works of Jung, though it is nearly impossible to do justice in a few paragraphs to this penetrating and rich thinker. Since his extensive writings cover many borderland areas among psychology, psychiatry, medicine, history of religion, theology, and cultural anthropology (20, 21, 22, 23), it would be tempting to confine ourselves here to Jung's contribution to the psychology of religion proper. However, his own demonstration of the interweaving among so many diverse themes, constructs, observations, and symbols makes such a restriction intolerable. They are all relevant to the psychology of religion, though some more peripherally than others.

One will search in vain for the classical chapter headings of psychology of religion in Jung's works. There are no systematic treatises on the religion of adolescence or on conversion. There is very little material on individual differences in religion. All these and many other topics are scattered throughout his works, sometimes in relation to religion, sometimes in connection with non-religious aspects of living.

But there is an abundance of rich, searching, and sometimes daring propositions from which the psychology of religion could greatly benefit.

While several thinkers have stated that people *use* their gods, there is probably no one who has come so close as Jung has to saying that people also *make* their gods. Lest one be frightened or repelled by the implications of this position, it should be noted that Jung is one contemporary psychologist who does not shrink away from the word "soul," which he at times even seems to prefer to the more neutral and technical term "psyche." Added to this is his conception of human life as a process of individuation in which the self and its destiny are actively sought and nurtured. The journey of the self is described as a road toward salvation—indeed, the soul and the self (though objects of empirical study) have by postulate been given a sacramental and pseudo-divine status! Hence Jung is able, from this position, to study the psychological side of the whole process in which man lives with his God and God with "his" men, in terms of the religio-psychological borderline concept of "archetypes."

God is here no longer an abstraction, no mere "Prime Mover" or "Summum Bonum," but something to which people feel related *in tension* (13). In other words, psychology of religion can be a psychology of interaction and interpersonal relationships with supernatural beings in which not only man but also God and the dialogue between them become objects for analysis. For God is not the projection of a thought or idea onto another person (as the paranoid patient may project some quality of himself onto someone else), but he is projected *as a person.* Thus he is within reach of personality theory. In his *Answer to Job* Jung is indeed consequent enough to describe God as a changing, developing Being who learns to respond to one man's exemplary morality. He also discusses the difficult problem of God's sexual identity.

No doubt there are reasons to worry about the solidity of Jung's premises and conclusions, but nevertheless it remains true that his propositions "will stand as a watershed between the traditional and the coming psychology of religion," as Hofmann (13) has said.

But psychotherapy is only one area in which the hand of dynamic psychology and psychiatry is shown. There is another, and perhaps much wider, field of professional endeavor in healing relevant to the psychology of religion. That is the field of hospital psychiatry. I think that the development of modern hospital psychiatry, as distinct from mere custodial care, has also some important implications for the psychology of religion. I will take these up under two headings: the composite of professional specialties on the psychiatric team and the nature of psychiatric case study.

First, the modern psychiatric team shows division of labor and specialization of functioning with the preservation of a common goal—healing. But the division of labor is not complete; there is indeed much overlap between the functions of the team members and considerable unity in basic scientific theory. Psychiatrist, psychologist, social worker, and chaplain, to mention only a few team members, all work together in the evaluation and the treatment of the patient under the integrating aegis of the psychiatrist. The modern mental hospital is also, more than it ever was, a social institution which maintains many intimate ties with the community. It interacts, more or less intensely, with many professional and social groups: local physicians, judges, ministers and priests, civic groups, welfare agencies, and various religious organizations such as churches and councils of churches. Many different persons and forces are marshaled on behalf of "total care" for the patient. Some of these groups or individuals have an obvious and direct concern with the religious welfare of the hospitalized patient before, during, and after his temporary isolation. Much of this activity has become channelized and epitomized in a new professional specialty—the mental-hospital chaplain. And this is the place to highlight one more chapter in the history of the psychology of religion written by Anton Boisen.

In his profound book, *The Exploration of the Inner World* (2), Boisen put a new stamp on psychopathology and religion by placing both in the framework of the life-crisis. Religious experience can best be understood if it is seen in the same order of intensity and depth that attaches to severe mental illness. Both are processes of disorganization and reorganization of personality, of transformation, dealing with man's potentialities and ultimate loyalties. I think that this is a position which places religious experience functionally and experientially most clearly at the nexus of holistic, integrating tendencies of the organism. In this theoretical framework religion is not an adjuvant to integration; it *is* integration. It is one way of solving problems, sometimes successfully. Religion and mental illness, and of course by implication also mental health, are to be approached as existential conditions. Specific categories of experience obtain the focus in mental illness and in religion: world catastrophe, death and rebirth, the feeling of cosmic importance and of personal responsibility and mission. Religious language is close to the "primary-process" language known from psychoanalysis.

Whatever one may think of Boisen's propositions in detail, they certainly stress a dimension that is much needed in the psychology of religion. The mental-hospital chaplain with special clinical-pastoral training as a part of the psychiatric team is chiefly Boisen's creation. His is a unique function: he represents religion in all its aspects on the psychiatric team and to the patients. We must ask what implications this has for the psychology of religion.

The chaplain is first of all a pastor not a theologian. His task lies in shepherding, co-ordinate with the healing goal of the psychiatric team, which goal he shares. But he is the only member of the team whose contact with the patients is voluntary—he cannot be made part of a therapeutic regime even if this would involve clear benefits toward the patient's healing. For our purposes the most significant part of his function is that it brings him into contact with persons who have met with utter failure in problem-solving, with or without religion or pseudo-religion, and at times with failure in earlier attempts at religious problem-solving, which has resulted in specific resistances to even the faintest religious allusions. If Boisen's thesis is correct, the chaplain is forced to *seek* religion in psychopathology; and he finds it— sometimes in obvious manifestations of psychopathology *of* religion, sometimes in seemingly non-religious processes, and at other times nowhere. I believe that this has some major consequences. While James and the traditional body of the psychology of religion focused on the more obviously and indisputably religious experience—on the "pure cases," so to speak—the chaplain is, as all ministers of the faith are, broadening the range of religious data immensely by including all potentially religious phenomena. The old question was: Which are the significant data of religious experience? The new question is: Which data of experience are of religious significance?

Now let us look at the clinical psychologist on the psychiatric team. Can he assess and evaluate the religious experience of his patients, if any? My personal experience as a member of such a team has been enigmatic, perhaps even shocking. I have been intrigued by the absence of spontaneous religious references in test responses and interviews, even among ardent churchgoers. Some of our tests seem able to tap fairly deep levels of personality functioning, and yet we rarely encounter a clearly religious response to our Rorschach and Thematic Apperception tests. Patients say many things and sometimes indulge in a large amount of moralizing; they may even see a church steeple in an inkblot, but this appears on further scrutiny to be purely an architectural or a scenic-idyllic item. Where in the tests do we find their religion? Is it a failure of our tests, or is it proof of the negligible role of religion in the life of many people, admitting that we actually deal with a selected group? Or is it perhaps the result of the patient's social perception which compartmentalizes all encounters with people in terms of specific roles? Does the patient seek out the chaplain to talk about religion, only to ignore this dimension of his life in his meeting with other team members? I do not know the full answer to these questions, but I surmise that they can all be answered with a partial "Yes."

For the psychology of religion this situation means that the clinical psychologist will not readily be able to furnish new data. As a matter of fact, the first datum is negative: there is not as much religion as we might have thought.

But here again we have to heed the question: Which data of experience are of religious significance? Could it be that the patients are giving us religious responses without our knowing it? And perhaps without their own conscious knowledge? There was a time when sexual references in language, action, and fantasy went by unrecognized, because the power of sex and the role of symbolism were not understood. At that time sex was, by the civilized, delegated to a separate and remote chamber of the mind or, rather, the body. Perhaps we are in the psychology of religion in the same state at which sexology was in the days of Havelock Ellis and Krafft-Ebbing.

A second comment about psychologists may be in order. In several of my colleagues who are articulate, introspective, and sensitive people and who subscribe to an integrated set of religious propositions, the reading of standard texts on the psychology of religion elicits disappointment. I have always shared their reaction; we sense keenly that the heart of the matter has not been reached. In the same vein there is even among some writers of these books, a hardly hidden overtone of hopelessness with regard to the relevance of their own works. Does it mean that they feel psychology is still too young to tackle such a formidable task? Or must we think of the possible role of repression which handicaps even psychologists in coming to grips with religion? Perhaps we can learn something from that mighty prescientific psychologist Feuerbach (6), who put all his emphasis on the given existence, that is, the sensing, thinking, and self-actualizing person, and who had the temerity to say, "Theology is anthropology," because in the object of religion nothing but the essence of man is expressed. Of course, Feuerbach's "nothing but" is dogmatic and to that extent unscientific, but his temerity, rigor, ardor, and immense curiosity are to be envied this day.

The effectiveness of hospital psychiatry depends in very large measure on the adequacy of the case study. What is psychiatric case study? Several books have been written on the subject (26, 28), but the essence of it lies in what psychiatrists do, which is, according to Menninger, "try to understand their patients." The case study is a formulation of that understanding. It is written purposefully, with the double aim of communicating the understanding to others and of marshaling all the available forces and knowledge to change the patient's condition. A good case study usually involves all the specialists on the team, but first of all it requires the observational powers, the analytic acumen, the persistence in pursuing significant detail, the synthesizing ability of the psychiatrist. Our question is: How can a psychiatric case study be made relevant to the psychology of religion? Note that I do not speak here of *psychopathology* of religion, although it is likely that, in a patient population, religion may be part of the presenting symptoms. I am assuming that mental illness need not engulf the whole person—in other words, that religion may be an area of healthy functioning in a person quite aberrant in other spheres or aspects of life.

A good many psychiatric case studies begin with phrases like this: "This is the case of a white, thirty-five-year-old, prim, Methodist, midwestern housewife," only to omit any further reference to the religious dimension in this person's life, except perhaps for a note on the role that the choir or the Sunday school played in getting her acquainted with her husband. Meanwhile the phrase itself is a perfect stereotype and sets up all kinds of expectancies which may help channelize possible interpretations. On the other hand, some books on the psychology of religion make use of the case-study method (as, e.g., Johnson [15, 16] does quite effectively) only to emphasize all possible aspects of experience relevant to religion, but with a neglect of the person's sexual history, his infantile and childhood experiences, his economic history, etc. I think that in both instances the psychology of religion does not really profit from the clinical case-study method, and this judgment stems from my ardent belief that it could profit so much if the case study were done with care, holistically, existentially, and following the natural articulations of the patient's subjective and objective reality. Nor should my allusion to the phrase "prim, Methodist housewife" be taken as a persiflage of the writing of case studies. I admit—nay, I am even proposing—that the psychiatric assessment of the religious dimension in the life of a patient is an extremely difficult business. And let me add that it is very difficult for the patient's pastor too.

But we must make an attempt, and our procedures must be fair to the reality which we want to assess. We need not assume that everyone is deeply religious, but neither may we assume that religion is a compartmentalized area of a patient's life and, consequently, delegate its assessment to the chaplain or some other specialist or simply ignore it. To be sure, in some people religion *is* compartmentalized, but that is psychologically an interesting phenomenon which merits special mention and interpretation. Above all, it seems to me that we can in no case expect "religious data" just to pop up. Strictly speaking, there are no religious data, ready to take, just as little as there are any sexual data. Rather *all* data—events, processes, actions, objects, and object relations —may have either or both a religious and a sexual significance for the patient, or for the examiner, or for both.

There is still a different angle on this problem. Even in well-documented and well-integrated psychiatric case studies religious references are often missing. Sometimes this may be because of the examiner's lack of interest, but sometimes it happens despite attempts at obtaining religious relevancies from the patient. I cannot quite explain this, except that I have a hunch that the faith of many people may be completely inarticulate, and in others it may rarely reach a level where explicit references to it can be made. I also surmise that in some patients, and perhaps in many normal people, specific religious qualities and numinous values have shifted from traditional and suitable objects to what theologians would call idolatrous objects, concerns, pursuits, and values (3). The chromium-plated car with the juke-box rear, the life-style of suburbia, the pursuit of conformism, the aspiration to orgastic potency, and the zealous search for mental health are cases in point. If there is some validity in this speculation, the psychology of religion may be greatly enhanced and enriched by a meticulous study of people's idols and idolatries. The scientific study of religion must include *all* gods, *all* numina, *all* ultimate concerns, even those that may turn out to be false ultimates. I know of no better way to accomplish this than by a thorough application of the clinical method in psychiatric case study—a method which attempts to portray and conceptualize "what men live by." Why not assess, as part of the case study, what a person considers holy?

If we are indeed concerned with all gods, we must also deal with *all* the ways of man in worship, prayer, and ritual. Books on the psychology of religion have usually emphasized the diversity of styles and types of such religious actions. But there is a conspicuous limitation of approach in relation to prayer. Entirely typical is the following statement which I found in the 1958 textbook to which I have already alluded: "In studying prayer we have the additional difficulty of surveying an area of the inner life of which the average person is loath to speak. If one prays at all, the matter is apt to concern his very dearest wishes."

**67**

The conclusion drawn from this observation is that the psychologist's curiosity should therefore be tempered by his reverence; in regard to prayer, he must content himself with "soft techniques" such as questionnaires and gentle interviews.

I am entirely at odds with such a policy. Prayer has been widely considered as "the heart of religion." The phenomenologist Heiler (11) has said that it is the most spontaneous and the most personal expression of religion. If this is so, the psychology of religion must look for ways of coming to grips with it. And again I believe that the psychiatrist and clinical psychologist are here in a unique position to contribute, because of their rich knowledge of, and total concern for, their charges. Meanwhile, the psychologist of religion can learn another lesson from the history of psychoanalysis: if observations on others are difficult to make, he can observe himself. Freud (9) analyzed his own dreams and published them in order to advance the science of dream interpretation. I would invite the religious ones among the curious scientists of religion to study their own prayers, including just these "dearest wishes" about which the "average person is loath to speak."

So far, I have stayed within the framework of the psychology of religion in the formal professional sense. I mentioned psychiatry and the mental-hospital chaplaincy only in terms of how they contribute to the process of assessing and evaluating the role of religion in life, the nature of an individual's faith, and the possible distortions thereof. The aims of psychiatry, and particularly of the chaplaincy, do not coincide with the aims of psychology. This review cannot be brought to a conclusion without considering at least one more discipline, the aims of which are widely different from those of psychology, but from whose matrix of observations, theories, and speculations exceedingly important contributions to the psychology of religion have been made. That discipline is theology, or the body of divinity.

We cannot go into the problem of how this vast body is internally articulated and how it relates to the arts and sciences. (In his recent book on pastoral theology, Hiltner [12] offers an interesting schema of these relations.) Nor can I venture here to review all the psychological relevancies of theological studies, although I am convinced that there are many. This would be beyond the scope of this presentation and perhaps beyond my competence. I say "perhaps" because I feel that it would take a *psychologist* to establish such psychological relevancies, but I also realize that this is a formidable task. Systematic theology usually contains more or less elaborate doctrines of man; moral theology presents values and goals for human behavior and includes admonitions and adhortations; pastoral theology presents aims and methods of shepherding. In all these there is at least an implied psychology, dealing with the actual and the ideal conditions of man, with origins, alienation, motives, values, conscience, goals, conflict, repair, and learning. It would take us too far afield to examine here any of these psychological implications of theology, but I think that it can and should be done for the advancement of the psychology of religion.

Some theologians have been quite explicit on psychological matters. While Schleiermacher (39) formulated his thesis on faith as the feeling of "utter dependency," still with a clearly apologetic aim, for some later theologians apologetics has given way to precise description and analysis of psychic states in faith for its own sake. Two of them, Otto and Tillich, must be mentioned here because of their immense value to the psychology of religion.

Otto's celebrated phenomenological study *The Idea of the Holy* (31) and his later work *Mysticism East and West* (32) have left a deep impression on readers in many different professions. His two-pronged approach to the subjective and objective pole of the core experience in religion, that is, the idea of the holy or numinous corresponding in each of its aspects with specific moments of human experience, is a master-piece of methodology. The emphasis is not on individual differences, although some striking differences are portrayed, but on the "common good" of religion, on the generalities that govern religious experience. But experience is related at every step with its object; the science of man as *Homo religiosus* and the science of God are not divorced. Otto's phenomenological analysis is a convincing answer to the fallacious assumption that the psychology of religion deals only with man—it must deal with God, for religion is the establishing, experiencing, and nurturing of a relation between God and man. There is no psychology of the artist apart from the artistic work and beauty that is given form; neither can there be a psychology of religion apart from the idea of God and the forms in which holiness becomes transparent. Just as theology deals also with man, psychology must deal also with the numinous.

And this is my reason for having quoted Allport's searching statement and for thinking that psychology of religion cannot, out of fear of the ontological question, avoid all references to God. Psychology cannot be theology or philosophy, but neither can it behave like the ostrich with its peculiar technique for shutting out fearsome objects. The truth of a religious assertion is a substantial part of the religious experience, for *Homo religiosus* is passionately involved in it and ulti-mately concerned with it. When a truth turns out to be disappointing, when it lets us down, we must reorganize our lives and seek a better truth; else we become ill. Whether God-in-general is real or not, the God-in-particular of this or that believer must at least be realistic. Not sensually and concretistically, in that "He walks with me and He talks with me" (this is Whitehead's "fallacy of misplaced concreteness"; or what Woodger labels the "finger and thumb philosophy"); neither as a loose thought or even as a concept, but in the psychological sense that God is loved and responded to by people who live with him. Freud's definition, "illusion," with the specifications that I mentioned, is not such a bad term after all.

A psychology of religion without some evaluation of God is a narrow undertaking. Though it is true that the reality of God cannot be asserted or denied by psychology, it is also true that a deliberately agnostic attitude on the part of the scientist cannot do full justice to the nature of the experience of God in believing subjects. I would hold that a humorless scientist cannot write a full psychology of humor; nor can the dreamless psychologist ever write the rich scientific text of dreams that Freud wrote. To know what aspects of experience have religious significance for a person presupposes some familiarity with possibilities and perplexities of religion in the investigator.

I think, then, that the psychology of religion may assume an attitude of naive realism toward the object of religious beliefs. All sciences take this attitude toward their direct and indirect objects. The philosophical critique of this position is a matter for the philosophy of science, not for the sciences themselves. To assume this attitude is not to place psychology in the service of religious apologetics. If, as Whitehead (44) holds, religion is one of the strong forces which influence man, and if believers place one source of this force in God, the psychologist must study Gods *for the sake of studying man*. I use the plural form here to indicate, moreover, that what is relevant to the believer is God's attributes in relation to himself rather than the general idea of God. And these are exactly some items of difference between various theologies. In some way, the problem of God's existence is to be approached as an individualized and particular, rather than a general, question. Woodger (46) has remarked that it is difficult to distinguish existing from existing *for someone*. Its parallel in the psychology of religion is that God is never a simple object, one among many, but always a *love* object to the devout person. Now love objects have a plus factor to the lover which outsiders cannot observe. To me, my spouse has attributes which my neighbors will never perceive. That is why my relationship with her is more dynamic than my neighbors'; it involves commitment, loyalty, exaltation, and a highly particularized order of reality. Again, Woodger states that it is impossible to know that something exists without knowing something else about it.

Existentially oriented thinkers have had far less trouble with the ontological problem than the classical theologians. They have seen that the arguments for God's existence are less relevant to religious vitality and truth than had been assumed. They have seen the profound but sublime irrationality of all religious propositions. They have noticed, moreover, that God-centeredness is not necessarily the opposite of man-centeredness. The various Cartesian splits between being and knowing, subject and object, natural and spiritual realms, are only some possible options of human thought. It is unscientific to take them as dogma. Hebrew genius produced another possibility, namely, that the knowledge of man and the knowledge of God are co-variants. To the extent that some religious men proceed on this premise, the psychology of religion may accept it as a postulate and knowingly assume the implied ontological position. I do not think that it will stop being a science for that matter.

Much affinity with the existential mode of thought is present in the works of Tillich. In *The Courage To Be* (42) and *Dynamics of Faith* (43) he stands in part on the shoulders of Otto. His expressions, "ultimate concern" and "centered act of the personality," have a strong appeal to dynamic psychologists, for they reach the motivational depths, the urge character, the directional qualities, and the forever-conflict-laden ways of human problem-solving. Tillich's emphasis on the cognitive process in religion, epitomized in his definition of faith as including the dynamics of doubt, offers much to the psychology of religion. Religion can now be seen as exploratory behavior, driven, among other things, by man's curiosity and by his perpetual attempts to maximize contact with a maximal environment to the full deployment of all his potentialities. The psychology of learning is interested in such propositions. Tillich's specifications of anxiety, and his emphasis on the dynamics of courage, have aroused considerable interest in psychological and psychiatric circles. I believe that the pursuit of just these subtle psychological processes implied in the terms "faith," "courage," "doubt," "concern"—and I would like to add "hope" (25) and "love" (29)—will, in the long run, provide exactly the enrichment of the psychology of religion that our science is waiting for. Our science is a sober but not inhibited, an imaginative but not fantastic, concern. The psychology of religion must be attuned to the double goal of using disciplined thought and of keeping religion in the equation.

# P. W. Pruyser

## BIBLIOGRAPHY

1. ALLPORT, G. W. *The Individual and His Religion.* New York: Macmillan Co., 1950.
2. BOISEN, A. T. *The Exploration of the Inner World.* New York: Harper & Bros., 1936.
3. CHERBONNIER, E. LA B. *Hardness of Heart.* Garden City, N.Y.: Doubleday & Co., 1955.
4. CLARK, W. H. *The Psychology of Religion.* New York: Macmillan Co., 1958.
5. COE, G. A. *The Psychology of Religion.* Chicago: University of Chicago Press. 1916.
6. FEUERBACH, L. *The Essence of Christianity.* With an introductory essay by KARL BARTH. New York: Harper & Bros., 1957.
7. FREUD, S. *From the History of an Infantile Neurosis* (1918). In Vol. III, *Collected Papers.* ("International Psychoanalytic Library," No. 9.) London: Hogarth Press, 1933.
8. ———. *The Future of an Illusion,* trans. W. D. ROBSON-SCOTT, HORACE LIVERIGHT, and the INSTITUTE OF PSYCHOANALYSIS. ("International Psychoanalytic Library," No. 15.) London: Hogarth Press, 1928.
9. ———. *Interpretation of Dreams.* Vols. IV and V in *The Standard Edition of the Complete Psychological Works of Sigmund Freud,* trans. JAMES STRACHEY *et al.* London: Hogarth Press, 1953.
10. ———. *Totem and Taboo* (1913). In Vol. XIII of *The Standard Edition of the Complete Psychological Works of Sigmund Freud,* trans. JAMES STRACHEY *et al.* London: Hogarth Press, 1955.
11. HEILER, F. *Prayer.* New York: Oxford University Press, 1932.
12. HILTNER, S. *Preface to Pastoral Theology.* New York: Abingdon Press, 1958.
13. HOFMANN, H. Review of C. G. JUNG, *Answer to Job, Christian Century,* LXXII (1955), 452-53.
14. JAMES, W. *The Varieties of Religious Experience.* New York: Longmans, Green & Co., 1902.
15. JOHNSON, P. E. *Personality and Religion.* New York: Abingdon Press, 1957.
16. ———. *Psychology of Religion.* New York: Abingdon-Cokesbury Press, 1945.
17. ———. "Psychoanalysis and the Christian Religion," in *Essays in Applied Psychoanalysis,* Vol. II. ("International Psychoanalytic Library," No. 41.) London: Hogarth Press, 1951.
18. ———. "A Psychoanalytic Study of the Holy Ghost," in *Essays in Applied Psychoanalysis,* Vol. II. ("International Psychoanalytic Library," No. 41.) London: Hogarth Press, 1951.
19. ———. *The Psychology of Religion: Essays in Applied Psychoanalysis,* Vol. II. ("International Psychoanalytic Library," No. 41.) London: Hogarth Press, 1951.
20. JUNG, C. G. *Answer to Job.* London: Routledge & Kegan Paul, 1954.
21. ———. *Modern Man in Search of a Soul.* New York: Harcourt, Brace & Co., 1933.
22. ———. *Psychology and Religion.* New Haven, Conn.: Yale University Press, 1938.
23. ———. Foreword to V. WHITE, *God and the Unconscious.* London: Haverhill Press, 1952.
24. LEUBA, JAMES H. *The Psychological Study of Religion: Its Origin, Its Function, Its Future.* New York: Macmillan Co., 1912.
25. MARCEL, G. *Homo Viator: prolégomènes à une métaphysique de l'espérance.* Paris: Aubier, Éditions Montaigne, 1944.
26. MASSERMAN, J. H. *The Practice of Dynamic Psychiatry.* Philadelphia: W. B. Saunders Co., 1955.
27. MEEHL, P. "Religion and the Maintenance of Mental Health," in *Society's Stake in Mental Health,* pp. 52-61. Minneapolis: Social Science Research Center, University of Minnesota, 1957.
28. MENNINGER, K. A. *A Manual for Psychiatric Case Study.* New York: Grune & Stratton, 1952.
29. MENNINGER, K. A., and MENNINGER, J. L. *Love against Hate.* New York: Harcourt, Brace & Co., 1942.

30. MUELLER-FREIENFELS, RICHARD. *Psychologie der Religion.* 2 vols. (Sammlung Goeschen, Bd. 805/806.) Berlin, 1920.
31. OTTO, R. *The Idea of the Holy.* New York: Oxford University Press, 1928.
32. ———. *Mysticism East and West.* New York: Living Age Books, Meridian Books, 1957.
33. PFISTER, O. *Christianity and Fear.* London: George Allen & Unwin, 1948.
34. ———. *Some Applications of Psychoanalysis.* London: George Allen & Unwin, 1923.
35. POLANYI, M. "Problem Solving," *British Journal of the Philosophy of Science,* VIII (1957), 89-103.
36. PRUYSER, P. W. "The Idea of Destiny," *Hibbert Journal,* LVII (1959), 380-85.
37. ———. "Is Mental Health Possible?" *Bulletin of the Menninger Clinic,* XXII (1958), 58-66.
38. ———. "Toward a Doctrine of Man in Psychiatry and Theology," *Pastoral Psychology,* March, 1958.
39. SCHLEIERMACHER, F. E. D. *The Christian Faith,* trans. and ed. H. R. MACKINTOSH and J. S. STEWART. Edinburgh: T. T. Clark & Co., 1928.
40. SHOBEN, E. J., JR. "Toward a Concept of the Normal Personality," *American Psychologist,* XII (1957), 183-89.
41. STRATTON, G. M. *The Psychology of the Religious Life.* London: George Allen & Co., 1911.
42. TILLICH, P. *The Courage To Be.* New Haven, Conn.: Yale University Press, 1952.
43. ———. *Dynamics of Faith.* New York: Harper & Bros., 1957.
44. WHITEHEAD, A. N. *Science and the Modern World.* New York: Macmillan Co., 1925.
45. WIEMAN, H. N., and WIEMAN, R. W. *Normative Psychology of Religion.* New York: Thomas Y. Crowell Co., 1935.
46. WOODGER, J. H. *Physics, Psychology and Medicine.* Cambridge: Cambridge University Press, 1956.

# METHOD IN THE PSYCHOLOGY OF RELIGION

# Introduction

## H. NEWTON MALONY

What are the ways and means by which psychologists have studied religion? These are the themes in this section.

A topical survey beginning with the last part of the nineteenth century and continuing through the 1950's is included in Flakoll's article. He introduces the major themes and thinkers of this period and provides a descriptive list of the various methods used.

Warren covers the decade from 1960 to 1970, giving special attention to definitions of religion, the study of religion and prejudice, and the personality correlates of religious behavior. The weaknesses of current approaches in research are also enumerated.

The final article in this section discusses a critical issue for the psychology of religion, i.e., whether personal experience is legitimate data for study. Havens compares several ways of gathering information and suggests that the experiences of participants provide the basis for religious research.

This portion of the book will, perhaps, awaken in the student a desire to do his/her own research.

# A History of Method in the Psychology of Religion (1900-1960)

DAVID A. FLAKOLL

## HISTORICAL ORIENTATION

It is difficult to appreciate fully some of the methods of investigation which have been used in the psychology of religion without briefly reviewing the historical times, trends, and men instrumental in facilitating them.

### Precursors

Psychological comments about religion stem from man's earliest history. Buddha, Jeremiah, Socrates, Paul, Plotinus, Augustine, Edwards—all these men reflected on their inner experiences. Søren Kierkegaard sought relief from the abstractions of speculative philosophy, and as Johnson (1959) suggested, "Psychologists who had dwelt in the halls of philosophy became restless and moved to the laboratories of science" (p. 17).

Other philosophical and theological assumptions which served to provide the background for the movement were furnished by certain European precursors (Stolz, 1937). David Hume in *The Natural History of Religion* (1755) viewed religion as arising out of man's nature. He also implied that religion could be studied objectively. August Comte advocated a positivistic philosophy and emphasized the sociological origin and nature of religion. Immanuel Kant denied traditional arguments for God and viewed the moral obligations within man as divine commands. Opposing the intellectual interpretation of the nature of religion, Friedrich Schleiermacher suggested that the domain of religion is intuition and feeling rather than thinking or behavior.

The "new psychology" of Wilhelm Wundt emphasized a natural science approach which experimentally dealt with man's conscious

Paper presented as part of the Special Symposium on Methods in the Psychology of Religion held at the annual meeting of the Society for the Scientific Study of Religion, New York City.

processes. From Wundt came fresh psychological concepts, and his students carried these and the scientific contagion to America.

Another important shift in thought occurred as a result of Charles Darwin. He viewed man as very much a part of the natural order, which meant that his behavior might be more significantly investigated by the methods of natural science.

E. B. Tylor was another intellectual precursor who gave impetus to the objective study of religion by suggesting, as the result of ethnological research, that animism might be the best explanation for the origin of religion.

It should also be said that the psychology of religion became particularly significant in America about the turn of the century because the spirit of the times continued to facilitate the spontaneous expression of religious feelings. The more traditional and formal religious observances of Europe could hardly compare with some of the bizarre kinds of religious phenomena generated in early American history.

## Pioneers

It was G. Stanley Hall who reported an empirical study of conversion in 1881. Later he founded Clark University, which at the turn of the century became the most productive center for the serious study of the psychology of religion. In 1904 Hall introduced *The Journal of Religious Psychology* —the first American journal in the field. By inviting Freud and Jung to lecture at Clark University in 1909, he did much to interest them in the origin of religious phenomena.

Two Clark University graduates made significant contributions. In 1899 Edwin Starbuck published the first systematic work in the field, entitled *The Psychology of Religion.* Despite opposition to his examination of religious experience, Starbuck did much to popularize the questionnaire method.

As a result of his "naturalistic" point of view and many of his published writings James Leuba generated considerable interest in the field. His main contribution was a comparison of the sources and methods of magic and religion.

The most influential of the pioneers was William James, and his *The Varieties of Religious Experience* is a landmark in the field. Material for these 1901–1902 Gifford lectures was drawn primarily from recorded cases of religious belief and behavior. Hiltner (1947) aptly summarized the major contributions that James made to the psychological understanding of religion.

First, he created enthusiasm for and interest in the subject, a matter of no small importance. Second, he used empirical material, but put it in a framework which made it clear that psychology was not sufficient by itself. Third, he gave impetus to a new vantage point for evaluating religious beliefs not so much in terms of their truth as in terms of their operational significance in human life, i.e., whether they were "healthy" or not. Fourth, he turned attention to more contemporary empirical methods in studying religion, to observable phenomena, and not merely to document accounts of primitivity. Fifth, to some extent he applied his study even to those types of religious functions that were fashionable, and not merely to those which were of the recent past. Sixth, he helped greatly to overcome the distrust of psychological study of religion as such by demonstrating that his own study had not made him lose interest in religion in a personal sense (p. 79).

George Coe (1900, 1916) was a pioneer whose special interest was religious education. A particular contribution of his was a study that identified various religious experiences as a function of the individual's temperament. This study is of particular interest because it provides a unique outline of some methods of investigation in use at the time. These methods are well summarized by Johnson (1959).

[Coe] constructed a list of questions not only to record facts but also to reflect the personality of the writer in anticipation of projective and personality tests used today. After securing these written personal documents he then had interviews to cross-examine, clear up doubtful points, and gain new important facts. A scale was constructed to guide him in "objective observation of temperamental manifestations." Interviews were had also with friends and acquaintances of the persons examined to gather impressions and observations from them. The reports of independent observers were collated and checked off against one another. Such observations were conducted in the manner of the recent "situational testing" to gain an all-around view of the person through his behavioral responses. Finally, he employed hypnotic experiments to get at the facts of suggestibility (p. 23).

Other pioneers were James Pratt (1907), Edward Ames (1910), and George Stratton (1911). Pratt focused on the nature of belief; Ames contributed an anthropological and sociological theory of the origin, growth and significance of religious behavior; and Stratton published a description of the conflicting forces in religious experience.

## Approaches

The functional point of view was important in the early history of the psychology of religion. Wilhelm Wundt (1916) had supported the theory that religion resulted from those influences which assist man in the struggles of life. He approached some of man's early mythical ideas from a genetic point of view, and lent credence to a psychology of religion based on anthropology. Others who concentrated more fully on the psychology of religion from a functional point of view were Hall, Coe, King, and Ames.

Pratt (1908) has claimed that the naturalistic attitude dominated in a general way all the writers of the field. But James Leuba was certainly the most consistent and dogmatic of the pioneers. For him the idea of supernatural intervention was discounted, and religious phenomena were the result of suggestion.

Though many of the classical studies were anecdotal in origin, attempts were still made to retain an empirical approach to the data. For example, the studies of Hall, Starbuck, Leuba, and Coe reflected a concern for obtaining empirical data, and William James with his work *The Varieties of Religious Phenomena* did much to popularize the examination of concrete religious phenomena.

Much of the literature in the history of the psychology of religion has reflected the psychoanalytic approach. Extensive reviews of some of this literature are available, including Cronbach (1926), Jones (1926), and Casey (1938). Later in this century Strunk (1959) also reported, "the majority of the current studies dealing with religious development are psychoanalytic and/or psychiatric in orientation" (p. 108).

The psychoanalytic approach tended to lead the psychological study of religion away from its already weak empirical moorings, and the behavioristic or Gestalt views of psychology were unable to anchor the young discipline in solid objective data. In fact, the behavioristic movement, with its oversimplified conceptual scheme, did much to distract scientists from the study of complex religious phenomena.

Finally, there was an approach to religion represented by Rudolf Otto which left behind empirical data altogether. The theory presented in Otto's book *The Idea of the Holy* is based on an intuitive hypothesis which ascribes religion to the apprehension of what Otto calls the "Wholly Other." This book probably reflected the spirit of the times more than any other in its attempts to de-empiricize the study of religion.

## Themes

Early studies in the psychology of religion focused on various phenomena of adolescence. Hall (1891) led the way with an article entitled "The Moral and Religious Training of Children." In 1904 he published *Adolescence,* which reflected on the religious difficulties of young people. Other psychologists who referred to the same subject included Burnham (1891), Daniels (1895), and Lancaster (1895).

Conversion phenomena were another popular topic of consideration. Early studies were made by Leuba (1896), Starbuck (1897, 1899),
Coe (1900), and Clark (1929). A more recent review of empirical studies
of religious conversion experience by Allison (1966) indicated that
there was still current research being done in this area.

William James made a great contribution to the psychology of
religion when he indicated that its subject matter ought to include other
kinds of experience besides that connected with adolescence and conversion (Trout, 1931). *The Varieties of Religious Experience* made reference to a great number of religious phenomena including mysticism,
prayer, healthy- and unhealthy-mindedness, the divided self, ecstasy,
and so on. Other important themes which came under the purview of
early investigators in the psychology of religion included religious education, belief, development, ceremonials, and the origin of religion.

## Trends

It is usually agreed that William James' *The Varieties of Religious
Experience* (1902) marks the high point in the field of the psychology of
religion. James was a brilliant and popular psychologist, and his work
provided a foundation on which the psychology of religion as an empirical discipline might flourish. And for a time it appeared to do just that as
other pioneers, like Starbuck, Coe, Pratt, Leuba, and Stratton, made
substantial contributions. During the second decade, while psychological studies concentrated on problems of origins, definition and sys-
tematization, the empirical study of religion was beginning to wane.
Even though there was optimism about the future of the discipline,
many articles appeared in the 1920's that showed evidence of strong
apologetic and applied interest in the field, written by men who had
neglected to develop more sophisticated methods of research. To a great
extent, the mass of inferior material which was produced either concentrated on interesting speculation or sought to defend the Christian
enterprise from the "threat" of psychology. In addition, much of the
research was imitative rather than innovative with respect to theory
and methodology. This trend continued in the 1930's and 1940's. Indeed, reviews by Page (1951) and Boisen (1953) indicated that the
subject was considered by those in academic psychology with almost
complete indifference, if not positive suspicion and disfavor. For
example, a survey of contemporary textbooks in psychology, e.g.,
Ruch's *Psychology of Living,* revealed that such works often made only
brief mention of religion as a possible source of racial prejudice. Page

also compared the content of the 1929 edition of Gardner Murphy's *Historical Introduction to Modern Psychology* to that of the 1949 edition. The early edition gave equal space and prominence to the psychology of religion and social psychology, but the later edition contained only two or three pages concerning James' *The Varieties of Religious Experience.*

## METHODS OF INVESTIGATION

Historically speaking, techniques of data collection in the study of the psychology of religion are varied, indicating the expansive way religious phenomena have been viewed by those desiring to understand them. The twenty methods reviewed in this paper overlap in places, but, because each is unique, they are dealt with separately.

1. *Questionnaires.* One of the leading techniques used in the psychological study of religion, the questionnaire method consists of compiling a list of queries designed to accumulate comparative data on specific topics.

Francis Galton had much to do with inventing the questionnaire method. G. Stanley Hall (1904) used the method in the "Adolescent Study of Conversion" by printing his questions in various church papers and making them available at colleges and revival meetings. Starbuck (1899) had implicit confidence in the questionnaire method, and his approach included going directly to the individuals themselves and obtaining records of their religious experience with the use of question lists. Clark (1929) employed a questionary to indicate how a shift in religious development had taken place in the thirty years since Starbuck's study.

Also, Leuba (1921) used the method to obtain information about belief in immortality and God, and Pratt (1907), in the appendix to his book, included a questionnaire which he used to study belief in God.

William James remarked in the preface of Starbuck's (1899) excellent volume that "the question-circular method of collecting information had already in America reached the proportions of an incipient nuisance in psychological and pedagogical matters." Nevertheless, Starbuck pursued his task, and James, to his chagrin, later had to admit that the results justified his student's faith in the method.

But it is evident that this method of research has certain limitations and detractions. Ligon (1956) repeatedly emphasized the difficulty of formulating good questions. Watson (1927) cited a resolution by a meeting of experimental psychologists at the University of Pennsylvania (1926), which passed with the approval of such notables as

Boring, Titchener, and Woodworth, to the effect that even scientists don't like to fill out questionnaires.

> Resolved, that this meeting deplores the increasing practice of collecting administrative or supposedly scientific data by way of questionnaires; and that the meeting deplores especially the practice under which graduate students undertake research by sending questionnaires to professional psychologists (p. 55).

Stolz (1937) has pointed out the defects of the questionnaire method of research more explicitly.

> Lapse of memory, unconscious exaggeration or suppression, suggestion, lack of spontaneity and descriptive inability may conspire to defeat the attempt to secure noteworthy accounts of religious belief, experience, and behavior (p. 136).

Yet Stolz has suggested that over the years certain refinements have been made to give the questionnaire method more credibility in the psychology of religion. Multi-choice, true-false, cross out, completion, and verbal association questionnaires have displaced the original "cumbersome direct question outlines" of the early pioneers, consequently making for higher degrees of reliability.

2. *Interview*. Several of the pioneers, including Coe (1900) and Starbuck (1899), used the interview method to collect their data. Johnson, in his book *Psychology of Religion,* has reported that James Leuba studied religious conversion for his doctoral research. He conducted interviews with a large number of Christian converts and gained firsthand information of their experiences. Johnson attributed to Leuba the introduction of this method of investigation and suggested that it "provides opportunity to explore questions further and secure more adequate information by sharpening issues in face to face conversation" (p. 21).

3. *Biographical*. G. Stanley Hall recommended that knowledge of teen-agers might be obtained through autobiographies and diaries. Pioneers in the psychology of religion, such as Starbuck (1899) and James (1902), used this method extensively. *The Varieties of Religious Experience* is filled with such case material.

To be sure, the biographical method provides vivid and dramatic testimonies, but indiscriminate and exclusive use of this method is likely to provide data which is only marginally reliable (Stolz, 1937).

4. *Content Analysis*. William James chose to allow much of his anecdotal material to speak for itself rather than to attempt analyzing or separating it into component parts. However, content analysis is a research technique for the objective, systematic, and quantitative de-

scription of any linguistic expression. Berelson (1952) provided a list of sixteen uses of content analysis of verbal material which further describes this method. Some of the pioneers used content analysis on their anecdotal material. Albert Coe (1900) used the method to examine eleven hundred hymns to assist him in clarifying the temperamental factors in religious experience. More recent users of content analysis include Arlow (1951) and Strunk (1958).

5. *Recreative*. Stolz (1937) described what he called the "re-creative method" as an "effort to reconstruct with the aid of anthropology, social psychology, and genetic psychology, early man's religious beliefs, attitudes, and behavior" (p. 139). Among the pioneers who employed this method were Ames (1910), Stratton (1911), King (1910), and Leuba (1925).

Stolz suggested that, although the method has added to an understanding of primitive religious origins and culture, it is very difficult to verify the comparisons made between the religious experience of primitive man and his modern counterpart because of the dearth of information on prehistoric peoples.

6. *Diary*. Oskar Kupky (1928) objected to the questionnaire method because answers often reflected an individual's stereotyped way of thinking about and expressing religious belief. He criticized the experimental method because of the experimental situation. As a result, he chose to collect and interpret more spontaneous expressions of religious experience contained in the diaries, letters, and poems of adolescents.

7. *Documentary*. Psychologists of religion have also been interested in the study of the world's sacred literature. The documentary method involves a critical psychological comparison of sacred writings in order to discover common and dissimilar elements embodied in various religions. A pioneer who particularly used the method of literary analysis was George Stratton (1911, 1923), who applied it to studying the religious significance of conflict and anger.

8. *Psycho-historical*. When James Pratt (1907) chose to study religious belief, he employed a psycho-historical analysis. Rather than confining his data to psychology, Pratt also used what he could of the results of anthropology and the history of religion. His examination indicated that though primitive religion as it develops in various contexts becomes more intellectualized, feeling always remains the fundamental basis of religious belief.

9. *Introspection*. E. L. Schaub (1926) has reported that Girgensohn (1921, 1923) was convinced that the psychology of religion could profit from studying living individuals rather than historical persons or

religious phenomena. Using systematic introspection under controlled conditions, he asked trained observers to express a judgment regarding a number of very different poems. Since he believed that the core of religion consists of an intuitively entertained God-consciousness, which the self, in turn, reflects, Girgensohn maintained that introspection is a key investigative method.

10. *Observation.* Stolz (1937) has suggested that "the method of personal observation applied unobtrusively and with the maximum elimination of bias and prejudice provides first-hand knowledge of specific forms of religious behavior and the conditions under which they have evolved" (p. 141). This method is particularly applicable to examination of group behavior, and Stolz recommended it for personal investigation of spiritistic seances, speaking in tongues, revival meetings, and the like.

Walter Houston Clark (1958) viewed "participant observation" as a "most promising technique for the psychology of religion." He cited an article by Kluckhorn (1940) as having set the stage of the increased use of this method, which encourages the investigator to identify himself with the group to be studied and to participate in some of its activities.

11. *Order of Merit.* Mark May (1915) has reported a preliminary attempt to apply the order of merit method to the study of "religious values." The research involved the presentation of twenty-five religious situations in which fifty seminary students were asked to imagine themselves as participating. The students were then told to rank these situations in order of religious and moral merit and in order of the pleasure that these situations conveyed to them. May concluded his discussion with the statement that the "order of merit" procedure "is a very satisfactory method of defining and bringing out of obscurity what we mean when we talk in such vague terms about the 'values of life.' "

12. *Scales.* It might be recalled that Albert Coe (1900) used the scale "to guide him in objective observation of temperamental manifestations." Some years later Thurstone and Chave (1928) described some of the issues involved in measuring attitudes and included in their discussion a scale for measuring attitudes toward the church. Except for those attitudes concerned with the dimension of religious orthodoxy and for those that indicate how the individuals perceive the church, Funk (1958) claimed that psychologists involved in measurement studies overlooked the study of religious attitudes. He therefore developed six religious attitude scales in a study of the relationship between religious attitudes and manifest anxiety. Other recent scales which have been devised are Brown and Lowe's Religious Belief Scale,

Levinson's Religious Conventionalism Scale, Wilson's Extrinsic Religious Values Scale, Hogge and Friedman's Scriptural Literalism Scale, and Broen's Religious Attitude Inventory.

13. *Tests*. William James' pragmatic test in *The Varieties of Religious Experience* to determine the value of the individual's religious feelings rested on an examination of their "fruits." In addition, during the history of the psychology of religion, investigators have concentrated heavily on paper and pencil tests. For example, in 1927 Goodwin Watson's *Experimentation and Measurement in Religious Education* discussed methods of measurement and construction of tests. Watson also described nearly fifty paper and pencil tests and a variety of conduct and behavior tests that have been used to collect data.

14. *Statistics*. Francis Galton (1872) insisted that statistical methods should be applied to study the objective efficiency of prayer, and Talbert (1931) has suggested that Galton's pioneering efforts in the field of the psychology of religion deserve more recognition. Edwin Starbuck (1899) arranged quantitative data in statistical patterns with the use of charts and graphs. Although William James (1902) did not follow Starbuck's use of statistical methods, he remarked in the preface to Starbuck's book that:

> Such statistical arguments are not mathematical proofs, but they support presumptions and establish probabilities, and in spite of the lack of precision in many of their data, they yield results not to be got at in any less clumsy way (p. ix).

Another pioneer who illustrates the use of statistical method with questionnaire data is James Leuba (1921), who made an anthropological, statistical study of religious belief.

The use of statistics in the study of religious phenomena was examined by Clark (1958). He gave special attention to factor analysis as a useful technique for studying the diverse elements of religious phenomena. A study by Shand (1953) is referred to as an example of the use of the factor of analytic technique.

15. *Experimental*. Although Albert Coe (1900), a pioneer in the use of experimental methods, employed hypnosis to determine the suggestibility of various personality types with reference to religious states such as mysticism, the experimental method in the history of the psychology of religion has not fared well. Stolz (1937) has written that "the laboratory type of experimentation in religion has not proved successful" (p. 145).

Ernest Ligon's *Dimensions of Character* provides a helpful orientation to research methods in the field of religious and character education and offers some illustrations of experimentation that are applicable to the psychology of religion. However, Klausner (1964) reviewed methods of data gathering as reported in articles that surveyed empirical studies published in the United States between 1950–1960 in the psychology and sociology of religion. He discovered that only 2% of 130 studies used laboratory experimental methods.

16. *Survey.* Studies by Allport, Gillespie, Young (1948), and Ross (1950) illustrate the use of the survey method to investigate religious beliefs. Braden (1954) used this method to study healing experiences known to pastors of Protestant churches.

Watson (1927) has provided a review of the use of survey methods and maintained that they are desirable in certain respects. They enable the psychologist to study problems which cannot be experimentally controlled, report the "natural experimentation" brought about by certain events in daily life, and make it possible to study certain factors that could not be ethically introduced into an experiment. However, there are difficulties inherent in the survey method, e.g., the large group that needs to be secured and studied and the object measurement of significant variables.

17. *Personal Documents.* In *The Use of Personal Documents in Psychological Science,* Gordon Allport wrote:

> One of the most subjective of all areas of experience is the religious life. It is safe to say that it has never been studied with even partial adequacy by other means than the personal document. . . . It is apparently impossible to take even the first steps in the psychology of religion without a sympathetic regard for subjective documentary records (p. 38).

This paper has examined the use of personal documents, such as questionnaires, autobiographies, interviews, diaries, etc., as a method of data collection. Indeed, Allport reaffirmed the usefulness of such personal documents in the tradition of William James. Allport, in his use of such material, was more critical than James, but each chose to examine what was unique in the religious experience of the individual (cf. Allport, 1950).

Although Allport (1951) recognized the limitations of relying on such "introspective protocols," he believed that "bold and radical experimentation" was needed, and that, "properly used, such documents anchor a discipline in the bedrock of human experience" (p. 191).

18. *Projective Techniques.* Recognizing that "most studies seem lacking in specific techniques for obtaining objective data needed in gaining a scientific description of religious factors," Helson and Jones (1957) adopted the Q-technique to the study of the Christian deity concepts of God and Jesus as compared with parent concepts of Mother

and Father. They concluded that the Q-technique (Stephenson, 1953) may have value for further study of religious concepts. Other studies that illustrate the use of a projective methodology were conducted by Lowe (1955), who studied religious beliefs and delusions with a Religious Projection Test, and Dreger (1952), who studied personality correlates of religious attitudes by using projective instruments such as the Rosenzweig's Picture Frustration Study, the Rorschach, and the Thematic Apperception Test.

19. *Clinical.* Reference has been made earlier in this paper to the great number of psychoanalytic studies of religion. The great progenitors of this movement were Sigmund Freud and Carl Jung. Paul Pruyser (1968) has suggested that psychoanalytic studies of religion have a "special character," conceptually as well as methodologically:

> They are basically studies of motivation for religion, and the person's set of beliefs and practices are approached from the point of view of wish fulfillment, drive control, primary- and secondary-process thinking, object relations, the genesis of conscience and the ego ideal, and the economics of individual and aggressive urges (p. 6).

In *A Dynamic Psychology of Religion,* Pruyser has made a strong case for the clinical perspective in the study of religious phenomena. Also, Paul Johnson (1959) has written a *Psychology of Religion* with special emphasis on the case study method.

20. *Timed Cross-Examination.* In recent years Orlo Strunk (1965) has been quite active in the psychology of religion. He has suggested a methodological innovation in the study of religious values and attitudes. The timed cross-examination test combines a traditional paper and pencil test with a device that measures the time it takes for a subject to respond to the test stimuli. This results in a record of conscious-voluntary reactions and in another record of those reactions that are subconscious-automatic. It is predicted that the use of this method will result in a more accurate study of religious beliefs and attitudes as well as of the motivational systems of religious practitioners.

## SUMMARY

The broad focus of this paper has been upon the methods of data collection in the psychology of religion from about 1900 to 1960. An historical orientation has dealt with some of the precursors, pioneers, approaches, themes, and trends that have served to facilitate the development of the twenty methods reviewed in the second section.

As the 1960's approached, there appeared to be increased interest in the psychology of religion. References might be made to systematic studies, e.g., Clark (1958), Johnson (1959), Strunk (1962), etc., which increased interest in the field. Also, studies of religion began to appear more frequently in the literature. Several journals were formed that dealt specifically with research in religion, among them the *Journal for the Scientific Study of Religion* (1961) and *Review of Religious Research* (1959). In addition, a new academic institution on the West Coast came into being, whose purpose is to relate psychology and religion in theory, research, and practice, i.e., the Graduate School of Psychology of Fuller Theological Seminary (1965).

An historical overview of the psychology of religion reveals methods of research which, for the most part, have been of the comparatively unsophisticated paper and pencil variety, with the questionnaire method dominating the field (cf. Klausner, 1964).

To be sure, the discipline has had a long pioneering period as a result of the limitations of the methods it has used. Indeed, little emphasis has been placed on experimental research. But with the advent of the 1960's conditions were about to change and research in the psychology of religion would, most likely, be characterized by an improved methodology.

## BIBLIOGRAPHY

Academy of Religion and Mental Health, *Research in Religion and Health:* Proceedings of the Fifth Academic Symposium, 1961. New York: Fordham University Press, 1963.

ALLISON, J. Recent empirical studies of religious conversion experiences. *Pastoral Psychology*, 1966, 17(166), 21–34.

ALLPORT, G. W. *The Use of Personal Documents in Psychological Science.* New York: Social Science Research Council, 1951.

ALLPORT, G. W.; GILLESPIE, J. M.; AND YOUNG, J. The religion of the postwar college student. *The Journal of Psychology*, XXV (1948), 3–33.

AMES, E. S. *The Psychology of Religious Experience.* Boston: Houghton Mifflin Company, 1910.

ARLOW, J. A. The consecration of the prophet. *Psychoanalytic Quarterly*, 1951, 20, 374–397.

BARRY, F. R. *Christianity and Psychology.* London: Student Christian Movement Press, 1923.

BERELSON, B. *Content Analysis in Communication Research.* Glencoe: The Free Press, 1952.

BERKOWITZ, M. I. AND JOHNSON, J. E. *Social Scientific Studies of Religion: A Bibliography.* Pittsburgh, University of Pittsburgh Press, 1967.

BOISEN, A. T. The present status of William James' psychology of religion. *Journal of Pastoral Care*, 1953, 7, 155–157.

BRADEN, C. S. Study of spiritual healing in the churches. *Pastoral Psychology*, 5, 1954, 9–15.

BROEN, W. E., JR. A factor analytic study of religious attitudes. *Journal of Abnormal and Social Psychology*, 1957, 54, 176–179.

# D. A. Flakoll

BROEN, W. E., JR. Personality correlates of certain religious attitudes. *Journal of Consulting Psychology*, 1955, 19, 64.

BROWN, D. G. AND LOWE, M. L. Religious belief and personality characteristics in college students. *Journal of Social Psychology*, 1951, 33: 103–129.

BURNHAM, W. H. A study of adolescence. *Pedagogical Seminary*, 1891, 1, 175–195.

CASEY, R. P. The psychoanalytic study of religion. *The Journal of Abnormal and Social Psychology*, 1938, 33, 437–452.

CLARK, E. T. *Psychology of Religious Awakening*. New York: The Macmillan Company, 1929.

CLARK, W. H. *The Psychology of Religion*. New York: The Macmillan Company, 1958.

COE, G. A. *The Psychology of Religion*. Chicago: The University of Chicago Press, 1916.

COE, G. A. *The Spiritual Life*. New York: Eaton & Mains, 1900.

CONKLIN, E. S. *The Psychology of Religious Adjustment*. New York: The Macmillan Company, 1929.

CRONBACH, A. Religion and psychoanalysis. *Psychological Bulletin*, 1926, 23, 701–713.

CRONBACH, A. The psychology of religion: a biographical survey. *Psychological Bulletin*, 1928, 25, 701–718.

DANIELS, A. H. The new life: a study in regeneration. *American Journal of Psychology*, 1895, 6, 61–103.

DREGER, R. M. Some personality correlates of religious attitudes as determined by projective techniques. *Psychological Monographs*, 1952, 66 (3).

FERGUSON, L. W. *Personality Measurement*. New York: McGraw-Hill Book Co., 1952.

FERGUSON, L. W. The evaluative attitudes of Jonathan Swift. *Psychological Reports*, 1939, 3, 26–44.

FESTINGER, L. AND KATZ, D. (Eds.). *Research Methods in the Behavioral Sciences*. New York: The Dryden Press, 1953.

FREUD, S. The future of an illusion. In J. Strachey (Ed.). *The Standard Edition of the Complete Psychological Works of Sigmund Freud*. Vol. XXI. London: Hogarth Press, 1961.

FUNK, R. A. Experimental scales used in a study of religious attitudes as related to manifest anxiety. *Psychological Newsletter*, 1958, 9, 238–244.

GALTON, F. Statistical inquiries into the efficiency of prayer. *Fortnightly*, August, 1872.

GEE, W. *Social Science Research Methods*. New York: Appleton Century Crofts, Inc., 1929.

GIRGENSOHN, K. *Der Seelische Aufbau Des Religioesen Erlebens*. Leipzig: Hirzel, 1921.

GIRGENSOHN, K. *Religionspsycholien Religionswissenschaft und Religion*. Leipzig: Antritisvorlesung, 1923.

GREGORY, W. E. The psychology of religion: some suggested areas of research to psychology. *The Journal of Abnormal and Social Psychology*, 1952, 47, 256–258.

HALL, G. S. *Adolescence*. New York: D. Appleton & Co., 1904, II, 292–362.

HALL, G. S. The moral and religious training of children and adolescents. *Pedagogical Seminary*, 1891, 1.

HAVIGHURST, R. S. AND TABA, H. *Adolescent Character and Personality*. New York: John Wiley & Sons, Inc., 1949.

HILTNER, S. The psychological understanding of religion. *Crozer Quarterly*, 1947, 24, 3–26.

HOGGE, J. H. AND FRIEDMAN, S. T. The scriptural literalism scale: a preliminary report. *The Journal of Psychology*, 1967, 66, 275–279.

JAMES, W. *The Varieties of Religious Experience*. New York: Longmans, Green and Co., 1902.

JOHNSON, P. E. *Psychology of Religion*. New York: Abingdon Press, 1959.

JONES, E. The psychology of religion. *British Journal of Medical Psychology*, 1926, VI, 264–269.

JOSEY, C. C. *The Psychology of Religion*. New York: The Macmillan Co., 1928.

JUNG, C. G. *Modern Man in Search of a Soul*. New York: Harcourt Brace & Co., 1933.

JUNG, C. G. *Psychology and Religion*. New Haven, Conn.: Yale University Press, 1938.

KING, I. *The Development of Religion*. New York: The Macmillan Co., 1960.

KLAUSNER, S. Methods of data collection in studies of religion. *Journal for the Scientific Study of Religion,* 1964, III, 2, 193–203.

KLUCKHORN, F. The participant observer technique in small communities. *American Journal of Sociology,* 1940, 46, 331–343.

KUPKY, O. *The Religious Development of Adolescents.* New York: Macmillan, 1928.

LANCASTER, E. G. The psychology and pedagogy of adolescence. *Pedagogical Seminary,* 1895, 5, 61–128.

LEUBA, J. H. *A Psychological Study of Religion.* New York: The Macmillan Co., 1912.

LEUBA, J. H. *Psychology of Religious Mysticism.* New York: Harcourt, Brace, & Co., 1925.

LEUBA, J. H. *The Belief in God and Immortality.* Chicago: University of Chicago Press, 1921.

LEUBA, J. H. The psychology of religious phenomena. *American Journal of Psychology,* 1896, 7, 309–385.

LEVINSON, D. J. The intergroup relations workshop: its psychological aims and effects. *Journal of Psychology,* 1954, 38, 103–126.

LIGON, E. M. *Dimensions of Character.* New York: The Macmillan Co., 1956.

LOWE, W. L. Religious beliefs and religious delusions: a comparative study of religious projection. *American Journal of Psychotherapy,* 1955, 9, 54–61.

MARET, R. R. *The Threshold of Religion.* London: Methuen & Co., 1909.

MAY, M. A. An experimental study of values. *The Journal of Philosophy,* XII, 1915, 691.

MUDGE, E. L. *The God Experience.* Cincinnati: Caxton Press, 1923.

MURPHY, G. A note on method in the psychology of religion. *The Journal of Philosophy,* 1928, 25, 337–345.

NELSON, M. D. AND JONES, E. M. An application of Q technique to the study of religious concepts. *Psychological Reports,* III, 293–97.

OLT, R. *An Approach to the Psychology of Religion.* Boston: The Christopher Publishing House, 1956.

OTTO, R. *The Idea of the Holy.* Trans. J. W. Harvey. London: Oxford University Press, 1928.

PAGE, F. H. The psychology of religion after fifty years. *Canadian Journal of Psychology,* 1951, V, 60–67.

PRATT, J. B. *The Psychology of Religious Belief.* New York: The Macmillan Co., 1910.

PRATT, J. B. *The Religious Consciousness.* New York: The Macmillan Co., 1920.

PRUYSER, PAUL W. *A Dynamic Psychology of Religion.* New York: Harper & Row, 1968.

ROSS, M. G. *Religious Beliefs in Youth.* New York: Association Press, 1950.

SANCTIS, S. de. *Religious Conversion.* New York: Harcourt, Brace & Co., 1927.

SCHAUB, E. L. The psychology of religion. *Psychological Bulletin,* 1926, 23, 681–700.

SCHAUB, E. L. The present status of the psychology of religion. *Journal of Religion,* 1922, II, 362–379.

SHAND, J. D. A factor-analytic study of Chicago protestant ministers' conceptions of what it means to be religious. Ph.D. dissertation, University of Chicago, 1953.

STARBUCK, E. D. A study of conversion. *American Journal of Psychology,* 1897, 8, 268–308.

STARBUCK, E. D. *Psychology of Religion.* New York: Charles Scribner's Sons, 1899.

STEPHENSON, W. *The Study of Behavior. Q Technique and Its Methodology.* Chicago: University of Chicago, 1953.

STOLZ, K. R. *The Psychology of Religious Living.* Nashville: Abingdon-Cokesbury Press, 1937.

STRATTON, G. M. *Anger: Its Religious and Moral Significance.* New York: The Macmillan Co., 1923.

STRATTON, G. M. *Psychology of the Religious Life.* London: George Allen & Co., 1911.

STRUNK, O., JR. A redefinition of the psychology of religion. *Psychological Reports,* 1957, III, 138.

STRUNK, O., JR. Humanistic religious psychology: a new chapter in the psychology of religion. *The Journal of Pastoral Care,* Vol. XXIV, June, 1970, No. 2, pp. 90–97.

# D. A. Flakoll

STRUNK, O., JR. (Ed.). *Readings in the Psychology of Religion*. New York: Abingdon Press, 1959.

STRUNK, O., JR. The psychology of religion: an historical and contemporary survey. *Psychological Newsletter*. New York: New York University, 1958, IX, 181–199.

STRUNK, O., JR. Theological students: a study in perceived motives. *Personnel Guidance Journal*, 1958, 36, 320–322.

TALBERT, E. L. On Francis Galton's contribution to the science of religion. *Scientific Monthly*, 1933, XXXVII, 205–249.

THOULESS, R. H. *An Introduction to the Psychology of Religion*. New York: The Macmillan Co., 1923.

THURSTONE, L. L. AND CHAVE, E. J. *The Measurement of Attitude*. Chicago: The University of Chicago Press, 1929.

TROUT, D. M. *Religious Behavior*. New York: The Macmillan Co., 1931.

TYLOR, E. B. *Primitive Culture*. New York: Brentano's, 1924.

WATSON, G. B. *Experiments and Measurements in Religious Education*. New York: Association Press, 1927.

WHITE, R. W. Black boy: a value analysis. *Journal of Abnormal and Social Psychology*, 1947, 42, 440–461.

WHITE, R. W. Value analysis: a quantitative method for describing qualitative data. *Journal of Social Psychology*, 1944, 19, 351–358.

WILSON, W. C. Extrinsic religious values and prejudice. *Journal of Abnormal and Social Psychology*, 1960, 60(2).

WUNDT, W. *Elements of Folk Psychology*. New York: The Macmillan Co., 1916.

# Empirical Studies in the Psychology of Religion: An Assessment of the Period 1960-1970

NEIL C. WARREN

From 1950 to 1960, one hundred thirty articles reporting on empirical studies in the psychology and sociology of religion were published in the United States (Klausner, 1964). Of these only some 30 percent were written by psychologists, while well over 50 percent were written by sociologists. Between 150 and 175 empirical studies in the psychology and sociology of religion were published between 1960 and 1970. Again, 25 to 35 percent were written by psychologists, and by far the majority were authored by sociologists.

More important, perhaps, is the fact that only 2 percent of the 130 articles in the 1950's reported on the use of experimental methodology. That is, only two or three studies employed a design that allowed for the manipulation of the independent variable(s) (Klausner, 1964). Likewise, this writer has been able to uncover only three such articles published during the 1960's. Thus, for twenty years the entire discipline has been dominated by correlational research and, as a result, the field has failed to move forward with vigor and certainty. Cline and Richards (1965) conclude that "significant empirical studies of the psychology of religion are a real rarity, and that this has certainly not been a popular area of study for psychologists."

This is not to deny that impressive gains have been made on at least two fronts. For instance, with regard to the definition of religion, several investigators have contributed significantly during the past ten years. In early studies an attempt was made to formulate a single, comprehensive definition of religion. (See Dittes' significant article, "Psychology of Religion," in the 1969 edition of Lindzey and Aronson's *The Handbook of Social Psychology* for an excellent review of this issue.) This "unidimensional" approach often focussed on the areas of

Part of the Special Symposium on Methods in the Psychology of Religion held at the annual meeting of the Society for the Scientific Study of Religion, New York City, October 22–27, 1970.

93

belief and behavior. Church attendance and orthodoxy of belief came to be looked upon as the marks of a religious man. But religion was far too complex to be treated so simply. When significant positive correlations between this type of religion and numerous unfavorable traits began to be reported, investigators looked more closely. Multidimensional structures of religious belief and behavior emerged from more sophisticated factor analytic studies (e.g., Allen & Hites, 1961; Fukuyama, 1961; Spilka, Armatas & Nussbaum, 1964; Cline & Richards, 1965; Faulkner & DeJong, 1966; King, 1967; Keene, 1967; Monaghan, 1967; Maranell, 1968; Gorlow & Schroeder, 1968; Gorsuch, 1968). A number of researchers formulated their own lists of heterogeneous items which, when responded to by large samples, were grouped according to their similarities. For instance, Glock (1962) differentiated five independent dimensions that have stimulated considerable research. These are: the ideological dimension, concerned with religious beliefs; the ritualistic dimension, relating to religious practice; the experiential dimension, referring to religious feelings; the intellectual dimension, corresponding to religious knowledge; and, finally, the consequential dimension, having to do with the "implications of religion for 'conduct' in 'secular' affairs" (Glock, 1962). These factors or dimensions provide a more thoroughly differentiated picture, and we can now relate other traits and qualities to religion without equating persons so grossly.

This progress in reference to definition of religion led to immediate gains on other fronts. The development of insight with regard to the relationship of prejudice and "religion" has often been traced, but because of its importance (especially because it turned out so well in the 1960's) it deserves to be repeated. That churchgoers are more prejudiced than nonchurchgoers is a fact that became well established in the late 1940's and early 1950's (Allport & Kramer, 1946; Adorno, Frenkel-Brunswik, Levinson, & Sanford, 1950). But in the late 1950's a number of researchers independently reported results which showed that the relationship of church attendance and prejudice is not nearly so linear as some originally thought (e.g., Holtzman, 1956). Instead, it was shown that frequent attenders are significantly less prejudiced than infrequent attenders. Further, it became clear that frequent attenders were often less prejudiced than nonattenders.

Then in the 1960's Gordon Allport and his students brought unusual insight to the issue. Refusing to treat religion in terms of church attendance alone, they talked about extrinsic and intrinsic motivations (Allport & Ross, 1967). Wilson (1960) first related the extrinsic-intrinsic dimension to ethnic prejudice. Feagin (1964) continued this work of differentiating between church attenders in terms of their motivation for involvement. The extrinsically motivated person was conceived of as a "user" of religion while the intrinsically motivated person was defined as "one who lives his religion." It was found that extrinsically motivated persons are significantly more prejudiced than the intrinsically motivated. Furthermore, in 1967 Allport and Ross found that "churchgoers who are indiscriminately pro-religious are more prejudiced than the consistently extrinsic, and very much more prejudiced than the consistently intrinsic types." Other researchers (notably Spilka & Reynolds, 1965; Allen & Spilka, 1967; Maranell, 1967; Glock & Stark, 1966), have shed considerably more light on the issue until the correspondence between religion and prejudice has become, perhaps, the most fully understood relationship in the entire field.

These gains with regard to the definition of religion and its relation to prejudice, though they were perhaps the most dramatic steps forward during the 1960's, were not the only ones on the positive side of the ledger. The relationship of religion and personality characteristics was explored with some success (see Sanua, 1969, for a review of this area). Unfortunately, many of these studies failed to take advantage of the more adequate definitions of religion which were uncovered. Other writers have reported on studies of the relationship between psychedelic drugs and religion (e.g., Leary & Clark, 1963). If nothing more, they have encouraged us to think about possible correspondences. Other areas of concern were conversion (e.g., Brock, 1962; Allison, 1968), death (e.g., Williams & Cole, 1968), and prayer (e.g., Long, Elkind & Spilka, 1967). Finally, developmental studies have turned up some interesting leads.

But, when one has collected and read the 175 or so empirical studies which were published during the past decade, one cannot help but lament the "poverty and primitive state of this field" (terms used by Dittes, 1969). More significantly, there is much that has happened during the past ten years which seems to indicate that the discipline is caught in unproductive approaches which it finds difficult, if not impossible, to overcome. One is struck by the apparent surrender to methodological limits that characterizes a large number of studies. Without question, there are some studies that provide hope, but simple problems with regard to experimental methodology greatly decrease the helpfulness of the studies reported. Let me comment on six methodological problems which occurred to me as I read the articles.

First, the paucity of experimental studies is immediately noticeable. If it weren't for the Pearson product moment correlation coefficient, 90 percent of the studies in this field could not have utilized statistical analysis. I am not unfamiliar with the ongoing debate about the relative merits of correlational and experimental approaches. I am not suggesting that a field as young and unexplored as the psychology of religion cannot profit significantly from carefully planned, thoughtfully designed correlational studies. Neither do I discount the difficulty of approaching this field experimentally. Randomly to assign subjects to groups and then to manipulate an independent variable so that one group receives one amount and another group receives a different amount is often an impossible order. Though we must in many instances settle for different amounts of the independent variable on the basis of selection alone, we can still profit from these efforts. But the real concern one develops in this field is that careful, experimental studies may be viewed as inappropriate or too difficult or too expensive. When twenty years pass and fewer than ten studies are reported in which the scientific method has been fully utilized, one immediately suspects strong resistance to the method itself. But when the experimental approach is not used, the causal relation of the independent and dependent variables is exceedingly difficult to ascertain. The use of more experimental designs is definitely called for in the years ahead.

Second, the problem of sampling attracts our attention. Although several studies during the past decade reported careful sampling procedures, the vast majority used inadequate sampling techniques. A high percentage of the studies utilized student populations, with all the risks this involved. Bender (1968) reported, for instance, that a group of 96 graduates of the Dartmouth College class of 1940 increased significantly in religious orientation over the years.

> While the group was in the college the average *Study of Values* score was highest in the political value and lowest in the religious. However, 15 years later, the religious had risen to the level of the political. As undergraduates, only a minority of the men attended church with any degree of regularity; 15 years later the majority attended either weekly or monthly. Now 62 percent are church attenders (Bender, 1968).

This argues strongly against using student samples unless one is interested in generalizing one's results to student populations. If students themselves change radically with the passing of twenty-five years, how much different must they be from individuals currently twenty-five years older. If a high percentage of our information about the psychology of religion is directly applicable to student populations and of doubtful accuracy when applied to other age and interest groups, we should carefully consider the wisdom of choosing student populations merely because of convenience or economics.

Other sampling errors were apparent. For instance, the use of volunteer subjects has always been of doubtful advisability, but a large number of studies utilized volunteers from churches, colleges, etc. A study by Wicker (1968) clearly indicates that there is a sampling bias when investigators use only the most easily obtained subjects. Some articles reported on studies in which announcements were made from the pulpit that research instruments were "on the table in the foyer" and anybody interested should pick up a set. Reasonably large numbers of sets were taken, but usually only a small percentage were returned. This approach to sampling clearly leaves any findings in grave doubt with regard to their meaning.

Careful, random samples are rarely reported. And since there are virtually no experimental studies, random assignment to groups is even rarer. This aspect of methodology can be greatly strengthened.

Third, the problem of controls should be discussed. Most experimental psychology books make control a matter of central importance. Experimenters are strongly encouraged to carefully list all extraneous variables and then to explain how each will be controlled. However, in most studies in the psychology of religion there is virtual silence on the subject of controls. Because one seldom reads of elimination procedures, balancing, constancy of conditions, or counterbalancing, one often concludes that the experimenter must be assuming that any extraneous variables will be controlled by randomization. But besides the fact that randomization is of less significance in correlational approaches, the type of sample usually selected makes randomization highly unlikely.

The value of continuing studies in the psychology of religion will be greatly enhanced if careful efforts are made to control extraneous variables. The goal should be to maintain equivalence between any two groups being studied, in all ways, except with regard to the independent variable. Then we will be able to have greater confidence that any changes or differences in the dependent variable are due to the influence of the independent variable alone. It is not possible, of course, to control all variables that threaten to confound the results of a study, but the current approach of denying the existence of extraneous variables must be altered if the field is to advance.

Fourth, there is a great need to employ more sophisticated experimental designs. A number of studies during the past decade utilized highly sophisticated approaches to factor analysis and cluster analysis. These studies make valuable contributions to the field. If correlational approaches are desired, no more helpful statistical tool could be used than factor analysis. But there are numerous other designs that should be considered. Simple designs involving two randomized groups are available. Well-developed statistical techniques are available for designs employing more than two randomized groups. The entire field of factorial designs and analysis of variance remains untouched. These designs allow for the study of one, two, three, four, and more independent variables at once, with opportunities to study main effects and interactional aspects. There is no end to the types of designs available. The experimenter must be encouraged to take advantage of this fact so that designs are not chosen exclusively out of habit or fear.

Fifth, the field as a whole seems to have suffered from an over-enthusiastic generalization of findings. Although a number of studies specifically caution against this tendency, other investigators tend to forget the populations sampled and focus exclusively on the findings that were uncovered. Thus, for instance, one study may sample from a student population in a church-related college in Tennessee; before long, the findings from this study are applied to all college students, or worse yet, to all American citizens. Again, it should be said that several studies stand out in respect of their strong effort to sample from a broad population. Thus, when they generalize more broadly, they are quite within their rights. But too many studies include samples consisting of freshmen from X college in Y state and begin immediately in the discussion section with an approach to generalization clearly beyond what is appropriate. The tendency seems to be to assume that people are alike on all variables, and that what is true for one is true for all. This is an aspect which can be improved considerably, either in terms of populations sampled or in connection with more precise generalizations.

Finally, a word should be said about programmatic research. In a field as small as the psychology of religion, where, as I mentioned earlier, psychologists produced only about an average of four studies a year between 1950 and 1960, the need to capitalize on every effort is apparent. When studies are completed in peripheral areas, the field as a whole may benefit slightly. But when critical studies are run that relate to other work in the field, leverage is possible and genuine gain in understanding becomes much more likely. When it is possible for colleagues in a given school or area to collaborate on topics of mutual interest, possibilities for more extensive data collection procedures are enhanced, mutual intellectual stimulation is available, and more concentrated gains are inevitable. In addition, programmatic research serves to attract student interest, and student effort and ingenuity can contribute significantly to the field.

Except for the two or three areas mentioned earlier in the paper, an analysis of the empirical studies within the decade of the 1960's in the psychology of religion would have to be negative. However, with the substantial interest in the individual fields of psychology and religion and the incredible interest in the integration of the fields, there is definite hope for the future. The challenge is at least threefold: (1) to use the most effective scientific tools in conjunction with the most critical theorizing possible; (2) to attract large groups of students to study psychology of religion, by the empirical approach in particular—undoubtedly on the basis of the enthusiasm and competence of those already working in the field; and (3) to align ourselves in such a way that we can both give guidance and support to students and colleagues and receive it ourselves.

## REFERENCES

ADORNO, T. W., ELSE FRENKEL-BRUNSWIK, D. J. LEVINSON, AND R. N. SANFORD 1950 *The authoritarian personality* (2 vols.). New York: Harper.

ALLEN, E. E. AND R. W. HITES 1961 Factors in religious attitudes of older adolescents. *Journal Soc. Psychol.,* 55, 265–273.

ALLEN, R. O. AND B. SPILKA 1967 Committed and consensual religion: a specification of religion-prejudice relationships. *Journal Scient. Stud. Religion,* 6, 191–206.

ALLISON, J. 1968 Adaptive regression and intense religious experiences. *Journal of Nervous and Mental Disease,* 145, No. 6, 452–463.

ALLPORT, G. W. AND B. M. KRAMER 1946 Some roots of prejudice. *Journal Psychol.,* 22, 9–39.

BENDER, I. E. 1968 A longitudinal study of church attenders and nonattenders. *Journal Scient. Stud. Religion,* 7, 198–203.

BROCK, T. C. 1962 Implications of conversion and magnitude of cognitive dissonance. *Journal Scient. Stud. Religion,* 1, 198–203.

CLINE, V. B. AND J. M. RICHARDS, JR. 1965 A factor-analytic study of religious belief and behavior. *Journal Pers. Soc. Psychol.,* 1, 569–578.

DITTES, J. E. 1968 The psychology of religion. In G. Lindzey and E. Aronson (Eds.). *The Handbook of Social Psychology.* Vol. 5. Reading, Mass.: Addison-Wesley Publishing Company. Pp. 602–659.

FAULKNER, J. E. AND G. F. DEJONG 1966 Religiosity in 5-D: and empirical analysis. *Soc. Forces,* 45, 246–254.

FUKUYAMA, Y. 1961 The major dimensions of church membership. *Review Religious Res.,* 2, 154–161.

GLOCK, C. Y. AND R. STARK 1966 *Christian beliefs and anti-semitism.* New York: Harper and Row.

GORLOW, L. AND H. E. SCHROEDER 1968 Motives for participating in the religious experience. *Journal Scient. Stud. Religion,* 7, 241–251.

GORSUCH, R. L. 1968 The conceptualization of God as seen in adjective ratings. *Journal Scient. Stud. Religion,* 7, 56–64.

HOLTZMAN, W. H. 1956 Attitudes of college men toward non-segregation in Texas schools. *Public Opinion Quarterly,* 20, 559–569.

KEENE, J. 1967 Religious behavior and neuroticism, spontaneity, and world-mindedness. *Sociometry,* 30, 137–157.

KING, M. 1967 Measuring the religious variable. *Journal Scient. Stud. Religion,* 6, 173–185.

KLAUSNER, S. Z. 1964 Methods of data collection in studies of religion. *Journal Scient. Stud. Religion,* 3, 193–203.

LEARY, T. AND W. H. CLARK 1963 Religious implications of consciousness expanding drugs. *Religious Educ.,* 58, 251–256.

LONG, D., D. ELKIND, AND B. SPILKA 1967 The child's conception of prayer. *Journal Scient. Stud. Religion,* 6, 101–109.

MARANELL, G. M. 1967 An examination of some religious and political attitude correlates of bigotry. *Social Forces,* 45, 356–362.

MONAGHAN, R. 1967 The three faces of the true believer: motivations for attending a fundamentalist church. *Journal Scient. Stud. Religion,* 6, 236–245.

SANUA, V. D. 1969 Religion, mental health and personality: a review of empirical studies. *Amer. Journal Psychiat.* 125: 9, 1203–1213.

SPILKA, B., P. ARMATAS, AND JUNE NUSSBAUM 1964 The concept of God: a factor-analytic approach. *Review Religious Res.,* 6, 28–36.

SPILKA, B. AND J. F. REYNOLDS 1965 Religion and prejudice: a factor-analytic study. *Review Religious Res.,* 6, 163–168.

WEBB, S. C. 1965 An exploratory investigation of some needs met through religious behavior. *Journal Scient. Stud. Religion,* 5, 51–58.

WICKER, ALLAN W. 1962 Overt behaviors toward the church by volunteers, follow-up volunteers, and non-volunteers in a church survey. *Psychol. Reports,* 22, 917–920.

WILLIAMS, R. L. AND S. COLE 1968 Religiosity, generalized anxiety, and apprehension concerning death. *Journal Soc. Psychol.,* 75, 111–117.

WILSON, W. C. 1960 Extrinsic religious values and prejudice. *Journal Abnorm. Soc. Psychol.,* 60, 286–288.

# The Participant's vs. the Observer's Frame of Reference in the Psychological Study of Religion

## JOSEPH HAVENS

There are many evidences of a thaw in the congealed canon of scientific method in American psychology. Sigmund Koch, in his "Epilogue" to Volume III of the monumental *Psychology: Study of a Science* (1959), reports a significant trend away from behavioristic and objectivistic methodology, and a return to "experiential data" as relevant to psychological science. As one outstanding example, he cites Edward Tolman's use of "intuition, common experience, . . . and my own phenomenology" as sources of the intervening variables which are central to his theory of learning. D. O. Hebb, in his 1960 Presidential Address to the American Psychological Association, calls for the analytic study of mind, consciousness, and thought processes as variables highly significant in their own right. "The self," he says, "is neither mythical or mystical, but a complex mental process." These changes are welcome ones to scientists concerned with religion as a part of man's experience; they allow us to move beyond questionnaire studies of church attendance or attitudes toward religion, without at the same time alienating ourselves from our more "tough-minded" scientific brethren! We may anticipate a significant renewal of interest and solid work in the field of the psychology of religion.

There are two fundamental issues highlighted by this change. The first is implicit in the above: How can scientific method legitimately be broadened to deal with religious phenomena? The other is related to it: To what extent can even a broadened scientific method adequately *comprehend* the essence or the roots of religious life and

Reprinted with permission of the author and publisher from:

*Journal for the Scientific Study of Religion,* 1961, 1 (1), 79-87, published by the SOCIETY FOR THE SCIENTIFIC STUDY OF RELIGION, University of Connecticut, Box U68A, Storrs, Connecticut 06268.

faith? The major portion of this paper is devoted to the first of these questions; the second is treated more briefly.

## THE PHENOMENOLOGICAL FRAME OF REFERENCE

A return to "experiential data" or to "the subjective frame of reference" refers of course to the relevance of the way in which the subject of psychological study perceives, experiences or understands himself or the world. Data of this sort are drawn from autobiography, clinical interview, projective tests, or other forms of self-report. In the psychology of perception, in personality study, and more recently in social psychology, it has been called "the phenomenological approach."[1]

Robert MacLeod defines the phenomenological approach as "the systematic attempt to observe and describe in all its essential characteristics the world of phenomena as it is presented to us . . . It requires the deliberate suspension of all implicit and explicit assumptions, e.g., as to eliciting stimulus or underlying mechanism, which might bias our observation" (MacLeod, 1947, p. 151). He recognizes clearly that "no psychologist ever achieves the ideal," and goes on to expound in lucid fashion the kinds of assumptions or biases in both the study of perception and in social psychology which interfere with a genuine phenomenological approach. (Interference refers both to the unconscious distortion of the scientist's own perceptions of the reality being studied, and to the interpretations which he unconsciously or consciously applies to phenomenological data supplied to him by other subjects.) In a discussion of attitudes of racial prejudice, for example, he indicates how our unexamined tendency to see prejudices as "belonging to" the subject who expresses the attitude interferes with our accepting the phenomena as it is experienced or reported. For example, as prejudiced persons, we may apprehend another person as brownfaced, dishonest, and stupid, and these properties may be *phenomenologically* objective.

> Our dislike will be felt as caused by, not as causing, the perceived properties of the person; and our dislike will continue until the person is apprehended in the kind of context which will present him with a different set of phenomenal properties.
> What we call an attitude is thus, *phenomenologically considered,* not a state of the self but a state of the "field," of which the self is a part; and it may well be that the most important components of the attitude are in this sense objective rather than subjective (italics mine) (MacLeod, 1947, p. 165).

MacLeod's paper concludes, "confusion (in the field of social psychology) can be considerably reduced if we profit from the history of the psychology of perception, suspend for the time being our present theoretical constructs and take a fresh look at the phenomena which are there for us" (MacLeod, 1947, p. 176).

It should be unnecessary to point out that, in contrast to most fields of psychology, in the psychology of religion phenomenological data have always occupied a central place. The work of William James, Rudolph Otto, Carl Jung all rely heavily on the subjective frame of reference, educing concepts and laws from data provided by it. We are indebted to MacLeod and other phenomenologists for further clarifying and codifying this approach for the use of psychology generally.

There are a number of philosophical problems implicit in phenomenological psychology which cannot be dealt with in this paper. A major one is whether it is even possible for one person to know that his experience or his "knowledge by direct acquaintance" approximates that of another. We simply assume that this is so on the basis of a fundamental similarity in the operation of cognitive processes. It should be noted that one intent of the phenomenological method is to reduce as far as possible the biases on the part of the hearer which interfere with empathic communication. Possible distorting factors within the speaker or subject are referred to below.

MacLeod and others (Kuenzli, 1959) are clear that the phenomenological approach is merely a means of gathering data, i.e., it is only the first step in the scientific enterprise. Many of the data utilized in psychological investigation come from a more objective frame of reference, i.e., from observations of the subject's behavior rather than from his self-reports. Objective scales of intelligence, quantitative measures of social class membership, observations of discriminatory behavior are examples of objective data relevant to the study of prejudice. The evolving of hypotheses and theories proceeds on the basis of the data gathered, and is of course a necessary aspect of any science. It clearly and properly takes place within the frame of reference of the scientist, given his existing knowledge of the field and the methods of science. The most adequate understanding of human behavior and experience will be based on constructs utilizing data from both ends of the subjective-objective continuum, aided by wide knowledge and creative inventiveness on the part of the investigator.

## CONTRADICTIONS IN ASSUMPTIONS OF SUBJECT AND OBSERVER

Certain problems implicit in the use of the phenomenological method in many fields come into sharper focus when it is applied to the study of religion. In the discussion of the phenomenological method in social psychology, MacLeod asserts that some of the biases or assumptions of contemporary psychology will be seriously modified or replaced by new ones more hospitable to data derived from a subjective frame of reference; but he stresses, quite properly, that the new assumptions or constructs must not be contradicted by data derived from the objective view. In his argument, MacLeod first discusses the biases which he feels the phenomenologists in the study of perception, especially the Gestalt psychologists, have had to combat. He then proceeds to indicate similar biases standing in the way of a fuller use of subjective data by the social psychologists. One of them is "the organism centered bias," of which the quotation concerning the locus of attitudes of prejudice is an example. Another is "the atomistic-reductive bias—the belief that something small is more fundamental than something large." MacLeod implies that such biases will eventually be relinquished under the steady pressure of facts, as they have to some extent already in the field of perception. The present situation in psychology gives some grounds for this hope, even though many psychologists continue to operate productively on the same questioned assumptions. The fact not fully developed by MacLeod, however, is the frequently evident contradictions between the assumptions implicit in the phenomenological approach and the more traditional ones.[2] This contradiction in assumptions is one of the tensions in psychology today, and it looms as one of the critical problems in the scientific study of religion.

Perhaps the nature of the tension can be illustrated by describing an attempt of the writer and his wife to understand the experience of members of the Society of Friends who had joined a Christian communal group, the Society of Brothers, or Bruderhof. Membership in this Protestant community of families demands not only full commitment of material resources but also the acceptance of the will of the community regarding matters of occupation, place of abode, standard of living, and religious *Weltanschauung*. Essentially it is a monastic vow of obedience, made not to a Superior but to the presumably democratic will of the group operating "under the guidance of the Holy Spirit." We shall take as an example the experiences of more intellectual, theologically-minded members of the group, described as one of these might report them.

1) "I found difficulty surrendering my theological liberalism to the New Testament view of the Brothers, because my view seemed truer to me. I had thought it through in college, and it meant much to me."

2) "But I saw the element of pride in maintaining *my* views, for I

was proud of what I had evolved. I felt uncomfortable in this pride-fulness."

3) "I began to feel that God was asking me to surrender my will to Him precisely at the point of my theological ideas. My pride more and more seemed to be blocking my willingness to surrender, and thus blocking my doing the work which God wished me to do. I knew that only by letting go this pride in my ideas could I truly let God guide me."

4) "Finally I surrendered my hold on my old ideas, and joined the Brothers, knowing for sure that this was God's will for me. At that point I felt great peace, joy, and new release of energy."

It is evident that the social scientist who holds to the traditional assumptions of psychological science would have difficulty "receiving" these phenomenological data in undistorted form.[3] He would have no trouble in comprehending and recording 1) and the first part of 2). It is likely that he could also comprehend the guilt of undue pride, but might have difficulty connecting this with his creative thinking processes! At 3) and 4) his assumption of determinism and his positivistic or naturalistic view of man would cause difficulty. He could record only that the subject "believes" or "thinks" that God is asking him to surrender his pride in ideas. But this is a crucial reduction of "feeling" or "knowing" in the depth of being to an intellectual or symbolic process. Anyone who has tried to conceptualize his own most profound aesthetic moments (e.g., experiencing a Beethoven symphony in the concert hall) or his interpersonal experiences (e.g., a love relationship) by such terms as "having an attitude of liking" or "having pleasant sensations" can comprehend the meaning of "reduction" here. An adequate use of phenomenological data demands some degree of empathy on the part of the investigator, i.e., it demands that he experience phenomena to some extent as the subject himself experiences them. This implies for the writer (as apparently for MacLeod) bracketing the assumptions which militate against such experiencing—in this case, the assumptions of determinism and the prevailing positivistic view of man and the universe. Such bracketing would at least leave the door open for the scientist to empathize more fully with what the words, "God was asking me" and "let God guide me" might mean experientially. To fail to bracket the prevailing assumptions would seem to the present writer to lead to drastic distortion in the understanding of the meaning of such phrases. If God's existence is denied *a priori,* the interpretation of the subject's phenomenal data by the investigator in the direction of disbelief is unavoidable—an instance of the kind of prejudgment the phenomenological approach was invented to avoid! How far phenomenology in this case demands the provisional assumption of

God's existence is not clear to the writer, but *some* movement in this direction seems indicated if empathy is to occur. The word "provisional" here protects the investigator's freedom to return to the more usual scientific frame of reference in the later steps of the research. The latter perspective is well illustrated by many recent religious community studies, most of which assume a social determinism of one sort or another.[4] One operating with such a view would stress the heavy "social coercion" which he would detect in the Bruderhof way of life. He would point, for instance, to the relative isolation from the rest of the culture, the several-times-a-week meetings, and the prominence of a few older members in forming community opinion. And he would weight such factors heavily in interpreting and explaining the conversion experience. He would normally use such constructs as "reference group," "role behavior," and "need: Affiliation" in interpreting his information. But the phenomenological reports seem to demand other categories: "self-surrender," "sense of the numinous," "sense of peace." To "let the data speak" it may be necessary to *continue* the suspension of certain assumptions in framing explanatory concepts. Hence the ultimate problem in the use of the phenomenological data is not the legitimacy of their admission at all (although this may be an issue), but the difference in assumptions used in framing constructs appropriate for the ordering of the various data.[5]

At the present juncture in the science of psychology, this dilemma seems to the writer to imply more of a "choice-between" than we would wish. The investigator may treat the phenomenological data with radical seriousness and hold in abeyance some of the traditional assumptions of behavioral science, as do MacLeod, Carl Rogers, and other phenomenologists. Or, he may choose to hold fast to those assumptions, and rule out subjective data, distort them as he receives them, or seriously delimit their importance or validity.

The position of the writer is that though such a state of affairs does indeed create tensions, it is not necessarily to be deplored, and may be unexpectedly fruitful in our fullest understanding of man. But before commenting further on this, it is necessary to discuss briefly the dangers inherent in the phenomenological approach.

By definition, phenomenology deals with conscious experience only; hence it omits from consideration the tremendously significant and sometimes decisive factors of personality not available to the subject's awareness. (This is the central criticism lodged against phenomenologists Snygg and Combs by M. Brewster Smith in his article in *The Phenomenological Problem*.) This fact in itself should make clear the ultimate inadequacy of constructs based wholly on phenomenological data. But there may also be distortion by the subject at the conscious level in reporting his experience. The motives of his reporting may lead him to want his experience to appear in a more favorable light to the investigator; this is especially likely in the study of a religious sect. Or his need to appear self-consistent may cause him to alter certain perceptions to make them "fit" better. We have progressed only a short way in discovering procedures for determining when such deceptions may be occurring. Gordon Allport's monograph, *The Use of Personal Documents in Psychological Science* (Allport, 1942), contains some good suggestions along this line. The "team approach" used in personality research at the Harvard Department of Social Relations gives some clues as to how corrections for distortion in self-report may be made (Murray, 1938). It is obvious that data drawn from a more objective frame of reference are of great significance in the final evaluation of phenomenological reports. But such corrections may not always resolve the problem created by differing sets of assumptions. The fact that certain data need correcting does not invalidate them, nor does it do away with the need for constructs appropriate to them. Apparently it is necessary that both frames of reference enter the scientific enterprise at some point.

## THE HEURISTIC VALUE OF TENSION

Some investigators will enter upon the study of religious phenomena with the traditional assumptions of social or behavioral science and find much of use in furthering our understanding. (Many current studies in the sociology and psychology of religion are of this nature.) Others will adopt an almost wholly phenomenological point of view, and likewise discover facts and relations of considerable consequence. Others will continue to struggle with some kind of integration, unwilling to relinquish either the rich data of phenomenology or the heretofore fruitful assumptions of behavioral science. Carl Rogers is one who in contemporary psychology has been most uncompromising in holding to both horns of the dilemma. His paper, "Persons or Science? A Philosophical Question" (Rogers, 1955) is almost a detective-story of the ferreting out of the two differing points of view and the searching and thoughtful attempt to bring them into unity. The resolution achieved by Rogers between the phenomenological viewpoint and the scientific one lays much heavier stress than usual upon the subjective and personal elements in science, especially in the hypothesis-making phase and in the applications of scientific knowledge. But the view may be defended that the decisive emphasis on *self* in the Rogerian theory of personality stems to some extent from the attempt to take full account of the phenomenology of freedom (Rogers and Skinner, 1956; Rogers, 1959). Laying stress upon the capacity of a mature person to choose and act on the basis of what he knows himself to be is to take full account of the subjective experience of self-determination. It might also be asserted that Rogers' extensive use of data drawn from tape-recorded therapy sessions is a reflection of his attempt to keep hold of both sets of assumptions. The words of the protocols are taken as a direct expression of the subject's phenomenology, but they are subjected to careful quantitative unit analysis, within the usual framework of deterministic science (Rogers, 1954).

At this very early stage in the attempt to understand religion from a scientific frame of reference, two things seem clear: We must try to be as explicit as possible as to what set of assumptions we are primarily working under; and we must allow other investigators *full freedom* to work under ones different from our own. Such attitudes as "That's not really science" (assuming the norms of physical science as the only legitimate ones), or "But you're not really studying religion" (assuming that religion can be studied *only* from the inside) have frequently blocked communication and have seldom furthered the cause of understanding. A comprehension of the possible creative function of tension between assumption-systems may help to change this.

## TWO KINDS OF KNOWLEDGE

It has been assumed in the above that scientific knowledge as such, whether based on subjective data, objective data, or a combination of the two, is not the only way of comprehending religion. Nor can it ever be a totally adequate way. In a chapter describing "The Scientific Approach to Personality," David C. McClelland makes these disclaimers (McClelland, 1951).

> After all, the scientific mode of apprehending reality is only one possible mode. A person may put it on or take it off according to the demands of the occasion. . . . A psychologist can love his wife without perceiving that she is "really" a mother figure for him. So in the following pages when we take a scientific analytic attitude toward personality we will not do so with the imperialistic notion that this is the only attitude which counts. . . . Many . . . problems can be solved only in terms of other modes of apprehending reality, in terms of aesthetic or religious modes, for instance. The scientific approach is only one among several (pp. 15-16).

The same needs to be said for any scientific study of religion.

Many writers have pointed to two different kinds of "knowing." Herbert Feigl, for example, distinguishes "descriptive knowledge" (e.g., scientific) and "knowledge by acquaintance" (immediate, direct knowledge, not publicly demonstrable or verifiable) (Feigl, 1958). The latter is sometimes referred to as "unitive knowing." "Unitive" stresses the personal and active involvement of the knower in the known. It is intended to go beyond a "transactional" view by indicating that, in some sense, both knower and known participate together in the same reality. The epitome of "unitive knowing" in religion is of course mystical experience. Descriptive or scientific knowledge, on the other hand, exists *in some sense* independent of the knower (e.g., the already established body of scientific knowledge). In his recent book, *Personal Knowledge,* Michael Polanyi (1958) states flatly that there is always some personal involvement in appropriating even the most "objective" of scientific facts, and Feigl makes quite clear that considerable knowledge-by-acquaintance is involved in the pursuit of scientific truth. Nonetheless it seems clear that the very great difference in the extent and duration of active commitment involved in the two types of knowledge allows for a clear and decisive distinction between them.

Both types of knowledge are involved in all religious traditions. Worship, and the religious sentiments of gratitude, of adoration, of being forgiven, are unitive. Theological statements, historical records, interpretations of Scripture are in some sense reflections upon unitive knowing after its occurrence. In this sense they are descriptive knowledge and closer to a scientific perspective. Many writers have been at pains to point out the great gulf between the immediate experience and reflections about it. In his spiritual autobiography, *Surprised by Joy,* C. S. Lewis (1955) has written sensitively of this. "Joy" is the term which Lewis uses to "point toward" his occasional direct experiencing of God. This he deeply treasured and sought after with the avidity of a miser. But all his attempts to pin down and make come the events of Joy were foredoomed to failure:

> I saw that all my waitings and watchings for Joy, all my vain hopes to find some mental content on which I could, so to speak, lay my finger and say "This is it," had been a futile attempt to contemplate the enjoyed. All that such watching and waiting ever could find would be either an image or a quiver in the diaphragm. I should never have to bother again about these images or sensations. I knew not that they were merely the mental track left by the passage of Joy—not the wave but the wave's imprint on the sand (pp. 217-218).

The long and tempestuous history of introspection in psychology has

**109**

documented the same problem (Boring, 1953). One of the most lucid discussions of the difference between immediate conscious experience and the attempt to catch and analyze it is given by William James in the first volume of his *Principles of Psychology* (1890). In it he says:

> Comte is quite right in laying stress on the fact that a feeling, to be named, judged, or perceived, must be already past. No subjective state, whilst present, is its own object; its object is always something else. There are, it is true, cases in which we appear to be naming our present feeling, and so to be experiencing and observing the same inner fact at a single stroke, as when we say 'I feel tired,' 'I am angry,' etc. But these are illusory, and a little attention unmasks the illusion. The present conscious state, when I say 'I feel tired,' is not the direct state of tire; when I say 'I feel angry,' it is not the direct state of anger. It is the state of *saying I-feel-tired,* of *saying-I-feel-angry,*—entirely different matters, so different that the fatigue and anger apparently included in them are considerable modifications of the fatigue and anger directly felt the previous instant (p. 190).

The obvious truth of both Lewis' and James' assertions makes clear to us the inevitable limitations of descriptive knowledge, even when it is deeply informed by data from the phenomenological method. For the latter also, and in fact any reflections I may make *about* my own experience, either during or after its occurrence, provide me with a view of it in some sense less than or different from the event itself.

Which of these ways of knowing has the higher claim to Truth? The ultimate answer depends upon one's "fundamental root intuitions" about life and reality. If we desire the fullest possible participation in Reality or Nature or God, "mere" descriptive knowing is not likely to appeal to us. On the other hand, an insistence on the surety and reliability of whatever portion of Truth we know, and a tendency to value supremely our own and others' rational functions, will make analysts or scientists of us. There is a third alternative: we may value most highly a grasp of Truth in as many aspects as possible. In this view, unitive knowing is valued for its own sake and not as a means to the end of descriptive knowledge, as it tends to be in science; and scientific knowledge is seen as an important corrective to the distortions and errors so frequently encountered in more direct knowing. It is evident that the phenomenological approach developed here partakes of knowledge-by-acquaintance in a different and fuller sense than is the case in the gathering of objective data, and hence it tends to support the third view mentioned above. The student of religion who is himself religious will be more concerned with phenomenological data for at least two reasons: his own "immersion" in the data should aid him in the evolving of constructs useful in ordering that data (just as Edward Tolman's own perceiving and learning helped him to sympathize with the inner dilemmas of rats in mazes); and he will be motivated to "take seriously" such data because he himself has taken seriously similar experiences.

## SUMMARY

The preceding remarks have spelled out three points relative to the psychological study of religion. First of all, they pointed to the central importance of the phenomenological method as a source of data concerning religious experience and behavior. But the gathering of such data undistorted by the assumptions of the investigator may demand the "bracketing" of certain presuppositions implicit in the prevailing scientific world-view, e.g., "the organism centered bias," or the naturalistic denial of the reality of God. Such bracketing may lead to a conflict of assumptions for the social scientist who takes seriously the phenomenological point of view. Though these difficulties are encountered in sociology, social psychology and the study of personality, they are especially evident in the study of religion, where the subjective experiences of the religious person are frequently central in his behavior, and may not be shared by the scientist.

Secondly, the possible fruitfulness of such tension was asserted; the case of Carl Rogers, especially his reflections on the nature of science, was cited as an example of such fruitfulness. The importance of some latitude in the nature of assumptions adopted by those studying religion, and the necessity of being clear what assumptions are in fact being made, was urged.

Thirdly, the frequently remarked distinction between knowledge-by-acquaintance and descriptive knowledge was noted in relation to the study of religion. Although the phenomenological approach as discussed above relies more heavily on knowledge-by-acquaintance than do other methods of data-gathering, it should still be seen as a part of the scientific enterprise. Science is only one of several ways of approaching religion, and is clearly to be distinguished from the "unitive knowing" of the religious participant.

### NOTES AND REFERENCES

[1] A recent book devoted wholly to this topic is *The Phenomenological Problem* (Kuenzli, 1959). Two highly useful articles in that book utilized in this paper are Robert B. MacLeod's "The Phenomenological Approach to Social Psychology" and M. Brewster Smith's "The Phenomenological Approach in Personality Theory: Some Critical Remarks." It is important to distinguish between phenomenology as it is used in recent

philosophy, especially by Edmund Husserl, and the phenomenological method as an approach in scientific psychology. The latter has been to a considerable extent inspired by the former, but differs sharply from it in several regards. Philosophical phenomenology, by a "bracketing" of the natural world, focuses on the study of "pure consciousness," or "pure Ego," with the intent of discovering the "essences" or fundamental constituents of all experience. The phenomenological method in philosophy is exclusively introspective: the consciousness of the philosopher becomes the focus of reflection. In phenomenological psychology, on the other hand, reports by subjects of their conscious experiences are taken as data for analysis. The "Author's Preface to the English Edition" of Husserl's *Ideas: General Introduction to Pure Phenomenology* (1931) attempts to clarify this distinction.

[2]The question of whether or not such assumptions as the subject-object dichotomy, reductionism, the "genetic bias," and determinism are in some sense dictated by data derived from the objective frame of reference is of course relevant, but a discussion of it would go beyond the concerns of this paper.

[3]The writer is indebted to William W. Rozeboom for pointing out the three steps involved in making use of phenomenological data, in all three of which distortion may occur. The first is the verbal reporting of immediate experience by the subject; the second is the "reception" of this, i.e., the giving of cognitive meaning to it in the immediate experience of the investigator; the third is the utilizing and communicating of it by the investigator in his scientific study.

[4]See, in this connection, a letter by R. W. White in *The American Psychologist,* November, 1958, in which he dramatizes the logical implications of social determinism in a recent community study.

[5]It has of course been charged that the data in themselves can never solve the problem of assumptions, and that the scientist must ultimately make his choice on other than empirical grounds. This may prove to be the case, but the writer prefers, at this very early stage in the investigation of man's "central" functions, to let the data speak to us as forcibly as we can rather than to make our decisions *a priori.* We are referring here of course to the investigator as scientist, and not in his personal religious or ultimate-value commitments.

ALLPORT, GORDON W., *The Use of Personal Documents in Psychological Science,* Social Science Research Council, Bulletin 49, 1942.

BORING, EDWIN G., "A History of Introspection," *Psychological Bulletin,* 1953, 50, 169-189.

FEIGL, HERBERT, "The 'Mental' and the 'Physical,'" in *Minnesota Studies in Philosophy of Science,* Vol. II. Minneapolis: University of Minnesota Press, 1958.

HEBB, D. O., "The American Revolution," *American Psychologist,* 1960, 15, 735-745.

HUSSERL, EDMUND, *Ideas: General Introduction to Pure Phenomenology.* New York: Macmillan, 1931.

JAMES, WILLIAM, *Principles of Psychology,* Vol. I. New York: Henry Holt, 1890.

KOCH, SIGMUND (Ed.), *Psychology: A Study of a Science,* Vol. III. New York: McGraw-Hill, 1959.

KUENZLI, ALFRED E. (Ee.), *The Phenomenological Problem.* New York: Harper, 1959.

LEWIS, C. S., *Surprised by Joy.* New-York: Harcourt, Brace, 1955.

MACLEOD, R. B., "The Place of Phenomenological Analysis in Social Psychological Theory," in J. H. Rohrer and M. Sherif (Eds.), *Social Psychology at the Crossroads.* New York: Harper, 1951.

———, "The Phenomenological Approach to Social Psychology," in Kuenzli, *The Phenomenological Problem,* First published in *Psychological Review,* 1947, 54, 193-210.

MCCLELLAND, DAVID C., *Personality.* New York: Holt-Dryden, 1951.

MAY, R., ANGEL, E. and ELLENBERGER, H. F. (Eds.), *Existence.* New York: Basic Books, 1958.

MURRAY, HENRY A., *Explorations in Personality*. New York: Oxford University Press, 1938.

POLANYI, MICHAEL, *Personal Knowledge*. University of Chicago Press, 1958.

ROGERS, CARL R. and DYMOND, R. F. (Eds.), *Psychotherapy and Personality Change.* Chicago: University of Chicago Press, 1954.

————, "Persons or Science: A Philosophical Question." *American Psychologist,* 1955, 10, 267-278; also published in *Cross Currents,* Summer, 1953, 3, 289-306.

———— and SKINNER, B. F., "Some Issues Concerning the Control of Human Behavior." *Science,* 1956, 124, pp. 1057-1066.

————, "A Theory of Therapy, Personality, and Interpersonal Relationships, as Developed in the Client-centered Framework," in Koch, *Psychology: Study of a Science,* 1959.

SNYGG, D. and COMBS, A. W., *Individual Behavior.* New York: Harper, 1949.

# ORIENTATIONS TO RELIGION

# Introduction

## H. NEWTON MALONY

The way people think about religion, the importance they place on it, the reasons they have for being religious—all provide the background for behavior. This section deals with the effect religious attitudes have on such nonreligious issues as prejudice. This contrasts with the next section, "Psychodynamics and Religion," in which the effects of personality differences on *religious* behavior are considered.

Allport was very concerned with the evidence that religious persons are more prejudiced than nonreligious persons. Attempting to understand this issue, he suggested that there are two types of religious persons—those who *use* religion (the extrinsic) and those who *live* religion (the intrinsic). He and Ross in their article report research comparing these types of persons. They suggest that persons who are churchgoers, for any and all reasons, are more prejudiced than any other types of persons.

Allport and Ross' study has exerted considerable influence during the last decade over the psychology of religion. Hunt and King survey and summarize this research and compare the intrinsic-extrinsic concept with many other similar ideas. They also discuss the Religious Orientation Scale, which has been widely used to measure these types of attitudes toward religion.

Dittes compares the intrinsic-extrinsic typology with theorizing by sociologists, such as Troeltsch and Weber. He notes that theorists have long been concerned with pure (sect) and historical (church) religion. He concludes that religion is much more complex than any twofold typology can encompass.

This portion of the book will acquaint the student with the continuing dialogue about various kinds of religious persons and ongoing efforts to differentiate them, one from another.

# Personal Religious Orientation and Prejudice

## GORDON W. ALLPORT AND J. MICHAEL ROSS

Previous psychological and survey research has established three important facts regarding the relationship between prejudiced attitudes and the personal practice of religion.

1. On the average, church attenders are more prejudiced than nonattenders.

2. This overall finding, if taken only by itself, obscures a curvilinear relationship. While it is true that most attenders are *more* prejudiced than nonattenders, a significant minority of them are *less* prejudiced.

3. It is the casual, irregular fringe members who are high in prejudice; their religious motivation is of the extrinsic order. It is the constant, devout, internalized members who are low in prejudice; their religious motivation is of the *intrinsic* order.

The present paper will establish a fourth important finding— although it may properly be regarded as an amplification of the third. *The finding is that a certain cognitive style permeates the thinking of many people in such a way that they are indiscriminately proreligious and, at the same time, highly prejudiced.*

But first let us make clear the types of evidence upon which the first three propositions are based and examine their theoretical significance.

## CHURCHGOERS ARE MORE PREJUDICED

Beginning the long parade of findings demonstrating that churchgoers are more intolerant of ethnic minorities than nonattenders is a study by Allport and Kramer (1946). These authors discovered that students who claimed no religious affiliation were less likely to be anti-Negro than those who declared themselves to be protestant or Catholic. Furthermore, students reporting a strong religious influence at home were higher in ethnic prejudice than students reporting only slight or no religious influence. Rosenblith (1949) discovered the same trend among students in South Dakota. *The Authoritarian Personality* (Adorno, Frenkel-Brunswik, Levinson, & Sanford, 1950, p. 212) stated that scores on ethnocentricism (as well as on authoritarianism) are significantly higher among church attenders than among non-attenders. Gough's (1951) findings were similar. Kirkpatrick (1949) found religious people in general to be slightly less humanitarian than nonreligious people. For example, they had more punitive attitudes toward criminals, delinquents, prostitutes, homosexuals, and those in need of psychiatric treatment. Working with a student population Rokeach (1960) discovered nonbelievers to be consistently less dogmatic, less authoritarian, and less ethnocentric than believers. Public-opinion polls (as summarized by Stember, 1961) revealed confirmatory evidence across the board.

Going beyond ethnic prejudice, Stouffer (1955) demonstrated that among a representative sample of American church members those who had attended church within the past month were more intolerant of nonconformists (such as socialists, atheists, or communists) than those who had not attended. It seems that on the average religious people show more intolerance in general—not only toward ethnic but also toward ideological groups.

Is this persistent relationship in any way spurious? Can it be due, for example, to the factor of educational level? Many studies show that people with education tend to be appreciably less prejudiced than people with low education. Perhaps it is the former group that less often goes to church. The reasoning is false. Sociological evidence has shown conclusively that frequent church attendance is associated with high socioeconomic status and with college education (Demerath, 1965). Furthermore, Stouffer's study found that the intolerant tendency among churchgoers existed only when educational level was held constant. Struening (1963), using as subjects only faculty members of a large state university (all highly educated), discovered that non-attenders were on the average less prejudiced than attenders. These studies assure us that the association between churchgoing and prejudice is not merely a spurious product of low education.

Turning to the theoretical implications of these findings, shall we say that religion in and of itself makes for prejudice and intolerance? There are some arguments in favor of such a conclusion, especially when we recall that certain powerful *theological* positions —those emphasizing revelation, election (chosen people), and theocracy (Allport, 1959, 1966)—have throughout history turned one religion against another. And among *sociological* factors in religion we find many that make for bigotry. One thinks of the narrow composition of many religious groups in terms of ethnic and class membership, of their pressure toward conformity, and of the competition between them (see Demerath, 1965; Lenski, 1961). It does seem that religion as such makes for prejudice.

And yet it is here that we encounter the grand paradox. One may not overlook the teachings of equality and brotherhood, of compassion and humanheartedness, that mark all the great world religions. Nor may one overlook the precept and example of great figures whose labors in behalf of tolerance were and are religiously motivated—such as Christ himself, Tertullian, Pope Gelasius I, St. Ambrose, Cardinal Cusa, Sebastian Castellio, Schwenckfeld, Roger Williams, Mahatma Gandhi, Martin Luther King, and many others, including the recently martyred clergy in our own South. These lives, along with the work of many religious bodies, councils, and service organizations, would seem to indicate that religion as such *unmakes prejudice.* A paradox indeed.

## THE CURVILINEAR RELATIONSHIP

If religion as such made *only* for prejudice, we would expect that churchgoers who expose themselves most constantly to its influence would, as a result, be more prejudiced than those who seldom attend. Such is not the case.

Many studies show that frequent attenders are less prejudiced than infrequent attenders and often less prejudiced even than nonattenders. Let us cite one illustrative study by Struening (1963). The curvilinear trend is immediately apparent in Table 1. In this particular study nonattenders had lower prejudice scores than any group, save only those devotees who managed to attend 11 or more times a month. Without employing such fine time intervals other studies have shown the same curvilinear trend. Thus, in *The Authoritarian Personality* (p. 212) we learned that in 12 out of 15 groups "regular" attenders (like nonattenders) were less prejudiced than "seldom" or "often" attenders. Employing a 26-item Desegregation Scale in three separate studies, Holtzman (1956) found the same trend as shown in Table 2. If more evidence for the curvilinear relationship is needed, it will be found in community studies made in New Jersey (Friedrichs, 1959),

## TABLE 1

CHURCH ATTENDANCE AND PREJUDICE AMONG FACULTY MEMBERS
OF A MIDWESTERN UNIVERSITY

| Frequency of attendance (times per mo.) | N | Prejudice score |
|---|---|---|
| 0 | 261 | 14.7 |
| 1 | 143 | 25.0 |
| 2 | 103 | 26.0 |
| 3 | 84 | 23.8 |
| 4 | 157 | 22.0 |
| 5-7 | 94 | 19.9 |
| 8–10 | 26 | 16.3 |
| 11 or more | 21 | 11.7 |

Note.—From Struening (1957).

## TABLE 2

CHURCH ATTENDANCE AND PREJUDICE AMONG STUDENTS
IN THE BORDER STATES

| | 1956 study % intolerant | Mean score on D scale | |
|---|---|---|---|
| | | 1958 study | 1960 study |
| Nonattenders | 37 | 41.3 | 38.1 |
| Once a mo. | 66 | 48.5 | 51.4 |
| Twice a mo. | 67 | 50.6 | 48.4 |
| Once a wk. or oftener | 49 | 44.5 | 44.3 |

Note.—Adapted from Holtzman (1956), Kelly, Ferson, and Holtzman (1958), Young, Benson, and Holtzman (1960).

North Carolina (Tumin, 1958), New England (Pettigrew, 1959), and Ohio and California (Pinkney, 1961). One could almost say there is a unanimity of findings on this matter. The trend holds regardless of religion, denomination, or target of prejudice (although the case seems less clear for anti-Semitism than for prejudice against other ethnic groups).

What are the theoretical implications? To find that prejudice is related to frequency of church attendance is scarcely explanatory, since it may reflect only formal behavior, not involvement or commitment to religious values. And yet it seems obvious that the regular attenders who go to church once a week or oftener (and several studies indicate that oftener than once a week is especially significant) are people who receive something of special ideological and experiential meaning. Irregular, casual fringe members, on the other hand, regard their religious contacts as less binding, less absorbing, less integral with their personal lives.

At this point, therefore, we must pass from external behavioral evidence into the realm of experience and motivation. Unless we do so we cannot hope to understand the curvilinear relationship that has been so clearly established.

## EXTRINSIC VERSUS INTRINSIC MOTIVATION

Perhaps the briefest way to characterize the two poles of subjective religion is to say that the extrinsically motivated person *uses* his religion, whereas the intrisically motivated *lives* his religion. As we shall see later, most people, if they profess religion at all, fall upon a continuum between these two poles. Seldom, if ever, does one encounter a "pure" case. And yet to clarify the dimension it is helpful to characterize it in terms of the two ideal types.

### Extrinsic Orientation

Persons with this orientation are disposed to use religion for their own ends. The term is borrowed from axiology, to designate an interest that is held because it serves other, more ultimate interests. Extrinsic values are always instrumental and utilitarian. Persons with this orientation may find religion useful in a variety of ways—to provide security and solace, sociability and distraction, status and self-justification. The embraced creed is lightly held or else selectively shaped to fit more primary needs. In theological terms the extrinsic type turns to God, but without turning away from self.

### Intrinsic Orientation

Persons with this orientation find their master motive in religion. Other needs, strong as they may be, are regarded as of less ultimate significance, and they are, so far as possible, brought into harmony with the religious beliefs and prescriptions. Having embraced a creed the individual endeavors to internalize it and follow it fully. It is in this sense that he *lives* his religion.

A clergyman was making the same distinction when he said,

> Some people come to church to thank God, to acknowledge His glory, and to ask His guidance. . . . Others come for what they can get. Their interest in the church is to run it or exploit it rather than to serve it.

## G. W. Allport and J. M. Ross

Approximate parallels to these psychological types have been proposed by the sociologists Fichter (1954) and Lenski (1961). The former, in studying Catholic parishioners, classified them into four groups: the dormant, the marginal, the modal, and the nuclear. Omitting the dormant, Fichter estimated in terms of numbers that 20% are marginal, 70% modal, and less than 10% nuclear. It is, of course, the latter group that would most closely correspond to our conception of the "intrinsic." Lenski distinguished between church members whose involvement is "communal" (for the purpose of sociability and status) and those who are "associational" (seeking the deeper values of their faith).

These authors see the significance of their classifications for the study of prejudice. Fichter has found less prejudice among devout (nuclear) Catholics than among others (see Allport, 1954, p. 421). Lenski (1961, p. 173) reported that among Detroit Catholics 59% of those with a predominantly "communal" involvement favored segregated schools, whereas among those with predominantly an "associational" involvement only 27% favored segregation. The same trend held for Detroit Protestants.

The first published study relating the extrinsic-intrinsic dimension directly to ethnic prejudice was that of Wilson (1960). Limiting himself to a 15-item scale measuring an extrinsic (utilitarian-institutional) orientation, Wilson found in 10 religious groups a median correlation of .65 between his scale and anti-Semitism. In general these correlations were higher than he obtained between anti-Semitism and the Religious-Conventionalism Scale (Levinson, 1954). From this finding Wilson concluded that orthodoxy or fundamentalism is a less important factor than extrinsicness of orientation.

Certain weaknesses may be pointed out in this pioneer study. Wilson did not attempt to measure intrinsicness of orientation, but assumed without warrant that it was equivalent to a low score on the extrinsic measures. Further, since the items were worded in a unidirectional way there may be an error of response set. Again, Wilson dealt only with Jews as a target of prejudice, and so the generality of his finding is not known.

Finally, the factor of educational level plays a part. Wilson used the California Anti-Semitism scale, and we know that high scores on this scale go with low education (Christie, 1954; Pettigrew, 1959; Titus & Hollander, 1957; Williams, 1964). Further, in our own study the extrinsic subscale is negatively correlated with degree of education ($r = -.32$). To an appreciable extent, therefore, Wilson's high correlations may be "ascribed" to educational level.

At this point, however, an important theoretical observation must be made. Low education may indeed predispose a person toward an exclusionist, self-centered, extrinsic, religious orientation and may dispose him to a stereotyped, fearful image of Jews. This fact does not in the least affect the functional relationship between the religious and the prejudiced outlooks. It is a common error for investigators to "control for" demographic factors without considering the danger involved in doing so. In so doing they are often obscuring and not illuminating the functional (i.e., psychological) relationships that obtain (see Allport, 1950).

Following Wilson the task of direct measurement was taken up by Feagin (1964) who used a more developed scale—one designed to measure not only extrinsic orientation but also the intrinsic. His scales are essentially the same as those discussed in a later section of this paper. In his study of Southern Baptists Feagin reached four conclusions: (*a*) Contrary to expectation, extrinsic and intrinsic items did not fall on a unidimensional scale but represented two independent dimensions; (*b*) only the extrinsic orientation was related to intolerance toward Negroes; (*c*) orthodoxy as such was not related to the extrinsic or intrinsic orientation; (*d*) greater orthodoxy (fundamentalism of belief) did, however, relate positively to prejudice.

Taking all these studies together we are justified in assuming that the inner experience of religion (what it means to the individual) is an important causal factor in developing a tolerant or a prejudiced outlook on life.

Yet, additional evidence is always in place, and new insights can be gained by a closer inspection of the rather coarse relationships that have been established up to now.

## THE PRESENT STUDY

We wished to employ an improved and broader measure of prejudice than had previously been used. And since direct measures of prejudice (naming the target groups) have become too sensitive for wide use, we wished to try some abbreviated indirect measures. Further, we wished to make use of an improved Extrinsic-Intrinsic scale, one that would give reliable measures of both extrinsic and intrinsic tendencies in a person's religious life. For these reasons the following instruments were adopted.

### Social Problems Questionnaire

This scale, devised by Harding and Schuman (unpublished[1];

see also Schuman & Harding, 1963, 1964), is a subtly worded instrument containing 12 anti-Negro, 11 anti-Jewish, and 10 anti-other items (pertaining to Orientals, Mexicans, and Puerto Ricans). The wording is varied so as to avoid an agreement response set.

## Indirect Prejudice Measures

Six items were taken from Gilbert and Levinson's (1956) Custodial Mental Illness Ideology Scale (CMI). Example: "We should be sympathetic with mental patients, but we cannot expect to understand their odd behavior. a) I definitely disagree. b) I tend to disagree. c) I tend to agree. d) I definitely agree."

Four items are related to a "jungle" philosophy of life, suggesting a generalized suspiciousness and distrust. Example: "The world is a hazardous place in which men are basically evil and dangerous. a) I definitely disagree. b) I tend to disagree. c) I tend to agree. d) I definitely agree."

In all cases the most prejudiced response receives a score of 5 and the least prejudiced response, 1. No response was scored 3.

TABLE 3

INTERCORRELATIONS BETWEEN FIVE MEASURES OF PREJUDICE

|  | Anti-Jewish | Anti-Other | Jungle | CMI |
|---|---|---|---|---|
| Anti-Negro | .63 | .70 | .20 | .25 |
| Anti-Jewish |  | .67 | .24 | .31 |
| Anti-Other |  |  | .33 | .36 |
| Jungle |  |  |  | .43 |

Note.—N = 309.

From Table 3 we see that while the indirect measures have a positive correlation with each other and with direct measures, the relationship is scarcely high enough to warrant the substitution of the indirect for the direct. The high correlations between prejudice for the three ethnic target groups once again illustrate the well-established fact that ethnic prejudice tends to be a broadly generalized disposition in personality.

## Religious Orientation Measure

The full scale, entitled "Religious Orientation," is available from ADI.[2] It separates the intrinsically worded items from the extrinsic, gives score values for each item, and reports on item reliabilities. In all cases a score of 1 indicates the most intrinsic response, a score of 5, the most extrinsic. While it is possible to use all 20 items as one continuous scale, it will soon become apparent that it is often wise to treat the two subscales separately. A sample item from the extrinsic subscale follows: "What religion offers me most is comfort when sorrows and misfortune strike. a) I definitely disagree, 1. b) I tend to disagree, 2. c) I tend to agree, 4. d) I definitely agree, 5." A sample item from the intrinsic subscale: "My religious beliefs are what really lie behind my whole approach to life. a) this is definitely not so, 5. b) probably not so, 4. c) probably so, 2. d) definitely so, 1.

## SAMPLE

While our sample of six groups of churchgoers shows some diversity of denomination and region, it is in no sense representative. Graduate-student members of a seminar collected the 309 cases from the following church groups: Group A, 94 Roman Catholic (Massachusetts); Group B, 55 Lutheran (New York State); Group C, 44 Nazarene (South Carolina); Group D, 53 Presbyterian (Pennsylvania); Group E, 35 Methodist (Tennessee); Group F, 28 Baptist (Massachusetts).

We labeled the groups alphabetically since such small subsamples could not possibly lead to valid generalizations concerning denominations as a whole. All subjects knew that they were invited to participate as members of a religious group, and this fact may well have introduced a "proreligious" bias.

## GROSS RESULTS

If we pool all our cases for the purpose of correlating religious orientation with prejudice, we discover that while the findings are in the expected direction they are much less impressive than those of previous studies, especially Wilson's.

### Correlations with Extrinsic Subscale

Since Wilson employed an extrinsic scale similar to ours, we first present in Table 4 our findings using this subscale and the various measures of prejudice. Whereas Wilson found a correlation of .65 between his extrinsic and anti-Semitic measures, our correlation falls to .21. In part the reason no doubt lies in certain features of Wilson's method which we have criticized.

## Correlations with Combined Extrinsic-Intrinsic Scale

From the outset it was our intention to broaden Wilson's undirectional (extrinsic) measure to see whether our hypothesis might hold for the total scale (combined scores for the 11 extrinsic and 9 intrinsic items). As Table 5 shows, matter do not improve but seem to worsen. The logic of combining the two subscales is of course to augment the continuum in length and presumably enhance the reliability of the total measure. It soon became apparent, however, that subjects who endorse extrinsically worded items do not necessarily reject those worded intrinsically, or vice versa. It turns out that there is only a very low correlation in the expected direction between the two subscales ($r = .21$). Obviously at this point some reformulation is badly needed.

## REFORMULATION OF THE APPROACH

Examination of the data reveals that some subjects are indeed "consistently intrinsic," having a strong tendency to endorse intrinsically worded items and to reject the extrinsically worded. Correspondingly others are "consistently extrinsic." Yet, unfortunately for our neat typology, many subjects are provokingly inconsistent. They persist in endorsing any or all items that to them seem favorable to religion in any sense. Their responses, therefore, are "indiscriminately proreligious."

TABLE 4

CORRELATIONS BETWEEN EXTRINSIC SUBSCALE AND PREJUDICE

| | |
|---|---|
| Anti-Negro | .26 |
| Anti-Jewish | .21 |
| Anti-Other | .32 |
| Jungle | .29 |
| CMI | .44 |

Note.—N = 309.

TABLE 5

CORRELATIONS BETWEEN TOTAL EXTRINSIC-INTRINSIC
SCALE AND PREJUDICE

| | |
|---|---|
| Anti-Negro | .26 |
| Anti-Jewish | .18 |
| Anti-Other | .18 |
| Jungle | .21 |
| CMI | .17 |

Note.—N = 309.

The problem is essentially the same as that encountered by the many investigators who have attempted to reverse the wording of items comprising the F scale, in order to escape an unwanted response-set bias. Uniformly the effort has proved to be frustrating, since so many subjects subscribe to both the positive and negative wording of the same question (see Bass, 1955; Chapman & Bock, 1958; Chapman & Campbell, 1959; Christie, 1954; Jackson & Messick, 1957).

An example from our own subscales would be: "My religious beliefs are what really lie behind my whole approach to life" (intrinsic). "Though I believe in my religion, I feel there are many more important things in my life" (extrinsic).

The approach used by Peabody (1961) offers us a model for analyzing our data in a meaningful way. Peabody administered both positive and negative F-scale items to subjects at two different testing sessions. By comparing each individual's responses to the same question stated positively at one time and in reverse at another he was able to separate out those who were consistently pro or anti toward the content of authoritarian items. But he found many who expressed double agreement (or disagreement) with both versions of the same question. Table 6 applies Peabody's paradigm to our data.

In assigning our 309 cases to these categories we employed the following criteria.

*Intrinsic type* includes individuals who agree with intrinsically worded items on the intrinsic subscale, and who disagree with extrinsically stated items on the extrinsic subscale. By the scoring method employed these individuals fall below the median scores on both subscales.

*Extrinsic type* includes individuals who agree with extrinsically stated items on the extrinsic subscale, and who disagree with items on the intrinsic subscale. By our scoring method these individuals all fall above the median scores on both subscales.

*Indiscriminately proreligious* includes those who on the intrinsic subscale score at least 12 points less than on the extrinsic subscale. (This figure reflects the fact that a subject gives approximately 50% more intrinsic responses on the intrinsic subscale than we should expect from his extrinsic responses to the extrinsic subscale.)

*Indiscriminately antireligious or nonreligious* includes those who would show a strong tendency to disagree with items on both subscales. Since nonchurchgoers are excluded from our samples, such cases are not found. (Some pilot work with markedly liberal groups indicates that this type does exist, however, even among members of "religious" organizations.)

TABLE 6

FOUR PATTERNS OF RELIGIOUS ORIENTATION

|  | Agrees with intrinsic choice | Disagrees with intrinsic choice |
|---|---|---|
| Agrees with extrinsic choice | Indiscriminately proreligious | Consistently extrinsic in type |
| Disagrees with extrinsic choice | Consistently intrinsic in type | Indiscriminately antireligious or nonreligious[a] |

[a]Not found in present sample.

Table 1 gives the percentage of the three types.

## RESULTS OF THE REFORMULATION

The five measures of prejudice were analyzed by a 6 (Groups) × 3 (Religious Types) analysis of variance. Table 8 presents the overall effects for religious types for each of the five measures of prejudice. The multivariate analysis of variance indicates that there is both a significant difference between the three types of religious orientation and between the six subsamples in the level of prejudice.[3] Examination of the means shows two trends: (a) The extrinsic type is more prejudiced than the intrinsic type for both direct and indirect measures; (b) the indiscriminate type of religious orientation is more prejudiced than either of the two consistent types. Statistically all these trends are highly significant.

TABLE 7

PERCENTAGE OF EACH RELIGIOUS TYPE IN
EACH SUBSAMPLE

| Religious group | N | Consistently intrinsic | Consistently extrinsic | Indiscriminately proreligious |
|---|---|---|---|---|
| A | (94) | 36 | 34 | 30 |
| B | (55) | 35 | 36 | 29 |
| C | (44) | 36 | 39 | 25 |
| D | (53) | 32 | 30 | 38 |
| E | (35) | 31 | 29 | 40 |
| F | (28) | 39 | 39 | 22 |

TABLE 8

PREJUDICE AND RELIGIOUS ORIENTATION

| Target of prejudice | Mean prejudice score | | | F ratio |
|---|---|---|---|---|
| | Intrinsic type N = 108 | Extrinsic type N = 106 | Inconsistent type N = 95 | |
| Anti-Negro | 28.7 | 33.0 | 36.0 | 8.6** |
| Anti-Jewish | 22.6 | 24.6 | 28.9 | 11.1** |
| Anti-Other | 20.4 | 23.3 | 26.1 | 10.9** |
| Jungle | 7.9 | 8.7 | 9.6 | 8.4** |
| CMI | 10.2 | 11.8 | 13.4 | 20.4** |

| Multivariate analysis of variance | | |
|---|---|---|
| Source of variation | F ratio | df |
| Religious type (A) | 5.96*** | 10,574 |
| Sample groups (B) | 3.19*** | 25,668 |
| A × B | 1.11* | 50,1312 |

*$p > .25$.
**$p > .001$.
***$p > .0005$.

We note especially that the scores of the indiscriminate type are markedly higher on all measures than the scores of the intrinsic type. Corresponding $F$ ratios for paired comparisons range from 8.4 for the jungle scale to 20.4 for the CMI scale. The differences between the indiscriminate and extrinsic types are smaller. For the anti-Jewish and CMI scales these differences are, however, beyond the .005 level; for the anti-Negro the difference falls below significance.

The relationship between the indiscriminately proreligious orientation and prejudice receives support (see Table 9) when we compare subjects who are *moderately* indiscriminate with those who are *extremely* indiscriminate. (In the first group the scores on the intrinsic subscale average 16 points lower than on the extrinsic subscale, whereas the extreme cases average 23 points less on the intrinsic than on the extrinsic subscale.)

The discovery that the degree of indiscriminateness tends to relate directly to the degree of prejudice is an important finding. It can only mean that some functional relationship obtains between religious muddle-headedness (for thát is what indiscriminate scores imply) and antagonism toward ethnic groups. We shall return to this interpretation in the concluding section of this paper.

## RESULTS FOR SUBSAMPLES

It would not be correct to assume that the variance is distributed equally over all the subsamples, for it turns out that the denominational groups differ appreciably in prejudice scores and in religious type, as Tables 10 and 11 indicate.

### TABLE 9
#### DEGREES OF INDISCRIMINATENESS AND AVERAGE PREJUDICE SCORES

| Target of prejudice | Moderately indiscriminate $N = 56$ | Extremely indiscriminate $N = 39$ | F ratio |
|---|---|---|---|
| Anti-Negro | 35.4 | 37.9 | .97 |
| Anti-Jewish | 28.0 | 30.1 | .90 |
| Anti-Other | 24.9 | 28.2 | 3.25* |
| Jungle | 9.5 | 10.2 | 1.11 |
| CMI | 10.2 | 14.6 | 3.99* |

*$p > .05$.

### TABLE 10
#### ANTI-NEGRO PREJUDICE: MEAN SCORES ON SOCIAL PROBLEMS SCALE

| Religious group | Intrinsic type | Extrinsic type | Indiscriminate type | Group M |
|---|---|---|---|---|
| A | 27.4 (34) | 34.8 (32) | 32.2 (28) | 31.4 (94) |
| B | 27.2 (19) | 32.3 (20) | 31.9 (16) | 30.4 (55) |
| C | 22.4 (16) | 36.2 (17) | 35.0 (11) | 30.9 (44) |
| D | 35.5 (17) | 28.7 (16) | 42.5 (20) | 36.1 (53) |
| E | 40.5 (11) | 35.5 (10) | 43.0 (14) | 40.1 (35) |
| F | 22.6 (11) | 27.9 (11) | 28.7 (6) | 26.0 (28) |
| Type M | 28.7 (108) | 33.0 (106) | 36.0 (95) | 32.5 (309) |

| Analysis of variance | | | |
|---|---|---|---|
| Source of variation | df | MS | F ratio |
| Religious type (A) | 2 | 1077.8 | 8.6** |
| Religious group (B) | 5 | 952.2 | 7.6** |
| A × B | 10 | 251.1 | 2.0* |
| Error (w) | 291 | 125.6 | |

*$p > .10$.
**$p > .001$.

It is true that when we combine subsamples all the trends are in the expected direction, but troublesome exceptions occur for single groups as indicated by the nearly significant interaction effects. The most troublesome contradictions appear in relation to the anti-Negro measures based on the Harding-Schuman scale. Table 10 discloses certain sore points, even though the average trend over all the sub-samples is in the predicted direction.

For Groups A, B, and C we note that the indiscriminate type is slightly less prejudiced than the extrinsic type, and for Groups D and E the extrinsic type seems actually less prejudiced than the intrinsic. (Groups D and E are consistently more troublesome than other sub-samples, perhaps because of some salient racial issue in the local community. It will be noted that both these groups are considerably more anti-Negro than the other subsamples.)

By way of contrast we present in Table 11 the results for the short (five-item) CMI scale. With the exception of the indiscriminate type in Group F, the progression of scores is precisely as expected. Each subsample shows that the intrinsic type is less prejudiced toward the mentally ill than the extrinsic type, and the extrinsic type is less prejudiced than the indiscriminately proreligious.[4]

TABLE 11

INDIRECT (CMI) MEASURE OF PREJUDICE

| Religious group | Intrinsic type | Extrinsic type | Indiscriminate type | Group $M$ |
|---|---|---|---|---|
| A | 11.2 (34) | 12.4 (32) | 13.6 (28) | 12.3 (94) |
| B | 10.1 (19) | 10.8 (20) | 13.4 (16) | 11.3 (55) |
| C | 9.5 (16) | 12.2 (17) | 12.6 (11) | 11.3 (44) |
| D | 10.6 (17) | 11.4 (16) | 14.8 (20) | 12.4 (53) |
| E | 8.6 (11) | 12.9 (10) | 13.6 (14) | 11.8 (35) |
| F | 9.2 (11) | 10.7 (11) | 9.2 (6) | 9.8 (28) |
| Type $M$ | 10.2 (108) | 11.8 (106) | 13.4 (95) | 11.9 (309) |

| Analysis of variance | | | |
|---|---|---|---|
| Source of variation | $df$ | $MS$ | $F$ ratio |
| Religious type (A) | 2 | 255.0 | 20.4** |
| Religious group (B) | 5 | 36.5 | 2.9* |
| A × B | 10 | 15.3 | 1.2 |
| Error (w) | 291 | 12.5 | |

*$p > .05$.
**$p > .001$.

Returning in a different way to the original question of whether consistent extrinsic and intrinsic orientations make for prejudice and for tolerance, respectively, we shall now examine this matter in each subsample separately. Inspection of the mean scores and variance for the total scale indicates that we are dealing with a relatively narrow range of variation. To minimize the effect of a narrow range of scores and skewed distributions, we used Kendal's (1955) tau as a measure of degree of relationship between prejudice and consistent religious orientation. The results are given in Table 12. While the correlations are not high (14 are significant in the expected direction), only one (in the troublesome Group E) is significant in the reverse direction.

## EDUCATIONAL DIFFERENCES

Computing the actual years of schooling for all groups we find that the indiscriminate type has significantly less formal education than the intrinsic cases ($p > .005$, $F = 18.29$), and somewhat less than the extrinsic type ($p > .10$, $F = 2.89$). Comparing extrinsic with intrinsic types we find that the former has finished fewer years of schooling ($p > .10$, $F = 3.45$). (Oddly enough the groups with highest average education are D & E, which also displayed the highest anti-Negro and anti-Semitic prejudice—perhaps because of particular local conditions.)

In our survey of earlier studies we saw that educational level is often a factor in the various relationships discovered between religion and prejudice. We have also argued that demographic factors of this sort should not be allowed to obscure the functional (psychological) analysis that the data call for. Granted that low education makes for indiscriminate thinking, the mental confusion that results from low education may have its own peculiar effects on religious and ethnic attitudes.

TABLE 12

CORRELATIONS BETWEEN COMBINED EXTRINSIC-INTRINSIC RELIGIOUS SCORES (FOR CONSISTENT SUBJECTS) AND PREJUDICE (KENDAL'S TAU)

| Religious group | Anti-Negro | Anti-Jewish | Anti-Other | Jungle | CMI |
|---|---|---|---|---|---|
| A | .31*** | .26*** | .24*** | .14* | .19*** |
| B | .19* | .13 | .15 | .05 | .03 |
| C | .32*** | .17* | .35*** | .14* | .28*** |
| D | −.12 | .05 | −.09 | .03 | .11 |
| E | −.24* | −.11 | −.13 | .26* | .46*** |
| F | .39*** | .13 | .25* | −.01 | .24* |

*p > .10.
**p > .05.
***p > .01.

132

## SUMMARY AND INTERPRETATIONS

At the outset we stated three propositions that seem to be firmly established: (a) Churchgoers on the broad average harbor more ethnic prejudice than nonchurchgoers; (b) in spite of this broad tendency a curvilinear relationship in fact exists; (c) the intrinsically motivated churchgoers are significantly less prejudiced than the extrinsically motivated. Our present research supplies additional strong support for the second and third of these propositions.

To these propositions we add a fourth: *churchgoers who are indiscriminately proreligious are more prejudiced than the consistently extrinsic, and very much more prejudiced than the consistently intrinsic types.*

The psychological tie between the intrinsic orientation and tolerance, and between the extrinsic orientation and prejudice, has been discussed in a series of papers by Allport (1959, 1963, 1966). In brief the argument holds that a person with an extrinsic religious orientation is using his religious views to provide security, comfort, status, or social support for himself—religion is not a value in its own right, it serves other needs, and it is a purely utilitarian formation. Now prejudice too is a "useful" formation: it too provides security, comfort, status, and social support. A life that is dependent on the supports of extrinsic religion is likely to be dependent on the supports of prejudice, hence our positive correlations between the extrinsic orientation and intolerance. Contrariwise, the intrinsic religious orientation is not an instrumental device. It is not a mere mode of conformity, nor a crutch, nor a tranquilizer, nor a bid for status. All needs are subordinated to an overarching religious commitment. In internalizing the total creed of his religion the individual necessarily internalizes its values of humility, compassion, and love of neighbor. In such a life (where religion is an intrinsic and dominant value) there is no place for rejection, contempt, or condescension toward one's fellow man. Such is our explanation for the relationship between extrinsic religion and prejudice, and between intrinsic religion and tolerance.

Our present task is to discover, if we can, some similar functional tie between prejudice (as measured both directly and indirectly) and the indiscriminately proreligious orientation. The common factor seems to be a certain cognitive style. Technically it might be called "undifferentiated thinking," or excessive "category width," as defined by Pettigrew (1958). Rokeach (1960) notes the inability of the "dogmatic" mind to perceive differences; thus, whereas some people distinguish in their thinking and feeling between Communists and Nazis, the undifferentiated dogmatist has a global reaction (cognitive and emotional) toward "Communazis."

We have no right, of course, to expect all our subjects to make discriminations exactly corresponding to our own logic. Nor should we expect them to read and respond to every item on the Extrinsic-Intrinsic scale according to its full meaning as intended by the investigators. Perhaps we should be gratified that two-thirds of our cases can be safely classified as "consistent" (i.e., having about the same strength of disposition toward an extrinsic or intrinsic orientation across most of the items). These consistent cases, as we have seen, support the hypothesis with which we started. It is the remaining (indiscriminate) one-third of the cases which obscure the trend (or diminish its statistical significance).

In responding to the religious items these individuals seem to take a superficial or "hit and run" approach. Their mental set seems to be "all religion is good." "My religious beliefs are what really lie behind my whole life"—Yes! "Although I believe in my religion, I feel there are many more important things in my life"—Yes! "Religion is especially important to me because it answers many questions about the meaning of life"—Yes! "The church is most important as a place to formulate good social relationships"—Yes!

There seems to be one wide category—"religion is OK." From the way in which the scale is constructed this undifferentiated endorsement can be the product of an agreement response set. Our inconsistently proreligious may be "yeasayers" (Couch & Keniston, 1960). But if so, we are still dealing with an undifferentiated cognitive disposition. We recall likewise that the inconsistent cases have a lower level of formal education than the consistent cases. This factor also is relevant to the formation and holding of overwide categories.

But why should such a disposition, whatever its source, be so strongly related to prejudice, in such a way that the *more* undifferentiated, the *more* prejudiced—as Table 9 shows?

The answer is that prejudice itself is a matter of stereotyped overgeneralization, a failure to distinguish members of a minority group as individuals (Allport, 1954, Chaps. 2, 10). It goes without saying that if categories are overwide the accompanying feeling tone will be undifferentiated. Thus, religion as a whole is good; a minority group as a whole is bad.

It seems probable that people with undifferentiated styles of thinking (and feeling) are not entirely secure in a world that for the most part demands fine and accurate distinctions. The resulting diffuse anxiety may well dispose them to grapple onto religion and to distrust strange ethnic groups. The positive correlation between the jungle items and other prejudice scales (Table 3) is evidence for this interpretation.

Our line of reasoning, readers will recognize, is compatible with various previous contributions to the theory of prejudice. One thinks here of Rokeach's concept of dogmatism; of Schuman and Harding's (1964) discovery of a "confused" type in their study of the relation between rational consistency and prejudice; of the same authors' work on sympathetic identification (1963); of studies on the dynamics of scapegoating, the role in insecurity, of authoritarian submission, of intolerance for ambiguity, and of related concepts.

All in all we conclude that prejudice, like tolerance, is often embedded deeply in personality structure and is reflected in a consistent cognitive style. Both states of mind are enmeshed with the individual's religious orientation. One definable style marks the individual who is bigoted in ethnic matters and extrinsic in his religious orientation. Equally apparent is the style of those who are bigoted and at the same time indiscriminately proreligious. A relatively small number of people show an equally consistent cognitive style in their simultaneous commitment to religion as a dominant, intrinsic value and ethnic tolerance.

One final word: our research argues strongly that social scientists who employ the variable "religion" or "religiosity" in the future will do well to keep in mind the crucial distinction between religious attitudes that are *intrinsic, extrinsic,* and *indiscriminately pro.* To know that a person is in some sense "religious" is not as important as to know the role religion plays in the economy of his life. (The categories of *nonreligious* and *indiscriminately antireligious* will also for some purposes be of central significance, although the present research, confined as it is to churchgoers, does not employ them.)

### NOTES AND REFERENCES

[1] J. Harding and H. Schuman, "Social Problems Questionnaire," Cornell University.
[2] The full Religious Orientation scale has been deposited with the American Documentation Institute. Order Document No. 9268 from ADI Auxiliary Publications Project, Photoduplication Service, Library of Congress, Washington, D. C. 20540. Remit in advance $1.25 for microfilm or $1.25 for photocopies and make checks payable to: Chief, Photoduplication Service, Library of Congress.
[3] The multivariate $F$ reported here is Wilk's lambda (Anderson, 1958). Statistical computations are summarized by Bock (1963) and programmed for the IBM 7090 by Hall and Cramer (1962). The univariate tests to be reported are adjusted for unequal

# G. W. Allport and J. M. Ross

Ns to obtain orthogonal estimates according to mathematical procedures described in Hall and Cramer.

⁴If we apply a more severe test, asking whether *all* differences between groups are significant, we find the following results. In four of the six groups (in both Tables 10 and 11) the extrinsic type is significantly more prejudiced than the intrinsic. Likewise in four out of six groups (Table 10) and five out of six (Table 11), the indiscriminate type is significantly more prejudiced than the intrinsic. However, in only two of the six groups (in both Tables 10 and 11) is the indiscriminate type significantly more prejudiced than the extrinsic.

ADORNO, T. W., FRENKEL-BRUNSWIK, E., LEVINSON, D. J., & SANFORD, R. N. *The authoritarian personality.* New York: Harper, 1950.

ALLPORT, G. W. Review of S. A. Stouffer, E. A. Suchman, L. C. De Vinney, S. A. Star, & R. W. Williams, Jr., *The American soldier.* Vol. 1. *Adjustment during Army life. Journal of Abnormal and Social Psychology,* 1950, 45, 168-173.

ALLPORT, G. W. *The nature of prejudice.* Reading, Mass.: Addison-Wesley, 1954.

ALLPORT, G. W. Religion and prejudice. *The Crane Review,* 1959, 2, 1-10.

ALLPORT, G. W. Behavioral science, religion, and mental health. *Journal of Religion and Health,* 1963, 2, 187-197.

ALLPORT, G. W. Religious context of prejudice. *Journal for the Scientific Study of Religion,* 1966, 5, 447-457.

ALLPORT, G. W., & KRAMER, B. M. Some roots of prejudice. *Journal of Psychology,* 1946, 22, 9-39.

ANDERSON, T. W. *An introduction to multivariate statistical analysis.* New York: Wiley, 1958.

BASS, B. M. Authoritarianism or acquiescence. *Journal of Abnormal and Social Psychology,* 1955, 56, 616-623.

BOCK, R. D. Programming univariate and multivariate analysis of variance. *Technometrics,* 1963, 5, 95-117.

CHAPMAN, L. J., & BOCK, R. D. Components of variance due to acquiescence and content in the F-scale measure of authoritarianism. *Psychological Bulletin,* 1958, 55, 328-333.

CHAPMAN, L. J., & CAMPBELL, D. T. The effect of acquiescence response-set upon relationships among the F-scale, ethnocentrism, and intelligence. *Sociometry,* 1959, 22, 153-161.

CHRISTIE, R. C. Authoritarianism re-examined. In R. C. Christie & M. Jahoda (Eds.), *Studies in the scope and method of the authoritarian personality.* New York: Free Press of Glencoe, 1954. Pp. 123-196.

COUCH, A., & KENISTON, K. Yeasayers and naysayers: Agreeing response set as a personality variable. *Journal of Abnormal and Social Psychology,* 1960, 60, 151-174.

DEMERATH, N. J., III. *Social class in American Protestantism.* Chicago: Rand McNally, 1965.

FEAGIN, J. R. Prejudice and religious types: A focused study of southern fundamentalists. *Journal for the Scientific Study of Religion,* 1964, 4, 3-13.

FICHTER, J. H. *Social relations in the urban parish.* Chicago: University of Chicago Press, 1954.

FRIEDRICHS, R. W. Christians and residential exclusion: An empirical study of a northern dilemma. *Journal of Social Issues,* 1959, 15, 14-23.

GILBERT, D. C., & LEVINSON, D. J. Ideology, personality, and institutional policy in the mental hospital. *Journal of Abnormal and Social Psychology,* 1956, 53, 263-271.

GOUGH, H. G. Studies in social intolerance: IV. *Journal of Social Psychology,* 1951, 33, 263-269.

HALL, C. E., & CRAMER, E. *General purpose program to compute multivariate analysis of variance on an IBM 7090.* Washington, D. C.: George Washington University Biometric Laboratory, 1962.

HOLTZMAN, W. H. Attitudes of college men toward non-segregation in Texas schools. *Public Opinion Quarterly,* 1956, 20, 559-569.

JACKSON, D. H., & MESSICK, S. J. A note on ethnocentrism and acquiescence response sets. *Journal of Abnormal and Social Psychology,* 1957, 54, 132-134.

KELLY, J. G., FERSON, J. E., & HOLTZMAN, W. H. The measurement of attitudes toward the Negro in the South. *Journal of Social Psychology,* 1958, 48, 305-317.

KENDAL, M. G. *Rank correlation methods.* (2nd ed.) London: Griffin, 1955.

KIRKPATRICK, C. Religion and humanitarianism: A study of institutional implications. *Psychological Monographs,* 1949, 63(9, Whole No. 304).

LENSKI, G. *The religious factor.* Garden City, N. Y.: Doubleday, 1961.

LEVINSON, D. J. The inter-group workshop: Its psychological aims and effects. *Journal of Psychology,* 1954, 38, 103-126.

PEABODY, D. Attitude content and agreement set in scales of authoritarianism, dogmatism, anti-Semitism, and economic conservatism. *Journal of Abnormal and Social Psychology,* 1961, 63, 1-11.

PETTIGREW, T. F. The measurement and correlates of category width as a cognitive variable. *Journal of Personality,* 1958, 26, 532-544.

PETTIGREW, T. F. Regional differences in anti-Negro prejudice. *Journal of Abnormal and Social Psychology,* 1959, 49, 28-36.

PINKNEY, A. The anatomy of prejudice: Majority group attitudes toward minorities in selected American cities. Unpublished doctoral dissertation, Cornell University, 1961.

ROKEACH, M. *The open and closed mind: Investigations into the nature of belief systems and personality systems.* New York: Basic Books, 1960.

ROSENBLITH, J. F. A replication of "Some roots of prejudice." *Journal of Abnormal and Social Psychology,* 1949, 44, 470-489.

SCHUMAN, H., & HARDING, J. Sympathetic identification with the underdog. *Public Opinion Quarterly,* 1963, 27, 230-241.

SCHUMAN, H., & HARDING, J. Prejudice and the norm of rationality. *Sociometry,* 1964, 27, 353-371.

STEMBER, H. C. *Education and attitude change.* New York: Institute of Human Relations Press, 1961.

STOUFFER, S. A. *Communism, civil liberties, and conformity.* Garden City, N. Y.: Doubleday, 1955.

STRUENING, E. L. Antidemocratic attitudes in a Midwest university. In H. H. Remmers (Ed.), *Anti-democratic attitudes in American schools.* Evanston: Northwestern University Press, 1963. Ch. 9.

TITUS, H. E., & HOLLANDER, E. P. The California F scale in psychological research: 1950-1955. *Psychological Bulletin,* 1957, 54, 47-64.

TUMIN, M. *Desegregation: Resistance and readiness.* Princeton: Princeton University Press, 1958.

WILLIAMS, R. M. *Strangers next door: Ethnic relations in American communities.* Englewood Cliffs, N. J.: Prentice-Hall, 1964.

WILSON, W. C. Extrinsic religious values and prejudice. *Journal of Abnormal and Social Psychology,* 1960, 60, 286-288.

YOUNG, R. K., BENSON, W. M., & HOLTZMAN, W. H. Changes in attitudes toward the Negro in a southern university. *Journal of Abnormal and Social Psychology,* 1960, 60, 131-133.

# The Intrinsic-Extrinsic Concept:
# A Review and Evaluation

RICHARD A. HUNT AND MORTON B. KING

Allport's concept of Intrinsic (I) and Extrinsic (E) orientations to religion was a major contribution to the empirical study of religion (1950, 1954, 1959, 1960, 1966; Allport and Ross, 1967). His ideas have stimulated both empirical data collection and theoretical analyses which have proved fruitful. Preliminary stock-taking of these results is now appropriate. This paper will review selected research reports and other papers in an attempt to bring their findings and conclusions to bear on four questions:

1. *Is there an I-E dimension? Can it be identified operationally as a unidimensional, bipolar variable?*

2. *What components, in theory and in research practice, does the I-E concept contain? Can separate dimensions be operationalized?*

3. *To what kind or kinds of phenomena does the concept refer: a kind of religion or a way of responding to or orienting to religion? religious behavior or motive for behavior? a religious or a personality variable?*

4. *What is the present and possible future utility of the concept and of measures associated with it?*

The sources reviewed will be presented in chronological order, with no attempt to give a general summary of each nor to describe the methodology of research articles. Only those aspects which seem germane to the questions will be treated. A concluding section will attempt to derive from the survey summary answers to each question.

Reprinted with permission of the authors and publisher from:

*Journal for the Scientific Study of Religion*, 1971, 10(4), 339-356, published by the SOCIETY FOR THE SCIENTIFIC STUDY OF RELIGION, University of Connecticut, Box U68A, Storrs, Connecticut 06268.

## EARLY HISTORY AND DEFINITIONS

The germ of the I-E concept appeared undefined and unnamed in *The Individual and His Religion* (Allport, 1950, p. 59). In the *Nature of Prejudice,* Allport (1954, pp. 451-56) discussed "two kinds of religion" related to ethnic prejudice. The terms "interiorized" and "institutionalized" were used for I and E, respectively; but no formal definition was given. He first introduced I and E as labels in the Tufts lecture published as "Religion and Prejudice" (Allport, 1959). The first of his two succinct, formal definitions appeared in a preface written for a reprinting of that article (Allport, 1960). His most complete, and regretfully his last, discussions of the concept were in "The Religious Context of Prejudice" (Allport, 1966) and "Personal Religious Orientation and Prejudice" (Allport and Ross, 1967). In the former, two sets of labels were used (I-E and "associational" vs. "communal," citing Lenski, 1961); in the latter, I-E alone.

### Nature of I-E

What light do Allport's conceptual formulations throw on our questions? First, what is the bearing of his general discussions on the nature of the phenomena (Q.3) and how they are viewed (Q.1)? Before the 1960 preface, emphasis was on E as the kind of religion associated with the ethnic prejudice. I was a partially and poorly defined opposite. Those early statements referred variously to kinds of "religion," "religious sentiments," or "religious outlook." I and E referred to opposites, but not specifically on the same continuum. Beginning in 1960, but especially in 1966 and 1967, I and E received relatively equal emphasis. Eventually, a bipolar continuum was clearly conceptualized: I and E are "two polar types of religious affiliation" (1966); "most people, if they profess religion at all, fall upon a continuum between these poles" (1967). There was also a clear progression toward viewing the phenomena as a type of motivation. What was being studied came to seem as, not "religion" or behaviors considered "religious," but the motives associated with religious belief and practice.

### Components

Secondly, what do the definitions indicate about the components (Q.2) of the I-E concept? Allport (1959, pp. 264-5) stated that extrinsic

> ... religion is not the master-motive in the life. It plays an instrumental role only. It serves and rationalizes assorted forms of self-interest. In

> such a life, the full creed and teaching of religion are not adopted. The person does not serve his religion; it is subordinated to serve him. The master-motive is always self-interest.

About intrinsic religion he stated that

> . . . dogma is tempered with humility . . . A religious sentiment of this sort floods the whole life with motivation and meaning. It is no longer limited to single segments of self-interest. And only in such a widened religious sentiment does the teaching of brotherhood take root.

In 1960 (p. 257), were the first formal definitions of both I and E.

> *Extrinsic* religion is a self-serving, utilitarian, self-protective form of religious outlook, which provides the believer with comfort and salvation at the expense of outgroups. *Intrinsic* religion marks the life that has interiorized the total creed of his faith without reservation, including the commandment to love one's neighbor. A person of this sort is more intent on serving his religion than on making it serve him.

The following statement was extracted from Allport (1966, pp. 454-5):

> . . . we borrow from axiology the concept of *extrinsic* value and *intrinsic* value. The distinction helps us to separate churchgoers whose communal type of membership supports and serves other, nonreligious ends, from those for whom religion is an end in itself—a final, not instrumental, good. . . . the extrinsic type . . . have no true association with the religious function of the church. . . . they feel no obligation to attend church regularly nor to integrate religion into their way of life. . . . most extrinsics are casual and peripheral churchgoers. . . . a type of religion that is strictly utilitarian: useful for the self in granting safety, social standing, solace, and endorsement of one's chosen way of life. By contrast, the intrinsic form of the religious sentiment regards faith as a supreme value in its own right. It is oriented toward a unification of being, takes seriously the commandment of brotherhood, and strives to transcend all self-centered needs. Dogma is tempered with humility. . . . A religious sentiment of this sort floods the whole life with motivation and meaning. Religion is no longer limited to single segments of self-interest.

Allport and Ross (1967, p. 434) gave the most extended formal definition:

> *Extrinsic Orientation.* Persons with this orientation are disposed to use religion for their own ends. The term is borrowed from axiology, to designate an interest that is held because it serves other, more ultimate interests. Extrinsic values are always instrumental and utilitarian. Persons with this orientation may find religion useful in a variety of ways—to provide security and solace, sociability and distraction, status and self-justification. The embraced creed is lightly held or else selectively shaped to fit more primary needs. In theological terms the extrinsic type turns to God, but without turning away from self.

*Intrinsic Orientation.* Persons with this orientation find their master motive in religion. Other needs, strong as they may be, are regarded as of less ultimate significance, and they are, so far as possible, brought into harmony with the religious beliefs and prescriptions. Having embraced a creed the individual endeavors to internalize it and follow it fully. It is in this sense that he *lives* his religion.

In sum: "... the extrinsically motivated person *uses* his religion, whereas the intrinsically motivated *lives* his religion."

The definitions do not describe a single idea. Rather, Allport has introduced a number of variables. While they may be interrelated, conceptually they are separable, thus suggesting that I-E is not one relatively simple continuum. In order to explore these separate components, Chart A was developed from Allport's definitions. Words and phrases used to refer to I or E were assigned to categories. Each category was assigned a number and descriptive label. The Roman numerals indicate, roughly, the time sequence in which the ideas appeared, first by date of publication and then within each source. The number(s) after a word or phrase give the date(s) of the work(s) in which it appeared.

The eleven categories chosen are, of course, arbitrary. There could have been more. Numbers VI and VII, and perhaps VIII and IX, might be combined to give fewer categories.

## CHART A

### COMPONENTS OF I-E DEFINITIONS

| INTRINSIC | EXTRINSIC |
|---|---|
| I. *Reflective* vs *Uncritical* | |
| reflective (1950) | unreflective, uncritical (1950) |
| II. *Differentiated* vs *Undifferentiated* | |
| highly differentiated (1950) | undifferentiated (1950) |
| III. *Personal* vs *Institutional* | |
| "interiorized" (1954 label; 1960) | institutional (1950, 54) |
| | "institutionalized" (1954 label) |
| vital, deeper level (1967) | |
| devout, internalized (1967) | external (1954) |
| IV. *Universal* vs *Parochial* | |
| universalistic (1954) | |
| infused with the character of ethics (1954) | exclusionist (1950, 59) |
| | ethnocentric, exclusive, in-group (1954) |
| creed, ideals of brotherhood (1954, 66) | at expense of out-groups (1960) |
| conditioned to love one's neighbor (1960) | |
| compassion (1967) | favors provincialism (1966) |

141

V. *Unselfish* vs *Selfish*
    not self-centered (1959)
    strives to transcend self-centered needs (1966)

self-centered (1950)
self-interest (1959)
self-serving, protective (1960)
useful to self (1966)
uses for own ends (1967)

VI. *Relevance for all of Life*
    distilled into thought and conduct (1954)
    floods whole life with motivation and meaning (1959, 66)
    not limited to single segments (1966)
    other needs brought into harmony with religious beliefs and prescriptions (1967)
    follows creed fully (1967)

single segment (1959)

not integrated into their way of life (1966)
favors compartmentalization (1966)

VII. *Salience*
    faith really matters (1954)
    sincerely believing (1954)
    accepts total creed (1960)
    without reservations (1960)
    follows creed fully (1967)

full creed and teaching not adopted (1959)
faith, beliefs lightly held (1967)

VIII. *Ultimate* vs *Instrumental*
    an end in itself (1954, 66)
    "intrinsic" (1959, 60, 66, 67 label)
    intent on serving his religion (1960)
    a final good (1966)
    faith is supreme value; the master motive (1967)
    ultimate significance (1967)

utilitarian, means to ends (1954)
"extrinsic" (1959, 60, 66, 67 label)
not master motive (1959)
instrumental (1959, 66, 67)
supports and serves non-religious (1966)
uses religion (1967)
serves other than ... ultimate interests (1967)

IX. *Associational* vs *Communal*

    "associational" (1966 label; 1967)
    seeking deeper values (1967)
    involved for religious fellowship (1967).

political and social aspects (1954)
"communal" (1966 label; 1967)

sociocultural (1966)
affiliates for communal identification, need to belong (1966)
no true association with the religious function of the church (1966)
involved for sociability and status (1967)

X. *Humility* vs *Dogmatism*
    humility (1959, 67)

dogmatic (1959, 66)

XI. *Regularity of Church
Attendance*
constant (1967)                        casual and peripheral churchgoers
(1966)
feel no need to attend regularly
(1966)

Five of the components dominated the definitions. Others were mentioned, but none seemed as central as these:

IV. *Universal-Parochial:* brotherhood and love of neighbor vs ethnocentrism and exclusion of those unlike oneself.

V. *Unselfish-Selfish:* effort to transcend self-centered needs vs self-serving, protective use for own ends.

VI. *Relevance for all of Life:* floods whole life with motivation and meaning vs compartmentalized, not integrated into one's way of life.

VII. *Ultimate-Instrumental:* ends vs means; master motive vs utilitarian uses; intrinsic vs extrinsic in the axiological sense.

IX. *Associational-Communal:* involved for religious fellowship and deeper values vs affiliation for sociability and status.

Two components, emphasized in 1950, did not appear in Allport's later descriptions: *I. Reflective-Uncritical* and *II. Differentiated-Undifferentiated.*

One, *V. Personal-Institutional,* provided the 1954 labels. "Institutionalized" was the key feature of E in 1950 and 1954. The component disappeared from the definitions, until 1967 when the "Internalized" aspect of I was emphasized.

*VI.Salience* (faith really matters, sincere belief vs faith lightly held) was identified in most of the definitions, especially of I; but was nowhere emphasized.

*X. Humility-Dogmatism:* appeared only occasionally and without emphasis.

*XI. Regularity of Church Attendance:* became an explicit component only in 1966 after empirical research established it as a correlate of prejudice. It was probably implicit in III as "devout" behavior. It is a sample of the several forms of congregational participation which might be either associational or communal (IX).

## Summary

Allport attempted to describe two orientations to religion as poles of a continuum. However, in his own definitions we discovered an expanding bundle of component variables. To deal with these complications, we now examine the content of items used to operationalize the I-E concept.

## OPERATIONAL DEFINITIONS

### Wilson

Wilson (1960) made the first report of empirical research based on the I-E concept. With Allport's help, he developed an "Extrinsic Religious Values Scale" (ERV) of 15 items to contain items of two kinds, corresponding to categories III and VIII, institutional and instrumental. All items, however, were treated as one scale with one pole as the "extrinsic religious value." The other pole was "not positively defined, but simply reflects the absence" of E. Support for treating the items as one scale was found in "corrected equivalent halves" reliability quotients of .51 to .86 for 10 groups of subjects.

Considered in terms of the 11 components, six items could be classified as instrumental, five of which were also selfish. Four items were institutional. The remaining five resist classification because of vagueness or mixed content. Other components in the early definitions were absent: unreflective, undifferentiated, parochial, non-salient.

Wilson's study shed some light on all four questions. Q1. Rather than being clearly undimensional, ERV had at least two components and only one pole. Q2. It seemed to be an index of E alone; with I undefined and unmeasured. Q3. Wilson (1960, p. 288) stated that ERV did not measure "the content of religious beliefs," but "attempts to measure . . . the motivations for affiliating with a religious institution." Thus, he established early the view that what was being measured was motivation for religion, not a kind of religion or a dimension of religion. Q4. That ERV had some validity and research utility was shown by the fact that it was significantly correlated with a measure of anti-semitism in all 10 subject groups (.41 to .72).

### Feagin

Feagin (1964) made a major forward step in operationalizing the I-E concept. He used an "Intrinsic/Extrinsic Scale" of 21 items, developed by Allport's seminar. It contained only two items from Wilson's ERV. According to Feagin, 12 were "extrinsically stated," six "intrinsically stated," while three belonged to an unnamed residual category. The I items seem only reverse statements of E, but were a first, small attempt to define another end of the continuum.

## CHART B

### Items to Measure I-E[1]

*Intrinsic:*

2. *I try hard to carry my religion over into all my other dealings in life. (A&R, K&H) [VI].

7. Quite often I have been keenly aware of the presence of God or of the Divine Being. (A&R) [III].

8. *My religious beliefs are what really lie behind my whole approach to life. (A&R, K&H) [VI].

9. *The prayers I say when I am alone carry as much meaning and personal emotion as those said by me during services. (A&R, K&H) [III].

16. Religion is especially important to me because it answers many questions about the meaning of life. (A&R, K&H) [VII].

20. *It is important to me to spend periods of time in private religious thought and meditation. (A&R, K&H) [III].

   (Unlabeled by Feagin, but called I by Allport and Ross)

13. *If not prevented by unavoidable circumstances, I attend Church at least once a week or oftener, two or three times a month, once every month or two, rarely. (A&R, K&H) [XI].

14. If I were to join a church group I would prefer to join A) a Bible Study group or, B) a social fellowship. (A&R) [IX].

18. *I read literature about my faith (or church) frequently, occasionally, rarely, never. (A&R, K&H) [?].

*Extrinsic:*

1. *What religion offers most is comfort when sorrow and misfortune strike. (A&R, K&H) [V, VIII].

3. *Religion helps to keep my life balanced and steady in exactly the same way as my citizenship, friendships, and other memberships do. (W, K&H) [V, VIII].

4. *One reason for my being a church member is that such membership helps to establish a person in the community. (W, A&R, K&H) [V, VIII].

5. *The purpose of prayer is to secure a happy and peaceful life. (A&R, K&H) [V, VIII].

6. *It doesn't matter so much what I believe as long as I lead a moral life. (A&R) [?].

10. Although I am a religious person, I refuse to let religious considerations influence my everyday affairs. (A&R) [? VI].

11. *The Church is most important as a place to formulate good social relationships. (A&R, K&H) [V, VIII].

12. Although I believe in my religion, I feel there are many more important things in life. (A&R) [VII].

15. I pray chiefly because I have been taught to pray. (A&R) [III].

17. A primary reason for my interest in religion is that my church is a congenial social activity. (A&R) [IX].

19. Occasionally I find it necessary to compromise my religious beliefs in order to protect my social and economic wellbeing. (A&R) [?].
21. *The primary purpose of prayer is to gain relief and protection. (A&R) [V, VIII].

*Items selected by Feagin for factorially-derived I and E scales.
1. The items are identified by their numbers in Feagin (1964). The letters after each item indicate other studies in which it was used: W, Wilson (1960); A&R, Allport and Ross (1967); K&H, King and Hunt (unpublished).
Roman numerals in brackets after each item indicate the conceptual component (Chart A) to which it is assigned.

These items (hereafter identified as "Allport-Feagin") were the basis of subsequent research and deserve careful attention. Charts B (list of items) and C (item-scale correlations) were prepared to aid the analysis. Examined in terms of the components in Chart A, six of the E items can be classified as both VIII and V, instrumental/selfish. Most of the other E items are hard to classify. One each is considered III (institutional), VI (non-relevant), VII (non-salient), and IX (communal). The other two are unclassifiable. Three of the I items are considered III (personal); two, VI (relevant); and one, VII (salient). The three unlabeled items are classified as XI (church attendance), IX (associational/communal), and unclassifiable. Thus, the total item content placed primary emphasis on instrumental/selfish. Three items each were devoted to the personal-institutional and the relevance components; two items each, to salience and associational-communal; and one, to church attendance. Three items were left unclassified.

Feagin's factor analysis produced separate I and E factors. From these, he selected two scales composed of six items each. All E items combined both instrumental and selfish components. The I scale was mixed, containing two items indicating relevance; two personal; and two, religious practices: church attendance and reading religious literature. The last had the highest factor loading and item-scale correlation. Chart C shows how these two variables were separated from the other items. Except for Number 21, item-scale correlations were consistently higher on the separate six-item scales, and lower on the total 21-item scale.

CHART C

ITEM-SCALE CORRELATIONS FROM THREE STUDIES[1]

|  | Feagin | | A & R | K & H | |
| --- | --- | --- | --- | --- | --- |
| *Intrinsic* | 21 Items | 6 Items | Total | I Items | E Items |
| 2 | .32 | .64 | .39 | .55 | — |
| 7 | .33 | * | .44 | * | — |
| 8 | .45 | .67 | .50 | .62 | — |
| 9 | .26 | .54 | .30 | .20 | — |
| 13 | .31 | .56 | .47 | .36 | — |
| 14 | .34 | * | .49 | * | — |
| 16 | .26 | * | .28 | .55 | — |
| 18 | .38 | .71 | .41 | .46 | |
| 20 | .37 | .66 | .58 | .51 | — |
| *Extrinsic* | | | | | |
| 1 | .47 | .65 | .49 | — | .41 |
| 3 | .47 | .61 | * | — | .33 |
| 4 | .50 | .56 | .47 | — | .38 |
| 5 | .50 | .68 | .51 | — | .44 |
| 6 | .34 | * | .39 | — | * |
| 10 | .40 | * | .31 | — | * |
| 11 | .41 | .59 | .44 | — | .39 |
| 12 | .37 | * | .32 | — | * |
| 15 | .35 | * | .31 | — | * |
| 17 | .22 | * | .33 | — | * |
| 19 | .32 | * | .18 | — | * |
| 21 | .54 | .48 | .50 | — | * |

*Item not included in study.
1. As in Chart B, Feagin (1964) numbers are used. Other sources: Allport and Ross (1967) and King and Hunt (unpublished data).

## Implications

Feagin's findings bear directly on the questions. *Q1.* He demonstrated that the 21 items were "not unidimensional." His separate factors pointed toward separate I and E dimensions. *Q2.* His items illustrated several components. His factorially derived E scale clearly defined "extrinsic" as instrumental and selfish. The I scale, containing three components, provided a less useful definition of "intrinsic." He was uncertain "whether any of the items are measuring 'intrinsic-devout' religiosity." (p. 12) Correlations of the 21-item scale, I scale, and E scale with a measure of anti-Negro prejudice were + .25, − .01, and + .35 respectively. These findings indicate that: *Q1.* I and E scales do in fact measure different things; *Q2.* they are more useful separately than the 21 items combined; and *Q4.* they have some validity and research utility.

## Allport and Ross

Allport and Ross (1967) reported a study using 20 of the same items, divided into two "subscales" (E, 11; I, 9) based apparently on subjective evaluation of item content. (See Charts B and C.) Neither factor nor item-scale analyses are reported beyond item correlations with the combined I-E scale. Two findings led them to question the utility of I and E items combined into one scale. The E items alone were more highly correlated with prejudice. There was "only a very low correlation" (−.21) between the I and E items scored separately. It was, they said, "apparent . . . that subjects who endorse extrinsically worded items do not necessarily reject those worded intrinsically, or vice versa." Many subjects "persist in endorsing any or all items that to them seem favorable to religion in any sense." Such subjects were called "indiscriminately proreligious."

Allport and Ross (1967) used the I and E items, scored as separate scales, to divide the subjects into three groups: "intrinsic," those who were above the median on I and below on E; "extrinsic," those in reverse categories; "indiscriminately proreligious," a subject who gave "approximately 50% more intrinsic responses on the intrinsic subscale than we should expect from his extrinsic responses on the extrinsic subscale." Comparing mean scores of the three groups on five measures of prejudice, they found that intrinsic subjects were least prejudiced and indiscriminately proreligious, most prejudiced. Those who were "extremely indiscriminate" were more prejudiced than those moderately so.

### Implications

This study indicated that: *Q1.* I-E is not one unidimensional variable. *Q2.* The authors concluded that the items could be used to measure "indiscriminately proreligious" as well as I and E. They considered it a third dimension or orientation, and presented a separate psychodynamic explanation to account for its high correlation with prejudice. The same multiple components found in Feagin's 21 items are present in their 20, of course. *Q3.* Allport and Ross made clear that they were measuring "motivation" for or "orientation" to religion, not its types or forms. I-E was discussed as if it were a personality variable. *Q4.* Correlations of I and E with prejudice and other variables to form explanatory patterns of theoretical interest indicated some validity and research utility for the measures.

## King and Hunt

King and Hunt (1969) reported results of factor and item-scale analyses on a large number of items indicating varied aspects of religious belief and practice. The questionnaire contained about 15 I-E items: Feagin's (1964) numbers 3 and 11 and others such as "The purpose of worship and prayer is to ask God to help us" and "The purpose of worship and prayer is to find out what God wants us to do." A six-item scale composed of E-type items was developed. It contained Feagin Number 11 and three other instrumental/selfish items, plus two whose content fit none of the 11 components. Nothing that could be called an "intrinsic" factor or scale appeared. The I-type items were scattered among several factors, including a quite general first factor.

In 1968 items from that study, together with many new items, were contained in a questionnaire returned by 1356 members of four Protestant denominations. Charts B and C show that seven I and five E items were included from the Allport-Feagin list. All procedures were similar to those previously reported (King, 1967; King and Hunt, 1969; Hunt, 1970). Two E-type scales were derived. One with seven items had six belonging to the instrumental/selfish component, five of which were Allport-Feagin items. Another five-item scale contained no Allport-Feagin items, but three which were instrumental/selfish. The other two were unclassified.

The seven Allport-Feagin I items did not form a stable, homogeneous cluster. They were scattered among several factors, including a first, general factor. Two of the scales derived contained some Allport-Feagin I items, but were given names to represent the total item content: "Orientation to Growth and Striving" and "Salience: Cognition" parallel to "Salience: Behavior."

The Allport-Feagin items, when treated as separate I and E scales (see Chart C), showed a positive correlation of .24 which was significantly different from zero, statistically. Our seven-item E scale had positive correlations of .26 and .37 with our scales containing Allport-Feagin I items. Their E items and our E scale showed no significant association with our measure of prejudice. The two scales containing I items had a low, statistically significant association (both .16) with tolerance.

### Implications

What are the implications for our questions? *Q1*. No I-E continuum was apparent. I and E were clearly not opposites, but rather two somewhat related but separable variables. *Q2*. Our findings, like Feagin's, indicated that E can be isolated and specified as instrumental/selfish. Neither the Allport-Feagin I items, nor any subset of them,

**149**

were successfully isolated by factor analysis. Our findings, like Feagin's, failed to define I with any clarity or homogeneity. Q3. In our study the I and E items appeared to indicate orientation to, or the way a person relates to, religion. Q4. Our E scale was not useful in relation to the tolerance/prejudice variable. However, its correlation with other variables, including + .49 with Intolerance of Ambiguity, indicated some analytical power. The I-type scales, while conceptually fuzzy, had some use through a positive relation to tolerance.

## OTHER RELATED STUDIES

### Using Allport Items

Three other studies used the 20 Allport and Ross items in empirical studies. Hood (1970) used them, as Allport and Ross (1967) suggested, to divide his subjects into four categories: I, E, and indiscriminately pro- and anti-religious. He found that the I and E subscales were not significantly correlated. I was significantly correlated with his "religious experience episodes measure" (REEM); E was not. Hood reported difficulty in distinguishing "intrinsically oriented" from "indiscriminately proreligious" persons, because of the "methodological problem of distinguishing a genuine report . . . from a response set." Relating his findings to our questions: Q1. Hood did not treat, and had no basis for treating, I-E as a single continuum. He did not find I and E related, as bipoles or otherwise. Q2. His REEM seemed to measure the I aspect of the Personal-Institutional component (III), and he treated indiscriminately religious, both pro- and anti-, as useful dimensions. Q3. He considered I and E to be orientations to religion. Q4. Despite careful attention to the reliability and validity of REEM, Hood presented no such evidence for the I and E subscales.

McConahay and Hough (1969) used the 20 items in a study with 48 original items. The latter were designed to indicate perspectives based on love, guilt, and forgiveness themes in Christian theology, plus a "culture-oriented" or "conventional" orientation. Factor analysis and Likert scaling techniques were used. Several of their findings bear on our questions: Q1. "Third factor was . . . clearly the Allport and Ross factor with Extrinsic items loading high positively and the Intrinsic low negatively." However, they used the I and E items separately as subscales and reported a statistically significant correlation of −.25 between them. Q2. Their "conventional" scale contained 5 original items, all of which have E-like content. Two can be classified as instrumental/selfish (V and VIII), and one as communal (IX). The other two were unclassified. This scale had a significant r of +.35 with the

Allport and Ross E items. Items on their "Love Oriented-Other Centered" scale had content similar to definitions of I. Three of the 5 items could be classified is IV, universal (brotherhood of all men). However, neither the I or E subscales were significantly correlated with it. Items were not shown for their "Church Involvement in Social Action" scale. However, the description of it sounds like component VI, relevance for all of life. Surprisingly, its correlation with the I items was − .38. Q3. McConahay and Hough considered that the I-E items measured "motivation for religious practices," in contrast to the "theological content" of their love-guilt scales. However, all their scales seemed to be of the "orientation to" or "perspective on" type. Q4. The pattern of correlation between their scales led to theoretically interpretations. Therefore, the I, E, conventional, love oriented-other centered indices had enough utility to encourage their testing through further use.

Strickland and Shaffer (1971) used the 20 items in a study with "Adorno's Fascism scale" and Rotter's scale measuring "belief in internal as opposed to external control of reinforcement." Q1. In a small pilot study, I and E were found to have a negative correlation of .54. The authors were persuaded that I and E were poles of a continuum and the "two subscales were combined into one overall extrinsic score." Q3. I and E, like the other variables, are considered "belief systems." Q4. The I-E scale was significantly correlated with control of reinforcement, I being related to belief that "behavior will have an impact on . . . life situations." It was not related to an authoritarian belief system.

## Using I-E Concept

Brown (1964), Tisdale (1966), and Vanecko (1966) conducted empirical studies using the I-E concept, but not the Allport-Feagin items. Tisdale used Wilson's ERV and the others used original items and methods. Some light was thrown on our questions. Q1. Brown (1964) and his judges were unable to classify sentence-completion-data as either I or E. Instead, seven categories were proposed. However, no obvious continuum emerged. Q2. He treated I and E as separate, mutually exclusive categories. Two of his categories were "self-serving extrinsic" and "extrinsic through conventional acceptance." These correspond to the instrumental/selfish (V, VIII) and institutional (III) components. VII, salience, was also implicit in his discussion. Q3. Brown proposed that disbelief, as well as belief, had its intrinsic and extrinsic orientations. His proposal that "more research is needed to show whether the origins and functions of extreme belief and disbelief are in fact the same" suggested that I-E refers to a pervasive personality process.

Tisdale (1966). *Q1.* thought that ERV measured one variable, an "extrinsic orientation." *Q3* and *Q4.* The ERV correlation with personality variables led to the conclusion that this religious orientation was related to certain "manifest needs in normal individuals," supporting Allport and Adorno theories of the relation of religion, personality, dynamics, and prejudice.

Vanecko (1966) used original measures of several religious dimensions to study their relation to prejudice. While his items and scales were not given, the description of some variables sound like components of I and E. "Acceptance of ethical norms," "acceptance of social teachings," and "devotional practices" could be considered I-aspects of the "relevance" (VI) and "personal" (III) components. His "instrumental" was E, and may be interpreted as "instrumental/ selfish" (VIII, V). *Q1.* Vanecko presented his scales as measures of separate variables. *Q2.* They were similar to several I-E components. *Q3.* Vanecko thought of his variables as forms of "religious behavior." *Q4.* "Acceptance of ethical norms" was negatively associated with prejudice and "instrumental" was positively associated, thereby supporting Allport's theory.

## Other Factor Studies

Studies by Keene (1967) and Monaghan (1967) used factor analysis on item pools quite different from Feagin's (1964). Both developed typologies which overlap with the I-E concept and with its components. Keene (1967) sought to identify "the basic dimensions of religious behavior" in studying Baha'is, Jews, Christians, and unaffiliated subjects. He distinguished four dimensions: a) Salient/Irrelevant, b) Spiritual/Secular, c) Skeptical/Approving, and d) Orthodox/Personal. Examination of his item content allows conclusions regarding *Q2:* Some items in his "salient" were similar to our "salience" (VII), but it also contained a "church attendance" (XI) and other participation items. "Spiritual" items were partly creedal, and partly the "personal" or I aspect of component III. "Orthodox" was primarily the "institutional" or E aspect of III.

Monaghan (1967) attempted to discover "motivations" for church membership and attendance. He distinguished three "hypothetical type[s] of person[s]": the "authority-seeker," "comfort-seeker," and "social participator." *Q2.* The latter two were similar to the E aspects of several components. "Comfort-seeking" had much in common with instrumental/selfish (VIII, V), non-relevant (VI), and non-salient (VII). "Social participation" contained inner conflicts. Some items pointed toward the E and others toward the I aspects of IX, and thus did not distinguish communal and associational motives for participation.

Finally, reference should be made to Allen and Spilka's (1967) careful attempt to measure orientations to religion in relation to prejudice. Their committed/consensual (Cm/Cs) dimension had some relationship to I-E (see Dittes, 1969a). In relation to Q2: three of the five Cm/Cs categories were similar to I-E components: "Clarity" and "reflective-unreflective" (I); "Complexity" and "differentiated-undifferentiated" (II); "Importance" and "relevance" (VI). None of these components was operationalized by the Allport-Feagin items. The first two were not mentioned by Allport after 1950. In Allport and Ross (1967) unreflective was explicitly and undifferentiated was implicitly assigned to the new "indiscriminately proreligious orientation." Cm/Cs did not correlate with Wilson's (1960) ERV. As conceptualized and especially as operationalized, I-E and Cm/Cs are largely different variables. Q3. In one way, however, they are similar. I and E are most usefully viewed as orientations to or motivations behind religion. Allen and Spilka conceived of Cm/Cs as a composite of five "cognitive dimensions." That is, both I/E and Cm-Cs seem to be pointing to pervasive personality characteristics. Q4. Cm was associated with prejudice and Cs with tolerance, which parallels the prediction of I-E theory.

## CONCLUSION

Allport's I-E concept has generated fruitful scholarly activity, both theoretical and empirical, among sociologists as well as psychologists. Their work has added to an understanding of the relationship between religion and ethnic prejudice. (See Allport and Ross, 1967, and Dittes, 1969a, in particular). Some contribution may have been made to the psychology of personality itself. On the other hand, we believe the time has come to abandon the early generalized definitions and rough measures in favor of more specific definitions and a complex set of measuring tools. To justify those conclusions, what can we conclude regarding the four questions proposed?

*1. Is there a single I-E dimension? Can it be identified operationally as a unidimensional, bipolar variable?*

The preponderance of evidence says "No." Feagin (1964) found two factors, and our own data produce several. Feagin (1964) and Allport and Ross (1967) found that I and E used separately were better

**153**

predictors of prejudice than the two combined. Brown (1964) concluded that two and perhaps three dimensions were involved. Factor analysis (Keene, 1967; Monaghan, 1967; King and Hunt, 1969 and unpublished data) revealed a complex structure. Examination of item content indicated several components, even in the Wilson (1960) ERV scale. Evidence in favor of unidimensionality is slight. Strickland and Shaffer (1971) combined I and E items into one scale, based on a correlation of .54 in a pilot study. McConahay and Hough (1969) obtained what they call "the Allport and Ross factor." From their description (the items are not shown), it is dominated by E items, the I items having low loadings.

The evidence indicates, secondly, that I and E are separate dimensions, not bipoles of one. Feagin (1964) stated that his I and E factors were "orthogonal" to each other. The Strickland and Shaffer (1971) finding that r = −.54 seems to support the idea of a bipolar continuum. However, there were only 24 pilot subjects and they report no test based on their study data. The r of .54 indicated that 71% of the variance was unassigned. The other studies reported no correlation or low correlations between I and E, with both plus and minus signs. Hood (1970) reported no correlation; Allport and Ross (1967), −.21; McConahay and Hough (1969), −.25; King and Hunt (unpublished) found low positive correlations between the Allport-Feagin I and E items (.24) and among scales containing them (.26 to .37). The highest, .37, accounts for only 14% of the variance.[1]

I-E, we conclude, has not been successfully operationalized as one dimension with I and E as its poles.

2. *What components, in theory and in research practice, does the I-E concept contain? Can separate dimensions be operationalized?*

Examination of Allport's definitions revealed a number of conceptually separable components. The 11 displayed in Chart A might be expanded or contracted. Other minds would produce different lists; but, we believe, they would discern several components. Our list proved useful for the classification of the content of items prepared in the Allport tradition. It was much less useful in classifying other items. The main components seen in the items were: III, Personal-institutional; V, Unselfish-selfish; VI, Relevance for all of life; VIII, Ultimate-instrumental; and IX, Associational-Communal. In addition to those, IV, Universal-Parochial, was prominent in the later definitions.

Which components have received separate operational definition by a useful or potentially useful scale? Only one, the instrumental/

selfish combination, is clearly established. Since Feagin (1964), "extrinsic" has had no other useful definition, and his six items are still its best measure. Support for this definition of E was found in Brown (1964), Vanecko (1966), Monaghan (1967), and King and Hunt (1969 and unpublished data). In general, two kinds of item matrices have been factored, or otherwise analyzed. When a small number of items was selected to meet Allport's definitions, an E factor composed primarily of instrumental/selfish items appeared. Most of the remaining items appeared as a first or general factor which, in that limited context, seemed to be a relatively homogeneous definition of I. However, in a larger, more heterogeneous matrix, the structure was different. An E factor or factors appeared, dominated by selfish/instrumental items. The I items, however, were scattered among several factors. Operational definition of I is still lacking; no one satisfactory scale has been developed.

The studies reviewed have indicated several other variables of potential utility, including both I and E components. All these warrant further study to test their research utility. Indicators of VI, Relevance for all of life, were found in Feagin (1964), Monaghan (1967), in McConahay and Hough's (1969) "Church Involvement in Social Action," and perhaps in their "Love oriented-other centered" dimension. The latter, however, also has the "brotherhood" aspects of IV, Universal-parochial. Indicators of VII, Salience, were present in Feagin (1964), Keene (1967), Monaghan (1967), and King and Hunt (unpublished data). The Personal (not institutional) aspect of III appeared in Feagin (1964), Keene (1967), Hood's (1970) REEM, and the "Personal Religious Experience" scale of King and Hunt (1969 and unpublished data). All these are similar to Lenski's (1961) "Devotionalism." Feagin (1964), Monaghan (1967), and King and Hunt (1969 and unpublished data) had items or scales measuring one or more aspects of congregational participation. However, none seem to measure the motivation for such behavior, which is what makes the idea of IX, Associational-Communal, interesting. Brown (1964) and McConahay and Hough (1969) identified a "conventional" dimension which is related to the E aspect of III, Personal-Institutional. Allport and Ross (1967) introduced and Hood (1970) supported the idea of two "indiscriminately pro- and anti-religious" dimensions.

## 3. To what kind(s) of phenomena does the I-E concept refer?

As early as Wilson (1960) emphasis was placed on I-E as orientation to or motivation for religion, rather than as a kind of religion or of religious behavior. That emphasis was clearer in definitions and in the discussion of research findings, than in item content. It was found in Allport and Ross (1967), McConahay and Hough (1969), and in King and Hunt (1969 and unpublished data). Monaghan's (1967) types of religious motivation shared components with I and E. However, it is in Allport and Ross (1967) and the parallel work of Allen and Spilka (1967) that the I-E phenomena began to look more like a personality variable and less like "religion." Allport and Ross (1967) referred to both I-E and prejudice as "state of mind," "enmeshed with" each other, "deeply embedded in personality structure." Prejudice, explicitly, and I-E, implicitly, were considered "a consistent cognitive style." Allen and Spilka (1967), engaged in the same search for the relation of religion to prejudice, arrived at a similar terminus: five categories of cognitive style. Brown (1964) proposed that I-E is a variable which cut across disbelief as well as belief. His discussion suggests a pervasive personality process. Dittes (1969a) summarized the interrelations between "religious" and "personality" variables. Duncombe (1969) defined "faith" as a "freeing sense of security" and the measures he proposed apply to "secular" more than to "religious" situations.

What social scientists have tried to measure under the label of "real," "internalized," "intrinsic" religion and its extrinsic opposite may prove to be basic, pervasive personality variables. If so, it would help to understand and predict all behavior, not just "religious" behavior. Read the items in Feagin's instrumental/selfish scale. Could these not be rewritten to apply just as well to any area of institutional behavior: work relationships, education, even the family? Is it only the church and religious behavior which one uses for selfish purposes? Indeed, in some theological perspectives *all* behavior is religious, since by implication it expresses one's faith perspective, his orientation to the ultimate meanings of life.

*4. What is the present and possible future of the I-E concept and of measures associated with it?*

How does one evaluate utility? We have used conceptual clarity and, especially, ability to explain the variance in other variables as our criteria. On both grounds, we found I-E lacking as a single variable. The label, certainly, and probably the gross idea should be abandoned. It has served a useful purpose. Now attention should be focused on labels, ideas, and scales of greater specificity. The supporting evidence includes: the variety of conceptual components identified in definitions, item content, and empirical findings; general failure to find one homogeneous set of items; Feagin (1964), Allport and Ross (1967), and others found that the E items alone were more closely related to prejudice than all items combined.

As noted above, however, "extrinsic" as measured by Feagin's (1964) instrumental/selfish scale is definitely useful. It produced informative correlations for Feagin (1964), Allport and Ross (1967), Vanecko (1966), and King and Hunt. No other definition of E has proved so useful. The McConahay and Hough (1971) "conventional" scale may be refined as a measure of another E component.

We conclude that I as a single religious dimension should be abandoned, as a label and as an idea. First, its conceptual complexity is supported by the fact that items chosen to measure it turn up on several separate factors. Some such dimensions may be interpreted in the I-E context (e.g., relevance, devotionalism); others may not (e.g., congregational participation). Second, it is hard to distinguish from "indiscriminately proreligious" (see Hood, 1970). Third, serious problems of reliability and validity are involved. The root meanings of I have been "inner," and "real," and "ultimate." All require inferences made from observed and reported behaviors which are believed to be symbols, indicators of something beyond themselves. Deciding what is "real" is a metaphysical, not empirical operation. Deciding what is "ultimate" is even harder. Who has the perspective from which to decide what is in fact ultimate, even in the psychic economy of one person? What indices should be used? Will they be consistent when comparing persons?

As noted above, separate I components were identified or measured in Allport and Ross (1967), McConahay and Hough (1971), Strickland and Shaffer (1971), and King and Hunt (unpublished data). Efforts to refine them should continue.

The idea of indiscriminately pro- and anti-religious dimensions deserves careful theoretical and empirical attention. Allport and Ross (1967) and Hood (1970) derived measures from their I and E scales. What they measured may be only a pro-religious response set encouraged by church-oriented research procedures. Our data share the same problem, and most of our scales developed for different religious dimensions have low positive correlations, even I and E. Future research reports should attempt to report correlations corrected for this bias. The phenomenon may be an expression of general yea- or nay-saying, as Allport and Ross suggest (p. 441). Couch and Keniston (1960) report that nay-sayers have good internal controls and high ego-strength. Yea-sayers are impulsive and low in ego-strength, with their "behavior determined more by external factors in the immediate situation." Is this a personality syndrome which explains differences in both prejudiced and religious behavior? Here, again, "religious" scales may be pointing us to those basic personality variables related to perception, cognition, and patterns of response which should be the central focus of "religious" research (see Pruyser, 1968).

Evaluation of research related to the I-E concept and other religious dimensions points to a paradox. Some scholars try to identify and measure the kind of religion which does, can, or should provide a master motive for all of life. Others aim at discovery of the motive(s) behind kinds of behavior called "religious." They, and personality psychologists, find that motivation which explains "religious" behavior is a pervasive variable which explains "secular" behavior also.

There seems little doubt that what deserves to be called "religious" behavior is involved in the personality structure at its deepest levels, and probably in multiple ways. That view is consistent with the thought of those like Luckmann (1967), Pruyser (1968), Yinger (1969), and Dittes (1969b) who seek to define religion by its function in life, rather than by historical and/or institutionalized substance. For example, Luckmann (1967) states that the "social processes that lead to the formation of the self are fundamentally religious."

Starting at any of several points on the research circumference, we are led to a common center for the social psychological study of the person and his relations with all other persons, things, and events. Work on the I-E concept, started by Allport, now points empirical students of religion to these research opportunities and to the need to join with other social scientists in common tasks.

## NOTES AND REFERENCES

[1]Correlation between variables is a function of the subject as well as item content. Therefore, much more attention should be given to whether I and E vary sufficiently, within a sample or across samples, to permit observation of their relationship. As the variability about the mean of a scale becomes less, correlation of that scale with others approaches zero.

ALLEN, R. O. AND B. SPILKA 1967 Committed and consensual religion: a specification of religion-prejudice relationships. *Journal for the Scientific Study of Religion* 6: 191-206.

ALLPORT, G. W. 1950 *The individual and his religion.* New York: Macmillan. 1954 *The nature of prejudice.* Cambridge, Mass.: Addison-Wesley. 1959 Religion and prejudice. *Crane Review* 2:1-10. 1960 *Personality and social encounter.* Boston: Beacon Press. 1966 The religious context of prejudice. *Journal for the Scientific Study of Religion* 5:447-57.

———, and J. M. ROSS 1967 Personal religious orientation and prejudice. *Journal of Personality and Social Psychology* 5:432-43.

BROWN, L. B. 1964 Classification of religious orientation. *Journal for the Scientific Study of Religion* 4: 91-99.

COUCH, A. AND K. KENISTON 1960 Yeasayers and naysayers: Agreeing response set as a personality variable. *Journal of Abnormal and Social Psychology* 60: 151-174.

DITTES, J. E. 1969a Psychology of religion. *The Handbook of Social Psychology.* Reading, Massachusetts: Addison-Wesley Publishing Company; edited by G. Lindzey and E. Aronson; second edition, 5: 602-59. 1969b Secular religion: dilemma of churches and researchers. *Review of Religious Research* 10: 65-80.

DUNCOMBE, D. C. 1969 *The shape of the Christian life.* Nashville: Abingdon Press.

FEAGIN, J. R. 1964 Prejudice and religious types: a focused study of southern fundamentalists. *Journal for the Scientific Study of Religion* 4:3-13.

HOOD, R. W. JR. 1970 Religious orientation and the report of religious experience. *Journal for the Scientific Study of Religion.* 9: 285-91.

HUNT, R. A. 1970 A computer procedure for item-scale analysis, *Educational and Psychological Measurement* 30: 133-35.

KEENE, J. E. 1967 Religious behavior and neuroticism, spontaneity, and worldmindedness. *Sociometry* 30: 137-57.

KING, M. B. 1967 Measuring the religious variable: nine proposed dimensions. *Journal for the Scientific Study of Religion* 6: 173-190.

———, AND R. A. HUNT 1969 Measuring the religious variable: amended findings. *Journal for the Scientific Study of Religion* 8: 321-23.

LENSKI, G. 1961 *The religious factor.* Garden City: New York: Doubleday.

LUCKMANN, T. 1967 *The invisible religion: the problem of religion in modern society.* New York: Macmillan.

MCCONAHAY, J. B., JR., AND J. C. HOUGH, JR. 1969 *Love and guilt oriented dimensions of religious belief.* Paper read to Society for the Scientific Study of Religion, Boston, October.

MONAGHAN, R. R. 1967 Three faces of the true believer: motivations for attending a fundamentalist church. *Journal for the Scientific Study of Religion* 6: 236-45.

PRUYSER, P. W. 1968 *A dynamic psychology of religion.* New York: Harper and Row.

STRICKLAND, B. R., AND SHAFFER 1971 I-E, I-E, & F, *Journal for the Scientific Study of Religion* 10: 366-369.

TISDALE, J. R. 1966 Selected Correlates of Extrinsic Religious Values. *Review of Religious Research.* 7:78-84.

VANECKO, J. J. 1966 Religious behavior and prejudice: some dimensions and specifications of the relationship. *Review of Religious Research* 8: 27-37.

WILSON, W. C. 1960 Extrinsic religious values and prejudice. *Journal of Abnormal and Social Psychology* 60: 286-88.

YINGER, J. M. 1969 A structural examination of religion. *Journal for the Scientific Study of Religion* 8: 88-99.

# Typing the Typologies:
# Some Parallels in the Career of
# Church-Sect and Extrinsic-Intrinsic

## JAMES E. DITTES

In its short career, the extrinsic-intrinsic typology has recapitu-
lated much of the history of the church-sect typology. It has provoked
research and distress, preoccupation and disdain, in about the same
proportions among psychologists as its predecessor has among
sociologists. The two sets of concepts have some striking similarities in
their core idea (distinguishing pure from adulterated religion) and in
their formal properties (shifting agglutination). These similarities may
suggest some common ancestry and may also help to account for their
persistent appeal as well as for their persistent disfavor. Finding the
same troublesome cluster of characteristics in a larger sample ($N=2$) of
types may make those characteristics seem a bit more intelligible and
manageable, though not necessarily less annoying, than when we encounter them in a single case.

The two principal characteristics both these typologies possess,
to the consternation of most social scientists, are (1) a heavy contraband
load of value judgment that simply will not be sloughed off; and (2) a
formal untidiness — multiple defining categories, carelessly aggluti-
nated, shifting from one discussion to another, not integrated with each
other conceptually, and manifestly not correlated empirically. In this
note, I simply want to point out these similarities and to suggest that, in
both the typologies, these two characteristics (value judgments and
conceptual sloppiness) are understandably related with each other.
They both occur because the developers of the typologies have been
principally concerned about the purity of religion, not about the purity
of concept.

Reprinted with permission of the author and publisher from:

*Journal for the Scientific Study of Religion,* 1971, 10(4), 375-383, published by the SOCI-
ETY FOR THE SCIENTIFIC STUDY OF RELIGION, University of Connecticut,
Box U68A, Storrs, Connecticut 06268

## Historical Summary

Church-sect is generally credited to Troeltsch and extrinsic-intrinsic to Allport. It is, however, well recognized that neither created the idea and that much of the impact of the ideas is due to those who followed.

Weber had immediately preceded Troeltsch in making the distinction, though he gave the terms different definitions and his comments were relatively casual and never developed in his later work on sociology of religion. The typology achieved prominence in American sociology of religion through the work of Richard Niebuhr (1929), who was a close student of Troeltsch, and of Liston Pope (1942), who was Niebuhr's student. Niebuhr and Pope especially developed the hypothesis of evolution (or decay) from sect toward church.

In the aftermath of World War II, Allport was one of several psychologists attracted to the study of prejudice who found that the relationship of prejudice and religion required the distinction between two types of religion, one type associated with prejudice and one with tolerance. In the same year that Allport first published his intimations of the types (1950), the distinction was also noted in the reports of two empirical studies of prejudice (Adorno, *et al.* 1950; Bettelheim and Janowitz 1950). These two groups of researchers elaborated the difference more fully than did Allport (all agreeing that prejudice was less likely among those with more "genuine" or more successfully internalized religious belief) and related the distinction to empirical data. They did not subsequently develop the types, as did Allport (Hunt and King 1971, and Dittes 1969). The terms "extrinsic" and "intrinsic" were not to come until the end of the decade. The distinction got established in the research literature by the successive efforts of several of Allport's students to develop scales (see Hunt and King 1971). It was one of Allport's students, Clark (1958), who, using the terms "primary" and "secondary" ("extrinsic" and "intrinsic" had not yet been announced), developed the notion of evolution from one to the other, especially intergenerationally, paralleling the sect-to-church theory.

## ISOLATING THE PURITY OF RELIGION

Social scientists persistently try to purify these concepts, to strip away the unwanted value judgments and to peel down to the essential scientific core. But the persistent frustration this endeavor experiences suggests that the core, in each case, is not, after all, scientific but evaluational, perhaps evangelical. The typologies are animated by a prophetic ardor. They are inspired by a concern to identify the purity of religion in a relatively primitive state (sect, intrinsic) and to distinguish this purity from its contamination and dilution by non-religious elements of culture and of personality (church, extrinsic).

Troeltsch (1931) opened page 1 of chapter 1, in a section called "Primitive Christianity an independent phenomenon" with these words: "In order to understand the foundation principles of Christianity as a whole, in its relation to social problems, it is of the utmost importance to recognize that the preaching of Jesus and the creation of the Christian Church were not due in any sense to the impulse of a social movement." This primitive Christianity was concerned with matters that were "purely religious" and was controlled by "the vision of an ideal ethical and religious situation, of a world entirely controlled by God, in which all the values of true spirituality would be recognized and appreciated at their true worth." Christianity was at first stalwartly independent, unshaped by, but also not shaping, society. But it soon accepted the fact that it was in a society; in order to influence that society (later sociologists would say, survive in it), Christianity had to make accommodations and compromises with it. This is the drama Troeltsch analyzes for 1000 pages, with the help of the sect-church distinction, and which he summarizes with these sentences that conclude the book:

> The truth is—and this is the conclusion of the whole matter—the Kingdom of God is within us. But we must let our light shine before men in confident and untiring labour that they may see our good works and praise our Father in Heaven. The final ends of all humanity are hidden within His Hands. (1931: 1013)

But to make its light visible to men, the church accommodates to what they will notice. This emphasis on accommodation as the distinguishing mark of the church is an abrupt shift (as Eister 1967 points out) from the distinction between inclusiveness and exclusiveness of membership for which Weber had invoked the sect-church terms.

Johnson vividly portrays this drama of the debasement of the sectual impulse:

> the extent to which a religious body accepts the culture of the social environment . . . is the single most generally agreed upon criterion of church and sect that we have. . . . The sect is depicted very much like a young maiden venturing forth into the world. If she is not careful she will lose her virtue. Would-be rapists and seducers lurk everywhere. . . . From reading formal descriptions of (churches and denominations) one is apt to get the impression that they are lukewarm, over-administered bodies that have given in, as it were, to the dominant interests and values

of the secular society or to some important segment of it. Compromise, accommodation, minimal commitment—these are among the adjectives that easily come to mind in describing them. (Johnson 1971: 128-131)

Allport's way of thinking about extrinsic-intrinsic is exactly parallel, except that the psychologist finds the contamination not in the social environment but in baser motives within the person. These capture and exploit the religious motive and compromise its purity, as culture captures and compromises the purity of the sect. The selfish, instrumental quality of extrinsic religion is what Allport emphasized and is what stands empirically as the defining characteristic of the type (Hunt and King, 1971). In one of Allport's earliest formulations, he said that the extrinsic type of religion "serves and rationalizes assorted forms of self-interest. In such a life, the full creed and teaching of religion are not adopted." (1959: 264) Eventually he was even to use language suggesting a kinship with church-sect.

> The distinction helps us to separate church-goers whose communal type of membership supports and serves other, nonreligious ends, from those for whom religion is an end in itself. . . . The extrinsic type . . . have no true association with the religious function of the church. (1966: 454)

## The dismayed voice of the prophet

The mistrust of established, acculturated religion and the celebration of primitive purity is the classic prophetic posture. It is hardly surprising that these two typologies adopt that posture. The Americans who developed them were self-consciously in the prophetic tradition. So was Troeltsch, insofar as a conservative supporter of the establishment can be. Troeltsch was a professor of theology who, just after the *Social Teachings,* was to move to Berlin and become increasingly active in German political life. He was struggling in the book with the question of whether and how church teaching has social impact. He based his study on his concern for "the social and ethical tasks and possibilities of Christianity at the present day." (1931: 992). He was to recognize (though not to regret—he was far more conservative than the American ethicists who would follow) that influence on society meant compromise with society. This was the church's bargain and burden.

Niebuhr and Pope, who were both to become professors of ethics at Yale Divinity School, more openly assumed the classic prophetic attitude: churchly accommodation represents corruption of the Christian mission, especially as it deadens sensitivity to social issues.

Allport's first and final academic appointments at Harvard were

to a chair in social ethics, giving (he once remarked in private correspondence) a welcome definition to his career. His typology was still
more "prophetic" than church-sect was for the American ethicists, if
"prophetic" means being animated principally by passion for social
values and religious integrity and if it means confounding these value
concerns with conceptual analysis. Almost certainly he would not have
come to his religious typology except out of his search to understand
and undo ethnic bigotry. He never clearly distinguished extrinsicness-
intrinsicness and prejudiced-tolerance as two separate variables. It
is undoubtedly for this reason that his research, attempting to demonstrate correlation *between* prejudice *and* extrinsic religiousness, was
relatively clumsy and indecisive (Allport 1954: 452; Allport and Ross
1967). He found entrenched, constricted, inhumane, selfish attitudes
intimately part of contaminated and diluted religious expression—as
had, before him, the developers of church-sect, other social ethicists,
other church reformers, and other prophets. The conceptions of
"church" and of "extrinsic" religion stand in succession to "Woe to
those who are at ease in Zion" (Amos 6) and "Woe to you, scribes and
Pharisees, hypocrites" (Matthew 23).

## The paradox of historical religion

But the two typologies appear to be animated not just by a persistent ethical vision, but also by a pervasive religious dilemma. Beyond
the ethical vision of a purged religion yielding enlightened social
attitudes, these types seem to participate also in a dialectic tension fundamental in western religious outlook. Western religions pivot on a
profound ambivalence between the transcendent and the immanent.
The religions move by the rhythms of incarnation and purge. The Holy
dwells in man (or *a* man), in history, in people ( or *a* people), in visible
sacraments and institutions and roles; indeed the Holy does not,
perhaps even can not, dwell apart from these forms; holiness is to be
found only in such forms. Yet the dwelling places must contaminate
the Holy, and holiness is to be found in withdrawal and purification
from them. Holiness is in them; holiness is in separation from them.
The promised land and the defiled land, the chosen people and the
exiled people, priest and prophet, priest and mystic, priest and ascetic,
sanctuary in Egypt and slavery in Egypt, Moses the Law-giver and
Moses the rebellious leader of exodus, Incarnation and Crucifixion,
the Body of Christ and the Spirit of Christ, works and faith, sacral
religion and secular religion, forms and reforms, relevance of ministry
and faithfulness of ministry, Hegel and Kierkegaard, bishops and Bon-

hoeffer, religion as establishment (Durkheim?) and religion as autonomous (Weber?). Images and slogans flood to mind. For the religious spirit, expression in forms, in a body, is necessary; and for the religious spirit, expression in forms, in a body, is defiling. Judaism and Christianity have tended to make the tension normative and to regard one-sided expression of either half of the dialectic as aberration needing correction from the other half.

These two typologies—church-sect and extrinsic-intrinsic—seem to be two more expressions of the same pattern, and we would expect the typologies to find favor among social scientists most immersed in these religious patterns. Both types call attention, within the structures discernible by social scientists, to the elusive, if not ephemeral ideal (sect and intrinsicness have never been so clearly described or defined as their counterparts) and to the rhythms by which it becomes expressed in forms and breaks free of forms.[1]

This dialectic between the historical and the transhistorical animated and preoccupied Troeltsch with a single-minded and persistent intellectual quest. And while it may not be entirely inaccurate (as in the preceding section) to see Troeltsch, refracted through his American interpreters Niebuhr and Pope, assuming a prophetic posture of concern for the proper social impact of Christian teaching, he is in better focus when seen as the philosopher-theologian trying to develop a theory of history. The *Social Teachings* and its church-sect typology must be seen as only one portion in a life-time struggle to locate the absolute and the historical in proper relation to one another. "This deeply religious man, in Baron von Hügel's words, this 'so realistic believer in God,' struggled to find within the ebb and flow of history a stable basis for universally significant values." (O'Dea 1968: 154) As Troeltsch was to write near the end of his life, his search was for a "vital and effective religious position, which alone could furnish my life with a center or reference for all practical questions and could alone give meaning and purpose to reflection upon the things of this world." (Troeltsch 1957: 37)

Troeltsch begins to point some of these more general conclusions towards the end of the *Social Teachings* (well beyond the limits of church-sect analysis):

> The Ethos of the Gospel is a combination of infinite sublimity and childlike intimacy . . . But it is an ideal which cannot be realized within this world apart from compromise. Therefore the history of the Christian Ethos becomes the story of a constantly renewed search for this compromise, and of fresh opposition to this spirit of compromise . . . Today, therefore, the main problem of the Christian Ethos is still the problem

**165**

of supernaturalism and of . . . how to supplement this religious one-sidedness with an ethic of civilization which can be combined with it. (1931: 999-1001)

> *In conclusion:* The Christian Ethos gives to all social life and aspiration a goal which lies far beyond all the relativities of this earthly life . . . The idea of the future Kingdom of God, which is nothing less than faith in the final realization of the Absolute (in whatever way we may conceive this realization) does not, as short-sighted opponents imagine, render this world and life in this world meaningless and empty; on the contrary, it stimulates human energies, making the soul strong through its various states of experience in the certainty of an ultimate, absolute meaning and aim for human labour. Thus it raises the soul above the world without denying the world. (1931: 1005f)

Something of the same rhythms and tensions are fundamentally present in Allport's thinking, though less prominently so than in the case of Troeltsch—Allport is more clearly the prophet than the philosopher. His lifelong struggle as psychologist was to find ways to understand personality that held in balance the unique richness of personality and the universal laws by which that personality becomes registered in a scientific psychology.[2] The characteristics of a personality *can* be expressed in terms of various general "laws," in fact *must* be—Allport's own research was chiefly of this "nomothetic" variety. But in this process, something of rich, unique importance in the personality is neglected or distorted. Allport writes in the concluding paragraph of his principal book: "The human person . . . is more than a bundle of habits, more than a point of intersection of abstract dimensions. He is more than a representative of his species, more than a citizen of the state, more than an incident in the movements of mankind. He transcends them all." (1961: 573)

It is understandable that the same psychologist who struggled to preserve the sense of this transcendence—with "functional autonomy", the "proprium", and all the other concepts that themselves took the forms of general principles—should be particularly sensitive to the integrity of personal religious impulse and its submergence under forms of expression.

## NEGLECTING THE PURITY OF CONCEPTUALIZATION

If the two typologies share a heritage, as just proposed, it is not surprising that they resemble each other in characteristics that follow from that heritage. If the expression of prophetic and religious concerns has been a principal purpose of these types, then the development of scientifically appropriate conceptualizations has clearly been of secondary importance. The form of the concepts reflects the primary purposes better than the secondary purposes.

### Agglutination

The shifting, loose accumulation of characteristics that are neither conceptually integrated nor empirically correlated is poor science, but is admirably suited to the prophet. It permits him to emphasize by varied repetition his concern for pure (or genuine, or real) religion, separated from cultural contaminants. There *is* a consistency in usage. Reading through Allport or Troeltsch or Niebuhr or Pope, it is not difficult at all to read in all the shifting characterization of the types the same persistent one root concern for separating out acculturated alloys and isolating the unacculturated religious impulse.

### Uni-dimensional polarity

Given the heterogeneity evident in these concepts, it would be logical and good science to abandon uni-dimensional thinking and develop multi-dimensional frameworks. This transformation has been persistently neglected or resisted. The sharper focus of uni-dimensionality, with its distinct polarity, serves the prophet's purposes better.

### Confounding with correlates

The description of both types has persistently become confounded with the description of variables that are more properly regarded as *correlates* of the types. Extrinsic-intrinsic religiousness has been confounded with social attitudes and cognitive rigidity, the church-sect religious organization with social attitudes and social class characteristics. Extrinsic-intrinsic may be better as a personality variable than as a religious type (Hunt and King 1971), and church-sect might have at least as much utility with non-religious institutions (Johnson 1971). The scientist regrets the confounding and urges the conceptual separation of religious type and its correlates; let the correlation be tested empirically. But it is precisely the prophet's intuitive perception of the correlation that simultaneously enlists his interest in the religious type, and also prevents him from distinguishing one from the other.

### Church attendance

Church attendance has played an awkward role in the history of both these typologies. Participation in established liturgical and ecclesiastical forms looks suspicious to the prophet; he is disposed to look for purity of religion elsewhere. Yet the facts have proved less simple (e.g., Dynes 1957), have provoked debate (e.g., Goode 1967, Demerath 1967) that seems unnecessary except for this prophetic bias (Can anything good come from church attendance?), and have compelled Allport eventually to include church attendance as an item on the intrinsic side (Allport and Ross 1967).

### Cultural limits

Both typologies are manifestly culture-bound. They are restricted to western Christianity; church-sect is seemingly most appropriate in a well-stratified society or in periods of immigration; extrinsic-intrinsic makes distinctions especially reminiscent of issues on the conscience of small-town Middle America. This may or may not be poor science but it makes a good social ethics or good philosophy of history, because it keeps a specific cultural target in view.

### NOTES AND REFERENCES

[1]Intriguingly, the very concept of "ideal type", often applied to the church-sect typology, reflects precisely the same dialectic pattern between immanence and transcendence: The ideal type is meaningless except as it points to empirical phenomena; yet these will always represent it only imperfectly, and the ideal type has a meaning that transcends any empirical referent. More intriguingly, even ironically, critics of the typology (whose criticism most often is of the value judgments and prophetic ardor embedded in the concepts) are themselves urging a purification (of the concept) precisely analogous to the purification ascribed to the sect and the intrinsic religionist, the purging away of accreted contaminants and the isolation of the purified concept.

[2]Troeltsch, too, expressed his concern with the dialectic between the historical and transhistorical also in discussion of methodology in the social sciences, even employing terms that have been rendered, as those Allport favored, "nomothetic" and "ideographic." (See the introduction to *Social Teachings* and Adams 1961.)

ADAMS, J. L. 1961 Ernst Troeltsch as analyst of religion. *Journal for the Scientific Study of Religion*, 1, 98-109.

ADORNO, T. W., E. FRENKEL-BRUNSWIK, D. J. LEVINSON, & R. N. SANFORD 1950 *The authoritarian personality.* New York: Harper.

ALLPORT, G. W. 1950 *The individual and his religion.* New York: Macmillan. 1954 *The nature of prejudice.* Cambridge, Mass.: Addison-Wesley. 1959 Religion and prejudice. *Crane Review* 2:1-10. 1961 *Pattern and Growth in Personality.* New York: Holt, Rinehart, Winston. 1966 The religious context of prejudice. *Journal for the Scientific Study of Religion* 5:447-457.

ALLPORT, G. W. & J. M. ROSS 1967 Personal religious orientation and prejudice. *Journal of Personality and Social Psychology* 5:432-443.

BERGER, P. L. 1961 *The noise of solemn assemblies.* New York: Doubleday. 1967 A sociological view of the secularization of theology. *Journal for the Scientific Study of Religion* 6:3-16. 1969 *A rumor of angels.* New York: Doubleday.

BETTELHEIM, B. & M. JANOWITZ 1950 *Dynamics of prejudice.* New York: Harper.

CLARK, W. H. 1958 *The psychology of religion.* New York: Macmillan.

DEMERATH, N. J. 1967 In a sow's ear. *Journal for the Scientific Study of Religion* 6:77-84.

DITTES, J. E. 1969 Psychology of religion. In G. Lindzey & E. Aronson (Eds.). *Handbook of Social Psychology*, second edition. Reading, Mass.: Addison-Wesley. 5:602-659.

DYNES, R. R. 1957 The consequences of sectarianism for social participation. *Social Forces* 335:331-334.

EISTER, A. W. 1967 Toward a radical critique of church-sect typologizing. *Journal for the Scientific Study of Religion* 6:85-90.

GOODE, E. 1967 Some critical observations on the church-sect dimension. *Journal for the Scientific Study of Religion* 6:69-76.

GUSTAFSON, P. M. 1967 UO-US-PS-PO: A restatement of Troeltsch's church-sect typology. *Journal for the Scientific Study of Religion* 6:64-68.

HUNT, R. A. & M. KING 1971 The intrinsic-extrinsic concept: A review and evaluation. *Journal for the Scientific Study of Religion* 10:339-356.

JOHNSON, B. 1971 Church-sect revisited. *Journal for the Scientific Study of Religion* 10:124-137.

NIEBUHR, H. R. 1929 *The social sources of denominationalism.* New York: Holt.

O'DEA, T. F. 1968 Ernst Troeltsch. In D. Sills (Ed.). *International Encyclopedia of the Social Sciences.* New York: Macmillan & Free Press. 16:151-155.

POPE, L. 1942 *Millhands and preachers.* New Haven: Yale University Press.

TROELTSCH, E. 1931. *Social teachings of the Christian churches.* Trans. Olive Wyon. New York: Meridian. 1957 *Christian thought: its history and application.* New York: Meridian.

WEBER, M. 1930 *The protestant ethic and the spirit of capitalism.* trans. Talcott Parsons. New York: Scribner's.

# PSYCHODYNAMICS AND RELIGION

# Introduction

H. NEWTON MALONY

What persons are religious? Do they differ in important ways from those who are not religious? What can be said about the personalities, character traits and underlying attitudes of those who are religious? Articles in this section deal with these questions.

A thorough review of studies on religion and personality is included in Sanua's article, where topics such as adjustment, mental health, deviancy, authoritarianism, prejudice, and social concern are considered. He concludes that the general belief which identifies religion as the basis of virtue and health is not supported by research.

These relationships between beliefs and behaviors are further explored in the Bock and Warren article. They report a study in which neither very religious nor anti-religious persons obeyed harmful commands as much as did moderately religious persons.

Another facet of the personality and religion question is considered in the article on emotion. Stoudenmire deals with the relationship between basic physiological reactions and differences in religious behavior and arrives at some very suggestive conclusions.

Barkman's article is concerned with a different aspect of the issue, i.e., how an emphasis on one or more personality traits determines the unique way a person experiences his/her religion. The four personality modes he considers are the verbal, the affective, the social-relational and the transcendental.

Finally, the relation between one's image of God and personality traits is discussed in the Benson and Spilka article. They report research in which high self-esteem was related to loving images of God.

This portion of the book will introduce the student to the many unanswered questions concerning the uniqueness of persons. We can assume that faith and personality are related even though the connections are not simple and are by no means well known.

# Religion, Mental Health, and Personality: A Review of Empirical Studies

VICTOR D. SANUA

My purpose in this paper is to review a number of studies which have tried to relate religion with mental health and other major aspects of personality. Psychiatry and religion share a common concern for the improvement of mental health. Yet, until a few years ago, there was little interaction or cooperation between these two areas in exchanging available information. To encourage such collaboration, the Academy of Religion and Mental Health was established in 1957. The Academy has since published an annotated bibliography (36) to aid

> ... the psychologists and psychiatrists in relating the knowledge and activities of their scientific disciplines to the concerns and demands of religious workers. Conversely, it is hoped that religious workers will be helped to better understand the purposes and techniques of these psychological sciences and consequently facilitate the utilization of psychological information in the services of souls.

We are all aware of the rather common theory that religion is a basis of sound "mental health." Numerous articles have been published, most frequently in the *Journal of Pastoral Counseling,* regarding the benefits derived from introducing religious aspects into counseling. However, most of these reports are anecdotal and lack empirical support. The contention that religion as an institution has been instrumental in fostering general well-being, creativity, honesty, liberalism, and other qualities is not supported by empirical data. Both Scott(55) and Godin(22) point out that there are no scientific studies which show that religion is capable of serving mental health. On the other hand, Godin feels that mental health can assist Christian life. While many professional workers in the mental health field, such as psychologists and psychiatrists, have been engaged in studies to validate the efficacy of their efforts in fostering better mental health conditions, the validation of the efficacy of religious teachings and religious counseling seems to be lacking.

In 1959 Argyle(7) discussed the relationship between religion and mental disorders. Jung(28) had pointed out that religion is a necessary adjunct to psychotherapy. However, the empirical evidence available, according to Argyle, seems to indicate that an inverse relationship between religion and mental disorders exists only for older people. There are no well-controlled studies in psychotherapy in which religious encouragement has been used as one of the independent variables. Argyle concluded that there is little evidence to support the hypothesis that religion ever causes mental disorders or that religion prevents such disorders.

The present review includes studies which have tried to relate religiousness and aspects of mental health, such as psychological adjustment, as measured by objective tests, and other indicators, such as deviancies. Studies of certain aspects of the personality, such as authoritarianism and prejudice, which are indicators of mental health, have also been included. A third major section of this review is devoted to a discussion of the relationship between religiousness and one's involvement in social issues.

## RELATIONSHIP BETWEEN RELIGIOUSNESS AND PSYCHOLOGICAL ADJUSTMENT

Jahoda(26) devoted an entire volume to a discussion of the criteria used to define mental health. Due to the limited scope of this paper, I have not discussed the various definitions which appear in the literature but have used the commonly operational definition of adjustment as measured by psychological tests. Thus, a very poor score obtained by a subject on an objectively standardized test of adjustment or poor results on a projective technique would indicate maladjustment.

In this section a number of studies are reviewed which have attempted to test the hypothesis that the person with strong religious beliefs can find "peace of mind" through his faith and thus be a well-adjusted person.

Funk(21) administered a scale of religious attitude and the Taylor Manifest Anxiety Scale to a group of college students who were representative of the three major religious groups (Protestants, Catholics, and Jews) and were majoring in the sciences. Anxiety was found to be unrelated to orthodoxy, religious preference, belief in a philosophy of life not founded on a religion, hostility to religion, or change of religious attitudes during years spent on the college campus.

However, high scores on the Taylor Manifest Anxiety Scale were found to be characteristic of students who had expressed religious doubts and who felt guilty about not living up to expectations of their religious teachings.

Wright(67) correlated the McLean Inventory of Social and Religious Concepts with the Heston Personal Adjustment Inventory. The latter scale includes six subscales. He found a positive correlation between the religious scale and sociability for male subjects. On the other hand, those men who appeared more liberal in their religious attitude, and those who seemed less certain of their religious opinions, tended to be better adjusted in the area of personal relations.

Lantz(31), on the other hand, found no correlation between religious activities and personal satisfaction with social conditions among college students. Porterfield(45), using vital statistics, studied the relationship between indices of well-being and religious activity as measured by church membership per 100,000 population and the number of ministers in the community. He stated that:

> It is clear to everyone that many factors enter into making of social conditions, favorable and unfavorable to man. The Church is only one institution among many, and religion is not the only force infringing upon us. Furthermore, our data do not indicate that the Church "makes things worse." But they do raise the important question as to "why things are not better."

In the following studies the authors tried to relate psychological adjustment and religious practice among the aged.

Moberg(39) found among institutionalized aged a significant correlation of .59 between personal adjustment and a religious activities score based on past and present religious activities. O'Reilly(42) confirmed this positive relationship with noninstitutionalized Catholic aged. He found that more than half of those who were "very happy" were more active in religious practices, while only 11 percent of the "unhappy" group indicated being active in religious affairs.

Ranck(49) hypothesized that, while authoritarianism and submissiveness are related to specific religious ideology, psychopathology is not. He assumed that religious ideology was primarily a cultural phenomenon. He administered an extensive battery of tests to 800 theological students in 28 schools across the United States, representing the entire continuum from conservatism to liberalism. The results confirmed his hypothesis, showing that while authoritarianism was related to religious ideology, psychlogical adjustment as measured by the Bell Inventory and some of the MMPI subscales was not related to religious ideology. Thus, beliefs were found to be unrelated to patholog-

**175**

ical symptoms. Instead, beliefs were found to be primarily a cultural phenomenon, related to early environment and specifically to family influences.

McGrath(35) used the semantic differential type of questionnaire to measure personal adjustment; he administered it to three groups of students who were members of religious organizations on campus. He found, in comparing group scores, that the Catholics had the highest personal adjustment scores, the Unitarian group had the poorest adjustment scores, and the Baptist group was in the middle of this range. However, when each group was studied separately, it was found that Catholic female students expressed a very low self-esteem and very low self-satisfaction. The interpretation of such findings could be more significant if, in addition, the investigator had used three groups with the same religious affiliations but not attending religious organizations on campus.

A well-designed research study on the relationship between religious attitude and emotional adjustment was conducted by Armstrong and associates(8). The sample included normal men and women and a group of psychotic subjects. Both groups included Catholics, Protestants, and Unitarians, which is a continuum in terms of orthodoxy, conservatism, and liberalism. Osgood's Semantic Differential (consisting of 23 bipolar adjective pairs) was used as a measure of personal adjustment. Each subject first rated himself as he saw himself and then as he wished he were. The discrepancy score was computed so as to obtain an index of distance between self and ideal self. The psychological adjustment or, in this particular case, the discrepancy score between actual self and ideal self was not markedly different for any of the three normal groups.

Rokeach(50) devoted a whole volume to the study of the nature of belief systems and personality systems. He found that people with formal religious affiliation are more anxious. Believers, compared to nonbelievers, complain more often of working under great tension, sleeping fitfully, and similar symptoms. Dunn(16) found that religious individuals tended to be more perfectionistic, withdrawn, insecure, depressed, worrisome, inept, and the men were somewhat feminine in interest. Women, on the other hand, tended to have somewhat masculine interests.

Gurin, Veroff, and Feld(24) conducted a nationwide study designed to find out whether there was a relationship between frequency of church attendance and answers to the question: "Did you ever feel you were about to have a nervous breakdown?" No relationship was found between these two variables. However, when the sample was reclassified into major income groups, a combination of higher income and regular church attendance showed a lower rate of affirmative answers to the question. The general finding was that belonging to a higher income group and a higher education group is more conducive to one's "happiness" than frequent church attendance.

The following studies related religiousness with different aspects of the personality, not yet discussed, which are usually linked to mental health.

Strunk(61) found that divinity students were more aggressive in social contacts than business administration students. Dreger(15), using a projective technique, found that the only difference between religious and nonreligious subjects was the dependency feelings shown by the former.

Bateman and Jensen(9) found that a person with extensive religious training tends to express less anger toward the environment and is more apt to turn it upon himself. Grunes(23) found that individuals highly characterized by realistic repressive traits exhibit lower intelligence than those showing such traits to a lesser degree. Studying attitude toward death, Alexander and Adelstein(2) found that religious subjects tend to escape to the satisfying concept of an afterlife, while the nonreligious subjects are more likely to banish the topic from consciousness.

In all of the aforementioned studies the investigators tried to relate religiousness to certain aspects of mental health. In one major study Srole and associates(60) tried to relate the religiousness of the parents with the mental health of their offspring. They hypothesized that the extent of religious practice of the parents would affect the mental health of their offspring. Respondents in the survey were asked about the importance of religion to their parents. While 31 percent of the Jewish respondents indicated that their parents attached importance to their religion, 40 percent of the Protestant respondents and 67 percent of the Catholic respondents indicated similarly. The data presented no significant findings pertaining to the relationship between parental religiousness of the Jewish respondents and their own mental health. For the Protestant and Catholic samples, a positive correlation was found only for the lower- and middle-class respondents. In general, the findings show that the "unchurched" individuals, from all three religious groups, seem to show a less favorable mental health picture.

The results of the above review seem to indicate, therefore, that most studies show no relationship between religiousness and mental health, while others point out that the religious person may at times show greater anxiety and at times less anxiety. What may be said at this point is that a substantial number of additional empirical findings would be necessary before any valid conclusions could be drawn as to the relationship between religiousness and mental health.

## DEVIANCY, SOCIAL PATHOLOGY, AND RELIGIOUSNESS

While the scales of adjustment may not represent an ideal criterion for differentiating religious from nonreligious subjects, it might be possible to use manifestations of antisocial behavior as a valid discriminating variable. The assumption could be made that the individuals reared in homes devoid of religion would be more likely to transgress ethical codes. Research studies, however, have failed to support such an assumption.

Middleton and Fay(38) compared the attitudes of delinquent and nondelinquent girls toward religion. They found that the delinquent girls had more favorable attitudes toward Sunday observance and the teachings of the Bible.

Scholl and Beker(54) investigated the religious beliefs of delinquent and nondelinquent Protestant adolescent boys. They found that the expressed religious attitudes and beliefs of delinquent adolescent boys do not differ greatly from those held by nondelinquent boys. The authors conclude, therefore, that no evidence was found to support the contention that the adoption of a delinquent behavior pattern is significantly related to religious attitudes.

In a more recent study Middleton and Putney(37) found no evidence that the religious variables are correlated with antisocial behavior, either positively or negatively. It appears that religious sanctions are not essential for basic social norms. They report that, in certain instances, religious skeptics who believe that certain antiascetic actions are wrong are likely to adhere to the ascetic norms to the same extent as believers. When skeptics violate ascetic norms, it is because of their greater tendency to reject such norms.

Although he did not use a control group, Smith(58) found that the majority of a group of inmates at a Michigan state reformatory had been regular church members, had studied the Bible in church schools, and had come from church-going families. One-half of them felt that churches were effective forces for good and would make a doomed man feel at home.

Schofield and Balian (53) compared the frequency of church attendance of a group of schizophrenic patients and a matched group of nonschizophrenics. The two groups were not differentiated as to frequency of church attendance. Using the ecological approach, Smith(57) reviewed a number of studies which tried to relate religiousness and crime. He reported that, despite the claims of religion, there is no convincing evidence that conventional religion in itself has proved to be an effective antidote to crime.

In 1939 Thorndike(62) tried to determine the factors which make a city "good" to live in. He selected 37 separate factors such as infant mortality, percentage of illiterate population, percentage of youngsters enrolled in schools. He correlated these criteria of "goodness" with a number of other variables including the percentage of the population who were church members. From a sample of 295 cities, Thorndike found a negative correlation of .22 (which was slightly above the level of significance) between the "goodness" score and total church membership.

Angell(6) determined the factors he assumed would reflect the social health of the community, which he preferred to call the "moral integration of the community." Cities where people were actively concerned about their neighbors' welfare could be considered to have a high "moral integration." Statistics on crime represented a second major index of "moral integration." Angell combined the scores of 28 cities on the basis of the 1936 Census of Religious Bodies. His hypothesis was that the larger the proportion of church members in a given community the greater the "moral integration." As in Thorndike's study, Angell found that church membership as such did not affect the social health of a city population. A replication of his study today, in light of current developments, would be highly relevant. Weir(65) selected one aspect of social pathology-delinquency and church membership but failed to find any significant correlation.

Walters(63) questioned the patients in a treatment center for alcoholics about the religious environment they were exposed to during their childhood, as well as their present attitudes toward religion. He found that, compared to parents in a control group, a larger number of the parents of these alcoholics were church members. While no differences in religious activities were found between the fathers in the two groups, mothers of alcoholics were more active in religious activities than those in the control group. It was also found that most alcoholics retained, in adulthood, the religious beliefs formulated during their childhood.

In the discussion of his results, Walters suggested that his group was not truly representative of alcoholics in general. It was his contention that a three-month voluntary hospitalization would more likely be sought by individuals with strong religious convictions, thus sorting them out from the ranks of the larger alcoholic population. However,

Walters still posed the question that "Since religion appears to be a deterrent to excessive drinking, why did not religious influence during the development period of those men protect them against becoming problem drinkers?"

Thus, while psychological testing has not been very conclusive as to the relationship between psychological adjustment and religiousness, the evidence regarding the relationship between social pathology and religion points out that the latter may not necessarily fulfill the function ascribed to it—namely, that of an integrating force in society and a contributor to the mental health of the members of that society.

While the aforementioned results may be startling, further research regarding the effectiveness of church membership in curbing social pathology would still be needed. We are all well aware that pathology is highly correlated with social class. It is suggested, therefore, that a clearer indication of the effectiveness of church membership may be obtained by conducting studies in cities matched for socioeconomic status but unmatched for church membership. Any difference between the social pathology of the two types of cities could be related to church membership.

## AUTHORITARIANISM AND RELIGIOUSNESS

Allport(3) reviewed the major findings of studies which tried to relate religiousness and authoritarianism; he also reported on his own research findings. His general conclusion was that

> This finding . . . not only . . . seems to belie the universalistic import of religious teaching, but it is contradicted by other evidence. Students were asked in the same investigation to tell how their religious training has influenced their ethnic attitude. Two types of report were given. Some said frankly that the impact was negative, that they were taught to despise other religious and cultural groups. But some said the influence was wholly positive . . . (p. 451).

In the light of our discussions the finding is easily understood. Belonging to a church because it is a safe, powerful, superior ingroup is likely to be the mark of an authoritarian character and to be linked with prejudice. Belonging to a church because its basic creed of brotherhood expresses the ideals one sincerely believes in is associated with tolerance. Thus, the "institutionalized" religious outlook and the "interiorized" religious outlook have opposite effects on the personality. In a recent paper Allport(4) further discusses this dichotomy.

Jones(27) administered the Allport-Vernon Scale of Values and the F scale to Navy cadets. There was marked tendency for authoritarian cadets to report strong religious background. Theoretic and aesthetic values were negatively related to authoritarianism.

Putney and Middleton(47), using a larger sample of 12,000 students majoring in the social sciences and enrolled at 13 colleges and universities in the northeastern and southern parts of the country, found that the students who are highly orthodox in religious beliefs tend to be authoritarian, highly concerned about their social status, and conservative on political and economic issues.

The positive correlation between religiousness and authoritarianism has been reported in many other studies. However, one study which challenges this hypothesis is mentioned here. High school students in a metropolitan area in Michigan, in a small town in Florida, and in a rural area in Alabama were administered the F scale. While differences were found on the F scale, no relationship was found between authoritarianism and frequency of church attendance. It should be pointed out, however, that this study was conducted with adolescents, while the majority of the other studies were conducted with adults. This may account for the difference in findings. It is possible that the frequency with which adolescents attend religious services may not be related to their own personaal inclinations but is likely to be influenced by extraneous pressures, such as parental fiat or social conformity.

The question may be raised at this point as to the relationship between authoritarianism and mental health. Aside from his negative social propensities, the authoritarian is not what we consider a healthy person. Maslow(34) found the authoritarian to be insecure and to possess other negative qualities such as drive for power, hostility, and prejudice. Fromm(20) found the authoritarian sadomasochistic, suffering from guilt feelings, and exhibiting homosexual trends.

## PREJUDICE AND RELIGIOUSNESS

Scales measuring ethnocentrism and authoritarianism have been the subject of innumerable papers and books during the past 18 years, following the publication of the book by Adorno and associates, *The Authoritarian Personality*(1). However, little interest has been expressed in measuring religiousness itself. Several criteria have been used to measure religiousness, but there are no standardized scales of religiousness. One difficulty involved is that religious beliefs are so varied among the different religious groups that the construction of one single over-all scale would be quite inadequate. Criteria which have been used in measuring religiousness include frequency with which an individual attends religious services, his membership in religious organizations, or the role that religion plays in his life. While the first criterion measures actual behavior, it may be influenced by variables other than religiousness. The second criterion indicates a formal association which may not necessarily be related to attitude or even behavior, while the third criterion, since it is based on self-reports, may be distorted. The ideal measure of religiousness would be based on the degree of ethical behavior in consonance with religious ideals.

Hartshorne and May(25) conducted such a study with children. They found no relationship between normal behavior and religious training, religious belief, or participation in religious ritual. Blum and Mann(10) administered a prejudice scale to undergraduates, half of whom belonged to religious organizations. Students belonging to such clubs were found to be more anti-Semitic than those who did not. Similar results showing a positive relationship between religion and prejudice were found by Eiseman and Cole(17), Maranell(32), Feagin(18), and Weima(64).

Kelly(29) found that there was a slight tendency for those with favorable attitudes toward the church to be less tolerant of the Negro; anti-Semitism and intolerance of the Negro were found to be correlated as well; Protestants were found to be more discriminatory toward the Negro. Other factors, besides religious preference and frequency of church attendance, significantly related to attitudes toward the Negro included geographic region, father's occupation, and major subject in college.

O'Reilly and O'Reilly(43) found that those who scored high on a religious scale favored the segregation of Negroes in their own parishes, while those who scored low on the religious scale were significantly less prejudiced and opposed to segregation. Allport and Ross(5) found that, on the average: 1) churchgoers are more prejudiced than nonchurchgoers; 2) people with extrinsic religious orientation are significantly more prejudiced than people with an intrinsic religious orientation; and 3) people who are indiscriminately proreligious are the most prejudiced of all. Findings to the contrary are reported by Marton and Nichols(33). Although they did not find the religious college student to be an exemplar of tolerance of humility, they did not find the generally negative picture to be inferred from previous studies either.

The studies just cited have used as criteria either attitude scales on religiousness or formal membership in a religious organization. Friedrichs(19) used frequency of church attendance as a criterion for measuring religiousness. He reported that while 67 percent of the subjects who were not members of a church were tolerant, only 45 percent of the subjects who were church members shared their views. However, when the samples were divided according to frequency of church attendance, a curvilinear relationship was found. Those subjects who attended 61 or more services per year were more tolerant than those who did not attend any religious services or those who attended such services with less frequency. It would appear, therefore, that very faithful churchgoers have attitudes which are more consonant with the ideals of their religion. Recently Allport and Ross(5) confirmed this curvilinear relationship.

Furthermore, Friedrichs tested the paradox of the American dilemma in which the prejudiced person imagines himself a good Christian. Findings based on interviews with 112 residents in a small town in New Jersey showed that, although three-quarters of the respondents felt that segregation is un-Christian, two-thirds argued that it would not be fair to rent or sell one's home to Negroes.

Rosenbloom(51) found that percentages of prejudiced and non-prejudiced subjects were almost equally divided among members of three church groups. His sample included Episcopalian, Presbyterian, and Jewish subjects in California. He found that social class was a more important variable in this study; those of higher socioeconomic status were more likely to be more prejudiced. Rosenbloom also reported more ethnic prejudices in respondents attending services less frequently than among those attending with greater regularity. No curvilinearity was found in this study.

The aforementioned studies were all conducted in this country. Siegman(56) attempted to test the hypothesis concerning the relationship between religiousness, ethnic prejudice, and authoritarianism in Israel. He administered a number of scales to Jewish adolescents in the United States and Israel. A correlation between religious beliefs and ethnic prejudice was found for the American but not for the Israeli sample. No evidence was found in the American sample that religiousness is associated with authoritarian personality. For the Israeli sample, a relationship was found between the authoritarian personality and certain religious beliefs, such as the nature of God, but not religious observance (Sabbath).

Siegman maintains that the failure to obtain a significant correlation between personality and religiousness in the American sample is attributable to the fact that social pressures for religious conformity leave little room for personality determinants of religious behavior.

In recent years, Rokeach(50) developed a research study in the area of rigidity and dogmatism. He found that, on the average, those who identify themselves with a religious organization express greater intolerance toward minority groups than do those who identify themselves as nonbelievers.

## RELIGIOUSNESS, HUMANITARIANISM, SOCIAL VALUES, AND SOCIAL ISSUES

Kirkpatrick(30) studied the relationship between religiousness and humanitarianism. He prepared 22 humanitarian and nonhumanitarian propositions concerning such problems as the treatment of criminals, unmarried mothers, and conscientious objectors. The correlation between religiousness and humanitarianism scores was found to be very low and predominantly negative. He concluded that the common assumption that religion is a source of humanitarianism was not supported by his data.

Pugh(46) administered the Allport-Vernon Scale of Values to Negro Baptist ministers, church members, and non-church members. The scale tests for six values—theoretic, economic, aesthetic, political, religious, and social. He found that all three groups obtained high scores on the religious scale. On the other hand, the social scale ranked second with non-church members and fifth among the ministers. Thus, most Southern Negroes are predominantly religious in interest. Social values were highest among non-church members. The author concluded that ministers might well reexamine their values for adequacy to enable them to meet the problems which they, by the very nature of their work, are forced to face.

Another area of interest is the relationship between religiousness and attitudes toward social issues. Obenhaus(41) tried to relate church affiliation and attitudes toward selected public questions; he found an almost complete failure, among his subjects, to think theologically about social issues. According to Obenhaus, this raises serious doubts about whether the church leadership is fulfilling its function in social and ethical development. However, this does not appear to be limited to the United States. Nowlan(40), a European Jesuit, feels that there is no standard Catholic attitude toward different aspects of social life.

Devolder(14), inquiring into the religious life of Catholic intellectuals in Belgium, indicated that "religious conviction based more on sentiment and tradition rather than on logical ground is apt to lead to misunderstandings."

Pyron(48) tried to correlate the scales on the Allport-Vernon Scale of Values with "openness to change." He found that those with a high religious score would tend to oppose change. Cline and Richards(12), using factor analysis, reported that there was a "close to

0-order relationship" between the major religiousness factors (high church attendance, frequency of prayer, contributions of money, etc.) and such variables as "having love and compassion for one's fellow men," "being a good Samaritan," and "possessing humility." It would seem that religious teachings had failed to induce much sense of responsibility toward one's fellow men.

Salisbury(52) conducted a large-scale study among college students in the North and South to explore which attitudes and behavior of the religiously orthodox are similar to or different from the attitudes and behavior of the religiously unorthodox or the religiously liberal. He found that the religiously orthodox personality differs consistently from the liberal personality. Among his findings were the following: 1) "The orthodox personality interacts within a religious system removed and remote from the problems of the social milieu." 2) "Internalization of doctrine is not reflected in external behavior, i.e., more tolerant, more democratic, etc." 3) "Religion to the orthodox person is a personal and private affair with little or no social implications." 4) "Where the sacred ideology is in conflict with the secular ideology, the orthodox personality finds it possible to retain or to reject individual values within the value system that characterizes his particular religious system."

The most striking present-day example is the one pointed out by Campbell and Pettigrew(11). Despite the number of preachers and ministers in the North who fight and speak out for Negro rights and their cause in the South, Campbell and Pettigrew found that religious leaders in Little Rock, Ark., preferred to sidestep the social reform issues in order to keep peace in their congregations. Certain institutional arrangements helped the ministers to control the development of guilt while they remained inactive during the racial crisis.

This concern about the failure of religion to fuse its higher values with basic functions in institutionalized life in the United States was expressed by Pemberton(44). He stated that this failure exists because Protestantism has no ethical method requiring its ideals to bear confirmable results within these basic institutionalized functions.

One fruitful way of approaching the problem would consist in the evaluation of the philosophy of present-day teachers of religion, both lay and clerical, since it is their own teachings that will probably determine the course of the values held by their students. Crawford(13) suggested the use of the "Q-sort" method to determine areas of concern in religious education. He found that rural churchmen tended to place least emphasis on social action and leadership training. He interpreted these findings in terms of these churchmen's satisfaction with the status quo. It would seem, therefore, that if churchmen themselves do not consider a given social issue or reform to be of major importance, their congregations cannot be expected to think otherwise. Some research evidence has already been mentioned which shows that churchgoers have little concern about such problems. By extension, then, we may say that consideration of social issues is either not an important part of clerical training or that the clergy are failing to instruct their congregations in social concerns.

Spilka(59) tried to test Allport's hypothesis about the existence of two types of religiousness. He administered the Thurstone Scale of Attitude Toward the Church and the E scale to a sample of college undergraduates. They were separated into two groups: those with high ethnocentric scores and those with low ethnocentrism and religious nonethnocentrism. He then administered another battery of tests and found that the religious ethnocentric group scored higher on manifest anxiety, rigidity, and self-concept instability than did the religious nonethnocentric. There was no difference in intelligence between the two groups. The study, however, remains incomplete, since Spilka selected only those subjects who scored above the median in religiousness. It would have been worthwhile to include two other groups, both nonreligious, but with one group being ethnocentric and the other nonethnocentric.

Following Allport's lead, Wilson(66) devised the Extrinsic Religious Values Scale (ERV) and correlated it with the Anti-Semitic Scale after he had administered the battery to ten different groups of subjects belonging to various religious groups. He found that the ERV-AS correlation was .66 on the average, but when homogeneity and alternations were corrected for, the correction coefficient would be .80. The validity of the ERV Scale, according to Wilson, is greater than the AS Scale because its content is more ambiguous in terms of social acceptability.

The two studies above represent a needed development in the scientific study of religion, since they differentiate religiousness which is based on rituals and religiousness which reflects the ideals of religion. Naturally, much more research is needed in this area.

## SUMMARY AND DISCUSSION

A number of empirical studies, which do not support the general belief that religion is the fountainhead of all moral tenets of our society, have been reviewed in this paper. According to Allport(3) religious instruction seems to include a contradictory set of beliefs. He stated that "most religious persons tend to internalize the divisive role of religion, whereas only a small minority are able to accept the unifying bond, moral and ethical principles underlying religion." Thus, on the one hand, religious leaders advocate love of all mankind and the equality of men as being children of God, while, on the other hand, certain religious teachings hold that only those who possess the "truth" may be saved.

As a result, religious education as it is being taught today does not seem to ensure healthier attitudes, despite its emphasis on ethical behavior. This should raise a major point of discussion among religious leaders to determine whether possibilities exist to remedy this failure to communicate the ethical aspects of religion rather than its ritual. In other words, would it be possible to alter aspects to the religious teachings in order to maximize the "intrinsic orientation" and minimize the "extrinsic orientation"? To undertake such a task would be rather difficult, since it would require that basic changes be made to eliminate contradictions in the content of religious teachings.

While it has been shown that nonbelievers may have strict moral values, the question could be raised as to the origin of such values. From the recent development in research which differentiates the two types of religiousness, it could be assumed that the irreligious person had been exposed to religious teachings during his formative years and that such teachings included both the negative and positive aspects, but that for one reason or another only the positive aspects have remained. The hypothesis presented at this point is that an ethical individual, while rejecting the tenets of the church, may both observe and practice its ethical teachings. However, such a hypothesis remains to be tested.

## REFERENCES

1. Adorno, T. W., Frenkel-Brunswik, E., Levinson, D. J., and Sanford, R. N.: The Authoritarian Personality. New York: Harper & Bros., 1950.
2. Alexander, J. E., and Adelstein, A. M.: "Studies in the Psychology of Death," in David, H. P., and Brengelman, J. C., eds.: Perspectives in Personality Research. New York: Springer Publishing Co., 1960, pp. 65-92.
3. Allport, G. W.: The Nature of Prejudice. New York: Addison-Wesley, 1954.
4. Allport, G. W.: The Religious Context of Prejudice, J. Sci. Study Religion 5:448-451, 1966.
5. Allport G. W., and Ross, J. M.: Personal Religious Orientation and Prejudice, J. Personality Soc. Psychol. 5:432-443, 1967.
6. Angell, R. C.: The Moral Integration of American Cities, Amer. J. Sociol. 57: (monogr.), 1951.
7. Argyle, M.: Religious Behavior. Glencoe, Ill.: The Free Press, 1959.
8. Armstrong, R. C., Larsen, G. L., and Mourer, S. A.: Religious Attitudes and Emotional Adjustment, J. Psychol. Studies 13:35-47, 1962.

9. Bateman, M. M., and Jensen, J. S.: The Effect of Religious Background on Modes of Handling Anger, J. Soc. Psychol. 47:133-141, 1958.
10. Blum, S. B., and Mann, J. H.: The Effect of Religious Membership on Religious Prejudice, J. Soc. Psychol. 52:97-101, 1960.
11. Campbell, E. O., and Pettigrew, T. F.: Racial and Moral Crisis: The Role of Little Rock Ministers, Amer. J. Sociol. 64:509-516, 1959.
12. Cline, V. B., and Richards, J. M.: A Factor Analytic Study of Religious Belief and Behavior, J. Personality Soc. Psychol. 1:569-578, 1965.
13. Crawford, A. A.: "Q-Sort" as a Method of Determining Areas of Concern in Adult Religious Education, Religious Education 58:366-371, 1963.
14. Devolder, P. M.: Inquiry Into the Religious Life of Catholic Intellectuals, J. Soc. Psychol. 28:39-56, 1948.
15. Dreger, R. M.: Some Personality Correlates of Religious Attitudes as Determined by Projective Techniques, Psychol. Monogr. 66: No. 335, 1952.
16. Dunn, R. F.: Personality Patterns Among Religious Personnel, Rev. Catholic Psychol. Rec. 3:125-137, 1965.
17. Eiseman, R., and Code, S. N.: Prejudice and Conservatism in Denominational College Students, Psychol. Rep. 14:644, 1964.
18. Feagin, J. R.: Prejudice and Religious Types: A Focussed Study of Southern Fundamentalists, J. Sci. Study Religion 4:3-13, 1964.
19. Friedrichs, R. W.: Christians and Residential Exclusion: An Empirical Study of a Northern Dilemma, J. Soc. Issues 15:14-23, 1959.
20. Fromm, E.: Psychoanalysis and Religion. New Haven: Yale University Press, 1950.
21. Funk, R. A.: A Survey of Religious Attitudes and Manifest Anxiety in a College Population, Dissertation Abstracts 15:2569, 1955.
22. Godin, A.: Mental Health in Christian Life, J. Religion and Health 1:41-51, 1961.
23. Grunes, M.: Some Aspects of Conscience and Their Relationship to Intelligence, Dissertation Abstracts 16:1282-1283, 1956.
24. Gurin, G., Veroff, J., and Feld, S.: Americans View Their Mental Health. New York: Basic Books, 1960.
25. Hartshorne, H., and May, M. A.: Studies in the Nature of Character: I. Studies in Deceit. New York: Macmillan Co., 1928.
26. Jahoda, M.: Current Concepts of Positive Mental Health. New York: Basic Books, 1958.
27. Jones, M. B.: Religious Values and Authoritarian Tendency, J. Soc. Psychol. 48:83-89, 1958.
28. Jung, C. G.: Psychology and Religion. New Haven: Yale University Press, 1938.
29. Kelly, J.: The Measurement of Attitudes Toward the Negro in the South, J. Soc. Psychol. 48:305-317, 1958.
30. Kirkpatrick, C.: Religion and Humanitarianism: A Study of Institutional Implications, Psychol. Monogr. 63:123, 1949.
31. Lantz, H.: Religious Participation and Social Orientation of 1,000 University Students, J. Sociol. Soc. Res. 33:285-290, 1948-49.
32. Maranell, G. M.: An Examination of Some Religious and Political Attitude Correlates of Bigotry, Social Forces 45:356-362, 1967.
33. Marton, C., and Nichols, R.: Personality and Religious Belief, J. Soc. Psychol. 56:3-8, 1962.
34. Maslow, A. H.: The Influence of Familiarization on Preference, J. Exp. Psychol. 21:162-180, 1937.
35. McGrath, J. E.: Religious Group Differences in Value Orientations, Interpersonal Perceptions and Personal Adjustment, read at the meeting of the Society for the Scientific Study of Religion, Cambridge, Mass., October 1961.
36. Meissner, W. W.: Annotated Bibliography in Religion and Psychology. New York: Academy of Religion and Mental Health, 1961.

37. Middleton, R., and Putney, S.: Religious, Normative Standards and Behavior, Sociometry 25:141–152, 1962.
38. Middleton, W. C., and Fay, P. J.: Attitudes of Delinquent and Non-Delinquent Girls Toward Sunday Observance, the Bible, and War, J. Educ. Psychol. 32:555-558, 1941.
39. Moberg, D.: Religious Activities and Personal Adjustment in Old Age, J. Soc. Psychol. 43:261-267, 1956.
40. Nowlan, E.: Le Portrait du Catholique a partir des tests d'attitudes, Lumen Vitae 12:284-295, 1957.
41. Obenhaus, V.: Church Affiliations and Attitudes Towards Selected Public Questions in a Typical Midwest County, Rural Sociol. 28:34–37, 1963.
42. O'Reilly, C. T.: Religious Practice and Personal Adjustment, Sociol. Soc. Res. 42:119-121, 1958.
43. O'Reilly, C. T., and O'Reilly, R. J.: Religious Beliefs of Catholic College Students and Their Attitudes Towards Minorities, J. Abnorm. Soc. Psychol. 56:3-8, 1962.
44. Pemberton, P. L.: The Protestant Minister's Role and Contemporary American Values, read at the meeting of the Society for the Scientific Study of Religion, New Haven, Conn., October 1959.
45. Porterfield, A. L.: The Church and Social Well Being: A Statistical Analysis, J. Sociol. Soc. Res. 31:213–219, 1946.
46. Pugh, T. J.: A Comparative Study of the Values of a Group of Ministers and Two Groups of Laymen, J. Soc. Psychol. 33:223–235, 1951.
47. Putney, S., and Middleton, R.: Dimensions and Correlates of Religious Ideologies, Social Forces 39:285–290, 1961.
48. Pyron, B.: Belief, Q-Sort, Allport-Vernon, Study of Values and Religion, Psychol. Rep. 8:399-400, 1961.
49. Ranck, J. G.: Some Personality Correlates of Religious Attitudes and Beliefs, Dissertation Abstracts 15:878-879, 1955.
50. Rokeach, M.: The Open and Closed Mind. New York: Basic Books, 1960.
51. Rosenbloom, A. L.: Ethnic Prejudice as Related to Social Class and Religiosity, Sociol. Soc. Res. 43:272-275, 1959.
52. Salisbury, W. S.: Religious Orthodoxy and Social Behavior, read at the meeting of the Society for the Scientific Study of Religion, New Haven, Conn., October 1959.
53. Schofield, W., and Balian, L.: A Comparative Study of the Personal Histories of Schizophrenics and Non-Psychiatric Patients, J. Abnorm. Soc. Psychol. 59:216-225, 1959.
54. Scholl, M. E., and Beker, J.: A Comparison of Religious Beliefs of Delinquent and Non-Delinquent Protestant Adolescent Boys, Religious Education 59:250-253, 1964.
55. Scott, E. M.: Presumed Correlation Between Religion and Mental Health, Guild of Catholic Psychiatrists Bull. 8:113-121, 1961.
56. Siegman, A. W.: A Cross-Cultural Investigation of the Relationship Between Religiosity, Ethics, Prejudice and Authoritarianism, Psychol. Rep. 11:419-424, 1962.
57. Smith, P. M.: Organized Religion and Criminal Behavior, Sociol. Soc. Res. 33:363-367, 1949.
58. Smith, P. M.: Prisoners' Attitudes Toward Organized Religion, Religious Education 51:462-464, 1956.
59. Spilka, B.: Some Personality Correlates of Interiorized and Institutionalized Religious Beliefs, New York University Psychological Newsletter 9:103-107, 1958.
60. Srole, L., Langner, T., Michael, S. T., Opler, M. K., and Rennie, T. A. C.: Mental Health in the Metropolis: Midtown Manhattan Study, vol. 1. New York: McGraw-Hill Book Co., 1962.
61. Strunk, O.: Interest and Personality Patterns of Pre-Ministerial Students, Psychol. Rep. 5:740, 1959.
62. Thorndike, E. L.: American Cities and States, Ann. N.Y. Acad. Sci. 39:213-298, 1939.
63. Walters, O. S.: The Religious Background of Fifty Alcoholics, Quart. J. Stud. Alcohol 18:405-416, 1957.

64. Weima, J.: Authoritarianism, Religious Conservatism and Sociocentric Attitudes in Roman Catholic Groups, Human Relations 18:231-239, 1965.
65. Weir, E.: Criminology: A Scientific Study. Joliet, Ill.: Institute for the Scientific Study of Crime, 1941.
66. Wilson, W. C.: Extrinsic Religious Values and Prejudice, J. Abnorm. Soc. Psychol. 60:286-288, 1960.
67. Wright, J. C.: Personal Adjustment and Its Relationship to Religious Attitude and Certainty, Religious Education 54:521-523, 1959.

# Religious Belief as a Factor in Obedience to Destructive Commands

DAVID C. BOCK AND NEIL C. WARREN

A perennial and current conflict involves a man's response to authority when that authority demands that he harm another human being. In past times legitimate authorities have demanded that witches be burned, Jews be exterminated, and the mentally unbalanced be chained and beaten. More recently, American students have experienced intense conflict over their required role in Viet Nam. Oversimplified, the question becomes: How do I choose between two demands when they are *in opposition*—the demand of an external, legitimate authority and the demand of my own commitment to the protection of the welfare of others?

Laboratory experiments have been devised involving realistic situations in which an authority orders an individual to obey commands which appear to result in destructive consequences for another person (Buss, 1961; Milgram, 1961, 1963). In Milgram's study an ethical dilemma is created which forces the individual to choose between an experimenter's demand to administer increasingly painful shocks to a fellow subject and defiance of the presiding authority which apparently disrupts the experiment. Over two-thirds of the subjects dealt with the conflict by obeying to the end the destructive commands (Milgram, 1963).

Several variables have been identified which relate to an individual's resolution of this conflict. Subjects tend to resolve the conflict through obedience to the authority when they score high on measures of hostility (Haas, 1966; Buss, 1961; Youssef, 1968), when group pressure is applied (Milgram, 1964, 1965; Kudirka, 1965), when the victim is male or of a different race (Youssef, 1968), when the experimenter is viewed as high status (Gladstone, 1969), and most sig-

Reprinted with permission of authors and publisher from:

*Review of Religious Research,* 1972, 13(3), 185-191, copyright 1972 by the RELIGIOUS RESEARCH ASSOCIATION.

nificantly when their scores on measures of authoritarianism are high (Elms and Milgram, 1966; Abrams, 1964). On the other hand, subjects tend to defy the experimental authority when they score high on measures of moral judgment (Kohlberg, 1968), when their scores on social responsibility scales are high (Elms and Milgram, 1966), when the victim is high status (Williamson, 1967), and when guilt is induced experimentally (Carlsmith and Gross, 1969; Freedman, Wallington, and Bless, 1967).

It is the interest of this study to assess the influence of an individual's religious commitment on his choice of obedience or resistance. In an experimental situation in which the conflict is clearly experienced, will subjects with more pronounced religious commitment show stronger resistance to authority?

The Christian religion emphasizes man's responsibility to obey legitimate authority; but it places primary emphasis on man's responsibility to treat a fellow human being with respect and care. From a Biblical perspective, the press for obedience by an authority must always be assessed in light of the effects such obedience would have on the persons involved.

However, religious believers in America have often placed primary emphasis on obedience and have relegated man's responsibility for the protection of his neighbor to a position clearly secondary. For instance, within the religious structure children have been taught to obey authority unquestioningly; they have not been taught to assess critically the legitimacy of that authority's demands. Thus, individuals who are deeply embedded in this structure would be expected to obey authority to the exclusion of other values.

At the same time, nonreligious extremes can become committed to an authoritarian structure of their own. They may find themselves caught in the web of excessive submission to the authority of their own value structure. Perhaps with respect to authoritarian systems, religious and nonreligious extremes hold similar positions.

On the other hand, it might be theorized that religious moderates have their values more in balance—i.e., while they recognize the importance of obedience to authority, they evaluate that authority in light of their concern for other men. If this is accurate, they would be expected hastily to terminate their participation in any procedure involving the infliction of pain on another person.

## METHOD

### Hypothesis

Persons scoring at the extremes on religious scales will be more obedient to an authority commanding destructive behavior than individuals scoring in the mid-range.

### Subjects

Thirty subjects ranging in age from 18 to 33 were selected from a local two-year college. Seventeen were male and thirteen were female. No attempt was made to discriminate on the basis of religious or racial criteria. Thus, the subjects represented a wide range of church affiliations and religious backgrounds.

### Procedure

Subjects came by individual appointment to a school facility. They were paid $5.00 for merely appearing. It was explained that this money was in no way contingent on their performance during the experiment.

Subjects completed two paper and pencil tasks:

1. Inventory of Religious Belief (Brown & Lowe, 1951). This is a brief 15-item measure highly discriminative of religious stances from believer to nonbeliever.

2. Religious Attitude Inventory (Broen, 1955). A 58-item scale which provides scores on two factors—a "Fundamentalism-Humanism" factor and a "Nearness to God" factor.

The subjects were subsequently introduced to a modified version of Milgram's (1963) procedure. At this point the subject was joined by a second "subject," actually an accomplice, and the pair were introduced to the experimenter. The purpose of the experiment was explained as an effort to judge the effects of punishment on human learning. A fake drawing elected the subject as "teacher" and the accomplice as "learner." The experimental apparatus was explained to the teacher and learner as a shock generator. This device was actually a panel of harmless switches graded from 15 to 450 volts.

The learner was strapped to a chair and connected to electrodes for receiving "shocks." He was out of view, but well within earshot of the teacher. He complained nervously of a heart condition and asked to be reassured concerning the punishment. The experimenter claimed, "the shocks may be painful, but they are not dangerous." The learning task, a paired-word association test, was administered by the teacher. When the learner made errors determined by a script, the teacher was instructed to administer increasingly elevated voltage as punishment. As the errors continued, the learner gave agonized screams appropriate to the shock level. These outbursts put the teacher under increased tension to defy the experimenter's authority and terminate the procedure. He was permitted to do so only after a clear break was made with the experimenter's repeated demands to continue. The measure of each subject's obedience was the highest shock value he administered.

When the procedure was terminated, the subject was reconciled to the learner. The learner was shown to be an accomplice and not to have received any shocks. Most subjects were greatly relieved.

A therapist debriefed each subject for a minimum of one-half hour during which subjects expressed their feelings about the experiment. The extensive debriefing was an attempt to meet Baumrind's (1964) complaint that Milgram gave only "casual assurance" to his subjects.

## RESULTS

Subjects experienced a wide range of emotions as the tension between fundamental ethical principles came into conflict with the experimenter's demand to continue punishment. The tension appeared in such forms as crying on the part of several female subjects, laughing when the learner groaned, anger toward the experimenter, and nervous fumbling and stalling before administering the shocks.

The hypothesis stated that obedient subjects would tend to be in the theological extremes, while defiant subjects would occupy the center of the theological spectrum. Prior to the collection of data, it was decided that a subject would be considered an "extreme believer" or an "extreme nonbeliever" if he scored in the upper or lower 20% of the range for each of the three religious scales. The "moderates," then, would be those subjects scoring in the middle 60% of each scale's range. These figures were altered slightly after the data were collected because of the number of subjects in each category. If subjects were limited for a given category, the range considered was sometimes increased slightly in order to include enough subjects to make data analysis possible. Table 1 compares the extremes and moderates on the Inventory of Religious Belief with regard to the highest shock level administered by subjects before terminating the experiment.

The mean of the maximum shocks for the extreme groups were

285.0 volts and for the moderate group, 409.0 volts. These data make it evident that the hypothesis was disconfirmed. However, the data suggest the reverse of the present hypothesis—namely that moderates are more obedient than extremes. In this connection the difference between the means was significant at the .05 level.

TABLE 1

COMPARISON OF MAXIMUM SHOCK FOR EXTREMES AND MODERATES
ON BROWN AND LOWE'S INVENTORY OF RELIGIOUS BELIEF

| Group | Sample Size | IRB Range | Standard Deviation | Mean Maximum Shock (Volts) | t value |
|-------|-------------|-----------|--------------------|----------------------------|---------|
| Extreme Non-Believers (N=4) | | 15-34 | 144.6 ⎱ | 319.3 ⎱ | |
| | 11 | | ⎰ 142.5 | ⎰ 285.0 | |
| Extreme Believers (N=7) | | 60-75 | 129.4 | 225.0 | 2.66* |
| Moderates | 19 | 35-59 | 48.2 | 409.0 | |

*p<.05

On the Fundamentalism-Humanism dimension, the extreme groups were again less obedient than the moderates. The difference between the means was significant at the .05 level, strengthening the possibility that religious moderates are indeed more obedient.

TABLE 2

COMPARISON OF MEAN MAXIMUM SHOCK FOR EXTREMES AND MODERATES
ON BROEN'S FUNDAMENTALISM-HUMANISM DIMENSION

| Group | Sample Size | F-H Range | Standard Deviation | Mean Maximum Shock (Volts) | t value |
|-------|-------------|-----------|--------------------|----------------------------|---------|
| Extreme Non-Believers (N=5) | | 0-6 | 138.0 ⎱ | 249.0 ⎱ | |
| | 11 | | ⎰ 141.4 | ⎰ 296.8 | |
| Extreme Believers (N=6) | | 25-31 | 133.9 | 337.5 | 2.22* |
| Moderates | 19 | 7-24 | 61.0 | 402.1 | |

*p<.05

TABLE 3

COMPARISON OF MEAN MAXIMUM FOR EXTREMES AND MODERATES
ON BROEN'S NEARNESS-TO-GOD DIMENSION

| Group | Sample Size | N-G Range | Standard Deviation | Mean Maximum Shock (Volts) | t value |
|-------|-------------|-----------|--------------------|----------------------------|---------|
| Extreme Non-Believers (N=5) | | 0-11 | 171.4 ⎱ | 312.0 ⎱ | |
| | 12 | | ⎰ 161.2 | ⎰ 323.8 | |
| Extreme Believers (N=7) | | 24-31 | 107.1 | 332.1 | 1.26 |
| Moderates | 18 | 12-23 | 79.8 | 390.0 | |

## TABLE 4

CORRELATION RATIO AND TEST OF NONLINEARITY FOR RELIGIOUS ATTITUDE
SCORES VERSUS MAXIMUM SHOCK ADMINISTERED

| Attitudes Correlated | Eta (n) | Pearson r | F test of Linearity (F Scores) |
|---|---|---|---|
| Inventory of Religious Belief with Maximum Shock Administered | .72* | .06 | 2.75* |
| Fundamentalism-Humanism with Maximum Shock Administered | .70* | .03 | 2.83* |
| Nearness-to-God with Maximum Shock Administered | .72* | .17 | 2.20 |

*$p < .05$

Extremes on the Nearness-to-God dimension were less obedient than moderates, but the difference was not significant ($.20 > p > .10$).

A scatterplot representation of the data suggested a curvilinear relationship; i.e., extremes on each of the three religious scales tended to administer lower maximum shocks than the moderates. On the basis of the observation a correlation ratio, eta, was computed between scores on each religious scale and maximum shock administered. The results are given in Table 4.

On each of the three religious dimensions eta was found to be significant at the .05 level. In order to establish curvilinearity each eta was compared with a Pearson r computed for the same data. For two of the three comparisons the differences were significant at the .05 level.

Finally, a comparison was made to see if sex was a factor in the administration of shock. Contrary to Youssef (1968), no differential levels of shock were observed, although the male mean (372.4 volts) was slightly higher than the female mean (351.9) volts. A difference between these means failed to reach significance ($t = 0.42$; $p > .50$).

## DISCUSSION

The aim of this investigation was to determine the relevance of a religious variable in choosing between obedience or resistance to destructive commands. The results suggest an unexpected relationship which requires explanation. Although it was hypothesized that persons scoring in the extremes on religious scales would perform more obediently, it was in fact found that they were significantly more resistant.

It is apparent that the theory initially presented in this paper is defective. Struening (1963) and Allport and Ross (1967), among others, found that *frequent* church-attenders and *non*-attenders are less prejudiced than *in*frequent attenders. In light of these results, a more accurate prediction would have been that the moderates of this study, perhaps comparable to the infrequent attenders, would show more submission to external norms. On the other hand, the religious extremes, comparable to the frequent attenders and non-attenders, should have been expected to behave more in accordance with humanitarian or moral directives.

One may theorize that the religious extremes consist of persons who have arrived at strong commitments. The ability to make firm decisions has perhaps become part of their life style. Thus, under experimental stress, they are both attitudinally and behaviorally capable of making decisions consistent with moral conscience.

Contrariwise, the religious moderates may be unaccustomed to firm decision-making. They are the "agnostics," those who do "not know for sure." In the presence of such indecision, they are willing to have the momentary decisions of life made for them. In this experiment, it was compelling to surrender moral conscience to a seemingly knowledgeable and decisive person. Only those accustomed to independent decision-making could resist.

The fact that this religious variable is significant suggests that an alternative explanation may arise from within the structure of religion itself. In the Judeo-Christian tradition a high value is placed on a strong, well-defined response to "the will of God." In fact, a decisive response even if negative is to be preferred over neutrality. The Biblical position is that the man who is undecided about basic religious issues is unable to be decisive when confronted by an ethical dilemma. His tendency is to forfeit his choice to any impinging power. On the other hand, having taken a definite religious stance, one is in a position to act in accord with conscience.

Finally, the unexpected direction of the results and the size of the sample limit the extent to which generalizations are valid. However, the provocative outcome of this study suggests the need for future research designed to clarify the relationship between religious variables and ethical decisions which involve the demands of authority.

# D. C. Bock and N. C. Warren

## NOTES AND REFERENCES

The authors express special thanks to Anne Zeisler, Alex Good, Jim Savage, but especially to Matthew Siebert (learner) and Thomas Elkin (experimenter) for their valuable time and energy.

ABRAMS, L. 1964 "Aggressive behavior in the authoritarian personality." Unpublished Ph.D. Dissertation, the University of Texas.

ALLPORT, G. W., and J. M. ROSS 1967 "Personal religious orientation and prejudice." Journal of Personality and Social Psychology 5: 432-443.

BAUMRIND, D. 1964 "Some thoughts on the ethics of research: After reading Milgram's 'Behavioral study of obedience'." American Psychologist 19: 421-423.

BROEN, W. E., Jr. 1955 "Personality correlates of certain religious attitudes." Journal of Consulting Psychology 19: 64.

BROWN, D. G. and W. L. LOWE 1951 "Religious beliefs and personality characteristics of college students." Journal of Social Psychology 33: 103-129.

BUSS, A. H. 1961 The Psychology of Aggression. New York, N.Y.: John Wiley.

CARLSMITH, J. M. and A. E. GROSS 1969 "Some effects of guilt on compliance." Journal of Personality and Social Psychology 11: 232-239.

ELMS, A. C. and S. MILGRAM 1966 "Personality characteristics associated with obedience and defiance toward authoritative commands." Journal of Experimental Research in Personality 1: 282-289.

FREEDMAN, J. L., S. A. WALLINGTON, and E. BLESS 1967 "Compliance without pressure: The effect of guilt." Journal of Personality and Social Psychology 7: 117–124.

GLADSTONE, R. 1969 "Authoritarianism, social status, transgression, and punitiveness." Proceedings of the 77th Annual Convention of the American Psychological Association 4 (part 1): 287–288.

HAYS, L. 1966 "Obedience: Submission to destructive orders as related to hostility." Psychological Reports 19: 32-34.

KOHLBERG, L. 1968 "Education for justice: A modern statement of the Platonic view." Ernest Burton Lecture on Moral Education, Harvard University, April 23.

KUDIRKA, N. Z. 1965 "Defiance of authority under peer influence." Unpublished Ph.D. Dissertation, Yale University.

MILGRAM, S. 1961 "Dynamics of obedience: Experiments in social psychology." Mimeographed report, National Science Foundation, January 25. 1963 "Behavioral study of obedience." Journal of Abnormal and Social Psychology 67: 371-378. 1964 "Group pressure and action against a person." Journal of Abnormal and Social Psychology 69: 137-143. 1965 "Liberating effects of group pressure." Journal of Personality and Social Psychology 1: 127-134.

STRUENING, E. L. 1963 "Antidemocratic attitudes in a Midwest university," Chap. 9 of H. H. Remmers (ed.), Anti-democratic Attitudes in American Schools. Evanston, Ill.: Northwestern University Press.

WILLIAMSON, D. S. 1967 "A study of selective inhibition of aggression by church members." Journal of Pastoral Care 21: 193–208.

YOUSSEF, Z. I. 1968 "The role of race, sex, hostility, and verbal stimulus in inflicting punishment." Psychonomic Science 12: 285-286.

# On the Relationship Between Religious Beliefs and Emotion

JOHN A. STOUDENMIRE

Sixty-four college students with conservative religious beliefs were used to conduct a modified replication of an experiment by Rosenberg (1965). An "Inventory of Religious Beliefs" (Brown & Lowe, 1951) was given each subject to determine his religious beliefs and his degree of conservatism. Later, 12 statements were presented to each subject. Four of the statements affirmed the subject's beliefs; four contradicted his beliefs; and four were neutral. The statements were presented in counterbalanced orders and were interspersed into non-religious, non-emotion-producing literature the subject was reading.

The subject's emotional reaction to each religious statement was recorded by a galvanic skin response (GSR) and by a subjective report of emotion.

Results showed that affirmation of one's religious beliefs produces a significant increase in emotion as measured by the GSR. The subject's verbal report of this emotion identifies it as pleasurable. Contradiction of one's religious beliefs also produces a significant increase in GSR, and this emotion is labeled as displeasure by the subject. Although both contradiction and affirmation of one's religious beliefs produce significant increases in emotion, it is noted that contradiction of beliefs engenders significantly more emotion than affirmation. Neutral statements, neither affirming nor contradicting religious beliefs, produced no significant change in emotion.

Reprinted with permission of author and publisher from:

*Journal for the Scientific Study of Religion,* 1971, 10(3), 254, published by the SOCIETY FOR THE SCIENTIFIC STUDY OF RELIGION, University of Connecticut, Box U68A, Storrs, Connecticut 06268.

## J. A. Stoudenmire

### REFERENCES

BROWN, D. G. and LOWE, W. L. 1951 Religious beliefs and personality characteristics of college students. *Journal of Social Psychology,* 33, 103-128.
ROSENBERG, M. J. 1965 Some content determinants of intolerance for attitudinal inconsistency. In S. S. Thomkins and C. E. Izard (Eds.), *Affect, cognition and personality,* New York: Springer.

# The Relationship of Personality Modes to Religious Experience and Behavior

PAUL F. BARKMAN

In the attempt to construct a psychological theory of personality it is customary to view man as having (a) a structure—the anatomy; which structure is related to (b) functions or processes—at least partly described by physiology and psychology; which processes are related to (c) the content of his environment. Man, furthermore, has (d) a history. Each of these is related to the others, and each is more or less dependent upon the others, and may be more or less modified by the interaction.

It is important to pause along the way long enough to state that process not only influences content, but content influences process as well. The behaviorists find no difficulty with that statement, but the more orthodox psychoanalysts have tended to deny it. A simple illustration of the influence of content on process is that of the violent death of a parent in the presence of a small child in which case the traumatic effect of that content may distort the child's psychological processes for life.

One dramatic example of the interrelationship of history, structure, function, and content is the wartime story of the athletic soldier who came to consciousness after battle and was told that he had lost two limbs; whereupon he exclaimed in despair, turned to the wall, and soon died, even though physicians regarded the physical trauma as inadequate to this effect.

It has been somewhat characteristic of psychologists to be more interested in structure and process than in other aspects of the person. They frequently disclaim interest or competence in content, preferring to leave that to the educational system, the parents, the culture, or whoever is interested. Their appropriate preoccupation, they feel, is

Reprinted with permission of author and publisher from:
*Journal of the American Scientific Affiliation,* 1968, 20(1), 27-30.

to assure a man that he will be able to reason efficiently, perceive well, relate realistically, tolerate frustration, and engage in other such processes without deficit or distortion. Or, in popular language, it is the psychologist's business to help men think straight, and it is a man's own business what he thinks about.

Because religion has so often been regarded as content, this preoccupation with process, together with a failure to recognize the reciprocal effects of content upon process, have caused religion to be brushed aside with such labels as "the unanalyzable residue" of psychoanalysis, or as "orthogonal with psychology."

Before pursuing that line of thought, we must recognize that for others religion has not been regarded as beside the point but as related process.

For the analysts it has often been regarded as either neurotic or psychotic process, and thus a displacement and distortion of reality. (Note that not all analysts take this position.) For some religionists it has been regarded as the dynamic panacea which transforms personality, sustains integration and creativity, heals physical ailments, and orients man to cope intuitively and effectively with reality.

If it were not for a recent fresh wind of scientific research and relatively unimpassioned theory which has blown through the emotional smog of ignorance and emotion in the past decade, such a discussion as this would rapidly descend into the familiar old exchanges which were characterized more by heat than light. Fortunately man's religious behavior has come under much more careful scrunity lately, with anthropologists and sociologists leading the way, and psychologists entering increasingly into the task.

The first awareness that has resulted is that religion has been grossly oversimplified by both its exponents and its detractors. Let me make a quick review of some of the discriminations which have begun to appear.

Michael Argyle (1959)[1] reviewing extensive research and theoretical literature has discussed the theories of religious behavior and belief under the following headings: Religion as social learning, as a response to frustration, as a reaction to intra-personal conflict and as conflict with the environment, as a fantasy father-figure, as obsessional neurosis, as a response to cognitive need, and as a response to physiological processes. Without entering into his findings, one may summarize his conclusions by saying that, in his opinion, most of these theories are descriptive and explanatory of certain groups of religious persons when they are classified into the usual sociological rubrics of church, denomination, sect, and protestant liberalism; but that no one theory is applicable throughout all religion.

For this paper, the single most significant awareness that comes from Argyle's work is the documentation that religion—even when defined as narrowly as the Judeo-Christian context—has a great variety of meanings and functions which differ for recognizable groups and classes of persons.

In view of the involvement of religious behavior in the psychoses and neuroses, such knowledge makes it possible to be more precise about the meaning of religious behavior in the disturbed personality, and the part it may or may not have had in the etiology of the disorder, and how (or whether) it should be included in the process of treatment.

Sociologist Gerhard Lenski[2] did a survey in 1961 in Detroit of the religious factor in the political, economic, and family life of the city, and found himself driven by the evidence to distinguish between two kinds of religious intensity that have previously been classified together. He found that "doctrinal orthodoxy" and "devotionalism" were both present among religious people, but not nearly so often in the same persons as one might have imagined. The Pearson product-moment correlation was only .23. A surprisingly low correlation. The sample included the usual American proportions of Catholics, Jews, and Protestants. Throughout the very extensive study these two factors of religiosity were repeatedly, though not always, related differently with various kinds of attitudes and behavior.

"Devotionalism" was defined by the frequency with which a person had individual prayer, or asked God what to do.

Quoting from Lenski's concluding chapter, "On the whole, doctrinal orthodoxy appears to be a type of religious orientation which is linked with (and we suspect fosters) *a compartmentalized view of life*. . . . one's religious commitments are irrelevant to one's political and economic actions and other aspects of secular life....Devotionalism, by contrast, seems linked both with the spirit of capitalism and with a humanitarian outlook when confronted with problems of social injustice."[3]

Gordon Allport has defined similar variables under the title of extrinsic and intrinsic religion. Extrinsic religion is "a dull habit, or a tribal investment to be used for occasional ceremony, for family convenience or for personal comfort. It is something to *use*, but not to *live*."[4] That is to say, "it is not a value in its own right, but is an instrumental value serving the motives of personal comfort, security, or social status."[5] It is the kind of religion responsible for the slogan, "Go to church and leave your troubles there."

Allport defines intrinsic religion as an orientation that regards faith as a supreme value in its own right.[6] ". . . it is not primarily a means of handling fear, or a mode of conformity, or an attempted sublimation of sex, or a wish-fulfillment. Earlier in life it may have been all of these things. But now these specific needs are not so much served by, as they are subordinated to, an overarching motive....intrinsic religion has nothing to do with formal religious structure."[7] He says there are intrinsically religious persons in all faiths.

He cites several studies which show a clear and unvarying positive correlation between extrinsic religion and prejudices toward race and religion; and a corresponding negative correlation between intrinsic religion and such prejudice. The subjects were drawn from both white and Negro, and from Jewish, Protestant, and Catholic churchgoers.

He continues to predict that, "mental health will vary according to the degree to which adherents of any faith are intrinsic in their interpretation and living of their faith,"[8] but he does not support this statement with research. His predictions challenge research.

Such discriminations as the foregoing are exceedingly useful in the scientific approach to religious behavior.

In the spirit of such efforts at refined discriminations, the following hypothesis is presented relative to the relationship of personality modes and religious experience and behavior.

It is proposed that there are at least four basic personality modes which are closely related to the central character of the varieties of Christian behavior. (Brief discussion with those who are acquainted with other religions seems to encourage the idea that these modes may apply elsewhere as well, but the theory does not say so at this time.) These four modes are verbal, affective, social-relational, and transcendental.

Modes can be thought of as relatively distinct and abiding characteristics of personality which are dynamic and somewhat determinative of behavior. For the purpose of this discussion, they are ways of cognition and of action or response. One might use the old term "personality traits," but the word "mode" is close to the concept of a "style of life," and more in keeping with the observations which prompt this theory.

There is considerable evidence in all of psychology to support the idea that we perceive and conceive in light of our needs and styles of life; and there is no reason to feel that this would not be the same with the religious behavior of a person; but not much has been done to explore that aspect of human behavior.

There is also some evidence that these modes are not arbitrarily arrived at, but may indeed represent fairly universal human modules of personality. For example, the evidence from the Wechsler Scales of intelligence seems to indicate that people do differ with respect to verbal and performance aspects of intelligence, and research would support the idea that they find their existence and expression in recognizable degrees in certain named categories of persons. (Schizophrenics, for example tend to be high on the verbal scales and low on the performance scales, while juvenile delinquents are low on the verbal and high on the performance scales. These are somewhat gross statements, but close enough for our example.)

Guilford gives another partial confirmation of the foregoing list of modes in his summary of the factor-analytic study of personality traits. "The primary traits of temperament can be grouped in three broad classes, depending upon whether they refer to a person's attitudes toward his general environment, to his emotional dispositions, or his inclinations in dealing with his social environment."[9]

When one thinks of verbal, emotional and social modes as possibly the basic human dispositions to perceive and deal with the world, and then regards the nature of the Protestant Reformation, there is suggested the idea that these modes may be closely related to the central emphases of the main segments of that great social and religious epoch.

At the time of the Reformation, perhaps for the first time in Christian history, large numbers of people were given relatively great freedom both to shape their religion and to shift their allegiance to the particular shading of Christianity which seemed most congenial to them as individuals. This freedom was far from complete, but sufficient to allow considerable alignment by personal choice. Thus, both reformers and adherents were free to shape and express religion in a manner that seemed most congenial to them as persons. All appealed equally to the Scriptures, and doubtless all were faithful to the Scriptures within their conscience. That personality modes were related to the results is rather evident, although no claim is made that Christianity was distorted thereby.

It would appear that those whose basic personality tendencies were more predominantly verbal tended to conceive of Christianity most readily and easily in words, and in verbally mediated concepts such as theologies—which are essentially verbal. They defined Christianity as the adherence to these verbally expressed ideas. Their watchword was "faith." For them, to be a Christian meant to *believe* the doctrines. The verbal mode found its strongest expression in the Reformed and Lutheran churches. They were the Believers. To the extent that congregations and individuals are orthodox Calvinists or Lutherans, this is probably still quite true.

A second mode is affective or emotional. For these people, Christianity was an experience. They developed a whole system of feelings and emotionally meaningful behavior by which they defined Christianity. Communion with God, conversion exprience, and the manifestations of the Holy Spirit by way of glossolalia and faith healing were some of the significant concepts and expressions of their Christianity. To them the great watchword was not "believe," but "experience." The Pietistic movement, in which this found its strongest expression, was not very much interested in theology. They were the *"born again"* ones, the *"converted,"* and the "saved ones." They scornfully stated that the devils also believed and trembled, and that the Reformers were cold intellectuals whose religion never went beyond their hearts, because they substituted intellectual pride for humble communion. The Methodists and the Pentecostalists are among the well-known heirs of tl_is tradition, and to the extent that they are orthodox, these attitudes and expressions are rather characteristic of them.

There is little meeting of minds (or hearts) between the Reformed and the Pietists to this day. One can hear a Presbyterian say that the Methodists have never produced a good theologian in their entire history; and hear a Methodist ask what that has to do with Christianity.

The third movement of the Reformation, that of the Anabaptists, contended that ideas and beliefs had their place, and emotional communion with God was good, but that a Christian is not measured primarily by these. He is ultimately measured by his relationship with people. Faith and experience were validated in observable behavior. Their mode was activist, or perhaps more correctly, in Guilford's phrase, social-relational. A Christian, to them, was a person whose character and behavior were modeled after the example of Christ and the Apostles. Among those congregations which remain closest to the Anabaptist tradition, even to this day, a person is not admitted into membership until he has demonstrated his Christian "walk," and has the public testimony thereto by the members of the congregation. The Anabaptists' emphasis on the personalness and relational quality of Christianity rejected formal theology with outright suspicion, and instead gave every man the right and obligation to think through to his own understanding of the Scripture, and his own relationship with God. Their watchword was "be," and by this they meant "do." They were the original social workers of the Protestant church, and consistent with their teachings, also the first active pacifists. They called themselves (and still do) the Brethren.

Carried over from the older stream of Roman Catholic Christianity (which did, and still does, contain all four of these modes, expressed in its various ranks and orders) was what appears to be a fourth mode which focuses on the transcendental. There is some question about whether this should be distinguished from the affective mode, but there is evidence that they are not really the same. It expresses itself both in the liturgy of the high church ritual, and in the life of the mystic. Both the ritual and the mystic experience focus on "worship," which is the watchword of the transcendental mode. This is not the emotional, individualistically involved experience of the Pietist, but the selfless absorption into the greater, all-comprehending being of an ineffable God, wherein the individual is submerged, and it is usually a passive and receptive state. This is the "mysterium tremendum,"[10] and the "wholly other" quality of God which Rudolph Otto, the anthropologist, has so well described, and which he proposes is the common element in all religions of every kind. It may be that Guilford's mathematical processes of factor analysis did not sort out this mode because the materials with which he was working did not contain so non-verbal a set of materials. The Episcopal church preserves much of this mode of religious experience and expression in our time, but it is also to some extent the heritage of some of the Lutherans. These are the Communicants.

Time and opportunity have broadened and blended the characteristics of the major denominations. This would be expected if, as in this theory, religious experience and expression are related to personality modes. It stands to reason that persons of following generations might not have quite the same predominant personality characteristics as their ancestors, while they still remain members of the same religious denomination. Thus there would be pressure to change the character of the congregation and the denomination. (This is not to exclude the intellectual pressures which come from competing theologies within the Christian church, but to add somewhat to our understanding of why they have an appeal.) Also, in so mobile a time as ours people move around and tend to join the churches which are geographically near their new location; thus the congregations tend somewhat to lose their identity. The typical large-city congregation of today has a bewildering mixture of denominational backgrounds among its members, and probably has many more adherents whose religion is extrinsic than intrinsic (to use Allport's categories). Thus, there are probably fewer "pure" congregation or denominations than formerly.

Furthermore, these modes do not exist in all-or-nothing quantities, but are likely all present in varying degrees in all people.

The theory is that where these modes are present in a manner that makes one or another particularly dominant, and where a person has reasonable choice of his religious expression, one will find that his religious expression is positively correlated with his personality mode.

It would seem that an approach of this kind to religious experience and behavior can help to explain how Christianity achieves its diversity while retaining its recognizable essential character. It could also help us to understand somewhat more accurately the meaning of Christianity to the individual.

For the churches it might open ways of consciously planning for the religious needs of their members in a somewhat more systematic manner; and it could probably help to understand and even eliminate some of the unnecessary frictions in the Christian church which arise essentially out of personal factors rather than the nature of Christianity.

This theory is presented for discussion in the hope that it can be refined for research.

## NOTES

[1]Michael Argyle, *Religious Behavior* (The Free Press, Glencoe, Illinois, 1959), 196 pages.
[2]Gerhard Lenski, *The Religious Factor, A Sociological Study of Religion's Impact on Politics, Economics, and Family Life* (Garden City, N.Y., Doubleday and Company, Inc., 1961), 367 pages
[3]Ibid., p. 297.
[4]Gordon W. Allport, "Behavioral Science, Religion, and Mental Health" in *Journal of Religion and Health*, Vol. 2, No. 3, April 1963, pages 187-197, esp. page 193.
[5]Gordon W. Allport, "Traits Revisited," in *American Psychologist*, Vol. 21, No. 1, January 1966, p. 6.
[6]Ibid.
[7]Allport, op. cit., "Behavioral Science, Religion, and Mental Health," p. 195.
[8]Ibid., p. 195.
[9]J. P. Guilford, "A System of Primary Traits of Temperament," in *Indian Journal of Psychology*, 1959?, p. 147.
[10]Rudolph Otto, *The Idea of the Holy*.

# God-Image as a Function of Self-Esteem and Locus of Control

PETER L. BENSON AND BERNARD P. SPILKA

The purposes of this study are twofold. First, it is intended to investigate theorized relationships between self-regarding attitudes and God-images. And second, it attempts to substantiate the interpretation that the hypothesized correlations can be explained as a process of such attitudes influencing the definition of God.

Cognitive consistency theory provides the basis for predicting and explaining these relationships. Consistency theory suggests that information which implies the reverse of one's usual level of self-regard tends to create dissonance (Bramel, 1968; Smith, 1968). In order to avoid the discomfort of such dissonant cognitions, techniques like selective perception, distortion, and denial can be used to keep information consonant with one's self-image. For example, a person with high self-esteem probably finds failure and interpersonal rejection inconsistent with his beliefs that he is basically successful and likeable. Hence, he may adopt perceptual and behavioral strategies to counter these kinds of experiences. The more interesting prediction is that an individual with low self-esteem who believes he is a failure and unlikeable will find success and social approval unpleasant. Consequently, he will attempt to disconfirm or avoid success and approval in order to keep his self-image and information about himself consistent. These hypotheses have gained some research support (Bramel, 1962; Fitch, 1970; Jacobs, Berscheid & Walster, 1971; Walster, 1965).

Accordingly, persons with different levels of self-esteem may find it difficult to share the same religious beliefs. A theology predicated on a loving, accepting God is cognitively compatible with high self-

Reprinted with permission of authors and publisher from:

*Journal for the Scientific Study of Religion,* 1973, 12(3), 297-310, published by the SOCIETY FOR THE SCIENTIFIC STUDY OF RELIGION, University of Connecticut, Box U68A, Storrs, Connecticut 06268.

esteem, but it could be a source of discomfort for a believer low in self-esteem. It does not make good cognitive sense to be loved when one is unlovable. Consequently, the latter person can march to a different theology, one that is more consistent with his self-image.

Dissonance theory can also be utilized to predict how feelings of personal control influence the interpretation of the causes of one's actions. If an individual views himself as the cause of his own behavior (internal control), belief in a God who intervenes in his life would be dissonant. Hence, God then would be perceived as freeing rather than restricting, and as uncontrolling rather than controlling. Alternatively, a demanding, powerful and controlling God should be consistent with the cognition that one is not the master of his own fate (external control).

In summary, it is argued that self-regarding attitudes influence God-images. A believer selects a "god" that is consistent with power-related (locus of control) and evaluative (self-esteem) self-images. In correlational terms, it is hypothesized that:

1. Self-esteem will be positively related to loving God-images, hence
2. Self-esteem will be negatively related to rejecting or nonloving images.
3. External control will be related positively to controlling God-images.

## METHOD

If the proposed associations are substantiated on a heterogeneous religious sample (where "heterogeneous" designates existing variations in religious background among subjects), three explanations are plausible: (a) As hypothesized, self-regarding attitudes influence God-images. (b) God-images influence self-regarding attitudes. A case for this interpretation depends on the argument that initial variations in God-images originate in differences in religious training. Consequently, these training-produced beliefs may differentially affect self-concept variables. (c) The relationships between self-regarding attitudes and God-images are due to a third variable or set of variables correlated with both.

The case for (a) depends on how well alternative explanations (b) and (c) can be dismissed. Therefore, several methodological strategies were adopted as attempts to eliminate these competing interpretations. Explanation (b) is plausible if it can be posited that belief variations have origins in religious training factors. If a group of subjects (Ss) is selected who have essentially identical religious training, and if noteworthy correlations remain between self-regarding attitudes and God-images, it may be argued that these relationships are due to (*a*) or (*c*). A partial correlation analysis can be used to control a number of potential correlates of both self-regarding attitudes and the religious measures. If substantial correlations remain after this analysis, it may further be argued that alternative (*c*) above has been seriously questioned as the primary explanation for the data. Explanation (*a*) then would remain as a reasonably compelling interpretation of the results.

## Subjects

Two hundred and five male Ss attending a Catholic high school were initially tested. In order to obtain a highly homogeneous religious sample, Ss were selected from this subject pool who met the following criteria: S considered himself Catholic, both parents were Catholic, S has never been a member of a different denomination, had never associated with a non-Catholic religious organization, and had been a member of a local Catholic parish for at least the last ten years. This final criterion was adopted as a control for geographical differences in theological emphasis. In addition, only Ss who regarded religion as personally important (above the midpoint on a nine-point semantic differential item) and who designated that they believed in God (above the midpoint on a seven-point item) were used. These two items were utilized to eliminate Ss who might be religious "detractors."

One hundred and twenty-eight Ss met these criteria. The final sample had the following educational distribution: 44 Freshman, 31 Sophomores, 19 Juniors, and 34 Seniors. Mean S age was 15.4 years.

## Tests

The first 23 items were selected from Coopersmith's (1967) original 50 items to form a self-esteem scale. On a sample of 55 Catholic youth, this short form correlated highly with the other 27 items ($r = .78$). Consistent with Coopersmith's scoring procedures, each high self-esteem response was multiplied by four. Thus, the maximum score on this scale was 92. The original scale has been widely used with children and adolescents. It is concerned with self-attitudes in four areas found to be important at these age levels: peers, parents, schools, and personal interests. The short-form used in this study contains items related to each of these areas. Rotter's (1966) 23-item scale was used as a measure of internal-external control. One point accrued for each external option marked, so that the maximum score on the scale was 23. External control was designated as a high score on the scale, and internal control signified a low score.

Single items were used to obtain information regarding age, grade, father's occupation, and religious behavior. These were included to measure possible extraneous influences on the proposed personality and religion relationships. Father's occupation was used as an indicant of socioeconomic status (SES), based on procedures developed by Edwards (Miller, 1964). Occupations were categorized into one of six SES levels. From high to low status, these levels were: professional or technical, business managers or proprietors, clerical or sales workers, craftsmen or foremen, operatives, and unskilled. On this variable, a score of one was assigned to the highest status and a six was given to the lowest status. The three religious behavior items were used to measure frequency of devotion at home, frequency of religious discussions at home, and hours spent per month in church or church-related activities. Each question had six options scored 0 to 5 with 5 corresponding to the highest level of activity.

A thirteen-item semantic differential scale was developed to measure loving and controlling God-images. Scores on the following five pairs of adjectives were summed to yield a Loving God index: rejecting-accepting, loving-hating, damning-saving, unforgiving-forgiving, and approving-disapproving. Each item was scored 0 to 6. The maximum Loving God score was 30. Scores on the following five pairs of adjectives were summed to give a Controlling God index: demanding-not demanding, freeing-restricting, controlling-uncontrolling, strict-lenient, and permissive-rigid. The same scoring procedure was used, with 30 representing the maximum Controlling God score. On a sample of 50 Lutheran Ss, scale homogeneity was .72 for the Loving God scale and. 60 for the Controlling God measure.

A 64-adjective Q-sort developed by Spilka, Armatas, and Nussbaum (1964) was used to obtain other God-image measures. Scores were obtained on six factors selected from their eleven factor orthogonal solution for a sample of 200 Catholic girls. The Vindictive God factor measures a God-image that is based on such Old Testament descriptions of God as wrathful, avenging, and damning. The Stern Father factor defines God as unyielding, punishing, and restricting. Three impersonal factors measure different facets of a God who is "out there," as opposed to a God that is closely related to human affairs. The Allness factor defines this impersonal dimension in terms of God's infinite, absolute, and unchanging power and wisdom; the Distant factor defines this impersonal nature more in terms of God's inaccessibility; and the Supreme Ruler factor deals more with a majestic and sovereign God. The Kindly Father factor measures a more personal image, based on such New Testament notions as mercy, forgiveness, and patience. The Kuder-Richardson reliabilities (K-R 20) for these six factors are: Vindictive God, .60; Stern Father, .71; Impersonal Allness, .77; Impersonal Distant, .51; Impersonal Supreme Ruler, .56; and Kindly Father, .61.

Ss were tested at their school during classroom hours, and in order to elicit frank answers and assure that responses were confidential, they were not required to sign or otherwise code their test battery.

## RESULTS

### Self-esteem and God-images

As predicted (Hypothesis 1), self-esteem was significantly related to loving God-images (see Table 1). This relationship held for both the Loving God scale ($r = .51, p < .01$) and the Kindly Father factor ($r = .31, p < .01$). These two variables may be, to some degree, measuring the same beliefs. The scales are correlated ($r = .32, p < .01$) and both include "loving" and "forgiving" adjectives.

It was also hypothesized that self-esteem would be negatively related to rejecting God-images (Hypothesis 2). The obtained relationship between self-esteem and the Vindictive God factor ($r = -.49, p < .01$) confirmed this prediction. Self-esteem also correlated negatively with three other God measures, all of which were positively related to Vindictive God. These self-esteem relationships were as follows: to Impersonal Allness ($r = -.23, p < .01$), to Controlling God ($r = -.35, p < .01$), and to Stern Father ($r = -.21, p < .05$). The Vindictive God correlations to these belief measures were: to Impersonal Allness ($r = .28, p < .01$), to Controlling God ($r = .30, p < .01$) and to Stern Father ($r = .45, p < .01$). These intercorrelations suggest that impersonality, rigid control, and vindictiveness may have been to some degree perceived as dimensions or components of nonlove. Accordingly, they appeared antithetic to loving images. The negatively significant correlations between Loving God and Impersonal Allness ($r = -.32, p < .01$), Impersonal Distant ($r = -.30, p < .01$), Controlling God ($r = -.30, p < .01$), Stern Father ($r = -.21, p < .01$), and Vindictive God ($r = -.30, p < .01$) support this contention.

TABLE 1

MATRIX OF CORRELATIONS ($N = 128$)

| | 7 | 8 | 9 | 10 | 11 | 12 | 13 | 14 | 15 | 16 |
|---|---|---|---|---|---|---|---|---|---|---|
| 1. Age | 02[1] | 07 | − 16 | 14 | − 06 | − 06 | 14 | 02 | − 04 | − 01 |
| 2. Grade | 06 | 06 | − 15 | 19* | − 10 | − 04 | 11 | − 04 | 01 | − 05 |
| 3. Frequency of devotions | 12 | − 30** | 34** | 01 | − 05 | − 03 | − 09 | − 12 | 15 | − 08 |
| 4. Frequency of religious discussions | 19* | − 18* | 23* | − 14 | − 02 | − 01 | − 05 | 04 | 06 | 01 |
| 5. Church hours per month | 09 | − 19* | 19* | − 04 | − 06 | − 04 | − 07 | − 10 | 10 | − 07 |
| 6. SES | − 05 | 25** | − 02 | − 11 | 14 | 02 | 04 | − 01 | − 14 | 08 |
| 7. Self-esteem | | − 32** | 51** | − 35** | − 49** | − 21* | − 23** | − 17* | 31** | − 18* |
| 8. Internal-external control | | | − 28** | 02 | 23** | 10 | 18* | 16 | − 14 | 12 |
| 9. Loving God | | | | − 30** | − 30** | − 21* | − 32** | − 30** | 32** | − 06 |
| 10. Controlling God | | | | | 30** | 31** | 09 | − 17 | − 22* | 02 |
| 11. Vindictive God | | | | | | 45** | 28** | 13 | − 33** | 17 |
| 12. Stern Father | | | | | | | 13 | 17 | − 07 | − 16 |
| 13. Impersonal: Allness | | | | | | | | 07 | − 46** | 20* |
| 14. Impersonal: Distant | | | | | | | | | − 13 | − 07 |
| 15. Kindly Father | | | | | | | | | | − 47** |
| 16. Impersonal: Supreme Ruler | | | | | | | | | | |

[1]Decimal points not presented
*Significant at .05 level
**Significant at .01 level

Self-esteem was also correlated negatively with Impersonal Distant ($r = -.17, p < .05$) and Impersonal Supreme Ruler ($r = -.18$, $p < .05$). Overall, self-esteem was significantly related to all eight God measures. The pattern suggests that self-esteem is related positively to loving images and negatively to rejecting-impersonal-controlling views, thereby supporting both Hypotheses 1 and 2.

## Locus of control and God-images

The data do not support Hypothesis 3. Locus of control was un-related to the Controlling God scale ($r = .02$). It was, however, significantly related to three other measures: with Loving God ($r = -.28$, $p < .01$), Vindictive God ($r = .23$, $p < .01$), and Impersonal Allness ($r = .18, p < .05$). In all three instances, the direction of the relationship is opposite that obtained with self-esteem. One possible explanation is that a high score on the locus of control measure, which is an external orientation, is a measure of low self-esteem. The negative and significant relationship between self-esteem and locus of control ($r = -.32, p < .01$) tentatively supports this interpretation. It is also possible that the Controlling God scale is more sensitive to a loving-nonloving dimension than to a controlling-noncontrolling one. The intercorrelations among the scales support this contention. For example, the Controlling God index correlated negatively with both Loving God ($r = -.30, p < .01$) and Kindly Father ($r = -.22, p < .05$), and positively with Vindictive God ($r = .30, p < .01$) and Stern Father ($r = .31, p < .01$).

## Self-esteem, locus of control, and religious behavior

The three religious behavior items were related to internal control and one was associated positively with self-esteem. Frequency of religious discussion correlated with both self-esteem ($r = .19, p < .05$) and internal control ($r = -.18, p < .05$). Frequency of devotions ($r = -.30, p < .01$) and hours spent in church activities ($r = -.19, p < .05$) were both significantly related to internal control.

## Controlling for demographic variables and religious behavior

The reported results were obtained on a sample of Ss with highly similar backgrounds. Many theorists would argue that such Ss should espouse parallel beliefs. However, as the data indicate, beliefs vary with self-regarding attitudes. The structure of the sample, however, suggests that self-regarding attitudes may be more responsible for these variations than are teaching or training factors.

It could be that self-regarding attitudes and God-images are the common effects of a third variable or set of variables. Age, SES, or educational level may play such a role. Also, the quantity (frequency) or location of religious exposure can influence the relationships. In order to add support to the interpretation that self-regarding attitudes probably influence God-images, these variables are controlled via partial correlational means. Table 1 indicates the variables that should be partialled. Four that correlated with both self-esteem and a number of religious measures are: frequency of devotions, frequency of discussions, hours spent per month in church or church-related activities, and locus of control. Of these, frequency of discussions ($r = .19, p < .05$) and locus of control ($r = -.32, p < .01$) correlate significantly with self-esteem. While the relationships to church hours ($r = .09$) and frequency of devotions ($r = .12$) did not attain the .05 level of significance, they may still account for some of the variance shared by self-esteem and the religious variables. Partialling the above four variables affords a look at self-esteem and religious variable relationships when the influence of these correlates has been removed. It should also be noted that these indices do not correlate with all eight religious measures. Rather, the three behavior items correlated only with Loving

God. It is on this variable that partial correlations are most crucial for questioning explanations that the personality and religion relationships are spurious. However, the removal of these four correlates from self-esteem in those cases where their relationship to religious measures is minimal is quite useful. In these situations, partial correlation techniques clarify the amount of variance that is uniquely shared by self-esteem and the religious variables. In essence, a partial correlation in such cases reduces to a part correlation. Age, grade, and SES did not correlate significantly with self-esteem. While it is doubtful that extracting these variables will lead to noteworthy changes in the self-esteem-religious variable correlations, doing so reveals whether these measures function as "suppressors." Since in a few cases grade and SES correlate negatively (though nonsignificantly) with the religious variables, they may possibly suppress the self-esteem-religion relationships. Age and grade are highly correlated in this sample (.95); thus controlling for grade level essentially controls for age.

Table 1 also reveals that the locus of control and religious variable relationships could be influenced by six variables. Four that correlated with both locus of control and with some of the religious variables are frequency of devotions, frequency of discussions, hours spent in church, and self-esteem. These were also submitted to a partial correlation analysis. A fifth variable, SES, correlated significantly with locus of control, but with none of the religious measures. A partial analysis of this variable functions primarily to remove SES from locus of control. Grade level was also partialled out for reasons similar to the case with self-esteem discussed above.

In summary, six variables were partialled from self-esteem and the religious measures, and from internal-external control and the same indices. If relationships between the self-regarding attitudes and the religious measures exist after the partial correlation analysis, it can be argued that the explanation that the associations are spurious has been seriously questioned. However, a note of caution is in order. Two factors make it invalid to dismiss the "spurious" explanation in any absolute sense. First, the partial correlation does not simply represent the correlation between two variables when a third variable has been held constant. Rather, it can be interpreted "as a weighted average of the correlation coefficients that would have been obtained had the control variable been divided into very small intervals and separate correlations computed within each of the categories" (Blalock, 1972: 436). Therefore, the resulting partial correlation is affected by the ranges of the scores obtained on the controlled variables. In the present study, these ranges may have been restricted by the characteristics of the subjects sampled. Therefore, if relationships exist after the partials, it can only be said that the variables were controlled within certain restricted boundaries. Second, since only six variables were partialled in each analysis, other uninvestigated variables could possibly affect the self-regarding attitude and religion associations. Obviously, it is impossible to absolutely dismiss a "spurious" explanation of the data, since it is impossible to control for all correlates. At best, it can be argued that the variables actually controlled in a study were the ones that could have the greatest influence, based on theoretical or empirical information.

## Self-esteem and God-images

Tables 2 and 3 contain the results that emerge from these statistical controls. Before the partial correlation analysis, self-esteem was related significantly to all eight God measures. After all six variables (internal-external control, frequency of discussions, frequency of devotions, church participation rates, SES and grade) were removed, self-esteem remained significantly related to six measures. Relationships to Impersonal Distant and Impersonal Supreme Ruler did not attain the .05 level of significance. In both instances, however, the amount of shared variance declined negligibly. This suggests that these relationships were in fact minimal before the partial analysis was undertaken. The Loving God and self-esteem relationship changed from .51 to .47, indicating that the amount of shared variance fell from 26 percent to 22 percent. The correlation remains significant at the .01 level.

In all other cases the reduction in shared variance was 3 percent or less. Overall, it appears that the partialling of these six variables did not appreciably affect the original relationships. This could have been expected for all associations other than that of self-esteem and Loving God. In these other situations, the original correlations between the God measure and the partialled variables were small. Potentially, the greatest change could have involved Loving God since four of the six partialled variables correlated with this variable. Nevertheless this relationship remained intact.

P. L. Benson and B. P. Spilka

## TABLE 2

CORRELATIONS BETWEEN SELF-ESTEEM AND RELIGIOUS VARIABLES WHEN THE FOLLOWING VARIABLES HAVE BEEN REMOVED: FREQUENCY OF DEVOTIONS AT HOME; FREQUENCY OF RELIGIOUS DISCUSSIONS AT HOME; HOURS SPENT PER MONTH IN CHURCH OR CHURCH-RELATED ACTIVITIES; I-E, SES, GRADE

| Religious Variable | Before Partials | After Partials on all Variables | After Devotions Discussions and Attendance Removed | After Devotions Discussions Attendance and I-E Removed | After Devotions Discussions Attendance I-E and SES Removed |
|---|---|---|---|---|---|
| Loving God | .51** (.26)[1] | .47** (.22) | .49** (.24) | .46** (.21) | .46** (.21) |
| Controlling God | -.35** (.12) | -.37** (.14) | -.33** (.11) | -.34** (.12) | -.34** (.12) |
| Vindictive God | -.49** (.24) | -.46** (.21) | -.49** (.24) | -.46** (.21) | -.46** (.21) |
| Stern Father | -.21* (.04) | -.19* (.04) | -.21* (.04) | -.19* (.04) | -.19* (.04) |
| Impersonal: Allness | -.23** (.05) | -.20* (.04) | -.22* (.05) | -.19* (.04) | -.19* (.04) |
| Impersonal: Distant | -.17* (.03) | -.14 (.02) | -.17* (.03) | -.15 (.02) | -.14 (.02) |
| Kindly Father | .31** (.10) | .29** (.09) | .30** (.09) | .29** (.09) | .29** (.09) |
| Impersonal: Supreme Ruler | -.18* (.03) | -.15 (.02) | -.18* (.03) | -.15 (.02) | -.16 (.03) |

[1]Squared correlation coefficient
*Significant at .05 level
**Significant at .01 level

Self-esteem remains positively correlated with Loving God ($r = .47, p < .01$) and Kindly Father ($r = .29, p < .01$) and negatively with Controlling God ($r = -.37, p < .01$), Vindictive God ($r = -.46, p < .01$), Stern Father ($r = -.19, p < .05$), and Impersonal Allness ($r = -.20, p < .05$). These data, then, are consistent with the hypothesis that self-esteem influences these God-images. The influence can be understood in terms of both loving and nonloving images. It can be argued that this is a reasonable explanation since the data were obtained on subjects with highly similar backgrounds after a number of correlates were controlled.

TABLE 3

CORRELATIONS BETWEEN INTERNAL-EXTERNAL CONTROL AND RELIGIOUS
VARIABLES WHEN THE FOLLOWING VARIABLES HAVE BEEN REMOVED:
FREQUENCY of DEVOTIONS AT HOME; FREQUENCY OF RELIGIOUS DISCUSSIONS
AT HOME; HOURS SPENT PER MONTH IN CHURCH OR CHURCH-RELATED
ACTIVITIES; SELF-ESTEEM, SES, GRADE

| Religious Variable | Before Partials | After Partials on all Variables | After Devotions, Discussions, Attendance Removed | After Devotions, Discussions, Attendance, and Self-esteem Removed | After Devotions, Discussions, Attendance, Self-esteem, and SES Removed |
|---|---|---|---|---|---|
| Loving God | -.28** | -.07 | -.18* | -.05 | -.06 |
|  | (.07)[1] | (.00) | (.03) | (.00) | (.00) |
| Controlling God | -.02 | -.07 | -.01 | -.10 | -.08 |
|  | (.00) | (.00) | (.00) | (.01) | (.01) |
| Vindictive God | .23** | .07 | .22* | .10 | .07 |
|  | (.05) | (.00) | (.05) | (.01) | (.00) |
| Stern Father | .10 | .04 | .10 | .04 | .04 |
|  | (.01) | (.00) | (.01) | (.00) | (.00) |
| Impersonal: Allness | .18* | .10 | .15 | .10 | .09 |
|  | (.03) | (.01) | (.02) | (.01) | (.01) |
| Impersonal: Distant | .16 | .09 | .13 | .08 | .09 |
|  | (.03) | (.01) | (.02) | (.01) | (.01) |
| Kindly Father | -.14 | .02 | -.09 | -.01 | .02 |
|  | (.02) | (.00) | (.01) | (.00) | (.00) |
| Impersonal: Supreme Ruler | .12 | .04 | .10 | .05 | .04 |
|  | (.01) | (.00) | (.01) | (.00) | (.00) |

[1]Squared correlation coefficient
*Significant at .05 level
**Significant at .01 level

## Locus of Control and God-images

The partial correlation analysis was more influential in the case
of locus of control and God-belief relationships. Before the analysis,
locus of control was significantly correlated with three of the measures,
although not with Controlling God as predicted. After the analysis, all
three relationships failed to reach the .05 level of significance. The
original associations with loving God, Vindictive God, and Impersonal
Allness reduce to .10 or less. Table 3 shows that the removal of self-
esteem after the initial removal of the three religious behavior items
was most responsible for these changes. This step accounted for a 3
percent reduction in the variance originally shared by locus of control
and Loving God, and a 4 percent reduction in variance shared with
Vindictive God. Self-esteem may therefore be an important component

**219**

of locus of control. In summary, it does not appear that locus of control influences God-images, at least as they are measured in this study.

## DISCUSSION

The major finding of this study is that self-esteem is related positively to loving God-images and negatively to rejecting-impersonal-controlling definitions of God. Furthermore, it is argued that the data provide some support for the explanation that self-esteem is a major determinant of God-images. This interpretation was made after a consideration of the alternatives. By obtaining the results on Ss with nearly identical religious training, it was posited that a "belief influencing personality" position was seriously questioned as the primary explanation for the findings. And by partialling variables dealing with internal-external control, SES, grade, and frequency of participation in religious activities, it was further suggested that explanations based on the premise that both self-esteem and God-images were the common effects of other variables were considerably weakened.

By the processes of elimination, then, it seems appropriate to argue that self-esteem influences God-images. Several other explanations of the data need to be investigated, and refuted, in order to maximize the credibility of this position. Other religious training factors need to be controlled. Differences in parish emphases, teachers, clergy, and reading material could possibly affect beliefs, which in turn influence self-esteem. Parents and peers may influence both God-images and self-esteem. For example, rejecting parents might induce low self-esteem, and as previous research suggests (Siegman, 1961; Strunk, 1959), Ss may define God in terms similar to the way they view their parents (which could include a rejecting image in this case). It may also be true that those with low self-esteem engage in problem behaviors which elicit from parents and other authorities fear-provoking religious concepts used in an attempt to control the behavior. Accordingly, these Ss could receive a different religious "treatment" than those with high self-esteem. Thus, low self-esteem could be paired with rejecting God concepts.

While such processes may influence God-images and self-esteem in certain individual cases, it is proposed that they are not of sufficient general strength to account for any large portion of shared variance between self-esteem and God-images in a relatively large sample.

Other issues need to be raised. While the reported data suggest a broad interpretation of self-esteem influencing God-images, the results do not provide many details about the relationship. Table 4 presents frequencies and percentages of Loving God scale scores at three levels of self-esteem. The average scale score among all 128 Ss was 25.3. Ss were divided into low, medium, and high levels of self-esteem. The first row shows that 79 percent of the "highs" scored above the mean (scale score of 26-30) while only 30 percent of the "lows" scored similarly. A chi square performed on scores above and below the mean suggests that "highs" tend to perceive God as significantly more loving than "lows" ($X^2 = 21.45, p <.001$). Additionally, scores below 20 occurred only in the "low" group. Twenty-eight percent of the "lows" scored between nine and 20 points. Twenty-three percent of the "highs" and only 5 percent of the "lows" scored the maximum 30 points.

TABLE 4

FREQUENCIES AND PERCENTAGES OF LOVING GOD SCALE SCORES
AT THREE LEVELS OF SELF-ESTEEM

| Loving God Scale Score ($\overline{X} = 25.3$) | Level of Self-esteem | | |
| --- | --- | --- | --- |
| | Low N = 43 | Medium N = 42 | High N = 43 |
| Above 25.3 | 13 (30%)[1] | 26 (62%) | 34 (79%) |
| Below 25.3 | 30 (70%) | 16 (38%) | 9 (21%) |
| 30 (Maximum scale score) | 2 ( 5%) | 5 (12%) | 10 (23%) |
| Below 20 | 12 (28%) | 0 | 0 |
| Mean Scale Score | 22.40 | 26.21 | 27.23 |

[1]Percentage of total N in the corresponding self-esteem level
$x^2 = 21.45, p <.001$. Computed on the first two rows.

The combination of these figures and the previously cited correlations suggests that a majority of Ss tend to perceive God in a way that is congruent with self-image. Some God-images, however, do not fit this consistency pattern. Twenty-three percent of the "lows" score above 26 points. This may indicate that some Ss are motivated to attain approval rather than consistency. Persons with high self-esteem can meet consistency and approval needs simultaneously, while persons with low self-esteem find these needs in conflict. A highly accepting God communicates approval, while a more rejecting God preserves consistency. In this context, it would be important to explicate what factors determine which option is chosen, and whether or not these needs operate for the same S in different situations.

Interpreting how individuals actually develop these God-images is difficult. Several possibilities exist. "Highs" may internalize the preached axioms of a given theology. Accordingly, "lows" then tend to change or modify this theology to conform more consistently with their self-images. It could also be, however, that individuals are exposed to a variety of religious teachings. These teachings could variously present God as loving and punishing, supernatural and immanent, warm and impersonal. Thus, the believer may select the set of preached God-images which is most consistent.

The nonsignificant correlations between locus of control and God beliefs merit discussion. Rotter's (1966) scale defines external control in terms of luck, fate, and chance. While it seems reasonable to argue that one who places his fate in God's hands is externally controlled, he may find that options phrased in luck and chance terminology are irrevelant. Relationships between locus of control and God-images could have been masked by this measurement problem.

The consequences of holding a controlling God-image warrants further research. Belief in a God who controls the destiny of human events may lead an individual to view his own behavior as inconsequential for social change. Seeman's (1959) work on alienation implies that external control and powerlessness are conceptually similar. This may partially explain why some church members refuse to engage in social action and conform to approved expectations in order to gain some feeling of control.

## SOME IMPLICATIONS

It has often been charged that religious individuals use religion for purposes of comfort—at the expense of challenging and changing the secular world (Glock, Ringer & Babbie, 1967). If this criticism is valid, where should the blame be placed?

One possible explanation lies in the conservative emphasis of religious institutions. As O'Dea (1966) has indicated, organized institutions tend to be concerned with stability and continuity. In the service of self-maintenance, such institutions attempt to avoid conflict. Consequently, members may learn that a life of faith is personal and not social. Theology can be presented to justify such a nonsocial orientation.

The data from the present study, however, suggest that the problem may also have its source in the psychological processes of the individual. Low self-esteem may lead one to resist a loving God and a compassionate ethical orientation, even when both are emphasized in a particular institutional setting. Assuming that self-esteem influences the content of religious beliefs, we can hypothesize that religious belief functions in part to maintain or preserve one's level of self-esteem. Belief justifies good or bad self-images, providing relief from the struggle to find meaningful explanations for one's identity. One's self-esteem level affects what can and cannot be accepted as a tenent of faith. Church members with high self-esteem can understand and appreciate a loving, accepting God—and may also apply principles of love and acceptance to various social settings. Persons with low self-esteem, however, find both God and ethics based on love and acceptance as uncomfortably inconsistent. Consequently, their needs lead them to replace these images with a more rejecting God who does not command a loving orientation to the world. Thus, some of the social complacency attributed to church members may reflect personal inhibitions rather than church policy. This problem may be immense if, as previous research indicates, self-concept variables correlate negatively with religious attitudes and involvement (Cowen, 1954; Strunk, 1958).

While such an inference implies that level of self-esteem is an antecedent to specific belief content, it should be recognized that theology might (if known by the member) also influence self-concept. Perhaps self-concept and belief are antinomously related, where there is continual interaction between these variables.

## CONCLUSION

These findings and inferences must be regarded as tentative pending further investigation. It should be recognized that the present study is only a beginning in establishing and explaining personality-religion relationships. Future research should strive to utilize theoretical models and methodological designs which make both the causes and consequences of religiosity more understandable. By explicating when and how personality influences religion and when and how religion influences personality, the scientific study of religion will have produced findings that are of both theoretical and practical use for understanding the dynamics of personal religion.

### REFERENCES

BLALOCK, HUBERT M. 1972 *Social Statistics*. New York: McGraw-Hill.
BRAMEL, D. 1962 "A dissonance theory approach to defensive projection." *Journal of Abnormal and Social Psychology* 64: 121-129. 1968 "Dissonance, expectation, and the self." Pp. 355-366 in R. P. Abelson, E. Aronson, W. J. McGuire, T. M. Newcomb, M. J. Rosenberg, and P. H. Tannenbaum (eds.), *Theories of Cognitive Consistency: A Sourcebook*. Chicago: Rand McNally.

## P. L. Benson and B. P. Spilka

COOPERSMITH, S. 1967 *The Antecedents of Self-Esteem.* San Francisco: Freeman.

COWEN, E. L. 1954 "The negative concept as a personality measure." *Journal of Consulting Psychology* 18: 138-142.

FITCH, G. 1970 "Effects of self-esteem, perceived performance, and choice on causal attributions. *Journal of Personality and Social Psychology* 16: 311-315.

GLOCK, C. Y., B. B. RINGER, AND E. R. BABBIE 1967 *To Comfort and to Challenge: A Dilemma of the Contemporary Church.* Berkeley: University of California Press.

JACOBS, L., E. BERSCHEID, AND E. WALSTER 1971 "Self-esteem and attraction." *Journal of Personality and Social Psychology* 17:84-91.

MILLER, D. C. 1964 *Handbook of Research Design and Social Measurement.* New York: McKay.

O'DEA, THOMAS F. 1966 *The Sociology of Religion.* Engelwood Cliffs, N.J.: Prentice-Hall.

ROTTER, J. B. 1966 "Generalized expectancies for internal versus external control of reinforcement." *Psychological Monographs* 80 (1, Whole No. 609).

SEEMAN, MELVIN 1959 "On the meaning of alienation." *American Sociological Review* 24: 783-790.

SIEGMAN, A. W. 1961 "An empirical investigation of the psychoanalytic theory of religious behavior." *Journal for the Scientific Study of Religion* 1: 74-78.

SMITH, M. BREWSTER 1968 "The self and cognitive consistency." Pp. 366-373 in R. P. Abelson, E. Aronson, W. J. McGuire, T. M. Newcomb, M. J. Rosenberg, and P. H. Tannenbaum (eds.), *Theories of Cognitive Consistency: A Sourcebook.* Chicago: Rand McNally.

SPILKA, BERNARD, P. ARMATAS AND J. NUSSBAUM 1964 "The concept of God: A factor-analytic approach." *Review of Religious Research* 6: 28-36.

STRUNK, ORLO, JR. 1958 "Relation between self-reports and adolescent religiosity." *Psychological Reports* 4: 683-686. 1959 "Perceived relationships between parental and deity concepts." *Psychological Newsletter* 10: 222-226.

WALSTER, E. 1965 "The effect of self-esteem on romantic liking." *Journal of Experimental Social Psychology* 1: 184-197.

# RELIGIOUS EXPERIENCE

# Introduction

## H. NEWTON MALONY

What is it like to be religious? Is the experience different from all other events? How does one know if he is experiencing religion? Is there a special religious sense? These have been significant questions for the psychologist since the time of William James.

Clark has long been interested in the mystical experience. He sees it as the essence of religion, and his article reports research of his own on the "triggers" of religious experience. He also surveys what several modern psychologists, such as Freud and Jung, have written on the subject.

Kildahl compares the psychological background of two types of religious persons—those who were suddenly converted and those who experienced gradual religious development. This is a continuation of interest in William James' "once-born" and "twice-born" individuals.

One widely held opinion has been that conversion is related to crisis. Manifest anxiety (one index of crisis) should, therefore, be higher at the time of religious conversion. Spellman, Baskett, and Byrne investigate this possibility in their article.

Scroggs and Douglas summarize the evidence about conversion experience in answer to a number of strategic questions: (1) What is conversion? (2) Is conversion pathological? (3) Is one personality more likely to be converted than another? (4) Does conversion tend to occur at a certain age? (5) Can conversion be manipulated or striven for? (6) Can psychology fully describe conversion?

This portion of the book will introduce the student to the psychological study of religious experience. Though religious experience cannot be fully explained, it is apparent that it can be better understood.

# The Psychology of Religious Experience

## WALTER HOUSTON CLARK

A few years ago an inconspicuous member of one of my classes sought me out. The mother of a family, she told me about a religious experience of a mystical nature, a story she had confided to no other living person. Not understanding it, except in its general nature, I listened sympathetically but gave no advice. But the incident seemed to set in motion a psychological and religious process of surprising proportions. Shortly afterward she became more active in her church. Now others seek her out to take leadership in discussion groups, and, to her embarrassment, church members refer problems to her that, more appropriately, should go to the pastor. Besides being much more forceful, she is more attractive, and she herself is amazed to find that she is becoming a positive force for good in the community and in her family instead of just another aging housewife.

This is an illustration in a commonplace, contemporary person of the influence that religion may have in the transformation of personality. I have seen and studied such phenomena in ordinary men and women, and in many persons undergoing a religious experience under psychedelic drugs. The psychological study of religion is as fascinating as man himself, and as compelling as his fascination with God.

We have records of something happening in the personalities of eminent men and women of history—Socrates, Moses, the Buddha, St. Paul, St. Francis, Teresa of Avila, the French mathematician Pascal, John Wesley, and Jesus. In large part, it was to seek the source of this power in scores of intense souls that William James wrote his great treatise, *The Varieties of Religious Experience,* certainly the most notable of all books in the field of the psychology of religion and probably

Reprinted by permission of the author and publisher from:

*Psychology Today* Magazine, February 1968, Copyright© 1967 Ziff-Davis Publishing Company. All rights reserved.

destined to be the most influential book written on religion in the twentieth century.

It is a paradox that, in view of such evidence, modern psychologists should be so incurious about the dynamics involved and so neglectful of a force in human nature with the influence religion has for both good and evil in human personality and human history. Since the time of William James, the psychological study of religion has fallen on dull days. In our day, its prestige has gradually begun to revive, but the conventional psychologist still tends to observe it warily as a subject that he is not quite sure belongs in his field.

And this is not hard to understand. In the 1920's, behaviorism was obtaining a firm grip on psychology. The aim of shaping psychology into another natural science still seemed to be within reach if all psychologists would only agree to neglect the mind and to confine themselves to a study of environmental stimuli and its resulting behavior.

But religion, particularly if one wishes to probe its depths and make sense of it, requires the study of the inner life more than almost any other human activity. With its close associations to theology and philosophy (more universally acknowledged in William James' day, incidentally), considering the psychology of religion as a natural science seems far from ideal.

By far the most interesting, instructive, and yet puzzling phenomenon of religious experience is the mystical one. I would agree with William James that "personal religious experience has its root and center in mystical states of consciousness." This characteristic seems to me to separate religious consciousness from other forms of consciousness. All other aspects of the religious life have their counterparts in man's secular life. A mystical state alone is *sui generis* and is so different from any other psychological state that subjectively it is seldom mistaken for anything other than religion. A mystical state produces a particular kind of perception involving what is probably the most intense positive psychological experience known to man. It may be compared to romantic love. Yet mystics, in order to serve God, have been known to desert their possessions, their previous ways of life, and those whom they love. It is the very differentness of mysticism that causes trouble for the mystic. He finds no words to explain exactly what he has experienced unless he is talking to other mystics. Thus the mystic is often a lonely person, keeping within himself the expression of his pearl of great price, the thing that gives meaning to his life.

The psychologist, unless he is a mystic himself (which he seldom is), is forced to rely on the words of the mystic to describe the experience, though he also notes the sharp changes in behavior that frequently accompany mystical states. The feature most often reported and which seems to be at the core of the experience is a perception of unity, accompanied also by a sense of timelessness, of holiness, and by the feeling that one has directly encountered ultimate reality accompanied by a sense of great peace. It would be easy for the psychologist to pass off this strange state of ecstasy as just another aberration, were it not for the wholesome changes of personality that often follow it. Certainly, even if such transformations do not occur every day, one might suppose that a thorough study of them at least would throw some light on the nature of personality change and human creativity.

In the study of religious experience and personality change, I will venture to mention a controversial but incomparable tool for the study of this elusive area—psychedelic drugs. Formerly I was extremely critical of the religious value of the drugs. However, I have experimented on myself and have had an opportunity to participate with others in research. My conclusions were not unlike those of William James after he had tried nitrous oxide, the psychedelic of his day. He said:

> One conclusion . . . is that our normal waking consciousness, rational consciousness as we call it, is but one special type of consciousness, whilst all about it, parted by the filmiest of screens, there lie potential forms of consciousness entirely different. . . . We may go through life without suspecting their existence; but . . . no account of the universe in its totality can be final which leaves these other forms of consciousness quite disregarded. . . . My own experiences . . . all converge towards a kind of insight to which I cannot help ascribing some metaphysical significance.

Certainly if the psychedelics do not release genuine religious experiences, then the differences are so subtle that even religious experts cannot tell the difference, apart from knowing that a drug has been involved. The experiment that did the most to convince me that the psychedelics triggered mysticism was the following: Dr. Walter N. Pahnke, in a Harvard doctoral study, set up nine criteria of mystical experience using principally those of Princeton's expert, W. T. Stace, and William James. He then gave 30 milligrams of psilocybin to ten theological students, and to ten others he gave a placebo. None of the 20 were informed which they had received. All of them then attended the same Good Friday service. In their descriptions after the service, nine of the ten who had been given the drug reported unmistakable characteristics of mystical phenomena, while only one who had taken the placebo did, and his reaction was very mild.

What further supports many psychedelic experiences as being religious is that, when the subject reports a religious experience, therapeutic results are often more marked. This was the case with pioneer experiments in which massive doses of LSD were given to hopeless alcoholics in Saskatchewan by Humphrey Osmond and Abram Hoffer. After five years, half of the sample of 60 cases were still found to be nonalcoholic. "As a general rule," Hoffer reported, "those who have not had the transcendental experience are not changed; they continue to drink. However, the large-proportion of those who have had it are changed."

There also has been experimentation with criminals in Europe and the United States. In order to find out for myself what the results had been, I studied several convicts to whom Dr. Timothy Leary had given psilocybin and who, according to his report, had encountered religious experiences of a life-changing nature. Some of these convicts definitely had fallen by the wayside—through lack of follow-up after the controversial Leary project collapsed.

But I discovered a rather remarkable phenomenon. Those who had remained in jail had started what they called the "Self-Development Group," a very successful AA type of self-rehabilitation that continued on a nondrug basis. One middle-aged armed robber, serving a twenty-year term, in a drug session had seen a vision of Christ. Shortly afterward, he said, "All my life came before my eyes, and I said, 'What a waste!' " Now, five years later, this man, a group leader, is considered by the authorities to be completely rehabilitated.

The point of these experiments is that not only do subjects, after psychedelic therapy, talk like religious people but religion for them has had the effect of radically changing their values and attitudes. The drugs seem to do what the churches frequently only *say* they do in their talk of salvation, redemption, and rebirth. All this is not to minimize the real dangers and problems of the drugs, but to call attention to certain facts that have not appeared often in the news media and to point out the connection of the drugs with religion.

The psychologist of religion faces some formidable problems. Even the definition of religion is a matter of great dispute. Several years ago I asked a number of experts in the field of the scientific study of religion to define what they meant by the word *religion*. Of 68 replies, no two were exactly alike, and even when replies were grouped, the categories differed. This is hardly a happy situation for a discipline making any pretense to being a science.

Yet the psychology of religion is beginning to emerge from its long period of exile. Strangely enough, this discipline of psychology owes its emergence in no small measure to another genius who held religion in much lower esteem than did James. That man was Sigmund Freud, who was able to seduce large numbers of modern scientific psychologists through his own scientific background and through his insistence, which at least in his early days seemed completely sincere, that he was strictly a scientist and nothing more.

Actually, to an extent that Freud himself did not realize, he was an artist of the human soul. While his observations involved close study of the lives of his patients, his intuitions and speculations went far beyond pedestrian reports of stimuli and responses to them—the responses, of course, and some of the stimuli as well, being merely the products of his patients' inner lives. Aided by a clarity of style hardly matched in such a complex field, Freud opened the doors for many behaviorists to the study of man's subjectivity, whose studies and writing were thereby enriched. As examples I might mention the followers of the Yale behaviorist Clark Hull—men like John Dollard, Neal Miller, and O. Hobart Mowrer.

More directly, Freud set an example through his own writings on religion—through books like *Totem and Taboo, The Future of an Illusion,* and *Moses and Monotheism.* He dealt with religion as merely the search for a father image and as "the universal neurosis of mankind." But he wrote more about religion than any other single subject except sex. That this interest may have had its roots in the connection of his forebears with Jewish mysticism is suggested in a volume by David Bakan. Then Freud occasionally alarmed some of his close followers after conversations lasting into the early hours when he said he had times when he could almost bring himself to believe in many things, even "der liebe Gott!" Certainly this interest has led many Freudians and neo-Freudians to think and write of religion.

One of the most influential of the latter was the Swiss psychiatrist Carl G. Jung, whom Freud at one time had designated as his successor. Though a more obscure writer than Freud, Jung was more positively and openly religious. It was he who declared that, among his patients over the age of 35, there were none whose problems did not have their roots in religion. Like Freud, he found the principal roots of religion in the unconscious, especially in what he called the racial unconscious, by which he explained the universal aspects of much religious symbolism.

Somewhat nearer to the orthodox academic psychological tradition in America have been several scholars, all presidents of the American Psychological Association in their day, who have written on the subject, though none has worked in the psychology of religion as his major field. The list includes Gardner Murphy, the late Gordon Allport, O. Hobart Mowrer, and Abraham H. Maslow. Of these, perhaps Allport did most toward making the subject academically respectable, through his volume of lectures, *The Individual and His Religion*. Maslow includes religion among the "peak experiences" that are the fruits of what he calls B-cognition, the source of human creativity.

A somewhat different influence on the psychology of religion, one especially strong in theological schools and churches, has been exerted by clinical pastoral psychology. This movement in the United States has had an interesting history.

In the early 1920's a middle-aged clergyman, considering his life a failure, was hospitalized with the diagnosis of catatonic schizophrenia. Through his stay in the hospital, he became convinced of the need of many mental patients for adequate pastoral care. On his recovery, after some difficulty with conventional administrative ideas as to the value of religion for mental patients, he persuaded Dr. James A. Bryan, Superintendent of Worcester State Hospital in Massachusetts, to appoint him the first chaplain at a mental hospital in this country. Shortly after his appointment, the chaplain persuaded several theological students to study the ministry to the mentally ill under his direction.

Thus started the clinical pastoral counseling movement in the theological schools, a training now required in at least one-third of the Protestant theological schools and in some form optional with most other seminaries, including many of the Catholic and Jewish seminaries as well. The clergyman who started it all was Anton T. Boisen, who died a few years ago at the Elgin State Hospital in Illinois, where he was Chaplain Emeritus, honored and lamented by thousands of students and patients.

About the time that Boisen began his ministry to the mentally ill, one of the first of a long line of volumes in the field of religion and mental health appeared—*Pastoral Psychiatry and Mental Health*, by James Rathbone Oliver, both a psychiatrist and a clergyman. One of the most articulate contemporary writers in this field is Seward Hiltner of Princeton Theological Seminary. However, recently authors in religion have multiplied themselves in so many volumes that they have become increasingly repetitive and even boring.

There has been a fringe benefit, however, in enrichment for clinical psychology. Theologians usually not noted for their attention to the practical or empirical have been forced to take some notice of mental health and of the fact that the clinician may often lead his patient to consider matters of "ultimate concern." The best-known theologian to encourage dialogue with therapists was the late Paul Tillich, particularly in his book, *The Courage to Be*. And the greats in psychology all have responded to his dialogue. There are recordings of conversations with Carl Rogers, Hobart Mowrer, Erich Fromm, and with the man who perhaps was Tillich's closest friend, Rollo May.

But let us look again at Anton Boisen in another way. One of the striking facts in the lives of many great religious leaders has been abnormality, which sometimes has grown into full-blown psychosis. Ezekiel's visions of complicated flying beasts and "wheels within wheels" are only darkly understandable, while some of Jeremiah's words and actions mark him as, at the very least, a peculiar fellow. At one time Jesus' family and friends spoke of him as "beside himself," while George Fox, founder of the Society of Friends, probably would have been hospitalized in this day and age. William James discusses this subject in the first chapter of his *Varieties*. Of Boisen's psychic instability there is no doubt. He acknowledged it himself, and the records of the diagnosis and his stay still remain at Worcester State Hospital in Massachusetts.

His sickness gave him an incomparable opportunity to observe a psychosis from the inside. In addition to this, having a scholarly cast of mind, as he recovered he had an opportunity to observe his fellow sufferers and to reflect on his observations. The result was his *Exploration of the Inner World,* a contemporary minor classic filled with original observations on the nature of schizophrenia and on the value of religion as a dynamic aspect of many cures. He regarded catatonic schizophrenia, from which he suffered, as the presentation to the patient of a crisis in his life so profound as to drive him into a panic. The very profundity of the problem offered religious dimensions to be coped with only by a radical religious decision.

Thus, the crisis tended to "make or break" the individual, leading either to rapid cure or to continued deterioration. For this reason Boisen saw religion as an essential therapeutic tool for many patients, one that might make the difference between sickness and health, and out of which strength might come. In this way he explained the power of George Fox and other unstable religious leaders. Psychologists have acknowledged the originality of Boisen's theories, and while they would not for the most part generalize them to the extent that he did, most would grant that at least they fit his own case very aptly.

The relationship between religion and mental illness suggests a paradox with respect to religion and mental health, and thus leads to two schools of thought. On the one hand are those who see religion as a positive force leading to a sense of well-being and optimism, tending to reduce morbid human attitudes and to maximize healthy-mindedness. On the other hand are those who make much of the association between religion and mental illness. Psychiatrists in the latter camp frequently stress the fact that there are some patients in whom the very consideration of religion will touch off a psychosis, and the fact that almost any mental hospital can display a varied assortment of self-styled messiahs and Jesus Christs. An interesting example of three such personalities is found in Rokeach's *Three Christs of Ypsilanti.*

Actually, the situation is much too complex for either of these views to be the whole truth. It is worth mentioning William James' two famous types of religion, the "religion of healthy-mindedness" and that of the "sick soul." James sees them simply as two differing expressions of religion usually associated with differing types of temperament or life style, though these may alternate within a single personality. The healthy-minded person expresses his religion in a context of exuberance and joy. He minimizes the tragedies of life and may even systematically deny the existence of sickness and evil, as in Christian Science, according to James. James points out that this way of dealing with life works well for some people and thus empirically demonstrates its core of truth.

But there are others who cannot turn away from life's tragic elements, its sicknesses, strife, injustices, and its suffering. Men are not born equal with an equal chance in life, and death is the only leveler. An honest facing of such facts leads to a much deeper probing of the meaning of life than "the religion of healthy-mindedness," even though it may not produce cheery apostles. The title of one of Kierkegaard's books is *The Sickness Unto Death,* and one must acknowledge that this particular gloomy Dane produced some of the most searching religious observations of the last century. James, at least when he wrote *The Varieties,* looked on the sick soul as one who recognized a truer dimension of religion and life.

If one looks at these two religious styles, he may see them not as mutually exclusive but as two roads to religious growth. There are none of the great religious faiths that do not provide for the expression of both. The greatest literary production of the Hebrew Bible—and indeed one of the great pieces of world literature—is the Book of Job, a consideration of suffering and its relation to evil. But the same Bible is filled with an account of the triumphs as well as of the disasters of the Children of Israel. The theme of Death and Resurrection is a universal one in religion, derived from the depths of human nature. It is significant that the Passion of Christ's Crucifixion is followed by His

Resurrection. Good Friday is linked with Easter. This symbolizes that alternation in human destiny, that dialogue of opposites, through which religious development takes place.

This search for understanding of the process of religious growth will bring any religious psychologist worth his salt to the delicate and fascinating field of religious experience. I say *delicate,* for the churches have widely differing but nevertheless very positive convictions in the area. One runs the risk of offending some people no matter what one says or how carefully one phrases one's research and thought. This is one reason that psychology is somewhat gun-shy about religion. But such subjects as conversion, mysticism, possession, and prophecy need to be dealt with not only by the psychologist of religion but by any psychologist who pretends awareness of the total man.

It is an oversimplication, of course, but we can see religious life as containing two interrelated but very different psychological functions. Rudolf Otto, in *The Idea of the Holy,* has termed them the *rational* and the *nonrational.* If we liken the religious pilgrim to a ship in voyage, we might designate as the rudder the critical, directive, rational, and reasonable parts of the pilgrim's nature; the ship's propulsion then would be the nonrational, the feeling and intuitive elements, providing energy, liveliness, and movement. Perhaps in this respect religion is simply a special case of all of life. But we might note that a boat, no matter how strong its rudder, would get nowhere without an engine, while a rudderless ship with a powerful engine would be a hazard to itself and to all navigation. Thus religion through the ages has needed the prophet, the convert, the seer, the martyr, and the saint as well as the theologian and the priest.

This well may be why the more dynamic forms of religion often deprecate the scholar and the rationalist. It also helps explain why churches so often have been afraid of religion in its livelier forms. The church develops the conservatism typical of any institution, and it prefers saints to be dead before it begins to worship them.

Partly because the churches at about the turn of the century made more of the phenomenon of conversion, James (and E. D. Starbuck, his predecessor in the field of the psychology of religion) devoted many pages to this phenomenon. The bad name which conversion has acquired among scholars is due partly to the fact that some churches have forced on their members a highly emotional experience of unsettling shallowness, which has obscured the significance of many a sudden conversion of life-saving proportions. The founders of Alcoholics Anonymous are an outstanding example. Against a background of brainwashing and Pavlovian theory, William Sargant gives some reasons for the power of sudden conversion, both for good and for ill, in *Battle for the Mind*.

It seems to me that religion at its best can be illustrated well by contrasting the two great psychologists, Gordon Allport and William James. In *The Individual and his Religion*, Allport speaks of "mature religion" as self-critical and as possessing its own motivational force; as consistent in its moral consequences; as comprehensive and integrative; and, finally, as eternally questing.

James tries to define what he sees as religion at its best in the chapter "Saintliness," in *The Varieties*. He defines the best thus: (1) "A feeling of being in a wider life than that of this world's selfish little interests; and a conviction, not merely intellectual, of the existence of an Ideal Power." (2) "A sense of the friendly continuity of the ideal power with our own life, and a willing self-surrender to its control." (3) "An immense elation and freedom as the outlines of the confining selfhood melt down." (4) "A shifting of the emotional center towards loving and harmonious affections, towards 'yes, yes,' and away from 'no' where the claims of the non-ego are concerned."

James is not uncritical of some of the excesses of saintliness. Yet, when we compare his view of high religion with Allport's, we sense a wide gap. Allport is the rationalist.

Most college students take to Allport—the rudder. But some prefer James. These tend to be the more sensitive, more emotional ones, those who may have experienced the aesthetic and the mystical in their own lives, and who may be scorned a bit by their more rational classmates. Perhaps this is reminiscent of the situation on the Harvard campus in James' day, when his colleagues shook their heads at the vagaries of their attractive colleague.

We can trace this difference in emphasis to roots in James' own nature—half artistic and half intellectual, with mystical sensitivities of a profound nature, heightened through his experience with nitrous oxide and other experiences of which he spoke only to his intimates. Thus, we can bring these two students of religion into dialogue and take from each his characteristic contribution to theory as we derive from them the rational and nonrational components in religion at its best.

But, taken as a whole, the psychologist's contribution to religion is mainly a rational one. The psychologist is like the music critic, who can analyze and therefore help the hearer to appreciate. And so, as a psychologist of religion, I work to understand when I can. But ultimately I must stand in awe before what, as a psychologist, I cannot match—the authentic religious life. This is the subtlest, most profound, yet puzzling and paradoxical, of the achievements of the human spirit. It is religion *par excellence,* which has the power to transform human life and so give it meaning, and it is for these reasons that the religious consciousness is the most fascinating object of study of all human phenomena. At least, that is how one psychologist of religion sees it.

# The Personalities of Sudden Religious Converts

## JOHN P. KILDAHL

Henry Ward Beecher once wrote about his early religious experiences:

> There was the constant thought that I was an awful transgressor; every little fault seemed to make a dreadful sin; and I would say to myself, 'There, I am probably one of the reprobate.' For a sinner that repented, it was thought that there was pardon, but how to repent is the very thing I did not know. . . . So I used to live in perpetual fear and dread, and often wished myself dead. . . . My feeling (at the age of 15) was such that if dragging myself on my belly through the street had promised any chance of resulting good, I would have done it.[1]

On the other hand, Edward Everett Hale once wrote:

> I observe with profound regret, the religious struggles which come into many biographies, as if almost essential to the formation of the hero. I ought to speak of these, to say that any man has an advantage, not to be estimated, who is born, as I was, into a family where the religion is simple and rational; who is trained in the theory of such a religion, so that he never knows, for an hour, what these religious and irreligious struggles are. I always knew God loved me, and I was also always grateful to him for the world he placed me in. I always liked to tell him so, and was always grateful to him for the world he placed me in. A child who is early taught that he is God's child, that he may live and move and have his being in God, and that he has, therefore, infinite strength at hand for the conquering of any difficulty, will take life more easily, and probably will make more of it, than one who is told that he is born the child of wrath and wholly incapable of good.[2]

It would certainly seem that Beecher and Hale were two different kinds of people—and that the differences between them were not only confined to the nature of their religious experiences. Beecher certainly

Reprinted with permission of author and publisher from:

*Pastoral Psychology,* 1965, 16, 37-44, copyright 1965 HUMAN SCIENCES PRESS, 72 Fifth Avenue, New York, New York 10011.

had a different view of the world and of himself than did Hale. It probably could be surmised that Beecher was more depressed and fearful; he was certainly more depreciating of himself; in a word, he was much more anxious than Hale. On the other hand, Hale seemed to be more confident about his abilities, he was much more grateful toward life, and less preoccupied with any inner emotional turmoil.

In describing these kinds of experiences, and these kinds of people, William James used the terms "once-born" and "twice-born" individuals. He described these individuals as representing "two ways of life which are characteristic of what we called the healthy-minded, who need to be born only once, and of the sick souls, who must be twice-born in order to be happy."[3]

## TWO DIFFERING APPROACHES TO THE RELIGIOUS LIFE

The question arises—what type of personality structure is typical of the once-born or twice-born person? What personality picture is related to one's preference for a certain variety of religious experience? Is there any consistent personality pattern among people who undergo sudden and dramatic religious conversions? And do such patterns (if they do exist) differ from the personality patterns of people with a less cataclysmic or more gradual religious development?

Because of the interest surrounding these two different kinds of religious experiences, the author undertook a study to differentiate personality patterns typical of two different varieties of religious experience. The purpose of the study was to determine personality differences between sudden religious converts, and persons of a gradual religious development. In other words, the differences between once-born and twice-born persons. The procedure and results of this empirical research project will be described in this paper.

## THREE PREVIOUS EMPIRICAL RESEARCH PROJECTS

Three important studies dating back to 1897 have shed light on the personality differences between sudden religious converts and persons of a gradual religious development. The study by Starbuck[4] was the first. Starbuck tabulated the experiences of 192 persons who had experienced sudden conversions, and 237 persons whose religious development had been a process of gradual growth. Starbuck did not directly describe the personalities of his subjects, nor was it his purpose to do so. However, there are many descriptions throughout his writings which give possible clues about personality differences between the two groups. For example, Starbuck stated, "The conversion group approach religion more from the subjective, emotional standpoint; but at the sacrifice of an intellectual comprehension of it, and of a rational appreciation of the relationship they sustain to the world."[5] Starbuck also said, "...the conversion group are persons who are more suggestible, more impressionable, and, accordingly, more liable to undergo mental crises."[6]

Coe carefully studied a group of sudden converts and a group of persons with a gradual religious development. He concluded:

> It has been shown that three sets of factors favor the attainment of a striking religious transformation: The temperament factor, the factor of expectancy, and the tendency to automatisms and passive suggestibility.—Given three factors, the fourth—the general character of one's religious experiences—can be predicted with a high degree of probability. In short, everything goes to show that the chief mental qualities and states favorable to these striking experiences are expectation, abundance of feeling, and passive suggestibility, with its tendency to hallucinations and other automatisms.[7]

A third study was that of Clark,[8] which was a replication of the studies of Starbuck type, but was undertaken a generation later. Clark described the sudden convert's feelings as including the sense of sin, depression, moral failure, and fear of death, hell, God, or simply some nameless dread.

Sigmund Freud also had something to say about sudden religious conversion. A paper by Freud on the subject of religious conversion was occasioned by his receipt of a letter from a medical colleague who had recently experienced a sudden religious conversion. After seeing the body of an old woman being taken to a dissecting room the colleague angrily felt that there must be no God who could let such a thing happen "to a sweet-faced dear old woman." In the following days after witnessing this scene, Freud's correspondent experienced a sudden and dramatic religious conversion. Freud commented on all this as follows:

> We may say that this is the way in which things happened. The sight of a woman's dead body, naked or on the point of being stripped, reminded the young man of his mother. It roused in him a longing for his mother which sprang from his Oedipus complex, and this was immediately completed by a feeling of indignation against his father. His ideas of father and God had not yet become widely separated; so that his desire to destroy his father could become conscious as doubt in the existence of God and could seek to justify itself in the eyes of reason as indignation about ill-treatment of a mother-object.

Freud then adds:

> It is of course typical for a child to regard what his father does to his mother in sexual intercourse as ill-treatment. The new impulse, which

was displaced into the sphere of religion, was only a repetition of the Oedipus situation and consequently soon met with a similar fate. During the actual conflict the level of displacement was not maintained: There is no mention of arguments in justification of God, nor are we told what the infallible proofs were by which God proved his existence to the doubter.—The outcome was displaced once again in the sphere of religion and it was of a kind pre-determined by the fate of the Oedipus complex.

After explaining that the fate of the Oedipus complex was complete submission to the will of God the Father, Freud concluded the paper with this summary:

> The young man became a believer and accepted everything he had been taught since his childhood about God and Jesus Christ. He had had a religious experience, had undergone a conversion. Since all of this is so simple and straightforward, we cannot but ask ourselves whether by understanding this case we have thrown any light on the psychology of conversion in general.[9]

Another psychoanalyst, Salzman, summarized his view of religious conversion as follows:

> In the case histories I have presented, the conversion experience has represented a method of solving the conflict arising from the hatred toward the father. I should make it clear that, in my opinion, conversion experiences may be used for conflict with any authority figure, whether the father, the mother, or other significant persons.[10]

## PRESENT RESEARCH PROCEDURE

### Hypotheses

On the basis of the literature noted above, plus other writings which will not be described here, seven different experimental hypotheses suggested themselves for the present research. It was hypothesized that the sudden converts (1) would be less intelligent; (2) would perceive authority figures as more threatening; (3) would be more authoritarian; (4) would be more hysteric; (5) would be more depressed; (6) would be less humanitarian; and (7) would be more religiously conservative.

### Definition of Conversion

A sudden conversion was defined as an experience in which the subject's very self seemed to be profoundly changed; the change seemed not to be wrought by the subject, but upon him; the change was in the attitudes which constituted the subject's mode and character of life.

A gradual religious development is one which is characterized by absence of such conversion experiences as are described above, and one in which the subject has never known himself to be irreligious. All the converts were from an admittedly irreligious condition to a religious one. No converts from Judaism or Roman Catholicism were included.

## Research Population

Twenty first-year students at the theological seminary who had had sudden religious conversions were equated with twenty seminarians who had had a gradual religious development. The particular seminary, which will remain anonymous, is a middle-of-the-road denominational seminary where sudden conversions are neither frowned upon, nor required as proof of one's Christian faith. The two groups of seminarians were equated for socio-economic status, rural-urban background, age, intact family, military experience, and marital status.

Two autobiographical statements fairly typical of the two groups are quoted below. One of the sudden converts described his experience as follows:

> This experience occurred in the Fall of my fourteenth year. I had been working in a field plowing. Suddenly a storm seemed to approach, and as though everything around me stopped—I felt the presence of God. The horses had come to a complete stop; the inky black sky rumbled and I prayed. The storm passed on quickly, but it was at this moment—as I prayed—that I decided I would be a Christian and serve the Lord if that was the Lord's desire.

A member of the gradual religious development group described his experiences as follows:

> It is difficult to explain when I became consciously religious. It would be quite as easy for me to account for the fact that some years ago I was born weighing ten pounds and that I now weigh considerably more. This growth is not unmarked by incident, but the process, at least in retrospect, blurs into a continuum so completely that I cannot isolate the point at which I became 'religious,' any more than I can remember the point at which I emerged into conscious awareness of myself; I believe the two events must be nearly simultaneous.

## Tests Administered

Both groups were administered these tests: American Council on Education Psychological Examination for College Freshmen, Strong Vocational Interest Blank, Minnesota Multiphasic Personality Inventory, selected subtests of the Elias Family Opinion Survey, Levinson-Lichtenberg Religious Conventionalism Scale, and the F Scale. In addition, the Stern Thematic Apperception Test was group administered, and the Rorschach was individually administered.

The A.C.E. was used to investigate the intelligence hypothesis; the Rorschach, T.A.T. and E.F.O.S. were used to investigate the subjects' perceptions of authority figures; the F Scale was used to investigate the authoritarianism hypothesis; the MMPI for the hysteria hypothesis; Rorschach and MMPI for depression; the Strong test for humanitarianism; and the Levinson-Lichtenberg Scale for the religious conventionalism hypothesis.

The Rorschach records were judged for depression and perceptions of authority figures; the T.A.T.'s were rated for perceptions of authority figures. The rating scales were prepared by the present investigator. The judges were three experienced clinical psychologists.

## Results of This Research

The first hypothesis, that sudden converts are less intelligent than persons of a gradual religious development, was confirmed.

The fourth hypothesis, that sudden converts score higher on the Hysteria scale of the MMPI, was confirmed.

The other hypotheses, relating to perceptions of authority, authoritarianism, depression, humanitarianism, and religious conservatism, were not supported. Nothing in the present data supports the view that there are significant differences between sudden converts and persons with a gradual religious development in regard to these personality variables.*

A word of caution about these findings is in order here. It is true that the sudden converts have, in general, lower scores on the intelligence test, and higher scores on the Hysteria scale of the MMPI. It should be noted, however, that the mean scores for both groups on the A.C.E. were in the superior range. (The mean A.C.E. score for the sudden converts ranked in the 74th percentile for male college freshmen, and the mean A.C.E. score for the gradual development group ranked in the 87th percentile for male college freshmen.) Furthermore, the mean MMPI Hysteria scores are within the normal range for both groups (a mean score of 60 for the sudden converts, and a mean of 55.7 for the graduals).

It is not possible to make any predictive statements about the intelligence or the hysteria score of any one *individual* within either

---

*The *t* test was used for testing the significance of the difference between the means of the two correlated samples. The five percent level of confidence, one-tailed test of significance, was used in interpreting the results.

group. It would be absolutely incorrect to assume that *every* sudden convert is less intelligent and more hysteric than *every* person with a gradual religious development. There is a great overlapping of the scores of the two groups.

It can safely be said that only in general, taking the groups as a whole, are the sudden converts less intelligent and more hysteric. Therefore, while interpreting the results of this study, one can only point out some general trends.

## CONCLUSIONS

Starbuck observed that sudden religious converts appeared to approach religion from a subjective, emotional standpoint, and at the sacrifice of an intellectual comprehension of it. Coe noted that for the gradual group, intellect seemed to predominate over affect.

The present investigator thus hypothesized that since the gradual development group seemed to have a more intellectual type of religion, perhaps they would actually be more intelligent. This hypothesis was supported during the present investigation. This is the first time that this relationship has been demonstrated empirically and statistically.

The sudden converts were also more hysteric. This is in accord with other findings that there is a negative correlation between intelligence and hysteria.[11]

The hysteric (when contrasted, for example, with the obsessive compulsive) has been characterized as a person who is emotionally labile, who is subject to mood swings, excitability, fearfulness, and other concomitants of being more easily dominated by one's affects than by one's intellectual efforts. The hysteric is described as a person who shows relatively less independence, creativity, and integrative ability. Naivete and moralism are particularly evident. A general tendency toward over-responsiveness to the emotional implications of events to the exclusion of rational events can be expected of the person with a predominately hysteric character structure.

Obviously, the general description above applies to a person clearly diagnosed as hysteric, and not necessarily to any member of the sudden conversion group in this investigation. Nevertheless, after re-stating that the mean hysteria score for the sudden converts is within normal limits, it can be pointed out that the sudden converts will *tend to* react in the above described direction to a *slightly* greater degree than will the person who has had a gradual religious development. These are the trends for the two groups as revealed in this investigation.

The hypothesis which resulted from the Freudian and psychoanalytic literature was not supported. There is nothing in the data from this investigation to indicate that sudden converts perceive father figures or authority figures any differently than persons of a gradual religious development. There are no data here to support the claim that the Oedipal situation is handled in any distinctive way by the sudden converts. There are probably many good reasons why the predicted result was not obtained. It was certainly a difficult hypothesis to test empirically, and it is perhaps only fair to say that nothing very definitive was established one way or the other in regard to the Oedipal situation. On the basis of the data here, it is possible to state only that the subjects who experienced a sudden religious conversion do not now perceive male authority figures in any consistent way. What other factors, or what other authority figures, are significant in the conversion process, cannot be determined from the data from this investigation. Personally, the author's own clinical and anecdotal experiences lead him to affirm Freud's appraisal of the relationship between the Oedipal and conversion situations, but this is not the place to discuss one's private opinions, particularly when the experimental evidence disagrees with one's collection of anecdotes.

## A FINAL PERSONAL REACTION

In conducting this research project, the author had occasion to read much of the literature concerning religious conversions. In summary, then, he would like to share his personal reactions to that large body of literature, plus his conclusions regarding his own research.

Religious conversion is an immensely complex phenomenon. It is well to keep in mind that conversions are rather widespread psychological phenomena, occurring within the Christian church, but also in non-Christian situations as well. They can occur in relation to other beliefs such as communism, or other religions. Or, there can be equally striking changes from a religious to an irreligious state. The psychological results may be the same: an abrupt change in the direction of one's life, and accompanying feelings of great peace, harmony, and contentment. William James, for example, has described many different cultural and ideological contexts in which conversions occur—and the psychological or emotional effects are astonishingly similar, regardless of what the context was in which those various conversions occurred. Salzman,[10] a psychoanalyst, notes that conversions occur in the realms of religious, moral, political, ethical, and esthetic views. For example, Whittaker Chambers in his book *Witness* gives a good description of the close relationship between political and religious conversions.

It is important also to note that conversions may or may not be conducive to better emotional integration. Dramatic religious conversions are invariably marked by great conflict. Boisen, a hospital chaplain, makes the point that:

> Pathological experiences are frequently attended by religious concern, and religious experience by pathological features. This is explained by the fact that both may be attempts to solve some difficult and vital problem. When the outcome is constructive, we are likely to recognize it as a religious experience. When it is destructive or inconclusive, we call it 'mental disorder.' The outcome of an acute disturbance is dependent upon the assets and liabilities which the individual brings to the crisis experience . . . and his previous preparation.[12]

Salzman has noted six post-conversion characteristics of what he calls regressive conversions:

> 1) The convert has an exaggerated, irrational intensity of belief. 2) The convert is concerned more with form and doctrine than with the greater principle of the new belief. 3) His attitude toward his previous belief is one of contempt, hatred, and denial, and he rejects the possibility that there might be any truth in it. 4) He is intolerant toward all deviates, with frequent acting out by denouncing and endangering previous friends and associates. 5) He shows a crusading zeal and a need to involve others by seeking new converts. 6) He engages in masochistic and sadistic activities, displaying a need for martyrdom and self-punishment.

Weininger, another psychoanalyst, says that the main problem of a person with a religious conversion is his inability to adjust to a group. The sense of social failure is the most prominent, and the conversion offers a new and better adaptation of having a relationship with people. Thereby, and for the time being, the sense of isolation disappears. Such a person has felt that he has been living wrongly, and that there is an opposite ideal to which he would like to conform. "When a person in inner conflict becomes exhausted with his struggle, or when he reaches the point where he has sunk to a very low feeling of self-esteem, feels utterly worthless and helpless, and thereby gives up the will power struggle, a religious conversion experience may take place."[13] Weininger then adds that when such a person meets someone else who shows a genuine interest in him, a radical change occurs. The second person shows that he does not find the person unacceptable, that there can be another solution to his problem, that he need not struggle fruitlessly, and that he can be helped by a religious approach. Religious conversions are brought about through the intervention and acceptance by another person. The other person acts as a catalyst. Being accepted by the other person, guilt and all, relieves the anxiety sufficiently so as to enable the compulsive struggle to decrease, and as the struggle stops, the remaining anxiety subsides. The acceptance by the catalyst person makes possible the cessation of the struggle.

This brief survey of some of the psychological factors in conversions is intended to point up the complexity of the phenomenon of conversion: it occurs in other realms than the religious; it may or may not bring about better emotional integration; it is probably most often a consequence of previous social isolation, and conversion itself may be an attempt to achieve closer contact with people.†

To conclude, then, sudden converts tend to fall into a certain personality type, i.e., the hysteric type. They also tend to be less intelligent than their counterparts with a gradual religious development. The relationship between sudden conversions and intelligence is significant (statistically and, I believe, also theologically). While a variety of religious experiences may reduce the monotony within the life of the church, the need for critical, reflective, and persistent thinking on the part of church people has never been greater than today. The naive attitude of the convert described by Freud ("the young man became a believer and accepted everything he had been taught since his childhood about God and Jesus Christ")—such an attitude is not what the church needs today. A naive acceptance of whole theological and social systems is hardly what this age demands—but it is the approach which the sudden convert usually adopts. To the extent that sudden conversions place a final stamp of approval on the denomination in which they occurred, they are depriving the convert of the impetus to examine and question his religious experiences. It would seem likely that a slower, more reasoned approach to one's religious faith provides a person with better equipment to deal with the questions that inevitably must occur to the believer. That person is ill-equipped who tends not to reflect on his beliefs. Any religious experiences which can help the believer to examine his beliefs should be encouraged. For this reason, the sudden and dramatic religious conversion falls short of optimally promoting mental or emotional growth and maturity.

†This evaluation is not meant to imply that conversion is either good or bad. It is not the purpose of this paper to enter into how or whether this may be the Spirit of God at work, nor to pass any other theological judgment on the phenomenon of conversion. This is simply a *psychological* attempt to explain one small part of a person's behavior—and to show how this bit of behavior may be explained on *psychological* bases.

# J. P. Kildahl

## NOTES

[1] H. Beecher, quoted in J. Leuba, "Studies in the Psychology of Religious Phenomena," *Amer. J. of Psychol.*, 1897, 7, p. 323.
[2] E. Hale, quoted in E. Starbuck, *The Psychology of Religion* (New York, 1912), pp. 305-306.
[3] W. James, *The Varieties of Religious Experience* (New York, 1902), p. 163.
[4] E. Starbuck, "A Study of Conversion," *Amer. J. of Psychol.*, 1897, pp. 268-308.
[5] E. Starbuck, *The Psychology of Religion* (New York, 1912), p. 370.
[6] *Ibid.*, p. 364
[7] G. Coe, *The Spiritual Life* (New York, 1900), p. 139.
[8] E. Clark, *The Psychology of Religious Awakening* (New York, 1929).
[9] S. Freud, "A Religious Experience," *Collected Papers*, Vol. V (London, 1950), pp. 244-45.
[10] L. Salzman, "The Psychology of Religious and Ideological Conversion," *Psychiatry*, 1953, 16, pp. 183-87.
[11] R. Schafer, *The Clinical Application of Psychological Tests* (New York, 1948), p. 33.
[12] A. T. Boisen, *Religion in Crisis and Custom* (New York, 1955).
[13] B. Weininger, "The Interpersonal Factor in Religious Experience," *Psychoanalysis*, 1955, 3, pp. 27-44.

# Manifest Anxiety as a Contributing Factor in Religious Conversion[1]

## CHARLES M. SPELLMAN, GLEN D. BASKETT AND DONN BYRNE

One aspect of human behavior that has attracted the interest of psychologists is the conversion phenomenon, whether it be political, economic, religious, or aesthetic conversion. Salzman (1953) pointed out that there are two kinds of conversion: a gradual conversion and a sudden or abrupt conversion. The gradual conversion represents maturation in the individual's personality development, tends to be integrative, and represents an internalization of new values and goals considered by the convert to be on a higher level than the previous ones. The sudden conversion is described by Salzman as "a pseudosolution for dealing with extreme disintegrating conflicts [p. 179]." It might be represented by a sightless grasping for a solution to whatever conflicts the individual experiences. That it is a pseudosolution is attested to by the fact that the sudden convert soon begins to "backslide" when he realizes that his problems have not been dealt with adequately. As a result, he abandons that solution and begins to seek new ones. According to Salzman, the sudden conversion, "because it is brought about by increasing anxieties and has a disjunctive effect on the personality . . . may either precipitate or be part of the psychotic process [p. 179]."

Religious conversion, either changing from one religion to another or from a nonreligious state to a religious one, has been a focal point for both theologists and psychologists. In attempting to understand this phenomenon, researchers have taken two related approaches: considering motivational factors which lead to conversion and studying the personality characteristics of the converts. Guilt feelings are among the motivational factors that have been investigated.

Reprinted by permission of authors and publisher from:

*Journal of Consulting and Clinical Psychology,* 1971, 36, 245-247, Copyright 1971 by the American Psychological Association.

### C. M. Spellman, G. D. Baskett, and D. Byrne

Whereas Clark (1929) found less than 10% of the general population reporting guilt feelings, both Clark (1929) and Roberts (1965) observed about half the converts (both sudden and gradual) in their samples suffering from feelings of guilt prior to their conversion. Roberts (1965) also found that sudden converts who remained within the same faith as their parents were more neurotic than those who were converted to a different faith.

Anxiety has received some attention as a possible concomitant of religious behavior. Williams and Cole (1968) found that highly religious Ss manifested less generalized anxiety (i.e., the frequency of extreme scores on the Minnesota Multiphasic Personality Inventory and galvanic skin response arousal) than the least religious Ss. However, no information as to the abruptness of their Ss' conversion was presented.

The studies by Clark (1929) and Roberts (1965) have suggested that feelings of guilt are often reported by converts. It might be argued that increased feelings of guilt should be associated with higher levels of anxiety and that reduction of the guilt should lead to a reduction of anxiety. However, since Salzman argues that sudden conversion is only a pseudosolution to the convert's problems, the sudden convert should not experience a permanent reduction of his anxiety. Therefore, the sudden converts should score higher on anxiety than should gradual converts. The present study was designed as a test of this hypothesis.

## METHOD

There are at least three categories into which the citizenry of a town can be placed with respect to religion. These categories are (a) the nonreligious or those not belonging to a church and showing no interest in institutional religion; (b) the regular attenders or those who belong to a church and attend frequently; and (c) those who experience a sudden religious conversion.[2] Typically, the lines between these three groups are easily drawn by clergymen particularly in small communities where the minister is likely to know all the residents.

These three categories were described to two ministers of a predominantly Protestant farming community in central Texas. The population of the town consisted of less than 150 persons, and the ministers were asked to suggest the names of 20 persons upon whom they could both agree might fit each category. They agreed on 92% of the persons they classified. These 60 persons were then asked to take the Taylor Manifest Anxiety Scale (MAS; Taylor, 1953). Twenty-three of the Ss were males and 37 were females.

The E (CMS), one of the town's ministers, approached the Ss and asked if they would take a test as a favor to him. They were told that the test was a "personality test having to do with my work at the university." No mention was made of religion even though all the Ss knew that the E was a minister. A copy of the MAS was left with the S one day and picked up the next day in order that the S could complete it at his leisure.

The converts consisted of 7 males and 13 females, ranging in age from 16 to 65, with a mean age of 36.9. The regular attendance group consisted of 8 males and 12 females, ranging in age from 17 to 75 with a mean age of 41.3. The nonreligious group consisted of 8 males and 12 females, and their ages ranged from 19 to 66 with a mean of 38.6. Six members of the regular attendance group were school teachers—the only professional workers in the study—the remaining 54 Ss were students, farmers, ranchers, or other types of unskilled or semiskilled laborers, and housewives.

## RESULTS

Since there were large age differences within each category as well as sex differences, the effects of age, sex, their interaction, and the interactions with religious category were tested to examine their influence on the MAS scores. The results of these tests indicated that neither age, sex, nor the interactions produced a significant contribution to the variance of the MAS scores. Thus, only the religious category was utilized as an independent variable. The resulting means for the groups were: 26.65 for the sudden converts, 17.81 for the regular attenders, and 18.40 for the nonattenders. The three means were significantly different ($F = 10.26$, $df = 2$, $57$, $p < .001$) and orthogonal comparisons indicated that the effect was due to the sudden converts being significantly higher ($t = 3.72$, $df = 57$, $p < .01$) than the other two groups combined, which did not differ significantly ($t < 1.0$, $df = 57$) from each other.

## DISCUSSION

These results provide tentative support for the hypothesis that those people having had a sudden religious conversion experience will score higher on anxiety than those not having the experience. The results suggest that conversion might be a pseudosolution for the sudden converts' problems, since for these individuals conversion has apparently failed to bring a permanent reduction, if any, in their anxiety. Therefore, when the sudden convert realizes that his anxiety remains high, he will probably abandon this attempt by backsliding and/or seeking new solutions (Salzman, 1953).

There are, however, a number of factors to consider about using the MAS as a dependent variable. First, one might wish to question whether or not the MAS measures the type of anxiety which would be associated with guilt as opposed to drive arousal. The MAS does correlate significantly with other measures of anxiety (Sarason, 1961), thus suggesting that the MAS scores reflect anxiety as well as drive arousal, and Lowe (1964) found substantial correlations between the MAS and his guilt scale.

Further considerations are due to the high correlations between the MAS and other variables. For example, since the MAS and social desirability (Edwards, 1957) are highly related, the results of the present study might be interpreted as evidence that individuals who undergo sudden conversion are low in social desirability response set. However, since Klein, Barr, and Wolitzky (1967) concluded that the psychological meaning of social desirability is unclear, this explanation seems less theoretically relevant than that which identifies anxiety as the underlying variable. It might also be argued that the converts' higher MAS scores reflect a lower defensiveness as a result of their being freed of their guilt (see Adelson, 1969, pp. 233-234; Klein et al., 1967). Although this explanation might seem desirable from a theological point of view, it would suggest that a more gradual conversion would not result in the same freedom from guilt, which from a theological position would seem undesirable. Thus, the lack of defensiveness interpretation seems unsatisfactory for the present data. Since Salzman (1953) described the sudden conversion as perhaps related to the psychotic process, one might wish to interpret the present data as suggesting that the sudden converts are less well adjusted. Their mean MAS score (26.65) is similar to that of psychiatric outpatients (Bailey, Berrick, Lachmann, & Ortmyer, 1960) and neuropsychiatric patients (Matarazzo, Guze, & Matarazzo, 1955), but higher than college students (Taylor, 1953).

In summary, even though a number of interpretations are plausible for the present data, other studies suggest that a reasonable interpretation would be that the higher MAS scores for the sudden converts reflect their higher levels of anxiety and are perhaps indicative of a less well-adjusted state of being.

### NOTES AND REFERENCES

[1]This article is based on data gathered by the first author for a master's thesis presented to the University of Texas at Austin and carried out under the direction of Donn Byrne.

Special thanks are due to the Reverend Louis Ketchum who helped in the classification of the Ss.

[2]It was assumed that the regular attenders were more gradual in their religious conversion. However, this assumption is questionable since the meaning of attendance has been shown to be a function of the person's religious orientation (Allport & Ross, 1967). Furthermore, individuals in the sudden conversion group might have been considering converting for a long time, hence the suddenness of their conversion might become questionable. Unfortunately, no information was obtained from the Ss in the present study as to either their religious orientation or the suddenness of their conversion.

ADELSON, J. Personality. *Annual Review of Psychology,* 1969, 20, 217-252.

ALLPORT, G., & ROSS, J. M. Personal religious orientation and prejudice. *Journal of Personality and Social Psychology,* 1967, 5, 432-443.

BAILEY, M. A., BERRICK, M. E., LACHMANN, F. M., & ORTMYER, D. H. Manifest anxiety in psychiatric outpatients. *Journal of Clinical Psychology,* 1960, 16, 209-210.

CLARK, E. T. *The psychology of religious awakening.* New York: Macmillan, 1929.

EDWARDS, A. *The social desirability variable in personality assessment and research.* New York: Dryden, 1957.

KLEIN, G. S., BARR, H. L., & WOLITZKY, O. L. Personality. *Annual Review of Psychology,* 1967, 18, 467-560.

LOWE, C. M. The equivalence of guilt and anxiety as pathological constructs. *Journal of Consulting Psychology,* 1964, 28, 553-554.

MATARAZZO, J. D., GUZE, S. B., & MATARAZZO, R. G. An approach to the validity of the Taylor Anxiety Scale: Scores of medical and psychiatric patients. *Journal of Abnormal and Social Psychology,* 1955, 51, 276-280.

ROBERTS, F. J. Some psychological factors in religious conversion. *British Journal of Social and Clinical Psychology,* 1965, 4, 185-187.

SALZMAN, L. The psychology of religious and ideological conversion. *Psychiatry,* 1953, 16, 177-187.

SARASON, I. G. Characteristics of three measures of anxiety. *Journal of Clinical Psychology,* 1961, 17, 196-197.

TAYLOR, J. A. A personality scale of manifest anxiety. *Journal of Abnormal and Social Psychology,* 1953, 48, 285-290.

WILLIAMS, R. L., & COLE, S. Religiosity, generalized anxiety, and apprehension concerning death. *Journal of Social Psychology,* 1968, 75, 111-117.

# Issues in the Psychology of Religious Conversion

## JAMES R. SCROGGS AND WILLIAM G. T. DOUGLAS

Conversion has probably received more attention from psychologists of religion than has any other topic, with the possible exception of mysticism. Since the turn of the twentieth century, there have been at least five hundred publications dealing with the psychological dynamics of religious conversion. In the first three decades of the century, major theoretical contributions were made by William James (1902), G. Stanley Hall (1904), Edwin D. Starbuck (1899), James H. Leuba (1912, 1925), James B. Pratt (1907, 1920), Edward S. Ames (1910), George A. Coe (1916), Sante de Sanctis (1927), Elmer T. Clark (1929), and others. But the ascendance of behaviorism in American psychology stifled further development until the late 1940's, when it again became possible for social scientists to express professional interest in these topics without losing scientific respectability.

Of course, considerable prescientific psychological wisdom is contained in the writings of the Apostle Paul, Augustine, Pascal, Kierkegaard, Jonathan Edwards (often referred to as the first American psychologist of religion), and many others within the Christian heritage. Certainly the process of personality change and reorganization has been of major concern to great mystics such as Teresa of Avila and Bernard of Clairvaux, as well as who have served as spiritual directors.

Psychological studies in the stricter sense have generally concentrated on surveys of relatively large numbers of people with defined characteristics (often the captive population of college students) yielding descriptive statistics on such issues as age of conversion. These studies, beginning with the pioneer investigations of Starbuck and Hall, and the creative theorizing of James on the basis of Starbuck's data, generally depended on questionnaire procedures. Seldom were data collected, however, according to systematic, replicable procedures, in

Reprinted with permission of authors and publisher from:
*Journal of Religion and Health,* 1976, 6(3), 204-216.

relation to clearly formulated hypotheses. Until ten or twenty years ago, there was little possibility of moving beyond superficial questionnaires the results of which were of unknown generalizability, supplemented by arm-chair reflection. Recently, however, the development of content analysis (as utilized by Schneider and Dornbush), structured interview schedules, standardized tests (like the Allport-Vernon-Lindzey Study of Values and the Myers-Briggs Type Indicator), projective techniques, participant-observer and group-process analysis schedules, and computer data analysis have made new developments possible.

*Potentially,* therefore, social scientists *could* make considerable contribution to knowledge of conversion through their specialized tool kit of standardized instruments and scientifically controlled methods or recording and analyzing data. However, there has been really little progress beyond James's creative intuitions in his 1901-02 lectures on *Varieties of Religious Experience,* which remains the classic in psychology of religion. Despite an expanded tool kit, the few empirical investigations that have been conducted have tended to rely on questionnaires in forms not much different from that employed by Starbuck in the 1890's. To use James's own typology, tough-minded method and theoretical rigor have seldom been associated with tender-minded concern for the basic issues of religion, such as conversion.

Solid empirical data—scientific "facts" and "laws"—regarding these matters are relatively few. The study of *When Prophecy Fails*[1] in a Minnesota millenarian group is one of the very few empirical studies based on clearly defined hypotheses. (Festinger found confirmation for his theory of cognitive dissonance.) The contributions of psychology and psychiatry to the understanding of conversion come primarily from training as skilled observers of human behavior and from wisdom gained from the library of living human documents. Moreover, since psychology is not a unified science using one common frame of reference, there are many "schools." Definition of issues will depend, therefore, on the psychological school of which one is a part. Indeed, major problems in the existing literature are lack of clarity concerning fundamental assumptions and the manner in which these assumptions bias treatment of conversion.

## THE ISSUES

A review of the literature on the psychology of conversion, representing a wide spectrum of schools of thought, reveals continued attention to a specific body of issues that can be outlined fairly simply and precisely. Though there is some change in focus, by and large books and articles written in the 1960's deal with the same issues, fight the same battles, and grind the same axes as those written in 1900. The issues listed below are abstracted from the literature. Whether or not they constitute the "right" questions, in the sense of generating hypotheses and promoting research, is beyond the scope of this article. These are the issues that have occupied the attention of psychologists writing about conversion. An indication of the major positions vis-à-vis each issue will be given, and some impression of what, if any, consensus exists.

1. *The definition issue.* What is conversion? How broad is the range of behavior that can be labeled "conversion"? More specifically:

A. For a process of change to be called conversion, must it be sudden, dramatic, about-face, or can it be a process of gradual change and growth? That is to say, are the psychodynamics involved in sudden, dramatic change the same as or so similar to those involved in gradual change that we are justified in regarding them as one and the same process, and hence denoting them with the same name—conversion? If, on the other hand, these two types of change are different, is the difference one of kind or merely of degree? I.e., is sudden change an exaggerated and intensified instance of gradual change, or is it something unique?

*Consensus.* Few psychologists have been willing to let go the possibility of gradual conversion despite the fact that the word generally connotes a sudden about-face. The contention that all conversions are gradual (being preceded by a long period of subconscious incubation) only begs the question. There is, in fact, little or no consensus on this, perhaps the oldest issue in the field. Most writers hedge. Few state definitely that sudden conversion is the one and only kind, and yet most apparently feel that it partakes more of the essence of conversion than what they term "gradual conversion."

B. For a process of change to be called conversion, must it be religious? Must it involve a change in commitment to metaphysical realities, religious values, or beliefs? Must certain religious accoutrements (the revival meeting, the spiritual discipline, or whatever) be present? Or may not such processes as brainwashing and psychotherapy be instances of conversion also? I.e., though intended goals differ, and methods may appear quite different, are the basic sociopsychophysiological processes involved in basic personality reorganization not fundamentally the same?

*Consensus.* This is a more recent issue, stimulated by the increasing frequency and importance of political and ideological "conversions." Those who choose to write on this issue are generally interested in advancing the thesis that religious conversion, brainwashing, and/or psychotherapy are fundamentally identical or very similar processes. Few, with the exception of theological conservatives, have taken the trouble to try to refute this thesis in print. Sargant holds that all these processes operate by driving the subject to the point of transmarginal inhibition of the brain, wherein he is hypersuggestible and may be easily indoctrinated.[2] Windemiller finds striking similarities between Chinese brainwashing and eighteeth-century Wesleyan revivals.[3] Both (1) are crisis experiences and problem-solving processes that aid in "maintaining ego identity and homeostasis; (2) involve emotional upheaval issuing in changed life and thinking; (3) rely on group pressures involving interrogation, confession, and discussion; (4) make use of highly structured organizations; (5) introduce new vocabularies; (6) involve exhaustion, surrender, and suggestion; (7) give rise to self-criticism, doubt, fear, and guilt; (8) bring feelings of cleanness, lightness, relief, gratitude, new truth, dedication, and zeal; and (9) involve repression or suppression of one psychic system and the coming into conscious control of another." Hiltner and Rogers suggest that the personality changes that occur during psychotherapy of the pastoral counseling variety are instances of what in an earlier age would have been called conversion.[4]

2. *The pathology issue.* Is conversion pathological, abnormal, regressive, a sign of mental illness or emotional instability? Or is it a constructive, healthy pattern of behavior leading to "true" maturity?

This is either a question of statistical normality depending upon cultural context or a value question betraying the writer's own commitment (regardless of the smoke screen of scientism he puts up to rationalize it). As Jahoda has indicated, the dominant conception of mental health held by American psychologists is that of the self-sufficient individualist who stands on his own two feet and is not a burden to others.[5] In this light, conversion to a theistic faith is likely to appear as a turning from independence to immature dependence.

*Consensus.* Generally speaking, those psychologists whose commitment is to the Christian faith tend to view conversion as healthy, normal, and leading to maturity, while those who do not share this commitment are more likely to see conversion as regressive and pathological. James avoids this issue by focusing attention on the "fruits" rather than the "roots."[6] Yet he does feel that a state of tension and inner conflict (the divided self or sick soul) necessarily precedes conversion. To this extent, then, conversion is initiated by at least the threat of pathological disintegration. At the same time, one gets the impression that James regards conversion as a satisfactory and positive response to this threat.

Freud regards conversion as a regressive defense against repressed hostility toward authority.[7] Salzman is a contemporary exponent of much the same view.[8] A recent wave of psychoanalytic papers and books assessing the beneficial aspects of regression (regression in the service of the ego) may signify a change of heart in that quarter.[10]

Allport, though he does not deal explicitly with conversion, is one of the foremost contemporary advocates of the fundamental healthiness of the mature religious sentiment.[11]

This issue has very practical consequences insofar as it determines, when one sets out to convert people, whether the strategy is one of increasing tensions and precipitating crisis (hell-fire and brimstone preaching) or whether some more gentle approach based on loving constraint is used (the acceptance of client-centered therapy).

3. *The convertible type issue.* Is one kind of person more likely to be converted and/or converted in a particular way than is another person? Can such a typology be specified? Are there some people who are "unconvertible," "anesthetic" on the religious side, to use James's phrase? How does a religious group determine which types of people, under which conditions, are most likely to be converted to its "brand" of life orientation?

*Consensus.* Sociologists stress the importance of such variables as social class, group expectations, and social change (as in American frontier society[12] or contemporary China[13]). Forms of religious expression vary according to culture and historical period. The implication, then, is that the most convertible type will be found, if he is found at all, to be culturally relative.

Sargant describes those most likely to be converted (or hypnotized or brainwashed) in terms of Pavlov's typology of his dogs, which in turn is parallel to the ancient Greek typology of the choleric, melancholic, sanguine, and phlegmatic. The first two types are more prone to conversion.[14] A variety of data, including Sheldon's somatotype research, indicates variability from birth in sensitivity to stimuli and modes of coping with stimuli. A number of studies have found that a high degree of suggestibility or hypnotizability is characteristic of sudden converts.[15]

James regarded the sick soul as the most likely candidate for conversion. The sick soul lives "close to the pain threshold." He is generally introverted and pessimistic in outlook, taking the evil of the

258

world profoundly to heart. The sick soul is brooding, steeped in existential *angst*. He is Kierkegaard's man who is in despair and knows he is in despair.

Freudian analyses suggest that sudden converts tend to have unsually great repressed resentment and hatred toward their fathers, or toward authority in general. The picture is not unlike that of the authoritarian personality, as conceived by Adorno *et al.* Salzman, for example, finds that sudden converts are characterized by "extreme dependency on strong, omnipotent figures."[16] He also finds that post-conversion behavior, in those cases that he regards as regressive conversions, exhibits: (1) "an exaggerated, irrational intensity of belief. . .; (2) more concern with the form and doctrine than with the greater principle . . .; (3) his attitude toward his previous belief is one of contempt, . . .; (4) he is intolerant toward all deviates, . . .; (5) crusading zeal . . .; (6) masochistic and sadistic activities, . . ."[17]

Freud himself saw conversion as related to the Oedipus complex. It is a matter of surrendering to the father's, or Father's, will. The period of doubt that often precedes conversion Freud saw as an expression of the subconscious wish to do away with the father. As the boy acknowledges the superior power of his father and so puts to rest the Oedipus complex, so the convert accepts the omnipotence of God and so resolves this Oedipal situation which has been displaced into the sphere of religion.[18]

Two rather telling points are made by Salzman in support of the Freudian theory that repressed hatred for authority is the basic dynamic in conversion. First he observes that the effect of "hell-fire and damnation" preaching is to inspire not love but hate. Secondly Salzman remarks upon the great observed coincidence of conversion with adolescence. This is perfectly understandable, he suggests, since "adolescence is often a period of the greatest turmoil and development; a period of struggle against authority in an effort to achieve independence."[19]

4. *The ripe age issue.* Is conversion most likely to occur at a certain age? Are there crisis points in human development that may represent more likelihood for conversion?

*Consensus.* There has been more research on age of conversion than on any other apsect. Early writers were unanimous in regarding adolescence as the most probable age for conversion. Johnson summarizes the major studies of average age of conversion as follows: Starbuck (1899), 1,265 cases, 16.4 yrs.; Coe (1900), 1,784 cases, 16.4 yrs.; Hall (1904), 4,054 cases, 16.6 yrs.; Athearn (1922), 6,194 cases,

14.6 yrs.; Clark (1929), 2,174 cases, 12.7 yrs.[20] In Clark's study, only 6.7 per cent reported a "definite crisis" conversion, vs. 27.2 per cent "emotional stimulus" and 66.1 per cent "gradual growth." He found that the more radical "awakenings" of a crisis variety tended to occur about the age of seventeen—which coincides with earlier reports of Starbuck and Hall. But when religion develops as a gradual process, the "awakening" comes as early as twelve years. The later the conversion comes, the more likely it is to be intense and revolutionary, for the changes called for are likely to be drastic and difficult.

Recent studies indicate that among some revivalistically oriented groups the age of conversion is dropping from the teens down into late childhood.[21] Ferm, on the other hand, believes the ripe age to be considerably higher.[22] He points out that by using college students as their subjects, many of the early studies unwittingly were operating with a truncated sample. In surveys of three churches, Ferm found the average age of conversion to be 43, 46, and 41 years respectively. Converts made by Graham's first British campaign averaged in their middle twenties.

Jung emphasized mid to late thirties as a period of moving from an extroverted, external-reality-mastery orientation to an introverted inner-reality-understanding orientation.[23] Hiltner writes that conversion "is most important, most likely, and most cultivatable in the thirties, rather than being regarded primarily as an adolescent phenomenon."[24]

Erikson has done the most thorough job of charting psychosocial crises and, in recent years, relating them to development of value-structures.[25] He stresses that secure identity rests on the foundation of trust, autonomy, initiative, etc., and that the identity crisis (which focuses in adolescence, but is repeated during middle age in the form of the integrity crisis) interacts with ideology. It is probably fair to conclude from Erikson's theories that both the identity crisis in adolescence and the integrity crisis in the middle years constitute ripe moments for conversion.

5. *The voluntaristic issue.* Is conversion the result of conscious striving and self-discipline, or does it happen to a person without his willing it, or even against his will? And if it occurs without conscious volition, is it the result of unconscious forces, beyond-individual-consciousness forces (God), or manipulation by other persons?

*Consensus.* The overwhelming majority of converts report the decisive operation of forces beyond their conscious control. Most psychologists agree with this. A recent study by a Roman Catholic psychologist, however, places strong emphasis upon conscious striving.[26]

A. What is the role of unconscious factors in conversion?

*Consensus.* James considered that the role of unconscious factors was extensive and often decisive in conversion, and that a long period of subconscious incubation preceded sudden conversions. Freud stressed that all behavior is motivated, and that most (if not all) of it is unconsciously motivated. The unconscious motives involved in conversion, according to Freud, are hatred of the father, fear of expressing this hatred, and fear of the father's taking revenge, with the consequent desire to propitiate him and be accepted by him.[27] Allport, Maslow, Rogers, and others stress the role of conscious, present decision, in contrast to the Freudian emphasis on unconscious, early-life determination. Nevertheless, it seems fair to say that the weight of opinion is with those who see unconscious factors as playing an important role in conversion.

B. What is the role of beyond-individual-consciousness forces in conversion?

*Consensus.* The incursions from beyond the margins of consciousness that James thought so important in producing religious experiences of all varieties were not so much the products of the individual unconscious mind in the Freudian sense as they were manifestations of a reality above and beyond the individual psyche ("the reality of the unseen"), which partakes much more of the nature of the Jungian collective unconscious. James was in fact a spiritualist; and it is these forces from the spirit world that he saw as influential in producing conversions. (This somewhat unacademic and "unscientific" aspect of James has been largely ignored. Another twenty years of psychical research may show him to have been even further ahead of his time than we had guessed.) Jung, of course, also saw the beyond-individual-consciousness forces of the collective unconscious and its archetypes as exerting pressure for personal integration or disintegration without individual volition.

Various theories associated with the Aristotelian concept of enteleché imply the operation of beyond-individual-consciousness forces, which, albeit natural, are still beyond conscious volition. Some psychologists, such as Progoff (quoting Smuts and the botanist Sinnott) refer to a "protoplasmic purpose." Progoff's and Maslow's emphasis on self-actualization is reminiscent of the Aristotelian enteleché—a built-in purpose or direction that the organism pursues and that will unfold invariably, unless something blocks or thwarts it.

The role of the Divine (theistically conceived) in conversion has been little dealt with by psychologists except as they have written for evangelical or devotional purposes, and even then rarely except within religiously conservative contexts. By and large, psychologists, whether they be atheists or believers, have studied conversion as though God had absolutely nothing to do with it.

C. What is the role of intentional manipulation, subtle coercion, and exploitation in conversion?

*Consensus.* Windemiller finds the primary distinctions between brainwashing and Wesleyan revivalism lying at precisely this point. Brainwashing employs intentional manipulation, whereas revival techniques allow for much greater personal freedom of choice. The implications of Sargant's presentation, on the other hand, are that conversions are quite explicitly the result of one person or team of persons "operating" upon another person or group with techniques that are very nearly irresistible to bring about whatever kind of change in behavior or ideology they desire. Recent research on sensory deprivation[28] and a paper by Alland[29] indicate how manipulation of sensory input may stimulate trance states and mystical-like experiences. Also, the powerful influence of group pressure, which can be intentionally structured and manipulated to achieve desired ends, has been repeatedly demonstrated experimentally.[30] On the whole, however, writers on religious conversion have preferred to ignore this topic—one that is certain to require increasing attention in the very near future.

6. *The science-versus-religion issue.* Can social science describe (let alone explain) the entire process of conversion, or only aspects or portions of it? How can a social scientific description handle issues connected with the theological doctrine of God at work in all of life, including conscious and unconscious motivation? Can conversion be described as a natural process, or are there supernatural factors involved that must be taken into account?

*Consensus.* Social scientists have tended to operate according to a nothing-but reductionism, while theologians (or other believers) have tended to take a something-more, hands-off-the-sacred-preserve approach. No solution to this very difficult problem appears in the immediate purview. Increasing dialogue between social scientists and theologians (Society for the Scientific Study of Religion, Academy of Religion and Mental Health, etc.), however, does indicate a growing concern with this issue.

A potential breakthrough is viewed by Leary and others as being provided by the development of "consciousness-expanding" (psychedelic) chemicals such as LSD.[31] These drugs, some hold, provide empirical evidence under controlled conditions of the existence and operation of divine or quasi-divine realities. Critics doubt either that such drugs do in fact expand consciousness or that they are relevant to religious experience.[32]

7. *The appropriate conceptual scheme issue.* What body of theories and methods is most appropriate to the study of conversion? Are some so inappropriate as to be useless? (This relates to issue 6 and to others mentioned.)

*Consensus.* Behaviorism, operationalism, and learning theory have rarely been applied to the study of religious conversion. The other dominant school of American psychology may be broadly termed "functionalism." The overwhelming majority of psychologies of conversion have been written from this perspective. The remainder have been written in a psychiatric context, which shares this functional, practitioner orientation—viz., what is true is what works. The consensus, then, has been very strongly in favor of functional analysis.

If one wants to "engineer" conversions, surely the functional approach promises great effectiveness. Is it not possible, however, that one may miss the fundamental aspect of religion (as distinguished from magic by Malinowski)—that religion is an end in itself—by following a functionalist tack? As long as the psychologist persists in asking and answering functional questions (How does it work? What is it good for?) about religious phenomena, the theologian will continue to insist that he has missed the point. The man of faith knows that his motive in becoming converted was not in order that his personality might become integrated, that he might put to rest the gnawing hatred for authority that consumed his energies, or that he might master his fears and compulsions. That his conversion had these fortunate by-products may well be true; but that desire to achieve them constituted the core of his motivation is a hypothesis that needs very careful reconsideration. That it is beginning to get such consideration is evident in a recent article by Allport wherein he stresses precisely this point.[33]

Psychologists, psychiatrists, and sociologists have only recently begun to recognize and admit that they are not, and cannot be, "objective" in the sense of being "value-free." One's own values (and is not a conceptual scheme a reflection of one's own values?) influence research design: what is studied, what is emphasized and de-emphasized, how data are recorded, analyzed, and interpreted. We cannot attain "pure objectivity" in science, for the observer affects the observation. (Cf. Heisenberg's principle of indeterminacy in physics, and the general principles of field theory.) We can, however, "calibrate our subjectivity" and make adjustments for our own biases and predilections. This would imply that not only interdisciplinary but interbias research is necessary in areas of high numinous-radiation, such as religious conversion.

# CONCLUSION

Such are the issues that two psychologists with theological training and ministerial ordination draw from social science literature as it relates to religious conversion. Few, if any, of these issues are settled definitively. There is a great need for solid, responsible research, not to prove or disprove, but simply to understand, predict, and, where desirable, control. For these are the goals of science. Before research can be productive, however, there is need for theoretical development. Inadequate conceptualization, especially of necessary distinctions and discriminations, has handicapped the scientific investigation of religion almost as much as a limited tool kit. But the signs of the times regarding social scientific investigation of conversion are hopeful. Especially to be recommended for further research by someone well acquainted with the field of religious conversion is the vast literature in social psychology on opinions, attitudes, and beliefs.[34] Perhaps we can continue the process of knowledge-building that began so promisingly in the first three decades of the century and then stopped on a plateau.

## REFERENCES

1. Festinger, L.; Riecken, H. W.; and Schachter, S., *When Prophecy Fails*. Minneapolis, University of Minnesota Press, 1956.
2. Sargant, William, *Battle for the Mind*. Garden City, N. Y., Doubleday & Co., 1957.
3. Windemiller, Duane A., "The Psychodynamics of Change in Religious Conversion and Communist Brainwashing: With Particular Reference to the 18th Century Evangelical Revival and the Chinese Thought Control Movement." Unpublished doctoral dissertation, Boston University, 1960.
4. Hiltner, Seward, and Rogers, William R., "Research on Religion and Personality Dynamics," *Research Supplement to Religious Education*, July-August, 1962, S-134.
5. Jahoda, Marie, *Current Concepts of Positive Mental Health*. New York, Basic Books, 1959.
6. James, William, *The Varieties of Religious Experience*. New York, The Modern Library, 1902.
7. Freud, Sigmund, "A Religious Experience," *Collected Papers*, Vol. V. London, Hogarth Press, 1950, pp. 244-245.
8. Salzman, Leon, "The Psychology of Religious and Ideological Conversion," *Psychiatry*, 1953, 16, 183-187.
9. Erikson, Erik H., *Young Man Luther*. New York, W. W. Norton, 1958.
10. Arlow, J. A., and Brenner, C., *Psychoanalytical Concepts and the Structural Theory*. New York, International Univ. Press, 1964; Gill, M. M., and Brenman, M., *Hypnosis and*

*Related States*. New York, International Univ. Press, 1961; Schafer, R., "Regression in the Service of the Ego." In Lindzey, G., ed., *Assessment of Human Motives*. New York, Grove Press, 1960, pp. 119-148.

11. Allport, Gordon W., *The Individual and His Religion*. New York, Macmillan, 1950.
12. Sweet, W. W., *Revivalism in America*. New York, Scribner, 1945.
13. Yang, C. K., *Religion in Chinese Society*. Berkeley, University of California Press, 1961.
14. Sargant, *op. cit.*
15. Starbuck, Edwin D., *The Psychology of Religion*. New York, Scribner, 1900, p. 364; Coe, George A., *The Spiritual Life*. New York, Eaton & Mains, 1900, p. 139; Kildahl, John P., "The Personalities of Sudden Religious Converts," *Pastoral Psychology*, 1965, *16*, 37-44.
16. Salzman, Leon, "Types of Religious Conversion," *Pastoral Psychology*, 1966, *17*, 8-20.
17. *Ibid.*, pp. 18-19.
18. Freud, *op. cit.*
19. Salzman, "Types of Religious Conversion," *op. cit.*, p. 19.
20. Johnson, Paul E., *Psychology of Religion*, rev. ed. Nashville, Abingdon, 1959, p. 127.
21. Drakeford, John W., *Psychology in Search of a Soul*. Nashville, Broadman, 1964, p. 261; Yoder, Deon, *Nurture and Evangelism of Children*. Scottdale, Pa., Herald Press, 1959.
22. Ferm, Robert, *The Psychology of Christian Conversion*. Westwood, N. J., Fleming Revell, 1959, p. 218.
23. Jung, Carl G., *Modern Man in Search of a Soul*. New York, Harcourt, Brace, 1933.
24. Hiltner, Seward, "Toward a Theology of Conversion in the Light of Psychology," *Pastoral Psychology*, 1966, *17*, 35-42.
25. Erikson, Erik H., *Insight and Responsibility*. New York, W. W. Norton, 1964.
26. Herr, Vincent V., S.J. *Religious Psychology*. Staten Island, N. Y., Alba House, 1965.
27. Freud, *op. cit.*
28. Solomon, P., *et al., Sensory Deprivation*. Cambridge, Harvard University Press, 1961.
29. Alland, A., "Possession in a Revivalistic Negro Church," *Journal for the Scientific Study of Religion*, 1962, *1*, 204-213.
30. Sherif, M., "Group Influences upon the Formation of Norms and Attitudes," *Readings in Social Psychology*, 3d ed.; Maccoby, Newcomb, and Hartley, eds., New York, Holt, Rinehart and Winston, 1958; Asch, S. E., "Opinions and Social Pressure," *Scientific American*, 1955, *193*, 31-35.
31. Leary, T., "Religious Experience: Its Production and Interpretation," *Dialog*, 1964, *3*, 215-220.
32. Hordern, W., "Theological Critique of the Psychedelic Experience," *Dialog*, 1964, *3*, 220 ff.
33. Allport, Gordon W., "Mental Health: a generic attitude," *Journal of Religion and Health*, 1964, *4*, 7-21.
34. Berelson, Bernard, and Steiner, Gary A., *Human Behavior: An Inventory of Scientific Findings*. New York, Harcourt, Brace and World, 1964. See chapter on opinions, attitudes, and beliefs.

# RELIGIOUS DEVELOPMENT

# Introduction

## H. NEWTON MALONY

This section examines the functions of religion at three critical periods: childhood, adolescence, and adulthood. It emphasizes changes that occur in the role which religion plays at these different stages.

Elkind suggests that Piaget's four cognitive capacities are expressed as elements in institutional religion. In children, being religious serves as a form of adaptation. Religion, through such answers as God, Scripture, worship and theology, gives children ready-made solutions to the problems of growing up.

Feldman reviews the last forty years of research on religious changes in students during college. The measures used to assess changes have differed widely, and few comparisons with non-college youth have been made. The results have been mixed but the issue continues to be significant.

Clippinger discusses the importance of a future-oriented model in which to view religion in adults. He believes that faith and moral values are closely linked. Religion is seen as the means by which persons fulfill themselves, and it plays a pivotal role in determining values.

This portion of the book will provide the student with insights about the ways in which religion functions in the lives of persons as they grow from birth to maturity.

# The Origins of Religion in the Child

## DAVID ELKIND

Every social institution, whether it be science, art, or religion, can be regarded as an externalized adaptation which serves both the individual and society. From the point of view of the group, social institutions provide the ground rules and regulations which make society and social progress possible. Looked at from the standpoint of the individual, social institutions afford ready-made solutions to the inevitable conflicts with social and physical reality which the individual encounters in his march through life. Social institutions, therefore, originate and evolve out of the adaptive efforts of both society and the individual. It follows that any complete account of the origins of religion must deal both with individual and social processes of adaptation.

In the present paper, I propose to treat the origins of religion solely from the perspective of the individual and not from that of society. It is not my intent, therefore, to give a comprehensive account of the origins of religion in general nor in any way to negate the central importance of social factors in the origination and historical evolution of religion. All that I hope to demonstrate is that religion has an individual as well as a social lineage and that this individual lineage can be traced to certain cognitive need capacities which emerge in the course of mental growth. To whatever extent religion derives from society's efforts to resolve the conflicts engendered by these individual need capacities, we are justified in speaking of the origins of religion in the child.

Briefly stated, the paper will describe four cognitive need capacities with respect to the age at which they first make their appearance, the problems of adaptation which they engender, and the corresponding resolutions offered by religion. A concluding section will take up the

Reprinted with permission of author and publisher from:

*Review of Religious Research,* 1970, 12 (1), 35-42, copyright 1970 by the Religious Research Association.

question of the uniqueness of religious adaptations from the point of view of the individual.

## EMERGENCE OF COGNITIVE NEED
## CAPACITIES IN THE CHILD

In describing the mental development of the child, this presentation will lean rather heavily upon the work of the Swiss psychologist, Jean Piaget. For more than forty years Piaget has been studying the mental development of the child. He has evolved a general theory of intelligence, wherein he derives the thinking of adults from the gradual elaboration of mental abilities in the child.[1] In effect, Piaget argues that each new mental capacity carries with it the need to realize itself through action and that, in the course of such realization, the individual comes into conflict with social and physical realities. The resolution of each such conflict results in structural changes which we call growth and which in turn pave the way for new conflicts and further growth in an unending dialectic.

Although Piaget's theory would seem to have rather direct implications for religious development, he has not himself, except for a few early papers (Piaget, 1923; 1930) dealt with the problem at length. It seems to me, however, that the major elements common to most religions provide comfortable solutions to some of the conflicts which Piaget's cognitive need capacities engender in the course of their realization. I must emphasize, however, that this is my way of viewing the problem and is not necessarily the way in which Piaget would deal with the issue, were he to attack it.

Before proceeding to the discussion of the cognitive need capacities themselves, it might be well to give a few concrete illustrations of the way in which their efforts at realization result in problems of adaptation. Once the child acquires language and a rudimentary understanding of causality, for example, he enters the notorious "why" stage. He soon discovers, however, that parents do not appreciate such questions, particularly when they are endlessly repeated. The child's attempts to realize his capacity for causal understanding thus bring him into conflict with the adult world. In the same way, when the child of four or five years begins to realize his emerging capacity to deal with quantitative relations, he again comes into conflict with others. His constant concern with "who has more" fails to endear him either to his parents or to his siblings. In short, every cognitive capacity is in itself a need which prompts behaviors that can create discord between the child and his social and physical milieu.

## INFANCY AND THE SEARCH FOR
## CONSERVATION

During the first two years of life, the human infant makes truly remarkable progress. From an uncoordinated, primarily reflex organism, he is within the course of a short two-year period transformed into an upright, talking semi-socialized being, more advanced intellectually than the most mature animal of any species. Of the many accomplishments during this period, none is perhaps as significant nor of such general importance as the discovery that objects exist when they are no longer present to the senses, that is to say, the discovery that objects are *conserved.*

To the adult, for whom the world and the self are clearly demarcated, it is hard to envision the infant's situation. The closest we can come to it is in a state of reverie or semi-consciousness when the boundaries of awareness waver and we are imbedded in the very pictures we are sensing. This is the perpetual state of the infant for whom all awareness can hardly be more than a series of blurred pictures following one another in an unpredictable sequence. Only gradually does the child begin to separate his own actions from things and to discriminate among different things, such as the human face. Even when the response to the human face occurs, usually in the second and third months of life, there is still no awareness that the face exists when it is no longer present. An infant, for example, who is smiling delightedly at an adult peering at him from the side of the crib will turn his head away immediately if the adult ducks out of sight. The infant does not cry; he behaves as if the adult drops out of existence when he disappears (Piaget, 1952).

Only toward the end of the second year and as a consequence of a series of progressive learnings and coordinations does the infant give evidence that for him objects now exist and have a permanence of their own quite independent of his immediate sensory experience. At this age, for example, the young child will search for objects, such as candy or a toy, which he saw hidden from view. This awareness of the permanence or conservation of objects comes about when the progressive coordinations of behavior give rise to internal representations or images of absent objects. It is the two-year-old's capacity to mentally represent absent objects which results in their conservation.

The construction of permanent objects is important because it is a prerequisite for all later mental activity. All of our concepts start from or involve objects in one way or another, so the recognition of their permanence is a necessary starting point for intellectual growth in general. Object permanence, however, is just the first of many such permanences or conservations which the child must construct. As his mental capacities expand, he encounters new situations which parallel, though at a higher level of abstraction, the disappearance of objects. Illusions are a case in point. A spoon in water looks bent or even broken, the moon appears to follow us when we walk, just as the sun appears to revolve around the earth. Similar problems present themselves on the social plane. The child must learn to distinguish, for example, a true invitation to stay at a friend's home from an invitation which is, in fact, a polite dismissal. In all of these cases the child has to distinguish between appearance and reality, between how things look and how they really are. Infancy thus bears witness to a new mental ability, the capacity to deal with absent objects, and to a corresponding need, *the search for conservation,* a life-long quest for permanence amidst a world of change.

One of the problems of conservation which all children eventually encounter, and to which they must all adapt, is the discovery that they and their loved ones must ultimately die. In contrast to the conservation of the object, which is first transient and only later permanent, the child begins by assuming that life is everlasting and is shocked when he finds out that it is transient. After the initial recognition, often accompanied by intense emotional outbursts, the child seeks means whereby life can be conserved, a quest which continues throughout his existence.

In many cases, the conflict between the search for conservation and the inevitability of death does not arise with its full impact until adolescence. Religion, to which the young person has already been exposed, offers a ready solution. This solution lies in the concept of God or Spirit which appears to be religion's universal answer to the problem of the conservation of life. God is the ultimate conservation since he transcends the bounds of space, time, and corporality. By accepting God, the young person participates in his immortality and hence resolves the problem of the conservation of life. Obviously, whether in any particular case the young person will accept the religious solution will be determined by a host of personal and sociocultural factors. All that I wish to emphasize here is that religion offers an immediate solution to the seemingly universal human problem posed by the search for conservation of life and the reality of death.

## EARLY CHILDHOOD AND THE SEARCH FOR REPRESENTATION

As was true for the period of infancy, the preschool period is one of rapid mental growth and of wide-ranging intellectual accomplishments. Foremost among these is the mastery of language. With the conquest of language the child goes far beyond the representation of things by mental images. Language is a series of conventional signs which bear no physical resemblance to that which they represent. The child must now painstakingly learn to represent all of those objects which were so laboriously constructed during the first years of life. The child is not, however, limited to representing things by language, he can now also employ symbols which bear some semblance to the objects which they represent. At this stage, the child creates his own playthings and transforms pieces of wood into boats, pieces of paper into airplanes, and odd-shaped stones into animals (Piaget, 1951). It is at this stage, too that the child dons adult clothes and plays house, store, and school. All of these behaviors, the mastery of language, and engagement in symbolic play activities bear witness to a new cognitive capacity, the ability to use signs and symbols, and to a new cognitive need, *the search for representation.*

The search for representation, which makes its appearance in early childhood, like the search for conservation, continues throughout life. At each point in his development, the young person seeks to represent both the contents of his own thought and those of his physical and social environment. As his knowledge of himself and his world grows more exact, he seeks more exacting forms of representation. Not only does his vocabulary increase at an extraordinary rate, but he also begins to acquire new tools of representation, such as mathematics and the graphic arts. Yet, the more exacting the child becomes in his search for representation, the more dissatisfied he becomes with the results. One reason, to illustrate, why children usually give up drawing in about the fourth or fifth grade is their disgust with the discrepancy between what they wish to portray and what they have actually drawn. In the same way as the child matures, he gradually realizes that language is a lumbering means at best for conveying his thoughts and is hopelessly inadequate for expressing his feelings.

For the young person who has accepted God, the search for representation poses special problems. If religion provided only a concept of God and nothing else, he would be at a loss to represent the transcendent. How, after all, does one signify that which is neither spatial, temporal, nor corporeal? Religion, however, affords more than a simple God concept; it also provides representations of the transcendent. In primitive religions the representations were totems or idols; whereas in modern "revealed" religions, the Transcendent finds its representation in Scripture. Here again, however, as in the case of the concept of God, the individual's acceptance of the religious solution is multi-determined and difficult to predict in the particular case. What must be stressed is that once the individual accepts the concept of God, the question of his representation is an inevitable outcome of the search for representation in general.

## CHILDHOOD AND THE SEARCH FOR RELATIONS

The school age period is one of less rapid intellectual growth than was true for the preceding two periods. During this epoch in the child's life he is, for the first time, exposed to formal instruction and must acquire a prescribed body of knowledge and special skills such as reading and writing. The acquisition of a prescribed body of knowledge, however, presupposes a mental system which is in part at least comparable to the mental systems of adults who transmit the knowledge. Such a system does come into being at around the sixth or seventh year, the traditional "age of reason." Research on children's thinking has shown that this is in fact quite an appropriate designation of the accomplishments of this age period. It is only at about the age of six or seven, for example, that the child manifests the ability to make logical deductions (i.e., to recognize that if A is greater than B, and if B is greater than C, then A must be greater than C even if he has not compared A and C directly); to nest classes (i.e., recognize that, say, boys + girls = children, and children − boys = girls, etc.) and to seriate relations (group elements systematically so that $A>B>C>D<E<F$, etc.) (Piaget, 1952; Elkind, 1961; 1965).

One general feature of this new ability to reason in a logical manner is that the child now tries to relate phenomena in the world about him in a systematic manner. The youngster at this stage wants to know how things work, how they are put together, where they come from, and out of what they are made. Moreover, his concepts of time and space have broadened, and he can now grasp historical time and conceive of such distant places as foreign countries. It is the age period during which Robinson Crusoe has his greatest appeal, because Crusoe describes in marvelous detail all the building, planting, hunting, and fishing activities in which he engages. In a very real sense, then, the child is trying to relate things to one another with respect to time, space, causality, and origin. It seems appropriate, therefore, to speak of the new ability that surfaces at school age as the capacity for practical reason and of the corresponding need as the *search for relations*.

The search for relations, which makes its appearance in childhood proper, continues throughout life. As the young person matures, he seeks to relate himself to his social and physical milieu and to relate the things and events in his world to one another. While this search for relations is often gratifying, it is also on occasion disheartening. There are many events in life which cannot be related to one another in any simple rational way. The quirks of fate and accident are of this kind and defy man's rational efforts. There is often no simple rational answer to the question, "Why did this happen to me?" So, while the quest for relations helps man to understand himself and his world better, it also makes him aware of how much he cannot know and understand.

Within the religious sphere, the young person who has accepted the concept of God and his scriptural representation, is confronted with the problem of putting himself in relation to the Transcendent. Here again, in the absence of a ready-made solution, the young person might flounder and his resolution of the problem would be makeshift at best. Religion, however, affords a means whereby the individual can relate himself to the deity, for it offers the sacrament of worship. By participating in worship, the young person can relate himself to the Transcendent in a direct and personal way. To be sure, the young person's acceptance of religion's answer to the problem will again be determined by a variety of factors. Indeed, some of our research (Elkind & Elkind, 1962; Long, Elkind and Spilka, 1967) suggests that many young people reject the formal worship service but nonetheless engage in individual worship in the privacy of their rooms. In any case, for the adolescent who has accepted God and his Scriptural representation the question of relating himself to God is an inevitable one, no matter how it is resolved.

## ADOLESCENCE AND THE SEARCH FOR COMPREHENSION

The physical and physiological transformations so prominent in adolescence frequently obscure the equally momentous changes undergone by intelligence during the same period. As a consequence of both maturation and experience, a new mental system emerges in adolescence which enables the young person to accomplish feats of thought that far surpass the elementary reasonings of the child. One feat that makes its appearance is the capacity to introspect, to take one's thought and feelings as if they were external objects and to examine and reason about them. Still another feat is the capacity to construct ideal or contrary-to-fact situations, to conceive of utopian societies, ideal mates, and preeminent careers. Finally, in problem-solving situations the adolescent, in contrast to the child, can take all of the possible factors

**D. Elkind**

into account and test their possibilities in a systematic fashion (Inhelder & Piaget, 1958).

Implicit in all of these new mental accomplishments is the capacity to construct and think in terms of overriding theories which enable the young person not only to grasp relations but also to grasp the underlying reasons for them. To use a biological analogy, the child is concerned with phenotypes, whereas the adolescent focuses his attention upon the genotypes, the underlying laws and principles which relate a variety of apparently diverse phenomena. It seems reasonable, therefore, to characterize the mental ability which emerges in adolescence as the capacity for theory construction and the corresponding need as *the search for comprehension.*

As in the case of the other need capacities we have considered, the search for comprehension persists throughout life, although it takes different forms at different stages in the life cycle. The search for comprehension is also like the other need capacities in the sense that it never meets with complete success. Whether it be in the field of science, art, history, or government, each new effort at comprehension uncovers new puzzles for the understanding. The same holds true on the personal plane. Although the adolescent, to illustrate, now has a conception of personality which enables him to understand people in depth, he still encounters human foibles and eccentricities which defy his generalizations. And, though his new-found capacity for comprehension enables him to hold a mirror to his mind, he still frequently fails to understand himself.

In the domain of religion, the problem of comprehension arises naturally to those who have accepted God, his Scriptural representation, and the sacrament of worship. Many young people often seek such comprehension on their own with the result that they become bewildered and disheartened by the failure of their efforts. Religion again provides a solution. Every religion contains a body of myth, legend, and history which provides a means for comprehending God in his various aspects. In modern religions, the resolution to the problem of comprehension is provided by theology. It may be, however, that the ferment within present-day theological discussions makes it more difficult than heretofore for the young person to accept the religious solution to the problem of comprehension. Be that as it may, for the individual who has accepted God, his representation, and his worship, the problem of comprehension must be faced regardless of how it may be resolved.

I am aware that the foregoing discussion probably raises many more questions than it has answered. All that I have tried to do is to present a scheme to illustrate the extraordinary fit between certain basic cognitive need capacities and the major elements of institutional religion. It is probable that this fit is not accidental and that religion has, in part at least, evolved to provide solutions to the problems of adaptation posed by these need capacities. To the extent that this is true, to that extent are we justified in speaking of the origins of religion in the child.

## CONCLUSION

Psychologists who have concerned themselves with religious phenomena (e.g., Allport, 1960; Dunlap, 1946; James, 1902) are in general agreement with respect to one point, namely, that there are no uniquely religious psychic elements. Insofar as anyone has been able to determine, there are no drives, sentiments, emotions, or mental categories which are inherently religious. Psychic elements, it is agreed, become religious only insofar as they become associated with one or another aspect of institutional religion. Nothing which has been said so far contradicts this position, with which I am in complete agreement.

Nonetheless, the view that there are no uniquely religious psychic elements does not preclude the possibility that there may be uniquely religious *adaptations*. Adaptations, by definition, are neither innate nor acquired but are instead the products of subject (individual or society) environment interaction. Every adaptation is thus a construction which bears the stamp of both nature and nurture, yet is reducible to neither one. The same holds true for religious adaptations. The concept of God, Spirit, or more generally, the Transcendent, cannot be reduced to the search for conservation any more than it can be traced to the phenomenon of death. Contrariwise, neither the search for conservation nor the phenomenon of death is in itself religious, although it may well take part in the production of religious elements. Like a Gestalt, such as a painting or a melody, the Transcendent is greater than the sum or product of its parts.

As suggested above, once the concept of God or Spirit is accepted as the ultimate conservation, it necessarily entails genuinely religious problems for the other emerging need capacities. These problems can, in turn, be immediately resolved by the ready-made constructions afforded by institutional religion, such as Scripture, worship, and theology. From the standpoint of the individual, therefore, the concept of God or of the Transcendent lies at the very core of personal religion. At the same time, however, whether the concept of God is a personal construction or one acquired from institutional religion, it is always

# D. Elkind

superordinate, transcending the particular individual or social needs as well as the phenomenal facts out of which it arose.

## NOTES AND REFERENCES

[1]For a comprehensive and detailed summary and interpretation of Piaget's work, see Flavell (1963). A briefer introduction is provided by Elkind (1967).

ALLPORT, G. W. 1960 The Individual and His Religion. New York: Macmillan.

DUNLAP, K. 1946 Religion: Its Function in Human Life. New York: McGraw Hill.

ELKIND, D. 1961 "The development of quantitative thinking." Journal of Genetic Psychology 98:37-46. 1964 "Discrimination, seriation and numeration of size and dimensional differences in young children" 104: 275-296.

ELKIND, D. (Ed.) 1967 Six Psychological Studies by Jean Piaget. New York: Random House.

ELKIND, D., AND ELKIND, SALLY F. 1962 "Varieties of religious experience in young adolescents." Journal for the scientific study of religion II: 102-112.

FLAVELL, J. H. 1963 The Developmental Psychology of Jean Piaget. New York: Van Nostrand.

INHELDER, BARBEL, AND PIAGET J. 1968 The Growth of Logical Thinking from Childhood through Adolescence. New York: Basic Books.

JAMES, W. 1902 Varieties of Religious Experience. New York: Longmans.

LONG, DIANE, ELKIND, D., AND SPILKA, B. 1967 "The child's conception of prayer." Journal for the scientific study of religion. VI: 101-109.

PIAGET, J. 1923 La Psychologie et les Foi Religieuses. Geneve: Labor. 1930 Immanentisme et foi religieuse. Geneve: Robert. 1951 Play, Dreams and Imitation in Childhood. New York: W. W. Norton. 1952 The Child's Conception of Number. New York: Humanities Press. 1954 The Construction of Reality in the Child. New York: Basic Books.

# Change and Stability of Religious Orientations During College

## KENNETH A. FELDMAN

Researchers have studied change and stability of college students during their undergraduate years along a wide variety of dimensions—including intellectual skills and dispositions; capacity for independent and creative thinking; skills necessary for moving into adult statuses; values and life goals; attitudes toward political, economic, social, and religious issues; authoritarianism and prejudice; and interpersonal and intrapersonal adjustments (including a number of personality dimensions). This article is a review and integration of the research literature in one of these areas: religious change and stability of undergraduate college students.

This article is based on a recent monograph (Feldman and Newcomb, 1969) the purpose of which was to integrate the published and unpublished research of the past four decades on the impacts of America's colleges on their students.[1] The search for published and unpublished literature was not intended to be a complete *omnium gatherum* nor a total flight into exhaustiveness, although there was an attempt to be as comprehensive as possible within the limitations of available resources. Information about the change and stability of students along the religious dimension is dispersed throughout this monograph. What I wish to do in this and the forthcoming second part is to gather together this scattered information and, more importantly, to present additional information about certain studies, to add new studies not previously summarized or cited, to pursue issues not previously discussed, and to draw out some implications for future research in the area of college impacts on students' religious outlooks.

In the two parts of this article, I have intentionally restricted my

Reprinted with permission of author and publisher from:

*Review of Religious Research,* 1969, 11 (1), 40-60, Copyright 1969 by the Religious Research Association.

attention to change and stability of college students' religious orientations and behaviors during their undergraduate years, particularly as various kinds of college experiences may have directly and indirectly influenced such change and stability. This focus—circumscribed by what can loosely be referred to as studies of "college effects on religion"—hardly exhausts the topics of interest in the study of the interrelationships among religion and higher education. Although the many other areas of interest will not be discussed in either part of this article, the following does list a few of them together with some selected readings in each:

(1) Comparison of different student generations on religious and moral attitudes (Allport, Gillespie, and Young, 1948; Cummins and Kissiah, 1968; Eddy, 1968; Gilliland, 1953; Heath, 1968; Hoge, 1967; Pressey and Jones, 1955; Rettig and Pasamanick, 1959a, 1959b, 1960; Young, Dustin, and Holtzman, 1966).

(2) Structure, functions, and impacts of sectarian colleges and universities (Greeley, 1962, 1963, 1967; Hassenger, 1965, 1967; Jencks and Riesman, 1968; Pattillo and MacKenzie, 1966; Trent, 1964, 1967; Weiss, 1964; Westoff and Potvin, 1967).

(3) Differential change on non-religious attributes by students of different religious affiliations (Brown and Bystryn, 1956; Dean and Reeves, 1962: Lehmann and Dressel, 1962; Payne, 1961; Raffel, 1965; Trent, 1967).

(4) Psychological and social correlates of students' religious beliefs and attitudes (Allport, Gillespie, and Young, 1948; Cline and Richards, 1965; Goldsen *et al.,* 1960; Hassenger, 1964, 1965; Hershenson, 1967; Katz and Allport, 1931; Kosa, Rachiele, and Schommer, 1962; McNamara, 1963; Symington, 1935; Trent, 1964).

## COMPARING SENIORS AND FRESHMEN

As an initial step toward discovering the effects of colleges on the religious outlooks of students, the following question may be posed: Do American students, regardless of who they are or where they go to college, typically change in certain ways in their orientation to religion during their undergraduate years? One way to answering this question is to determine the consistency in results of studies that either (1) cross-sectionally compare the religious attributes of freshmen and seniors at a certain college (or certain colleges) at a given point in time, or , preferably, (2) longitudinally compare the religious characteristics of students as entering freshmen with the characteristics of the *same* students when they are departing seniors.

In reviewing these studies, I shall assume—for the moment—full reliability and validity of the measures (including single-item indicators of religiosity) used in the studies. I shall also assume complete meaningfulness of the various findings. Certain measurement problems and interpretive difficulties, as well as concomitant conceptual issues, will be raised in later pages.

## Importance of religious values

One goal of research in this general area of freshman-senior comparisons has been that of finding out whether college students are likely to change in certain ways in the *degree* to which religious concerns serve as an important value to them relative to other values. For the present purposes, a value is considered to be a cluster of attitudes organized around a conception of the desirable (cf. Kluckhohn, 1951; Newcomb, Turner, and Converse, 1965).

The Allport-Vernon Study of Values (1931) and its revised form, the Allport-Vernon-Lindzey Study of Values (1951, 1960), offer an instrument for measuring the relative importance of six types of values suggested originally by Spranger (1928). Described in terms of "types of men," the six values are as follows:

(1) *Theoretical*. The dominant value of the theoretical man is the discovery of truth. His interests are empirical, critical, and rational. His chief aim in life is to order and systematize his knowledge.

(2) *Economic*. The economic man characteristically values what is useful and practical, especially the practical affairs of the business world. He judges things primarily by their tangible utility.

(3) *Aesthetic*. The aesthetic man sees his highest value in beauty and in form and harmony. Each experience is judged from the standpoint of grace, symmetry, or fitness. He finds his chief interest in the artistic episodes of life.

(4) *Social*. The highest value for the social man is other human beings in terms of love in its altruistic or philanthropic aspects. He prizes other persons as ends and is therefore himself kind, sympathetic, and unselfish.

(5) *Political*. The political man primarily values power and influence. Leadership, competition, and struggle are important aspects of his interests.

(6) *Religious*. The highest value of the religious man is unity. He is mystical, and seeks to comprehend the cosmos as a whole, to relate himself to its embracing totality.

This instrument measures the relative importance of these values to the individual, rather than the "absolute" importance of each value. For this reason, it is impossible to score highly on all six values; a preference for certain values must always be at the expense of the other values.

The strongest and most consistent changes across the studies using these six scales to compare freshmen and seniors—most of which are longitudinal in design—occur on the religious and aesthetic scales (Arsenian, 1943; Gordon, 1967; Heath, 1968; Huntley, 1965; Lane and Pemberton, n.d.; Miller, 1959; Stewart, 1964; Thompson, 1960; Twomey, 1962; Tyler, 1963; University of Delaware, 1965; Whitely, 1938). Nearly without exception, aesthetic values are of higher relative importance to seniors, whereas religious values are of lower importance. When students other than those who are in their senior year are compared to freshmen, results are the same: the average score on the religious scale decreases and the average score on the aesthetic scale increases, with year in college (Burgemeister, 1940; Hilton and Korn, 1964; Klingelhofer, 1965; Plant and Telford, 1966; Telford and Plant, 1963; Todd, 1941).

For all intents and purposes the *Poe Inventory of Values* (Poe, 1954) measures the importance of the same six values as the *Study of Values,* and in addition two others (Prestige and Humanitarian). The eight value areas are measured independently of each other using Likert-type scales. Thus it is possible to have low (or high) scores in all eight areas at once. In this sense the instrument measures change in the "absolute" importance of the several values. Using this instrument on a longitudinal sample of students at the State University of New York at Plattsburgh, Johnson (n.d.) found a trend toward freshman-senior decrease in the importance of religious values (but no freshman-senior increase in the importance of aesthetic values).

Another way of gauging the importance of religious values to students is to ask them to compare the importance of a number of possible life goals and life satisfactions. Research in this area—at least as conducted during the 1950s and the earlier years of the 1960s—reveals that the typical American student plans to search for the rich, full life within his future family, and from his friendships and his job or career. Of somewhat less importance, though still a major source of expected life satisfaction, are recreational and leisure activities. The student is much less likely to feel that he will derive major life satisfactions from religious beliefs and activities, participation in community affairs, or participation in activities directed toward national or international betterment.[3] To take a concrete example, in the early 1950s male students from all four college-class levels at eleven universities in the United States were asked what three activities (out of a list of six) they expected would give them the most satisfaction in their lives (Goldsen *et al.*, 1960). The percentage of students endorsing each of the activities as first, second, or third in importance as sources of major life satisfactions was as follows:

| | |
|---|---|
| Family relationships | 89% |
| Career or occupation: | 89% |
| Leisure time recreational activities: | 57% |
| Religious beliefs or activities: | 17% |
| Participation as a citizen in the affairs of the community: | 17% |
| Participation in activities directed toward national or international betterment: | 12% |

From the set of data just given and others like it, the amount and nature of change during the college years in the importance of religious activities and beliefs (in comparison with other sources of life satisfactions) cannot be determined. The few studies that do present freshman-senior comparisons in this area—all done, incidentally, during either the early or middle years of the 1960s—most generally reveal that religious beliefs and activities are of quite low importance to freshmen and are still unimportant in the senior year (Gaff, 1965; Katz, 1967; Katz *et al.*, 1968; Krulee, O'Keefe, and Goldberg, 1966). In only one of these studies were religious beliefs and activities of even modest importance as an expected source of satisfaction: some 38 percent of the freshman women at Mundelein College (a Catholic women's college in Chicago) indicated this source to be one of three most important activities out of a list of ten possible sources (Hruby, 1966b, 1967). Even here, by the time these women were seniors, only 13 percent indicated that religious beliefs and activities were important.

The studies reviewed so far focus on change and stability in the *general* importance of religious values, beliefs, and activities—either relative to other values and activities, or in some nonrelativistic sense. These studies do not tell us about change (or stability) of religious orientations in more *specific* terms, to which the discussion now turns.

## Religious orientation

There have been a number of studies dealing with average change in students' religious orientations, as determined by average change in scores on multi-item scales. These scales are usually interpreted in terms of religious "liberalism" and nonorthodoxy or, conversely, in terms of religious "conservatism" and orthodoxy (Barkley, 1942b; Brown and Lowe, 1951; Bryant, 1958; Burchard, 1964, 1965; Corey, 1940; Ferman, 1960; Flacks, 1963; Gilliland, 1940; Hall, 1951; Hassenger, 1965, 1966; Havens, 1964; Hites, 1965; Hruby, 1966a,

## K. A. Feldman

1966b, 1967; Hunter, 1942; Jones, 1938a, 1938b; S. King, 1967; McConnell *et al.*, forthcoming; Nelson, 1940; Symington, 1935; Thurstone and Chave, 1929; Trent, 1964, 1967; University of Delaware, 1965; West, 1965; Young, Dustin, and Holtzman, 1966). These studies generally show mean changes indicating that seniors, compared with freshmen, are somewhat less orthodox, fundamentalistic or conventional in religious orientation, somewhat more skeptical about the existence and influence of a Supreme Being, somewhat more likely to conceive of God in impersonal terms, and somewhat less favorable toward the church as an institution. Although the trend across studies does exist, mean changes are not always large, and in about a third of the cases showing decreasing favorability toward religion differences are not statistically significant (considering only those studies that give results of statistical tests of significance).

Other studies report cross-sectional differences or longitudinal changes on either a single questionnaire item or a series of such items not combined into a scale (Allport, Gillespie, and Young, 1948; Bain, 1927; Brown, n.d.; Dudycha, 1933b; Gaff, 1965; Garrison and Mann, 1931; Hassenger, 1965; Heath, 1968; Hruby, 1966a, 1966b, 1967; Jones, 1926; Katz and Allport, 1931; MacNaughton, 1966; Spady, 1967; Trent, 1964; Webster, 1958; Webster, Freedman, and Heist, 1962; Wickenden, 1932; Willoughby, 1930). These studies, too, generally show that seniors, as a group, are somewhat less likely to be indifferent or opposed to religion, somewhat more likely to conceive of God in impersonal terms, somewhat less orthodox or fundamentalistic in religious orientation, and somewhat more religiously "liberal." There are, however, a number of items showing no differences between seniors and freshmen, and a few reveal net religious changes in directions that are the reverse of those just given.

From the few studies in the above two sets that present information about attendance at religious services and participation in church-related activities, average change in behavior is consistent with average change in attitudes and beliefs (also see Wilson, 1968). That is, church attendance and religious participation typically decrease between the freshman and senior years in college.

Trends in changes in the area of ethics and morality are clearer and stronger than those in the more specific area of religious orientation, although it should be kept in mind that the distinction between ethical or moral orientation and religious orientation is not completely clear cut and thus is somewhat artificial. With respect to ethical issues and attitudes toward moral norms, upperclassmen are less moralistic, more liberal, and more flexible than lowerclassmen; at the same time, the first group is more morally consistent and manifests a higher level of judgment in its moral thought (Barkley, 1942a; Baur, 1965; Buck, 1936; Dudycha, 1933a; Foster *et al.,* 1961a; Glick, 1963; Kuhlen, 1941; Pressey, 1946; Pressey and Jones, 1955).

## Uniformity and patterning of students' religious characteristics

Average scale scores are not the only group characteristics of interest in the study of freshman-senior differences. For example, changes in the size of standard deviations (as indicators of the dispersion of scores around mean scores) give useful information from which to make inferences about the impact of college on students. Even if there are no mean differences between freshmen and seniors on some variable, it is still possible that there is a significant increase or decrease in the dispersion of scores. That is, even though a group of students has not shifted in average score, the college may still have had an impact of either "homogenization" or "heterogenization." Of course, there can be change in mean scores in addition to change in size of standard deviation.

Reviewing freshman-senior differences in standard deviations in a variety of change areas, Feldman and Newcomb (1969) have found that across colleges, in almost every change-area *including religious outlook,* decreases in homogeneity of scores are as likely as increases. Put otherwise, and contrary to Jacob's assertions in his much-quoted *Changing Values in College* (Jacob, 1959), increasing homogeneity of outlook is a *variable* outcome of the college experience rather than a *constant* one. This leads to a search for determinants of increase (or decrease) in homogeneity.

Change in the *distribution* of scores is another type of change in samples of students as a whole that merits future research. Scores may be distributed unimodally, with the highest frequencies of scores around the mean of the sample, as well as in other shapes, such as bimodal or even multimodal. Even if a group of seniors, compared to itself as a group of freshmen, has not changed in mean score or on dispersion of scores, it is still possible that the scores of these students now bunch in two (or more) peaks, rather than in one (as when they were freshmen). This might be called "factionalization." The change might be in reverse direction—from factionalization in the freshman year to "integration" in the senior year. There are still other possibilities—say from a curve approximating a "normal curve" to one approximating a rectangular distribution. Of course, any of these changes in distribution of scores may be accompanied by various combinations of directional trends in mean change and in changes in the dispersion of scores. Future investigations are needed to determine whether one of these kinds of changes typically predominates across different types of colleges, or whether certain kinds of changes occur at certain kinds of colleges.

## TIMING OF CHANGE
## AND CHANGE PATTERNS

Many of the studies giving average scores for freshmen and seniors on the several religious-value and religious-orientation scales also present mean scores for sophomores and juniors. This information can be used to examine the timing of change and to explore patterns of change.

By tracing out mean scores of contiguous college-class levels, the nature of the change-curve for any particular variable can be determined. For some change areas, these change curves are quite consistent across studies. Thus the predominant type of curve across various investigations for authoritarianism (including related variables of dogmatism, ethnocentrism, prejudice, and so on) shows progressive decrease; and the predominant type of curve across studies of political-economic liberalism shows progressive increase (Feldman and Newcomb, 1969, Chapter 4). Generally speaking, then, each class becomes progressively less authoritarian and each class becomes progressively more liberal in politico-economic orientation. In each of these areas, the curves that are not of this nature are almost always of the kind showing a junior "peak" (in increasing politico-economic liberalism), or a junior "trough" (in decreasing authoritarianism), and slight retrenching by seniors in both cases. For changes in religious outlook, however, no particular type of change-curve is predominant. Not only does the shape of the curve vary from study to study, but for some studies the curves are altogether irregular in pattern.

Comparison of the means of contiguous college-class levels can also be used to find out in what year change is typically the greatest. It might be expected that freshman-sophomore differences (in means) would be larger than either sophomore-junior or junior-senior differences (in means), thereby leading to the inference that the impact of college is greatest in the early months or the first year. This expectation is congruent with the view that the first year of college more than any other years is the major period of adjustment. It is reasonable to expect that the impact of the college would be greatest during this time. More than one investigator has argued that the major changes in college occur early in the college experience due to the special sensitivity of freshmen (and perhaps sophomores) to the influences they encounter. Juniors and seniors, in particular, are considered to be in a different developmental phase, one where change is leveling off and where little more happens to them. (For example, see Freedman, 1965; Lehmann and Dressel, 1962; Sanford, 1965.)

On the other hand, there are grounds for not expecting to find, as an invariable occurrence, that college effects are greatest during the freshman year. In the first place, there is no reason to anticipate that the curves of change will be the same in all change-areas or in all colleges. For some dimensions, the early college years may indeed provide the greatest impetus for change, but other areas of potential change may not become salient or relevant to students until their later college years. Likewise, at some colleges the challenges of the early years may be greater than those of the later years, whereas the structural arrangements of other colleges may create greater pressures for change on upper-division than on lower-division students.

Secondly, the timing of change depends upon individual rhythms of adaptations. Even if most students find the challenges of their first year to be heavier than those of later years, they may still differ in the degree and timing in which such challenges are "registered" in terms of change. For some, change may be almost immediate; for others there may be a longer period of "working through" with observable change being evidenced only in later college years. It is even possible that some students find the challenges of their freshman year so heavy that they become resistant to change, only to become less defensive and more likely to change in their junior or senior year.

Because of possibilities such as these, Feldman and Newcomb (1969, Chapter 4) were not particularly surprised not to find any indication that freshman-sophomore differences are larger than sophomore-junior or junior-senior differences in most of the change-areas they surveyed—*including religious orientation*. The major exception was in the area of authoritarianism where freshman-sophomore differences (decreases) are larger than sophomore-junior and junior-senior differences in the majority of studies.

All of this is not to say that religious changes occur only during college but not before. In point of fact, according to students' self-reports, marked change in religious orientation is as likely to begin in high school as in college (see Blau *et al.*, 1966; Bushnell, 1960; Educational Reviewer, 1963; Horton, 1940; Van Tuyl, 1938).

K. A. Feldman

# SOME PROBLEMS OF INTERPRETING
# FRESHMAN-SENIOR DIFFERENCES

## Multidimensionality of responses

Comparisons of average freshman and senior scores (or comparisons between any other college-class levels) on scales measuring religious outlook are not without interpretative problems. One such problem occurs when scales assumed (but not proven to be) unidimensional are in reality multidimensional. Students may differentially respond to different dimensions at different points in time, or they may change on certain of these dimensions and not others. These differentials are hidden in the average change score for a group of students, so that interpretation of an overall difference is not fully meaningful and may be misleading.

One way of discovering the basic dimensions that underlie a multi-item questionnaire or testing instrument is through the use of factor analysis or a similar methodological technique. Hites (1965) factor analyzed the responses of students as freshmen and as seniors at Birmingham Southern College to 37 Likert-type religious items. He found three factors on which four or more items loaded significantly for both freshman and senior testings and on which the factor structure was similar for all items: Factor 1, the function of religion and how revealed; Factor 2, literal-nonliteral acceptance of the Bible; and Factor 3, immortality and man's relation to the physical world. Change was strongest on the first two factors, the first representing average movement from more to less acceptance of certain functions of religion (insuring the survival of civilization, giving meaning to life, explaining the basis of the laws of nature and the mystery of life), and the second representing average movement from a more to a less literal interpretation of religion and from the belief that religion is changeless to a recognition of a constant change in religion. On the third factor, change, which was much less in degree than on the first two dimensions, was in the direction of a more naturalistic interpretation of the world.

In the same spirit of attempting to more fully and accurately interpret average-score change, it may be useful to determine on which individual items of a scale students change most and on which least. For example, Thompson (1960) found that a sample of Macalester College students between entrance and the end of their sophomore year changed on some of the items of the Religious Scale of the Allport-Vernon Study of Values and not on others. The items on which there was very little change involved those dealing with the basic acceptance of a religious point of view, whereas those items on which there was a great deal of change involved a redefinition of the aims of religion (from reverence and worship to humanitarian service).

It is also possible that one category of students changes primarily on one set of items on a multi-item scale or questionnaire, while a second category changes primarily on a different set. For instance, Burchard (1965) has noted that, in his study of freshman-senior change on a questionnaire of religious orientation, male and female students did not change in exactly the same ways on the same items. Men were more susceptible to change in specifically religious beliefs and attitudes, whereas women were more susceptible to change in the area having to do with inter-human or God-human relationships.

Multidimensionality of scales presumed to be unidimensional probably underlies the criticism that is sometimes made of the interpretation of change on scales measuring authoritarianism and politico-economic liberalism—and, by extension, religious liberalism and religious nonorthodoxy. The general criticism is that change scores on tests in these areas may be indicating changes in test-wiseness, sophistication and the like, rather than changes in authoritarianism and various kinds of liberalism. Thus George Smith (1948) writes the following about changes in political and economic liberalism:

> . . . it may be that on campuses, or at least in certain departments, the abler students learn their liberalism as an accommodation to professors, and absorb it from assigned readings in the same enterprising way that they learn French and history. They may, in fact, become "attitude scale wise" just as they become "test wise", and learn to make the expected answers (p. 78).

In a similar vein, others have emphasized the importance of distinguishing increases in liberalization of attitude, in the sense of increases in openmindedness, flexibility, and tolerance, from increases in sophistication of attitude in some genteel or superficial sense. "True" liberalization of attitude is to be distinguished from decreases in naiveté and provincialism (cf. Freedman, 1961, 1965; Brown and Datta, 1959; Bereiter, 1964; Stember, 1961). It is possible to take this sort of criticism as meaning that scales measuring authoritarianism and liberalism (including those concerning religious matters as well as political and economic matters) are simply invalid: they do not measure what they purport to measure, but only sophistication or attitude scale wiseness. Since investigators who construct or use instruments in this area usually offer at least some evidence of the validity of their instruments, it seems unlikely that such tests do not measure liberalism and authoritarianism at all. What seems more likely is that these scales are scored as though they were unidimensional when they may be measuring two or more underlying characteristics. Two likely characteristics that are being measured are liberalism (or authoritarianism) and sophistication (including attitude scale wiseness). Unfortunately, we rarely know the proportions in which the two are combined—although recent studies of change in degree of authoritarianism are beginning to fill in the gaps (Brown and Datta, 1959; Korn, 1967). One awaits similar studies in the religious area.

Multidimensionality of religious scales and questionnaires doubtlessly reflects the complexity of religious phenomena for college students and adults alike. Religious beliefs, attitudes, and feelings do not correlate perfectly with overt religious practices (see, for example, Goode, 1966). Religious orientations of individuals vary in the degree to which they are "intrinsic" rather than "extrinsic" (Allport, 1959, 1960; Wilson, 1960); "noninstrumental" rather than "instrumental" (McNamara, 1963, 1964); and "churchlike" rather than "sectlike" (Dynes, 1955). In factor analyzing 58 separate measures relevant to religious beliefs and practices (many of which were multi-item indices), Cline and Richards (1965) found twelve major religious factors for adult males and eleven for adult females. Glock (1962) posits the following five dimensions of religious commitment, each with its own components and subdimensions: ideological (religious belief); ritualistic (religious practice); experiential (religious feeling); intellectual religious knowledge); and consequential (religious effects). For other analyses of the multidimensionality of "religiosity," see Allen and Spilka (1967); Demerath and Hammond (1969); Fichter (1951); Fukuyama (1961); Goode (1968); Glock and Stark (1965); M. King (1967); Lenski (1961); Stark and Glock (1968). The general conceptual and methodological complexities described by these investigators have not as yet been *fully* and *systematically* considered in the study of change and stability of college students' religiosity—although some college studies, of course, have made efforts in this direction.

## Masking individual changes

A further problem of using differences between freshman and senior mean scores is that such differences may conceal the amount and nature of *individual* changes. Any observed freshman-senior difference is affected both by *extensity* and *intensity*—that is, by the number of individuals who change, and by the degree to which each of them changes. If for purposes of simplicity, group scores of freshman-senior differences are categorized as either high or low, the four cells in Figure

1 show the possible combinations. Assuming for the moment that all changes are in the same direction, then a large change score necessarily points to both high extensity and high intensity (Cell D), just as a small change score indicates small degrees of both (Cell A). Intermediate change scores, however, may result from high-low combinations of extensity and intensity, as in either Cell B or Cell C.

FIGURE 1.—TYPE OF GROUP CHANGE WITHIN A POPULATION, ACCORDING TO EXTENSITY AND INTENSITY OF CHANGE

|  |  | *Intensity of Change* | |
|  |  | LOW | HIGH |
| --- | --- | --- | --- |
| *Extensity* | LOW | Cell A | Cell B |
| *of* | | | |
| *Change* | HIGH | Cell C | Cell D |

The paradigm, though over-simple, illustrates the point that the processes by which change occurs are not the same when mean differences reflect large shifts by a comparatively few individuals and when they represent modest changes by many persons. Within most populations that are being studied, extensity will be somewhere between minimal and maximal, and there will be wide variations in individual intensity. One is not likely, therefore, to know what is responsible for observed differences in mean scores without information about both extensity and intensity.

Cell D is often of most interest to researchers, teachers, and administrators since it may indicate that a college or subgroup in the college is having a significant impact on students with respect both to extensity and intensity. The other cells, however, may also indicate types of impact and are important in their own right. Even Cell A—where most students do not change and the small proportion who do, change only a little—may indicate an impact of college. For example, if a large proportion of persons of college age who are not attending college are changing intensively on some dimension (say, the religious), the lack of such change on the part of college students could well indicate an impact of the college.

The problem of interpreting overall freshman-senior differences is even more complex when—as seems to be especially the case in the religious area—change among students is in more than one direction. A difference either between the percentage of students (at different college-class levels) endorsing a particular religious statement indicates *net change* in a particular direction. As such, these differences mask the amount and direction of individual change.

Data gathered by Eleanor Miller (1959) furnish one example. She randomly picked a small group of freshmen to study over a four-year period. For the twelve students given the Allport-Vernon-Lindzey Study of Values the freshmen received average scores of 41.75 and the seniors 41.57 on the scale measuring the relative importance of religious values. This small and statistically insignificant decrease of .18 obscures the amount and direction of change. The individual changes producing the average changes were as follows, listed from largest individual decrease to largest individual increase: − 19, − 16, − 14, − 12, − 2, +1, +3, +7, +11, +11, +12, +16. These individual changes in opposite directions are "cancelled out" in the average score. Most of them probably represent meaning shifts.

Corey (1940) likewise found little change in average scores over a one-year period on Thurstone's Attitude toward the Church and Attitude toward God scales for a sample of female students at the University of Wisconsin. Exploring individual changes in scale scores, rather than net changes for the group, he found that only ten percent of the students made no change whatsoever in their attitude toward the church as an institution; 48 percent became less sympathetic toward the church whereas 42 percent became more sympathetic. Similarly, 45 percent came to believe less in the reality of God whereas 37 percent increased their belief (18 percent).

Additional evidence of the masking of individual change by net change is offered by studies in which college students are asked directly whether or not they have changed in religious orientation while they have been in college and, if so, in what way. A large number of students in these studies feel that they have changed their orientation toward religion during college; in almost all of the studies, at least half or more of the students in the samples specify a perceived change. Moreover, students clearly do not picture themselves as changing uniformly in one direction. Some say that religion has become less important to them, that they are less committed to a set of religious beliefs, that doubts have been raised in their mind about their particular religious faith. Others report that they have an increased concern with religious questions, an increased attachment to religion, and are generally more favorable toward religion since entering college. In some studies the *net* perceived change is in the direction of strengthened religious beliefs and more interest in religion; in others the *net* perceived change is toward weakened religious faith and lessened religiosity. (See Arsenian, 1943; Blau et al., 1966; Burchard, 1965; Emme, 1941; Jacob, 1957;

Jacobson and Sharp, 1966; Lehmann and Dressel, 1962; MacGregor, 1967; Morgenstern *et al.*, 1965; Newcomb *et al.*, 1967; Trent, 1967; Trent and Medsker, 1967, 1968; for self-reported changes in religious attendance of students at Monteith and the University of Illinois, see Ramshaw, 1966.)

The obscuring of individual change by net change is further revealed in data on students' conceptions of God (Ferman, 1960). Students at Cornell were asked as freshmen and again as juniors to indicate which of the following statements of faith most closely described their ideas about the Deity:

> I believe in a divine God, Creator of the Universe, who knows my innermost thoughts and feelings and to whom one day I shall be accountable.
> I believe in a power greater than myself, which some people call God and some people call nature.
> I believe in the worth of humanity, but not in a God or a Supreme Being.
> I believe in natural law, and that so-called universal mysteries are ultimately knowable according to scientific method.
> I'm not quite sure what I believe.
> I'm an atheist.
> Other.

Table 1, adapted with slight modifications from a table given by Ferman (1960), shows the responses of students as freshmen and as juniors to this question. Additional information, which I have calculated from these raw data, is given in Table 2.

TABLE 1.—RELATIONSHIP BETWEEN THE CONCEPTIONS OF THE DEITY OF 893 CORNELL STUDENTS AS FRESHMEN (1950) AND AS JUNIORS (1952). ADAPTED FROM TABLE 1 IN FERMAN (1960).

| | *Response distribution (in absolute numbers) for freshmen in 1950* | | | | | | | |
|---|---|---|---|---|---|---|---|---|
| Response distribution (in absolute numbers) for juniors in 1952 | "Divine God" | "Power greater than myself" | "God as humanity" | "Natural Law" | "Not quite sure what I believe" | "Atheist" | Other (Agnostic) | 1952 Totals |
| "Divine God" | 246 | 41 | 2 | 8 | 16 | 2 | 1 | 316 |
| "Power greater than myself" | 64 | 166 | 14 | 12 | 35 | 0 | 2 | 293 |
| "God as humanity" | 2 | 22 | 13 | 7 | 12 | 5 | 1 | 62 |
| "Natural law" | 8 | 14 | 6 | 30 | 6 | 4 | 4 | 72 |
| "Not quite sure what I believe" | 35 | 30 | 6 | 9 | 32 | 1 | 7 | 120 |
| "Atheist" | 1 | 4 | 1 | 1 | 2 | 5 | 0 | 14 |
| Other (Agnostic) | 3 | 2 | 1 | 2 | 3 | 1 | 4 | 16 |
| 1950 totals* | 359 | 279 | 43 | 69 | 106 | 18 | 19 | 893 |

*1950 totals for first five categories incorrectly given in the original table as 361, 285, 46, 74, and 110 respectively.

TABLE 2.—TURNOVER IN THE CONCEPTIONS OF THE DEITY OF 893 CORNELL STUDENTS AS FRESHMEN (1950) AND AS JUNIORS (1952). CALCULATED FROM DATA GIVEN IN TABLE 1 IN FERMAN (1960).

| Response Category | (Col. 1) Original distribution of freshman response (in numbers) | (Col. 2) Original distribution of freshman response (in percentages) | (Col. 3) Distribution of junior response (in numbers) | (Col. 4) Distribution of junior response (in percentages) | (Col. 5) Net change (in numbers) Col. 1 minus Col. 3 | (Col. 6) Net change (in percentages): Col. 2 minus Col. 4 | (Col. 7) Number defecting from original choice | (Col. 8) Percentage defection (no. defecting as a proportion of original size of category): Col. 7 divided by Col. 1 | (Col. 9) Number recruited into each category | (Col. 10) percentage recruitment (no. recruited as a proportion of original size of category): Col. 9 divided by Col. 1 | (Col. 11) Ratio of number of recruits to no. of defectors |
|---|---|---|---|---|---|---|---|---|---|---|---|
| "Divine God" | 359 | 40% | 316 | 35% | −43 | −5% | 113 | 31% | 70 | 20% | 0.62:1 |
| "Power greater than myself" | 279 | 31% | 293 | 33% | +14 | +2% | 113 | 41% | 127 | 46% | 1.12:1 |
| "God as humanity" | 43 | 5% | 62 | 7% | +19 | +2% | 30 | 70% | 49 | 114% | 1.63:1 |
| "Natural law" | 69 | 8% | 72 | 8% | +3 | +0% | 39 | 57% | 42 | 62% | 1.08:1 |
| "Not quite sure what I believe" | 106 | 12% | 120 | 13% | +14 | +1% | 74 | 70% | 88 | 83% | 1.19:1 |
| "Atheist" | 18 | 2% | 14 | 2% | −4 | −0% | 13 | 72% | 9 | 50% | 0.69:1 |
| Other (Agnostic) | 19 | 2% | 16 | 2% | −3 | −0% | 15 | 79% | 12 | 63% | 0.80:1 |

If one simply referred to net percentage change (see Table 2, Column 6) based on the percentage of students endorsing each conception of the Deity as freshmen and as juniors (see Table 2, Columns 2 and 4), it would appear that very little happened during the students' years in college. As freshmen in 1950, 76 percent of the students endorsed one of the first three conceptions of God ("Divine God," "Power greater than myself," "God as humanity") while as juniors in 1952, 75 percent of these Cornell students selected one of these three categories. The largest net change was in the category of "Divine God" which received endorsement by 40 percent of the freshmen and 35 percent of the juniors—a net loss of 5 percent. "Power greater than myself" made a net gain of 2 percent, as did "God as humanity." Other categories showed even less percentage gain or loss. But these net changes camouflage the amount and direction of change. For example, the net loss of five percentage points for the "Divine God" category—representing a net loss of 43 persons—comes about because 113 persons who originally chose this conception no longer did as juniors, while 70 persons who did not choose this conception as freshmen did so as juniors (see Table 2, Columns 7 and 9). To give another example, the two percent or 14-person increase in the choice of the conception of God as a "Power greater than myself" is based on a defection of 113 students from this category and a recruitment of 127 students to this category. All told, during 1950 and 1952, of the 893 students of the sample of

Cornell students, 397 (or 45 percent) changed their responses to the question about conceptions of the Deity.

If one had information solely about net percentage changes, one obvious inference would be that the "Divine God" category had the largest net loss because it had the highest defection rate of the seven categories. Column 8 in Table 2 shows this *not* to be true. Comparing defection rates of the seven conceptions of the Deity, "Divine God" actually had the *lowest* defection rate—that is, the proportion of the original students selecting a category who then changed to another category was the lowest for "Divine God." The conception of "God as humanity," in contrast, had the highest net change (in absolute numbers) but also a very high defection rate. What is at work here is that the rate of recruitment into these categories differed; thus all the defectors from the "Divine God" category were obviously not replaced, whereas the defectors from the "God as humanity" category were more than replaced. This is shown directly in Column 10 of Table 2, which gives the recruitment rate (students who are recruited into a category as a proportion of the original entrants for each category). The "Divine God" category had the lowest and the "God as humanity" had the highest rate of recruitment by this index. Similarly, as shown in Column 11, the latter category had the highest ratio of recruits to defectors while the former had the lowest ratio.

In sum, data from studies using a methodology that does not obscure the amount of religious change indicate that there is rather extensive change during the college years but not in a uniform direction. This extensity of change is shown by freshman-senior changes on scale scores as well as by the fact that one-half or more of the students at most colleges are likely to say that they have changed their religious orientation during college. The fact that religious changes are in more than one direction most likely indicates that the influences of most colleges on religious orientations are neither direct nor uniform but, not surprisingly, are indirect and diffuse.

## Need for comparison groups

*Non-College students.* From the studies reviewed to this point—at least as they have been summarized herein—it cannot be determined whether the changes that occur during the college years are due to the college experience *per se*. It is true that some proportion of students do specify that aspects of college have directly or indirectly influenced their thoughts and feelings about religion—teachers, courses, outside reading, college friends, and the like (Arsenian, 1943; Educational

Reviewer, 1963; Katz and Allport, 1931; MacGregor, 1967; Ramshaw, 1966). However, it may be that there are analogous influences on non-college persons (of college age) effecting the same overall amount and kinds of change. The question therefore arises whether comparable changes are also occurring in young people of college age who do not attend college. If these persons change in ways similar to college attenders, it could be argued that the changes in both groups either reflect general maturational development within American society or are determined by general societal-wide cultural forces at work during the years under study and thus reflect a societal trend. To determine whether, and to what degree, change during the college years can be attributed to the experiences in college requires the availability of research data collected in ways designed to answer such questions. One way is to observe changes in a control group of noncollege persons at the same time that students at college are being studied.

Only two studies—by Plant (1962, 1965) and Trent and Medsker (1967, 1968)—have systematically studied four-year changes of control groups in addition to changes by college students. From these studies, the best generalization that can be made is that on such dimensions as intellectual dispositions and authoritarianism (and related variables of dogmatism, ethnocentrism, and so on) college experiences have a "facilitative effect" on changes that are occurring in lesser degree in the non-college group (although, in a few cases, the non-college group is not changing at all).

Little is known about the comparison between college and non-college groups with respect to change on religious attributes. Trent and Medsker (1968) longitudinally studied 10,000 young adults from 37 high schools in 16 communities from California to Pennsylvania—comparing (among other things) the group of persons who were to be consistently employed during that time. Unlike their information on other dimensions of change, they did not have before-after data on religious attitudes. However, they did ask persons in both groups (four years after high school) to give their opinions as to whether they valued religion the same, more, or less than they had in high school—with the following results:

> Proportionately more of those in college (approximately 75 percent) than those in jobs (62 percent) reported a change in their religious values, and in both directions. Among the men a greater proportion of the college students compared with the workers reported valuing religion less (26 percent and 12 percent, respectively) and also valuing it more (47 percent and 43 percent, respectively). Twenty-four percent of the college women placed less value on religion, and 7 percent of the

employed women valued religion less, but proportionately more employed than college women valued religion more (59 percent and 54 percent, respectively) (p. 174).

Comparing change over a two-year period by students who attended one of six public junior colleges (in California) with change during the same period by persons who applied to one of these same colleges but did not enter it or any other school, Plant and Telford (1966) found very little in the way of differential average change by the two groups on the Religious Scale of the Allport-Lindzey Study of Values (also see Telford and Plant, 1963). The college females decreased on this scale in about the same average amount as the non-college females. Both male groups also decreased on the average, although in this case the non-college males, having started lower, decreased slightly more than the college groups—perhaps in this case indicating a slight facilitative effect of the non-college environment.

*Alumni.* Apart from non-college comparisons, freshman-senior differences will also take on additional meaning when we know more about change and stability of college alumni. Bender (1958) has shown that between their senior year and fifteen years later Dartmouth alumni typically increased their score on the Religious Scale of the Study of Values. Since it is not known how these men scored as freshmen, it cannot be determined whether this average post-college change on their part is an *extension* or a *reversal* of the average trend during their college days. (It probably is a reversal since almost all studies—as presented earlier in this article—have shown average freshman-senior decreases on this scale.)

Nelson (1956) also found that in 1950 some nine hundred college alumni were on the average more pro-religious than they had been fourteen years earlier, when they were either freshmen, sophomores, juniors, or seniors at eighteen different colleges and universities. Although there was much stability in religious attitudes during the 14-year period, what change there was tended on balance to be in the direction of increased favorability toward the church and increased belief in the reality and influence of God. Given the cross-sectional freshman-senior comparisons of these same persons (and their compeers) when they were in college—presented in Nelson (1940)—this change probably represents a reversal of within-college change.

Likewise, Shand (1968) reports great stability of religious beliefs and attitudes for 114 Amherst alumni during a twenty-year period. The changes that did occur more often than not indicated decrease in doubt, consolidation of religious beliefs, greater conviction, and increased faith. Again, it may be hypothesized that this represents a reversal of

**297**

the typical change of these persons during college, although within-college changes are not given.

Longitudinal investigations of the same persons comparing average freshman-senior change with average senior-alumni change is needed to document these suggestions of a reversal in direction of religious change between that in college and that afterwards. Insofar as such reversals are genuine, they are probably to be accounted for primarily in terms of a shift from college environments, where students reinforce one another in questioning home and family values, to communities in which, as young adults, they are more subject to influences toward accepting than rejecting such values.

But what is really needed—more than comparisons between average freshman-senior differences and average senior-alumni differences—is exactly what Newcomb and his associates (1967) have given us in their study of the political and economic attitudes of female students when they were students at Bennington College and during their post-college life. These investigations separated out women who changed in different ways during college, then traced the change and stability of attitudes for these different alumnae, and finally determined the conditions of differential post-college change and stability. This has not yet been done for change in religious outlook. When it is, there will be answers to such questions as the following: Under what conditions do students who become less religiously orthodox during college persist in their new attitudes or make even further decreases (rather than reverting to prior orthodoxy) after college?

## ONLY A BEGINNING

The above has focused on the ways in which American students, regardless of who they are or where they go to college, typically change in their orientations to religion during their undergraduate years. In a very real sense, however, this is not the most important question to be posed or answered in the analysis of the effects of colleges on the religious attributes of students. American colleges are diverse, and so are their students—even within a single institution. Thus no generalizations could be expected to apply equally to all colleges, nor, *a fortiori,* to all individual students. Moreover, the more interesting questions (and, probably the more clearly answerable ones) are more specific, such as what kinds of students change in what kinds of ways, following what kinds of experiences, mediated by what kinds of institutional arrangements.

## NOTES AND REFERENCES

[1] The monograph is a revision and extension of an earlier report (Newcomb and Feldman, 1968) to the Carnegie Foundation for the Advancement of Teaching, which proposed and sponsored the three-year project.

[2] The lack of interest in public affairs, predominance of privatistic values, and certain forms of apathy and indifference among a relatively large proportion of college students have been observed, documented or analyzed by a number of investigators of the campus scene—including the following: Bolton and Kammeyer, 1967; Bryan, 1967; Bushnell, 1960, 1962; Eddy, 1959; Gaff, 1965; Gillespie and Allport, 1955; Goldsen, 1951; Goldsen et al., 1960; Hall, 1951; Hopwood, 1954; Jacob, 1957; Katz, 1965, 1967, n.d.; Katz and Sanford, 1966; Katz et al., 1968; Keniston, 1962-63; Knode, 1943; Krulee, O'Keefe and Goldberg, 1966; Lehmann and Dressel, 1962; G. F. Lewis, 1965; McCorquodale, 1961; Mogar, 1964; Morgenstern et al., 1965; Phillips and Erickson, 1964; Regan and Thompson, 1965; Richards, 1966; Riesman, 1960; Simon, Carns, and Gagnon, 1968; Trent, 1965, Trent and Craise, 1967; Trent and Medsker, 1967, 1968; Warren, 1964. Exceptions for certain subgroups of students have been noted. For example, in an investigation conducted in the early 1940's with humanities students enrolled predominantly in church-affiliated colleges, values of privatism typically received less emphasis than did more religious, welfare, and community oriented values (Dunkel, 1947, Chapter 2). Also, there has always been a minority of college students who expect to find primary satisfactions in less privatistic areas (or in conjunction with these areas), and thus have become socially and politically active in community and national affairs. This minority, which in recent years has become more vocal, vociferous, visible, organized, and probably proportionately larger, is not particularly committed to conventionally religious activities although it often concerns itself with ethical and moral questions.

ALLEN, R. O., AND B. SPILKA 1967 Committed and consensual religion: A specification of religion-prejudice relationships. Journal for the Scientific Study of Religion, 6, 191-206.

ALLPORT, G. W. 1959 Religion and prejudice. Crane Review, 2, 1-10.

ALLPORT, G. W. 1960 Religion in the developing personality. New York: New York University Press.

ALLPORT, G. W., J. M. GILLESPIE AND JACQUELINE YOUNG 1948 The religion of the post-war college student. Journal of Psychology, 25, 3-33

ALLPORT, G. W., P. E. VERNON 1931 Study of Values manual. Boston: Houghton Mifflin.

ALLPORT, G. W., P. E. VERNON AND G. LINDZEY 1951 Study of Values: manual (rev. ed.). Boston: Houghton Mifflin.

ALLPORT, G. W., P. E. VERNON AND G. LINDZEY 1960 Study of Values: manual (3rd ed.). Boston: Houghton Mifflin.

ARSENIAN, S. 1943 Change in evaluative attitudes during four years of college. Journal of Applied Psychology, 27, 338-349.

BAIN, R. 1927 Religious attitudes of college students. American Journal of Sociology, 32, 762-770.

BARKLEY, K. L. 1942a Development of the moral judgment of college students. Character and Personality, 10, 199-212. 1942b Relative influence of commercial and liberal arts curricula upon changes in students' attitudes. Journal of Social Psychology, 15, 129-144.

BAUR, E. J. 1965 Achievement and role definition of the college student. U.S. Department of Health, Education, and Welfare Cooperative Research Project No. 2605. Lawrence, Ka.: University of Kansas.

BENDER, I. E. 1958 Changes in religious interest: A retest after 15 years. Journal of Abnormal and Social Psychology, 57, 41-46.

BEREITER, C. 1964 Liberalism versus attitude sophistication. Journal of Social Psychology, 63, 121-127.

# K. A. Feldman

BLAU, JUDY, NANCY PITTS, BEV NOSANCHUCK, AND SUE RUSSELL 1966 Religious attitudes: A survey. Unpublished MS (University of Michigan).

BOLTON, C. D., AND K. C. W. KAMMEYER 1967 The university student: A study of student behavior and values. New Haven, Conn.: College and University Press.

BROWN, D. G., AND W. L. LOWE 1951 Religious beliefs and personality characteristics of college students. Journal of Social Psychology, 33, 103-129.

BROWN, D. R., AND DENISE BYSTRYN 1956 College environment, personality, and social ideology of three ethnic groups. Journal of Social Psychology, 44, 279-288.

BROWN, D. R., AND LOIS-ELLIN DATTA 1959 Authoritarianism, verbal ability, and response set. Journal of Abnormal and Social Psychology, 58, 131-134.

BROWN, M. E. n.d. The Sarah Lawrence Study. Unpublished ms (Sarah Lawrence College.)

BRYAN, C. D. B. 1967 1-A or 2-S: The draft and the student. New York Times Magazine (March 19), 26-27, 158-164.

BRYANT, M. D. 1958 Patterns of religious thinking of university students as related to intelligence. Unpublished doctoral dissertation. University of Nebraska.

BUCK, W. 1936 A measurement of changes in attitudes and interests of university students over a ten-year period. Journal of Abnormal and Social Psychology, 31, 12-19.

BURCHARD, W. W. 1964 Religion at a midwestern university: An interim report. Paper read at the annual meeting of the Society for the Scientific Study of Religion. 1965 Effects of college education on religious beliefs and behavior: A preliminary report. Paper read at the annual meeting of the American Catholic Sociological Society.

BURGEMEISTER, BESSIE B. 1940 The permanence of interests of women college students: A study of personality development. Archives of Psychology, 36 (Whole No. 255).

BUSHNELL, J. 1960 Student values: A summary of research and future problems. In Marjorie Carpenter (Ed.), The larger learning: teaching values to college students. Dubuque, Iowa: Brown. Pp. 45-61. 1962 Student culture at Vassar. In N. Sanford (Ed.), The American college: A psychological social interpretation of the higher learning. New York: Wiley. Pp. 489-514.

CLINE, V. B., AND J. M. RICHARDS, JR. 1965 A factor-analytic study of religious belief and behavior. Journal of Personality and Social Psychology, 1, 569-578.

COREY, S. M. 1940 Changes in the opinions of female students after one year at a university. Journal of Social Psychology, 11, 341-351.

CUMMINS, E. J., AND H. C. KISSIAH 1968 Trends in religious attitudes of college freshmen: 1961-1966. Journal of College Student Personnel, 9, 256-258.

DEAN, D. G., AND J. A. REEVES 1962 Anomie: A comparison of a Catholic and a Protestant sample. Sociometry, 25, 209-212.

DEMERATH, N. J., III, AND P. E. HAMMOND 1969 Religion in social context: tradition and transition. New York: Random House.

DUDYCHA, G. J. 1933a The moral beliefs of college students. International Journal of Ethics, 43, 194-204. 1933b The religious beliefs of college students. Journal of Applied Psychology, 17, 585-603.

DUNKEL, H. B. 1947 General education in the humanities. Washington, D. C.: American Council on Education.

DYNES, R. 1955 Church-sect typology and socio-economic status. American Sociological Review, 20, 555-560.

EDDY, E. D., JR. 1959 The college influence on student character. Washington, D. C.: American Council on Education.

EDDY, J. P. 1968 Report on religious activities at Harvard and Radcliffe. College Student Survey, 2, 31-34, 37.

EDUCATIONAL REVIEWER, INC. 1963 Survey of the political and religious attitudes of American college students. National Review, 15, 279-301.

EMME, E. E. 1941 Factors in the religious development of thirty-eight college students. Religious Education, 36, 116-120.

FELDMAN, K. A., AND T. M. NEWCOMB 1969 The impact of college on students. Vol. 1. An analysis of four decades of research. Vol. 2. Summary tables. San Francisco: Jossey-Bass.

FERMAN, L. A. 1960 Religious change on a college campus. Journal of College Student Personnel, 1, 2-12.

FICHTER, J. H. 1951 Dynamics of a city church: southern parish. Chicago: University of Chicago Press.

FLACKS, R. 1963 Adaptations of deviants in a college community. Unpublished doctoral dissertation. University of Michigan.

FOSTER, J. et al. 1961 The impact of a value-oriented university on student attitudes and thinking. U.S. Department of Health, Education, and Welfare Cooperative Research Program Project No. 729. Santa Clara, California: University of Santa Clara.

FREEDMAN, M. B. 1961 Measurement and evaluation of change in college women. U.S. Department of Health, Education, and Welfare Cooperative Reasearch Project No. 736. Poughkeepsie, N.Y.: Mellon Foundation, Vassar College. 1965 Personality growth in the college years. College Board Review, 56, 25-32.

FUKUYAMA, Y. 1961 The major dimensions of church membership. Review of Religious Research, 2, 154-161.

GAFF, J. G. 1965 Danforth study of the campus ministry: A report to the University of the Pacific community. Raymond College, University of the Pacific. (mimeo)

GARRISON, K. C., AND MARGARET MANN 1931 A study of the opinions of college students. Journal of Social Psychology, 2, 168-177.

GILLESPIE, J. M., AND G. W. ALLPORT 1955 Youth's outlook on the future: A cross-national study. New York: Doubleday.

GILLILAND, A. R. 1940 The attitude of college students toward God and the church. Journal of Social Psychology, 11, 11-18. 1953 Changes in religious beliefs of college students. Journal of Social Psychology, 37, 113-116.

GLICK, O. W. 1963 An investigation of changes in the normative system of students in a small liberal arts college. Unpublished doctoral dissertation, University of Kansas.

GLOCK, C. Y. 1962 On the study of religious commitment. Religious Education, 57, S98-S110.

GLOCK, C. Y., AND RODNEY STARK 1965 Religion and society in tension. Chicago: Rand McNally.

GOLDSEN, ROSE K. 1951 Report on the Cornell study body. Social Science Research Center, Cornell University. (mimeo)

GOLDSEN, ROSE K., M. ROSENBERG, R. M. WILLIAMS, JR., AND E. A. SUCHMAN 1960 What college students think. Princeton, New Jersey: Van Nostrand.

GOODE, E. 1966 Social class and church participation. American Journal of Sociology, 72, 102-111. 1968 Class styles of religious sociation. British Journal of Sociology, 19, 1-16.

GORDON, J. H. 1967 Value differences between freshmen and seniors at a state university. College Student Survey, 1, 69-70, 92.

GREELEY, A. M. 1962 The influence of religion on the career plans and occupational values of June, 1961, college graduates. Unpublished doctoral dissertation. University of Chicago. 1963 Religion and career. New York: Sheed and Ward. 1967 The changing Catholic college. Chicago: Aldine.

HALL, R. M. 1951 Religious beliefs and social values of Syracuse University freshmen and seniors, 1950. Unpublished doctoral dissertation. Syracuse University.

HASSENGER, R. 1964 Varieties of religious orientation. Sociological Analysis, 25, 189-199. 1965 The impact of a value-oriented college on the religious orientations of students with various backgrounds, traits and college exposures. Unpublished doctoral dissertation. University of Chicago. 1966 Catholic college impact on religious orientations. Sociological Analysis, 27, 67-79.

# K. A. Feldman

HASSENGER, R. (Ed.) 1967 The shape of Catholic higher education. Chicago: University of Chicago Press.

HAVENS, J. 1964 A study of religious conflict in college students. Journal of Social Psychology, 64, 77-87.

HEATH, D. H. 1968 Growing up in college: liberal education and maturity. San Francisco: Jossey-Bass.

HERSHENSON, D. B. 1967 Family religious background, secondary schooling, and value orientation of college students. Sociological Analysis, 28, 93-96.

HILTON, T. L., AND J. H. KORN 1964 Measured change in personal values. Educational and Psychological Measurement, 24, 609-622.

HITES, R. W. 1965 Change in religious attitudes during four years of college. Journal of Social Psychology, 66, 51-63.

HOGE, D. R. 1967 Trends in religious commitment of college students over several decades. Paper read at the annual meeting at the American Sociological Association.

HOPWOOD, KATHRYN 1954 Expectations of university freshman women. Personnel and Guidance Journal, 32, 464-469.

HORTON, P. B. 1940 Student interest in the church. Religious Education, 35, 215-219.

HRUBY, N. 1966a Comparative tabulations: one possible interpretation. Office of the Vice President, Mundelein College. (mimeo) 1966b Comparative tabulations of Mundelein College Student Questionnaire responses. Office of the Vice President, Mundelein College. (mimeo) 1967 Responses of Mundelein College's entering freshmen to the Student Questionnaire—compared with those of other Mundelein students. Office of the Vice President, Mundelein College. (mimeo)

HUNTER, E. C. 1942 Changes in general attitudes of women students during four years in college. Journal of Social Psychology, 16, 243-257.

HUNTLEY, C. W. 1965 Changes in Study of Values scores during the four years of college. Genetic Psychology Monographs, 71, 349-383.

JACOB, P. E. 1957 Changing values in college: An exploratory study of the impact of college teaching. New York: Harper.

JACOBSON, M., AND SHARP, H. 1966 The college student and the public. Wisconsin Survey Research Laboratory, University Extension, University of Wisconsin. (mimeo)

JENCKS, C., AND D. RIESMAN 1968 The academic revolution. New York: Doubleday.

JOHNSON, S. W. n.d. Progressive changes in educational values over four years of college. Report No. 44 of the Plattsburgh Study. Office of Institutional Research, State University College, Plattsburgh, New York. (mimeo)

JONES, E. S. 1926 The opinions of college students. Journal of Applied Psychology, 10, 427-436.

JONES, V. 1938a Attitudes of college students and the changes in such attitudes during four years in college. Journal of Educational Psychology, 29, 14-25. 1938b Attitudes of college students and the changes in such attitudes during four years in college, part II. Journal of Educational Psychology, 29, 114-134.

KATZ, D., AND F. H. ALLPORT 1931 Students' attitudes: A report of the Syracuse University Reaction Study. Syracuse, New York: Craftsman Press.

KATZ, J. 1965 The learning environment: societal expectations and influences. Paper read at the annual meeting of the American Council on Education. 1967 A portrait of two classes: the undergraduate students at Berkeley and Stanford from entrance to exit. In J. Katz (Ed.), Growth and constraint in college students: A study of the varieties of psychological development. U.S. Department of Health, Education, and Welfare Project No. 5-0799. Stanford, Calif.: Institute for the Study of Human Problems, Stanford University. Pp. 7-80. n.d. The role of the student dean in educational innovation. Claremont, Calif.: College Student Personnel Institute. (mimeo)

KATZ, J., AND R. NEVITT SANFORD 1966 17 to 22: the turbulent years. Stanford Today, Series L, No. 15, 7-10.

KATZ, J. et al. 1968 No time for youth: growth and constraint in college students. San Francisco, Calif.: Jossey-Bass.

KENISTON, K. 1962-63 American students and the "political revival." American Scholar, 32, 40-64.

KING, M. 1967 Measuring the religious variable: nine proposed dimensions. Journal for the Scientific Study of Religion, 6, 173-190.

KING, S. H. 1967 Personality stability: early findings of the Harvard Student Study. Paper presented at the American College Personnel Association Conference.

KLINGELHOFER, E. L. 1965 Studies of the General Education Program at Sacramento State College. Technical Bulletin No. 14. Sacramento, Calif.: Student Personnel Services, Sacramento State College.

KLUCKHOHN, C. et al. 1951 Values and value-orientations. In T. Parsons and E. A. Shils (Eds.), Toward a general theory of action. Cambridge, Mass.: Harvard University Press. Pp. 388-433.

KNODE, J. C. 1943 Attitudes on state university campuses. American Sociological Review, 8, 666-673.

KORN, H. A. 1967 Personality scale changes from the freshman to the senior year. In J. Katz (Ed.), Growth and constraint in college students: A study of the varieties of psychological development. U.S. Department of Health, Education, and Welfare Project No. 5-0799. Stanford, Calif.: Institute for the Study of Human Problems, Stanford University. Pp. 122-155.

KOSA, J., L. RACHIELE AND C. O. SCHOMMER 1962 The self-image and performance of socially mobile college students. Journal of Social Psychology, 56, 301-316.

KRULEE, G. K., R. O'KEEFE AND M. GOLDBERG 1966 Influence of identity processes on student behavior and occupational choice. U.S. Department of Health, Education, and Welfare Project No. 5-0809 (OE 3-10-044). Evanston, Ill.: Northwestern University.

KUHLEN, R. G. 1941 Changes in the attitudes of students and relations of test responses to judgments of associates. School and Society, 53, 514-519.

LANE, G. G., AND CAROL PEMBERTON n.d. Changes in values of college students. Unpublished manuscript. University of Delaware.

LEHMANN, I. J., AND P. L. DRESSEL 1962 Critical thinking, attitudes, and values in higher education. U.S. Department of Health, Education, and Welfare Cooperative Research Project No. 590. East Lansing, Mich.: Michigan State University.

LENSKI, GERHARD 1961 The religious factor: A sociological study of religion's impact on politics, economics, and family life. Garden City, New York: Doubleday.

LEWIS, G. F. 1965 "The new breed": A dissenting view. Saturday Review, 48, No. 37 (Sept. 11), 75-76.

MACGREGOR, A. 1967 Summary of a study of the religious values of 2,750 Brooklyn College students designed and administered by the Brooklyn College Student Committee on Student Values. Memorandum, Office of Student Activities, Brooklyn College. (mimeo)

MACNAUGHTON, W. S. 1966 Comparative profiles of emergent value patterns in undergraduate life at Dartmouth: A summary report on selected data from the Class of 1965 Study of Student Attitudes. Hanover, N.H.: Dartmouth College.

MCCONNELL, T. R., B. CLARK, P. HEIST, M. TROW, AND G. YONGE forthcoming Student development during the college years.

MCCORQUODALE, MARJORIE K. 1961 What They'll Die For in Houston. Harper's Magazine, 223, No. 10 (Oct.), 179-182.

MCNAMARA, R. J. 1963 The interplay of intellectual and religious values. Unpublished doctoral dissertation. Cornell University. 1964 Intellectual values and instrumental religion. Sociological Analysis, 25, 99-107.

MILLER, ELEANOR O. 1959 Nonacademic changes in college students. Educational Record, 40, 118-122.

# K. A. Feldman

MOGAR, R. E. 1964 Value orientations of college students: preliminary data and review of the literature. Psychological Reports, 15. 739-770.

MORGENSTERN, J., M. GUSSOW, K. L. WOODWARD, AND J. M. RUSSIN 1965 Campus '65: the college generation looks at itself and the world around it. Time, 65, No. 12 (March 22), 43-63.

NELSON, E. N. P. 1940 Student attitudes toward religion. Genetic Psychology Monographs, 22, 323-423. 1956 Patterns of religious attitude shifts from college to fourteen years later. Psychological Monographs: General and Applied, 70 (Whole No. 424).

NEWCOMB, T. M., AND K. A. FELDMAN 1968 The impacts of colleges upon their students: A report to the Carnegie Foundation for the Advancement of Teaching. University of Michigan. (mimeo)

NEWCOMB, T. M., KATHRYN E. KOENIG, R. FLACKS, AND D. P. WARWICK 1967 Persistence and change: Bennington College and its students after twenty-five years. New York: Wiley.

NEWCOMB, T. M., R. H. TURNER AND P. E. CONVERSE 1965 Social psychology: the study of human interaction. New York: Holt.

PATTILLO, M. M., JR., AND D. M. MACKENZIE 1966 Church-sponsored higher education in the United States: report of the Danforth Commission. Washington, D.C.: American Council on Education.

PAYNE, ISABELLE K. 1961 The relationship between attitudes and values and selected background characteristics. Unpublished doctoral dissertation. Michigan State University.

PHILLIPS, G. M., AND E. C. ERICKSON 1964 Marvin and Melinda Modal in Collegeville: A preliminary study in the measurement of student values. Washington State University. (mimeo)

PLANT, W. T. 1962 Personality changes associated with a college education. U.S. Department of Health, Education, and Welfare Cooperative Research Branch Project 348 (SAE 7666). San Jose, Calif.: San Jose State College. 1965 Longitudinal changes in intolerance and authoritarianism for subjects differing in amount of college education over four years. Genetic Psychology Monographs, 72, 247-287.

PLANT, W. T., AND C. W. TELFORD 1966 Changes in personality for groups completing different amounts of college over two years. Genetic Psychology Monographs, 74, 3-36.

POE, W. A. 1954 Differential value predictions of college students. Unpublished doctoral dissertation. University of Nebraska.

PRESSEY, S. L. 1946 Changes from 1923 to 1943 in the attitudes of public school and university. Journal of Psychology, 21, 173-188.

PRESSEY, S. L., AND A. W. JONES 1955 1923-1953 and 20-60, age changes in moral codes, anxieties, and interests as shown by the "X-O Tests." Journal of Psychology, 39, 485-502.

RAFFEL, S. 1965 Some effects of Columbia College on its students. Unpublished ms (Columbia College).

RAMSHAW, W. C. 1966 Religious participation and the fate of religious ideology on a resident and a nonresident college campus: an exploratory study. Unpublished doctoral dissertation, University of Illinois.

REGAN, MARY C., AND O. E. THOMPSON 1965 The entering student: College of Agriculture. Research Monograph No. 1. Davis, Calif.: Department of Agricultural Education, University of California, Davis.

RETTIG, S., AND B. PASAMANICK 1959a Changes in moral values among college students: A factorial study. American Sociological Review, 24, 856-863. 1959b Changes in moral values over three decades, 1929-1958. Social Problems, 6, 320-328. 1960 Differences in the structure of moral values of students and alumni. American Sociological Review, 25, 550-555.

RICHARDS, J. M., JR. 1966 Life goals of American college freshmen. Journal of Counseling Psychology, 13, 12-20.

RIESMAN, D. 1960 The uncommitted generation: "Junior Organization Men" in America. Encounter, 15, 25-30.

SANFORD, N. 1965 General education and personality theory. Teachers College Record, 66, 721-732.

SHAND, J. 1968 A twenty-year follow-up study of the religious beliefs of 114 Amherst College students. Unpublished manuscript. Gettysburg College.

SIMON, W., D. CARNS, AND J. H. GAGNON 1968 Student politics: continuities in political socialization. Paper read at the annual meeting of the American Sociological Association.

SPADY, W. G., JR. 1967 Peer integration and academic success: the dropout process among Chicago freshmen. Unpublished doctoral dissertation, University of Chicago.

SPRANGER, E. 1928 Types of men (translated by P. J. W. Pigors). Halle: Niemy.

STARK, R., AND C. Y. GLOCK 1968 Patterns of commitment. Vol. 1. American piety: the nature of religious commitment. Berkeley, Calif.: University of California Press.

STEMBER, C. H. 1961 Education and attitude change: the effect of schooling on prejudice against minority groups. New York: Institute of Human Relations Press.

STEWART, L. H. 1964 Change in personality test scores during college. Journal of Counseling Psychology, 11, 211-230.

SYMINGTON, T. A. 1935 Religious liberals and conservatives: A comparison of those who are liberal in their religious thinking and those who are conservative. Teachers College Contributions to Education, No. 640. New York: Bureau of Publications, Teachers College, Columbia University.

TELFORD, C. W., AND W. T. PLANT 1963 The psychological impact of the public two-year college on certain non-intellectual functions. U.S. Department of Health, Education, and Welfare Cooperative Research Branch Project SAE 8646. San Jose, Calif.: San Jose State College.

THOMPSON, R. W. 1960 Value changes among Macalester College students—1947 to 1951. Unpublished master's thesis. University of Chicago.

THURSTONE, L. L., AND E. J. CHAVE 1929 The measurement of attitude: A psychophysical method and some experiments with a scale for measuring attitude toward the church. Chicago: University of Chicago Press.

TODD, J. E. 1941 Social norms and the behavior of college students. Teacher College Contribution to Education, No. 833. New York: Bureau of Publications, Teachers College, Columbia University.

TRENT, J. W. 1964 The development of intellectual disposition within Catholic colleges. Unpublished doctoral dissertation. University of California, Berkeley. 1965 Personal factors in college choice. Paper read at the annual meeting of the College Entrance Examination Board, New York City, October 26. 1967 Catholics in college: religious commitment and the intellectual life. Chicago: Univ. of Chicago Press.

TRENT, J. W., AND JUDITH L. CRAISE 1967 Commitment and conformity in the American college. Journal of Social Issues, 23, 34-51.

TRENT, J. W., AND L. L. MEDSKER 1967 Beyond high school: A study of 10,000 high school graduates. Berkeley, Calif.: Center for Research and Development in Higher Education, University of California. 1968 Beyond high school: A psychological study of 10,000 high school graduates. San Francisco: Jossey-Bass.

TWOMEY, A. E. 1962 A study of values of a select group of undergraduate students. Unpublished doctoral dissertation. Colorado State College.

TYLER, F. T. 1963 A four-year study of personality traits and values of a group of National Merit Scholars and Certificate of Merit recipients. Center for the Study of Higher Education, University of California, Berkeley. (mimeo)

UNIVERSITY OF DELAWARE 1965 Summary of procedures. Commission to Study the Impact of the University on Its Undergraduates, University of Delaware. (mimeo)

VAN TUYL, MARY C. T. 1938 Where do students "lose" religion? Religious Education, 33, 19-29.

WARREN, J. R. 1964 Student characteristics associated with farm and nonfarm backgrounds. Unpublished ms (University of Nebraska).

WEBSTER, H. 1958 Changes in attitudes during college. Journal of Educational Psychology, 49, 109-117.

WEBSTER, H., M. B. FREEDMAN, AND P. HEIST 1962 Personality changes in college students. In N. Sanford (Ed.), The American college: A psychological and social interpretation of the higher learning. New York: Wiley. Pp. 811-846.

WEISS, R. F. 1964 Student and faculty perceptions of institutional press at Saint Louis University. Unpublished doctoral dissertation. University of Minnesota.

WEST, J. V. 1965 Characteristics and changes in the 1961 Class, Baylor University. In C. H. Bagley (Ed.), Design and methodology in institutional research: Proceedings of Fifth Annual National Institutional Research Forum. Pullman, Wash.: Office of Institutional Research, Washington State University.

WESTOFF, C. F., AND R. H. POTVIN 1967 College women and fertility values. Princeton, N.J.: Princeton University Press.

WHITELY, P. L. 1938 The constancy of personal values. Journal of Abnormal and Social Psychology, 33, 405-408.

WICKENDEN, A. C. 1932 The effect of the college experience upon students' concepts of God. Journal of Religion, 12, 242-267.

WILLOUGHBY, R. R. 1930 A sampling of student opinion. Journal of Social Psychology, 1, 164-169.

WILSON, K. M. 1968 Background document, meeting of the CRC Board of Directors, May 8, 1968. Poughkeepsie, N.Y.: College Research Center, Vassar College.

WILSON, W. C. 1960 Extrinsic religious values and prejudice. Journal of Abnormal and Social Psychology, 60, 286-288.

YOUNG, R. K., D. S. DUSTIN AND W. H. HOLTZMAN 1966 Change in attitude toward religion in a southern university. Psychological Report, 18, 39-46.

# Toward a Human Psychology of Personality

## JOHN A. CLIPPINGER

There is an emerging consensus in certain areas of psychology that sees man as a whole person containing a self, having both ontological and physical dimensions, motivated by present as well as future considerations, possessing the ability to be creative, and able to change his less adaptable patterns of behavior. Maslow saw this as a "third force" in psychology today as against behaviorism and psychoanalysis.[1] By some it is called humanistic psychology, by others proactive psychology, by still others the psychology of being or self psychology. The name of the approach is not important, but the emphasis on the humanity of the individual and his openness to experience constitute the hallmarks of this approach.

I shall present one example and then refer to a number of others. Bonner has developed a proactive psychology that sees man as a being-becoming. It contrasts sharply with classical psychoanalysis, which makes man a creature of the past, held down by his infantile impulses, and with modern behaviorism, which sees him bound by habits that he is never quite able to unlearn. This new approach to psychology emphasizes man's future intentions and his forward directedness. It claims among its adherents such psychologists as Rogers, Maslow, Bugenthal, Frankl, Moustakas, Jourard, Gibb, Allport, and Murphy.

> Proactive psychology is a synthesis and an interpretation of the mind of man derived from empirical science, ontological analysis and humanistic insight. Its methodology is pluralistic, relying on objective procedures, phenomenological description, and immediate cognition. The psychology which emerges from these integrated modes of investigation is a psychology of the total human being.[2]

Such an approach does away with the complete dualism between subject and object, between observer and observed. It recognizes that all

Reprinted with permission of author and publisher from:
*Journal of Religion and Health*, 1973, 12 (3), 241-258.

observations are fraught with subjectivity. Bugenthal has shown that any statement one makes about the world out there is intimately bound up with one's unstated assumptions about the observer's inner world. These include one's feelings about the validity of sense experience, the degree to which one is willing to trust his own feelings, one's own logic, and finally the possibility of the replication of the experiment, to name but a few influential items. Further, in personality study, which is the central facet of this approach, one deals with the object that is most subjectively perceived. Paul Tillich has expressed this idea most cogently:

> A truly objective relation to man is determined by the element of union, the element of detachment is secondary . . . there are levels in man's bodily, psychic and mental constitution which can and must be grasped by controlling knowledge. But this is neither the way of knowing human nature nor is it the way of knowing any individual personality in past or present, including oneself. Without union there is no cognitive approach to man.[3]

## THE WHOLE PERSON

Not only is the element of union important in knowing a person, but there is also the necessity for the appreciation of the unique individuality of the particular person. My late good friend and mentor, Gordon Allport, has made the point that there is both the general and the unique in the psychology of personality. There are certain aspects of behavior in which one is similar to all men. These are dimensional traits. On the other hand, there are certain traits that are unique to each individual; they are called morphogenic traits. There is a uniqueness about the way in which one's traits form an unrepeatable patterning in life that is completely different from one individual to another. Since much psychology of personality today is based on a mathematical assessment of those traits that individuals share in common, its predictions may hold for large groups, but it fails to capture the unique patterning of traits of the individual, thus missing any great degree of understanding of an individual's behavior.[4]

Many psychologists today have sold their souls for a "mess of galloping empiricism" that puts its faith in mathematics and fails to use other rational modes of inquiry. Such a so-called "scientific approach" has led Nevitt Sanford to remark: "The plain fact is that our young psychological researchers do not know what goes on in human beings, and their work shows it."[5]

What is the place of the individual person in a science of psychology? Orthodox science is ethnocentric, being Western rather than universal in origin and acceptance. It is a product, narrowly defined, of the thinking of the past several centuries in Europe and America. Its present methodology of observation, prediction, and control is primarily borrowed from the fields of the natural and biological sciences, where it has enjoyed much success. However, T. S. Kuhn has demonstrated that the style of normal science has not been established by the great "eagles of science," the discoverers, but by the majority of "normal scientists," who remind one of the tiny marine animals that build up a coral reef by slow and patient work. This slow, cautious, obsessional world view appears to many psychologists to be centered on safety rather than on a more mature, generally humane, comprehensive view of life.[6] This produces what Maslow terms "the desacralization of life." It sees life as subhuman and explains it in terms of part reactions. This tendency appears in such statements as "man is just an animal," "you are what you eat," "man's life can be fully explained in terms of operant conditioning," and "the human brain is merely a computer," to give but a few examples. The attempt to reduce the wholeness of life to the lower level of the part reaction is one of the great problems and mistakes of modern scientific psychology. Bertalanffy has pointed out:

> The acceptance of living beings as machines, the domination of the modern world by technology, and the mechanization of mankind are but the extension and practical application of the mechanistic conception of physics.[7]

This is where psychology must part company with the sciences of the past and develop a wholistic science of its own having humanistic dimensions.

Polanyi has shown the fundamental differences between a machine and a person and the resulting differences of study applicable to these two objects. He also points out the possible objectivity, and thus scientific justification, of "participating experience."[8] The late Abraham Maslow caught this very well when he wrote, "The basic coin in the realm of knowing is direct, intimate, experiential knowing." Earlier he affirmed, "I must approach a person as an individual, unique and peculiar, as the sole member of his class."[9]


## FREEDOM AND CHOICE

The most important element of the emerging new view of personality is that of freedom. Does man possess freedom to control his destiny? B. F. Skinner believes not:

> If we are to use the methods of science in the field of human affairs we must assume that behavior is lawful and determined. We must expect to discover that what a man does is the result of specifiable conditions and that once these conditions have been discovered, we can anticipate and to some extent determine his actions. [or again] By arranging conditions in ways specified by the laws of a system, we not only predict, we control; we "cause" an event to occur or to assume certain characteristics.[10]

Recently Skinner has carried his scientific determinism to its logical conclusion. He believes that freedom and human dignity are merely names that fail to control human behavior because they rely primarily on punitive approaches to life, and punished behavior is likely to reappear after the punitive contingencies are withdrawn, since the environment is responsible for the behavior. Thus, science or behavioral technology must design a world in which certain desired activities will be reinforced, with the result that the behavior of persons will be controlled. As Skinner so simply states his position:

> . . . our task is not to encourage moral struggle or to build or demonstrate inner virtues . . . [We must ] proceed to the design of better environments rather than of better men.[11]

The answer was given by Maslow, who pointed out that extremely obsessional people must live by control, by prediction, by law, by order, by manipulation. They are not able to let go. If science is a tool for allaying anxiety, this conception of active control fits very well. But if science is a path to the growth of human beings, we must enlarge our ideas of control. Maslow then suggested the need for "Taoistic science" or "understanding science," the key characteristics of which are receptivity to knowledge, understanding as the main goal of science, freer use of empathy, and a greater stress on experiential knowledge.[12]

The great biologist Theodore Dobzhansky feels that man does have freedom and sees choice as rooted in the biological nature of man.

> The ability of man to choose freely between ideas and acts is one of the fundamental characteristics of human evolution. Perhaps freedom is even the most important of all the specifically human attributes. Human freedom is wider than "necessity apprehended" which is the only kind of freedom recognized by Marxists. Man has freedom to defy necessity, at least in his imagination. Ethics emanate from freedom and are unthinkable without freedom.[13]

The center of man's activity has shifted from Descartes's *cogito* to Jaspers' *ich wahle*—from "I think" to "I choose."

How, then, do we fit the closed system of Skinner with the matter of choice that is characteristic of human personality at its best? Here Bertalanffy's "system theory" permits a relatively closed system such as Skinner's to operate in restricted areas of an open system that is controlled by choice and values. Notice that Skinner's research is primarily based on animal learning and smaller part reactions when human behavior is concerned.

There are closed systems that are mechanical and primarily static in nature. There are open systems that are organismic in nature and dynamic. There are four criteria of open systems: 1) there is intake and output of both matter and energy; 2) there is achievement and maintenance of steady states; 3) there is increase of complexity and differentiation of parts; 4) at the human level there is an extremely extensive transaction with the environment. As von Bertalanffy so aptly put it:

> The universe of symbols created by man's day personality distinguishes him from all other beings . . . Goal-seeking behavior is a general biological characteristic: true purposiveness is a privilege of man and is based upon an anticipation of the future in symbols. Instead of being a product, man becomes the creator of his environment.[14]

Man, then, is not a mere creature of his past conditioning or merely a delicate homeostatic balance of the id and superego maintained by means of a placating ego, as Freud pictured him. He is a creature who moves into the future and shapes that future.

## VALUES

Some 15 years ago I published a paper on "Recent Value Research and Its Significance for Religious Psychology,"[15] in which I cited some 30 articles or books that had shown, from either empirical or clinical findings, the importance of values. Several times that many empirically-oriented works on values have appeared since that time.

Most modern behaviorist psychology has been predicated on the assumption that biological needs are ultimate. However, certain recent anthropological and psychological investigations have shown that values both modify and organize the expression of our needs. Take the need for food. In our society it is more pronounced than in others. But now let us compare two primitive cultures. A laborer in a certain tribe in New Guinea needs a minimum diet of seven pounds of yams and some meat per day, while an Arapesh can lead a normal, healthy life on three pounds of yams a day and almost no meat. Since the size and energy output of individuals in both of these tribes is approximately the same, the difference in food consumption cannot be a mere matter of biological need. As Dorothy Lee has shown, it is the values of the individual that determine his food consumption.[16]

Again, breathing has always been considered an exclusively physiological matter. Studies by T. R. Brosse by means of the pneumograph used on yogis buried underground for ten hours indicated that breathing was actually suspended for periods of up to 15 minutes and that breathing was extremely light at other times. This was a religious exercise; again physiology was controlled by a person's values.[17]

Postman, Bruner, and McGinnies did an interesting experiment in which a person's values were shown to influence his perception of situations. A certain value orientation makes for "perceptual sensitization" to the value object. This in turn leads to "perceptual defense" against irrelevant objects. (How many professors have noted this mechanism at work when their students did not hear such irrelevant sounds as assignments!) Also, perception produces value resonance— the tendency of a person to respond in terms of objects valuable to him even when such objects are not perceptually present. (Here is the psychological explanation of one's response to God even though one has never seen Him.)[18]

Some questions have been asked concerning the set of concepts suggested by the study of the three psychologists, but more recent research seems to have supported the central finding of the experiment according to McGinnies.[19]

The influence of values on memory was demonstrated empirically by Bartlett. Using certain stories, he tested the subject's remembrance of their contents at varying intervals up to a year. As time progressed, the unique features of the original story were lost in recall by means of the individual's choice of details and socially acceptable clichés. In other words, as the material was remembered, it was distorted in terms of the individual's values.[20]

A study by Morgan and Morton has shown that in an area supposedly as rigid as logic, the personal values of the individual play an exceedingly important role. When syllogisms contained nothing to arouse personal convictions, the selection of a conclusion to two premises was determined about half by atmosphere effect and one-fourth each by logic and chance. However, when the syllogism related to the personal values of the individual, it was found that one-fourth of the conclusion was determined by atmosphere, one-fifth each by logic and chance, and a little more than one-third by personal convictions (values).[21]

But how does one's knowledge of values help in understanding human beings? Allport and Vernon developed a test of values based on Spranger's six fundamental types or ways of looking at life.[22] Using this Test of Values, they were able to predict, on a follow-up study of

Wellesley graduates after 15 years, that women significantly high in *economic* interest went into business; women with high *theoretical* interest went into medicine, government, and scientific work; those high in *esthetic* interest went into the fields of literature and art; those high in *social* values went into social work; and those with predominant *religious* values went into religious work. Thus, Allport has shown that even at college age it is possible to forecast in a general way modal vocational activity as a result of certain "basic value postures."[23]

Maslow roots values in biological needs in a very instructive way. He sees certain levels of needs, such as physiological needs, safety needs, belongingness needs, love needs, and self-esteem needs organized in terms of the value that he terms "self-actualization" making operative the potentialities and capacities of the individual in a unified, integrated way that is both understood and accepted by the individual himself. The individual who operates at this level does so not from a deficiency motivation but from a growth perspective.[24]

Meissner, in an excellent review article in the *Journal of Religion and Health* on "Values as Psychological," discusses their characteristics. Values are intrapsychic and nonobservable. They are more or less permanent aspects of personality organization. They are intentional structures, whether explicit or implicit, that are oriented toward a certain goal and involve action. Further, they require selection or decision and are normative. Although they are not sources of energy, they perform a directive and integrative function in human personality.[25]

Now, let us see how they operate in psychotherapy. Charlotte Buhler has done a careful study of values. She feels that Freud, Fenichel, and certain other Freudians as well as a modern Freudian such as Karl Menninger either ignore or deny the importance of values in the therapeutic relationship.[26] In Menninger's vivid picture of the healthy functioning ego he says nothing about the functioning of the patient's value system. Notice his words in describing the patient's ego:

> A sense of greater freedom, a capacity for more joy in life, a cessation of various compulsive activities and a diminution of the tendency to depression.[27]

On the other hand, Buhler feels that Frankl's logotherapy develops "the will to meaning" in patients, but by the very effort he replaces analysis with teaching. Frankl emphasized the central place of duty and meaning in human personality. From his own experience he learned that pleasure and success, two of the supposed basic drives in human nature, have no place in a prison camp. One wants to know the meaning of his suffering and how, as a responsible being, he should acquit himself. Should he commit suicide, and if not, why not?

Applying his hard-won insights to therapy, he feels that a neurotic or psychotic will regain health not by reshuffling memories, defenses, or conditioned reflexes, which are ordinarily self-defeating. He must break through to new horizons seen in terms of a new purpose and meaning for life. Man constantly seeks meaning and opening horizons. Thus he is guided by his values.[28]

But Buhler feels that there is a middle course between that of ignoring or explaining away values on the one hand and teaching values on the other. Her approach lies between these two other ways of looking at values.

> ... the therapeutic relationship becomes an effective *human* impact through the undercurrent of human values that both the therapist and the patient feel to be of the essence in their lives: while the therapeutic relationship becomes an effective *emotional* impact through the analysis of motivation.[29]

Paul Halmos has written a book in which he unmasks the values of various schools of therapy. He shows that even Dollard and Miller, who claim to have written a book of psychotherapy on the rational basis of learning theory and thus to have produced an "applied science," use value-laden terms. Listen to their words:

> The therapist *must believe*—and [had] better believe on the basis of his own experience—that repression can be evoked and that neurotic conflicts can be eliminated. How else can he have *courage* to drive and to help the patient along the blind way he must go? He *must believe* in the patient's capacity to learn. We must agree with Rogers that *faith* in the patient is a most important requirement in a therapist.[30]

No mechanistic learning theory accounts for such words as "must believe," "courage," "faith." These reflect values, and as Halmos observes:

> ... the authors' solemnity is not a sign of hypocrisy but an unconscious admission by them that they have the same kind of faith and courage as they expect of the counselor about whom they are writing. I should describe the condition in which they and so many other psychological writers and thinkers are in today as a condition of inverted hypocrisy. If the hypocrite is someone who professes what he does not believe, these inverted hypocrites are too shy to profess what they in fact believe.[31]

In closing this section on values it is well to note the opinion of the anthropologist, Clyde Kluckhohn, who felt that human culture is not so much a response to the total biological needs of a society as a system that stems from and expresses the basic values held by that society. It is his feeling that psychology has too much stressed the push of the past and tended to neglect the lure of the future as seen in human ideals, purposes, and values.[32]

## CREATIVITY

Buhler has pointed out that man's creativity is one of the most central concepts of humanistic psychology. Maslow as early as 1954 saw creativity as a "universal characteristic of all people" that was given at birth, lost by many as they became encultured, retained by a few in their fresh, naive, direct way of looking at life, and regained by others as they grew older.[33] This creativity led to all kinds of self-expressive activities that are the opposite of homeostasis, so much emphasized by psychoanalysis, and instead represent a heterostatic urge as delineated by Bernard.[34]

Contrary to relaxation of tensions as the end of all activity, research on creativity has discovered the creative person's desire for problems that have to be resolved and neither avoided nor disliked. Eiduson, in his study of chemists, found:

> Their happiness obviously cannot be defined in terms of absence of tension or unabated pleasure. On the contrary, they are very tense about their work, and are frequently impatient and filled with despair; but their discomforts do not dim their over-all notion that what they are doing is enjoyable, and that no other work can compete with it in this respect.[35]

Among humanist psychologists there is a shared conviction that the end goal of life is self-realization. This does not mean that everyone pursues this goal consistently, but most will eventually return to it. Goldstein has even shown that only in sickness does homeostasis become a goal.[36] However, Fromm[37] and Horney[38] suggested self-realization as the goal toward which human beings strive, and Goldstein[39] and Maslow[40] saw the end object as self-actualization. Rogers[41] spoke of it as a growth process in which one's potentialities and latent abilities are brought to realization, while Buhler[42] and von Bertalanffy[43] saw it as the actualization of values. Frankl further pointed out that human experience is self-transcending and that the human goal toward which one strives is the fulfillment of a personal meaning projected into something for which one lives.[44]

## PSYCHOTHERAPY AND THE SELF

Rogers introduced completely new procedures into psychotherapy, procedures that differ from the older psychoanalytic techniques or the recently developed behavior therapy principles. Rogers saw the therapeutic relationship as a person-to-person meeting rather than a transference situation or the relation of a superior knowledgeable creature training an inferior unknowing automaton. This person-to-person relationship develops trust through the patient's feeling of being accepted by the therapist. With this approach one does not talk as much about mental illness as about emotional problems and problems in the area of value choices that become increasingly complex in the changing era of Western civilization.[45]

Jourard has shown that one loses his mental health because he avoids becoming known by another human being. Self-disclosure to at least one other human being is both an indication of personality health and a means of ultimately achieving a healthy personality. One's self grows from the consequences of knowing and acting in terms of one's real self. This is basically a process of being.[46] Ruesch[47] has described neurotics, psychotics, and psychosomatic patients as persons having selective atrophy and overspecialization in various parts of the process of communication. Thus symptoms become devices to avoid becoming known. "The way out of the problem is self-disclosure and the maintenance of the transparent self."

## RELIGION

A number of followers of this approach see a place for religion. They do not subscribe to the tenets of the amended poem quoted below:

> For this is good old Eliteland,
> Home of the learned and the odd,
> Where the savants talk only to the scholars
> And the scholars never talk about God.

J. L. Moreno has pointed out that the scientific models of man are incomplete because they do not integrate man into a universal system except as a physical existence.[48] Man, in his origin, his birth, his death, his morals, and the furthest stages of his past and future evolution, is involved in the cosmos. Man does not live only within himself, within a society, or even within a biological evolution. The universe at large has its own cosmic evolution, and man is a part of it. He must have his relation to this larger happening spelled out and structured. When man has done this by myth and creed and covenant, he has felt at home in the world and has achieved an understanding not only of the meaning of his individual existence but also of the society in which he lives and of the universe that envelops him. These, then, are the functions of religion.

Almost two decades ago Gardner Murphy pointed out our neurotic attempts to escape from this deep-seated religious need which is within all of us.

> There may be a touch of neurotic phobia in the persistence with which the modern study of man has evaded the question of his need in some way to come to terms with the cosmos as a whole. Whenever people have stopped the dizzying round of earning a living or the fascinating task of taking one another to pieces physically or metaphorically . . . they have felt incomplete as human beings except as they endeavored to understand the filial relations of man to the cosmos which has begotten him. . . . Our study of man must include the study of his response to the cosmos of which he is a reflection.[49]

Interestingly enough there is an indication that college students are aware of the need for meaning in their lives that usually runs ahead of the same for the adult community. Poorbaugh and Smith remark:

> Most of today's students are not hostile to a minister's attempt to reveal meaning. . . . Many of the old barriers of cynicism and of nihilism in the intellectual community are crumbling fast; the world no longer seems cold or absurd . . . students have had—experiences especially of personal worth and of community.[50]

Thus religion may move from an institution-centered experience to a person-centered experience in which small, intimate groups seek meaning for their lives.

The late Abraham Maslow made a study of self-actualization in which he found that there were "healthy people"—those who could embody "full-humanness." The climax of their self-actualization is the peak-experience. Such an experience is similar to those found in religion and mysticism. It comes and goes, but it cannot be forgotten nor can it be summoned at will. It is a tying together of value and emotion. It transpires at the level of being rather than the level of deficiency on which most of the rest of our motivated behavior takes place. A peak-experience is a coming into realization that what "ought to be" *is*. There is a merging of subject and object without the loss of self. Further, all people have had such experiences but many, especially scientists, find it difficult to admit having them. These are not experiences taking place in some realm called "the sacred." The sacred is always apprehended in the ordinary and is to be found in one's daily life, in one's friends and family, or in one's own backyard. Further, travel in search of the sacred may many times be a flight from confronting the sacred. Thus Maslow legitimatizes and gives us the intellectual tools by which we learn about and begin to understand such experiences.[51]

Recently psychiatrist Robert Coles, after a careful study of the religious faith of black sharecroppers and white tenant farmers, of migrant workers and of the mountain people of Appalachia, has come to some telling conclusions.[52] He points out that as intellectuals we look down on their religion as we seldom do with the dozens of secular theologies that command compliance, belief, and real zealotry from educated and well-to-do people. Yet contrary to our pale, weak faith, in their religion something happens.

> In rural churches one is moved and transported, one is elevated and summoned, one uses arms and the hands and the legs, one bends and straightens out and twists and turns, and yes, arrives ... religious passions are unashamedly, indeed proudly, connected to man's physical and psychological nature, to his lusts and urges and wants and needs.[53]

Coles shows that in their religion through prayer and supplication, by means of protestation and affirmation, they make comparisons between what is and what might be; they seek and find a sense of coherence and reassurance that a person is noticed and somehow does matter. They experience joy through music, prayer, and singing. They read the Bible and become stronger, speak louder, and feel more certain about things. They fight on in the face of almost insurmountable odds and ally themselves with Him who offers them hope, redemption, and another chance. *This is the real thing.*

A half-century ago, George Coe pointed out that one of the special functions of religion was "the revaluation of values in terms of personal-social ends."[54] But Kluckhohn has gone even further by showing that there is a need for a moral order because there is a requirement for predictability in social behavior. The predictability of social behavior is not taken care of automatically by biologically inherited instincts, as in the case of bees and ants.

> ... there must be generally accepted standards of conduct, and these values are more compelling if they are invested with divine authority and continually symbolized in rites that appeal to the senses.[55]

That religion can and does do this for certain people is seen in a report by the Joint Information Service of the American Psychiatric Association and the National Association for Mental Health as reported by Jim Warren. Daytop Village in New York has seen thousands of drug users over the past five years, but only 130 (one to two percent) have been graduated from the program; of those who graduated, 90% are claimed as cured. On the other hand, the researchers investigated one of the "Jesus Freak" drug abuse centers and found they had much better results than that of Daytop.[56] Could it be that religion offers a transcendent meaning that helps one value both his life and the lives of others in a more dynamic way than does mere group therapy? Might it not also allow one real channels for sharing one's awareness of self and provide natural paths by which this sharing can lay hold on love and values?

Talcott Parsons has summed up the pivotal role of religion and morality as "boundary structures" that maintain society and promote personal integrity.[57] What we see in society today is a withdrawal from institutional religion by the young, but not a withdrawal from its ideals of love and brotherhood. This can be a time of purification and reassessment rather than total destruction of religion if older people can become less defensive and if youth can become less obsessed with the eternal now.

The criticism has been made by some analysts that morals and religion belong to the realm of the superego and as a result they are frozen remnants of the past that make for ill health and personality destruction. E. Mansell Patterson has shown that religion and morality are not necessarily only superego structures, but that they can be and are related to the ego and the ongoing life of the individual.

> Morality in these terms, then, is not a question of prohibitions, but rather the values and definitions of appropriate adaptation by which man governs his behavior.[58]

The foregoing pages have presented a third force that is emerging in psychology today and catching a more humane approach to human personality and the values by which one lives.

## REFERENCES

[1]Maslow, A. H., *Toward a Psychology of Being*. Princeton, New Jersey, D. Van Nostrand, 1962.

[2]Bugenthal, J.F.T., "The Challenge That Is Man." In Bugenthal, ed., *Challenges of Humanistic Psychology*. New York, McGraw-Hill Book Company, 1967, pp. 5-11.

[3]Tillich, P., *Systematic Theology*, Vol. I. Chicago, University of Chicago Press, 1951, p. 5.

[4]Allport, G., *The Person in Psychology*. Boston, Beacon Press, 1968, pp. 81-102.

[5]Sanford, N., "Will Psychologists Study Human Problems?" *Amer. Psychologist*, 1965, 20, 192-202.

[6]Kuhn, T. S., *The Structure of Scientific Revolutions*. Chicago, University of Chicago Press, 1962.

[7]Bertalanffy, L. V., *Problems of Life*. New York, Wiley, 1952, p. 202.

[8]Polanyi, M., *Personal Knowledge: Toward a Post-Critical Philosophy*. Chicago, University of Chicago Press, 1958.

[9]Maslow, *The Psychology of Science*. Chicago, Henry Regnery, 1966, pp. 45, 46.

[10]Skinner, B. F., *Science and Human Behavior*. New York, Macmillan, 1953, p. 6.

[11]_____, *Beyond Freedom and Dignity*. New York, Knopf, 1971, pp. 81-82.

[12]Maslow, Answer to B. F. Skinner, "The Design of Cultures," *Daedalus*, 1961, 90, 534-46.

# J. A. Clippinger

[13]Dobzhansky, T., *The Biological Basis of Human Freedom*. New York, Columbia University Press, 1956, p. 134.

[14]Bertalanffy, "Theoretical Models in Biology and Psychology." In Krech, D., and Klein, G., eds., *Theoretical Models and Personality Theory*. Durham, North Carolina, Duke University Press, 1952, pp. 24-28.

[15]Clippinger, J. A., "Recent Value Research and Its Significance for Religious Psychology," *Religious Education*, 1954, 49, 204-210.

[16]Lee, D., "Are Basic Needs Ultimate?" *J. Abn. and Soc. Psychol.*, 1948, 43, 391-5.

[17]Brosse, T., "A Psycho-Physiological Study," *Main Currents in Modern Thought*, 1946, 5, 77-84.

[18]Postman, L., Bruner, J., and McGinnies, E., "Personal Values as Selective Factors in Perception," *J. Ab. Soc. Psychol.*, 1948, 43, 142-54.

[19]McGinnies, E., *Social Behavior: A Functional Analysis*. Boston, Houghton Mifflin Company, 1970, pp. 153-61.

[20]Bartlett, F. C., *Remembering: A Study in Experimental and Social Psychology*. Cambridge, Cambridge University Press, 1932.

[21]Morgan, J. J. B., and Morton, J. T., "The Distortion of Syllogistic Reasoning Produced by Personal Convictions," *J. Soc. Psychol.*, 1944, 20, 39-59.

[22]Allport, G., Vernon, P., and Lindzey, G., *A Study of Values*. Boston, Houghton Mifflin, 1960.

[23]Allport, *The Person in Psychology*. Boston, Beacon Press, 1968, p. 514.

[24]Maslow, *Toward a Psychology of Being;* 2nd edition. New York, Van Nostrand Reinhold Co., 1968.

[25]Meissner, W. W., "Notes Toward a Theory of Values: Values as Psychological," *J. Religion and Health*, 1970, 9, 233-249.

[26]Buhler, C., *Values in Psychotherapy*. New York, Free Press of Glencoe, 1962.

[27]Menninger, K. A., *Theory of Psychoanalytic Technique*. New York, Basic Books, 1958, p. 166.

[28]Frankl, V. E., *Man's Search for Meaning*. New York, Washington Square Press Inc., 1963.

[29]Buhler, *op. cit.*, p. 4.

[30]Dollard, J., and Miller, N., *Personality and Psychotherapy*. New York, McGraw, 1950, 4b.

[31]Halmos, P., *The Faith of the Counselor*. New York, Schocken Books, 1966, pp. 87, 88.

[32]Kluckhohn, C., "The Limitations of Adaption and Adjustment as Concepts for Understanding Cultural Behavior." In Romano, J., ed., *Adaptation*. Ithaca, New York, 1949, Chap. V.

[33]Buhler, "Basic Theoretical Concepts of Humanistic Psychology," *Amer. Psychologist*, 1971, 26, 378-386.

[34]Bernard, H. W., *Human Development in Western Culture*, 3rd edition. Boston, Allyn and Bacon, 1970, pp. 555-558.

[35]Eiduson, B. T., *Scientists: Their Psychological World*. New York, Basic Books, 1962, p. 161.

[36]Goldstein, K., *The Organism*. New York, American, 1939.

[37]Fromm, E., *Escape from Freedom*. New York, Holt, Rinehart & Winston, 1941.

[38]Horney, K., *Neurosis and Human Growth*. New York, Norton, 1950.

[39]Goldstein, *op. cit.*

[40]Maslow, *Motivation and Personality*. New York, Harper, 1954.

[41]Rogers, C. R., *Client-Centered Therapy*. Boston, Houghton-Mifflin, 1951.

[42]Buhler, *Values in Psychotherapy, op. cit.*

[43]Bertalanffy, "General System Theory and Psychiatry." In Arieti, S., ed., *American Handbook of Psychiatry*. Vol. 3. New York, Basic Books, 1966.

[44]Frankl, *The Will to Meaning: Foundations and Application of Logotherapy*. New York, World, 1969.

[45]Rogers, *Counseling and Psychotherapy*. Boston, Houghton-Mifflin, 1942.

[46]Jourard, S., *The Transparent Self*. New York, Van Nostrand Reinhold Company, 1971.

[47]Ruesch, J., *Disturbed Communication*. New York, Norton, 1957.

[48]Masserman, J., and Moreno, J.L., eds., *Progress in Psychotherapy, III.* New York, Grune & Stratton, 1957, p. 7.

[49]Murphy, G., *Personality.* New York, Harper, 1947, p. 919.

[50]Poorbaugh, F., and Smith, R., "Dilemmas in the Campus Ministry," *Yale Alumni Magazine,* 1970, 33, 28-31.

[51]Maslow, *The Farther Reaches of Human Nature.* New York, The Viking Press, 1971, pp. 168-179, 260-266.

[52]Coles, R., "God and the Rural Poor," *Psychology Today,* 1972, 5, 33-41.

[53]*Ibid.,* p. 33.

[54]Coe, G., *The Psychology of Religion.* Chicago, University of Chicago Press, 1916, pp. 215-228.

[55]Kluckhohn, "Introduction." In Lessa, W. A., and Vogt, E. G., eds., *Reader in Comparative Religion: An Anthropological Approach.* New York, Harper & Row, 1966.

[56]Warren, J., "Pot-pourri," *Amer. Psychol. Assoc. Monitor,* 1971, 2, 3.

[57]Parsons, T., "Mental Illness and 'Spiritual Malaise': The Role of the Psychiatrist and the Minister of Religion." In Hoffman, H., ed., *The Ministry and Mental Health.* New York, Association Press, 1960.

[58]Pattison, E. M., "Ego Morality: An Emerging Psychotherapeutic Concept," *Psychoanal. Rev.,* 1968, 55, 187-222.

# THE MEASUREMENT
# OF RELIGION

# Introduction

H. NEWTON MALONY

This section reports several of the most recent attempts to assess religion. Three types of religious behavior are considered: (1) religious experience; (2) religious development; and (3) observable religious participation.

Hood has constructed a Religious Experience Episodes Measure (REEM). He describes a study in which intrinsically oriented religious persons reported more religious experiences than extrinsically oriented religious persons. The scale is suggestive as a means for probing the inner religious life of individuals.

Embree's Religious Association Scale (RAS) is a unique effort to study religious thinking through association with nonsense syllables.

Gorsuch and McFarland discuss an important issue. They ask, "Is religiosity best measured with answers to one or to many questions?" They suggest that single-item tests are best for measuring certain religious tendencies, e.g., intrinsic orientation, but that multiple-item tests more accurately assess orthodoxy.

A novel approach to the study of religion is the N = 1 method discussed by Malony. Although early investigators reported many "case studies," most recent research has been done on groups of people. Malony calls for a return to the study of individuals.

King and Hunt detail the results of several extensive studies on a number of different samples. Their scale is the most sophisticated in the literature, and is based on factor-analytic methods. They used it recently to study a national sample of Presbyterians. Prior investigation with other samples is included.

This portion of the book will acquaint the student with some of the major attempts psychologists are making to study religious be-behavior. Methods are varied and approaches are innovative.

# Religious Orientation and the Report of Religious Experience

## RALPH W. HOOD, JR.

*Introduction.* Religious experience has been a concern of the psychology of religion from the beginning (James 1902; Leuba 1925; Starbuck 1899). But empirical research has lagged. The more phenomenologically or existentially oriented writers such as King (1968) and Van Kaam (1964) have speculated about the *functions* of such experiences, as have depth oriented investigators working from their general personality theories (Freud 1928; Jung 1938; Fromm 1959). More empirically inclined investigators have been primarily concerned to distinguish religious experience from other dimensions of religiosity or to distinguish among types of religious experience. For instance, Glock and Stark (1965) have presented a complex taxonomy of types of religious experience which they consider indicative of one of the ways in which persons *can* be religious. Yet even for them the constructing of adequate operational measures has lagged behind this conceptualization. Thus far the *empirical efforts* of Glock and Stark mainly have been focused upon the mere use of structured Likert-type items which appear to be oversimplified operational measures of an interesting conceptual system.

The purely empirical investigation of religious experience need not be concerned with the issue of whether or not religious experience ought to be the major defining characteristic of religiosity as suggested by such diverse investigators as James (1902), Jung (1938), and Maslow (1964), or whether it is simply one important aspect of a complex dimension of religiosity.

The present research was intended to develop an adequate operational measure of the degree of reported religious experience and to

Reprinted with permission of the author and publisher from:

*Journal for the Scientific Study of Religion*, 1970, 9(4), 285-292, published by the SOCIETY FOR THE SCIENTIFIC STUDY OF RELIGION, University of Connecticut, Box U68A, Storrs, Connecticut 06268.

discover how this is related to empirically defined indicators of religiosity such as religious orientation (Allport 1950).

Accordingly, the first phase of this study was concerned with the construction of an operational measure of religious experience. Rather than being asked whether they had had a "religious experience"— definition left up to them—respondents were presented an array of reports of what had independently been defined as religious experience, and they were asked whether they had had similar experiences. These accounts were selected from those reported by James (1902) and presumably reflect James' own definition of religious experience as "the feelings, acts, and experiences of individual men in their solitude, so far as they apprehend themselves to stand in relation to whatever they may consider divine (1902, p. 42)." This instrument was called the Religious Experience Episodes Measure (REEM).

The second phase of this study was concerned with determining the relationship between religious orientation and the report of religious experience as determined by REEM. In a series of articles Allport (1959, 1963, 1966) has argued that an important indicator of religiosity is personal religious orientation, a concept which has been operationalized in the form of the *Religious Orientation Scale*. This concept essentially refers to the motivational basis for participation in organized religion which Allport views basically as either extrinsic or intrinsic. Most simply, the extrinsically motivated person is one who *uses* his religion for personal gain while the intrinsically motivated person is one who *lives* his religion (Allport and Ross 1967). Importantly, the concepts of extrinsic and intrinsic religious motivation have been empirically related to such variables as frequency of church attendance and prejudice (Allport 1959, 1963, 1966; Allport and Ross 1967).

Allport and Ross (1967) claim that intrinsically motivated persons receive special "experiential meanings" from their religion. Similarly, Maslow (1964) has stated that conventionally religious persons are *less likely* to have religious (transcendent) experiences than other types of persons, an hypothesis not inconsistent with that of Allport and Ross. These considerations yielded the prediction that intrinsically religious motivated persons would be more likely to report having had religious experiences than extrinsically religious motivated persons.

## DEVELOPMENT OF THE REEM

Data in the first phase of the study were collected from fifty-one volunteer introductory psychology students at SDSU. All Ss nominally identified themselves as Christians. Students at SDSU generally come from a rural background in which religion is an important aspect of their life. In this respect the Ss in this study may not be typical of many samples in more metropolitan areas or in other areas where religion is not necessarily of such importance and concern.

## The Instrument

Reports of religious experience described in James (1902) were culled, and on the basis of pilot research brief written descriptions of fifteen such experiences were edited, abbreviated, and presented, one description per page in booklet form.[1] The following is an example of a REEM item:

> The highest experiences that I have had of God's presence have been rare and brief—flashes of consciousness which have compelled me to exclaim with surprise—God is here!—or conditions of exaltation and insight, less intense, and only gradually passing away. I have severely questioned the worth of these moments. To no person have I named them, lest I should be building my life and work on mere phantasies of the brain. But I find that, after every questioning and test, they stand out today as the most real experiences of my life, and experiences which have explained and justified and unified all past experiences and past growth.

The Ss rated each episode in the REEM on a five-point scale, ranging from (1) "I have had absolutely no experience like this" to (5) "I have had an experience almost identical to this." Two weeks later the same Ss rated the REEM again, in order to determine its test-retest reliability. (Five of the original Ss did not appear at the second session so the test-retest reliability is based upon a total $N$ of forty-six.)

## Results

The test-retest reliability based upon the 46 Ss in the first phase of the study was .93. In addition a measure of reliability in terms of the internal consistency of the REEM was determined by the Kuder-Richardson method (Nunnally 1970). This reliability was .84. Analysis of the initial ratings ($N = 51$) indicated a range from 15 to 51 with a mean of 31.5 and a median of 30.5.

Ss interviewed informally after the final rating of the REEM considered the items as fairly adequate descriptions. No S indicated that he had had an experience self-defined as "religious" which did not relate in some fashion to at least one of the experiences described in the REEM. Accordingly, for the purposes of the second portion of this study, it was concluded that the REEM is a valid measure of reported religious experience insofar as it reliably distinguishes among persons claiming to have had religious experiences.

## RELATIONSHIP OF THE REEM TO EXTRINSIC AND INTRINSIC RELIGIOUS ORIENTATION

The second phase of the study consisted of determining the empirical relationship between the ROS and the REEM. Specifically, it was predicted that intrinsically religious motivated Ss would be more likely to report having had religious experiences than extrinsically religious motivated Ss where intrinsic and extrinsic motivations are defined according to their pattern of responses on the ROS (Allport and Ross 1967).[2]

Subjects were another group of eighty-nine volunteer introductory psychology students at SDSU.

### Results with Extrinsic and Intrinsic Scales

The mean response per REEM item for intrinsically motivated Ss ($N = 18$) was 2.58 and for extrinsically motivated Ss ($N = 18$) was 2.00. (See table 1.) The difference between these means was significant ($t = 3.31$, $p < .01$). A conservatively evaluated $r_m$ value of .47 ($p < .01$) further indicates the significance of the magnitude of the differences between these means (Friedman 1968).

Correlations between the intrinsic scale and the REEM was .51 ($p < .01$) and between the extrinsic scale and the REEM .06. (The correlation between the intrinsic scale and the extrinsic scale was .18, not significant.)

### Results with All Categories of Religious Orientation

Allport's ROS allows the identification of four categories of persons. On the basis of their patterns of response to the ROS Ss were classified as their extrinsic ($N = 18$), intrinsic ($N = 18$), indiscriminately pro-religious ($N = 27$)—upper right cell table 1—or indiscriminately anti-religious ($N = 26$)—lower left cell.[3] The mean response per REEM item for each of the four religious categories is reported in table 1.

TABLE 1. MEAN RESPONSE PER REEM
ITEM FOR EACH TYPE OF RELIGIOUS
ORIENTATION

|  |  | Extrinsic | |
|  |  | Low | High |
| --- | --- | --- | --- |
| Intrinsic | High | 2.58 | 2.19 |
|  | Low | 1.88 | 2.00 |

The 2 × 2 table was analyzed by a two-way least squares analysis of variance (Winer 1962). The results indicated a significant main effect for the intrinsic dimension ($F = 18.15$; $p < .01$) but not for the extrinsic dimension ($F = .96$). The interaction was significant ($F = 6.50$; $p < .05$).

In order to shed further light upon the least squares analysis an analysis was undertaken based upon the Newman-Keuls Range Test employing an harmonic mean (Winer 1962). The mean response per REEM item for the intrinsic category was significantly different ($p < .01$) from both the extrinsic and indiscriminately anti-religious categories but not from the indiscriminately pro-religious category. The indiscriminately pro-religious category was significantly different ($p < .01$) from the indiscriminately anti-religious category but not from the extrinsic category. No other combinations of paired categories were significantly different from each other.[4]

## DISCUSSION

As a whole the results of this study are encouraging. First, the REEM has been tentatively demonstrated to be a reliable measure that differentiates among persons on the basis of their reported religious experiences. The technique of measuring degree of religious experience by matching S's experience with descriptions of others' religious experiences seems to be fruitful. Importantly, it allows for an operational measure of religious experience (simply in terms of the descriptions employed in the REEM) and thus avoids the problem during research of defining religious experience a priori, abstractly, and in terms acceptable to all persons with a wide variety of faiths and non-faiths. Investigation of the relationship of the REEM to other empirically established measures of religiosity appears warranted.

Second, the results of this study indicate support for the hypothesis that report of religious experience and personal religious orientation covary: intrinsically oriented persons are more likely to report having religious experiences than are extrinsically oriented persons.

Third, the methodological difficulty of distinguishing between intrinsically oriented persons and indiscriminately pro-religious persons is highlighted. Allport and Ross (1967) argue that the indiscriminately pro-religious person is one who unequivocally endorses all statements concerning religion, however incompatible. It seems reasonable to assume that such persons are also likely to endorse descriptions of religious experiences simply because they "refer to religion." As such, the failure to differentiate between intrinsically oriented persons and indiscriminately pro-religious persons on the REEM may be interpreted to mean that the intrinsically oriented persons agreed with reported experiences similar to ones *they in fact experienced* while indiscriminately pro-religious persons agreed with reported experiences simply because they were "religious" in tone. The methodological problem of distinguishing a genuine report of religious experience from a response set to make such a report remains and obviously is a problem with the REEM in its present form.

The failure to distinguish between extrinsically motivated persons and indiscriminately anti-religious persons on the basis of their willingness to report religious experiences may be due to several factors. It may be the case that indiscriminately anti-religious persons and extrinsically oriented persons do not differ in their actual experiences. However, a more interesting possibility is that indiscriminately anti-religious persons may actually have religious experiences but do not identify them as such. This hypothesis is consistent with Maslow's (1964) contention that many persons who have religious experiences resist identifying them as such, an hypothesis worthy of further investigation.

Finally, these findings suggest the possibility of an interesting and perhaps unexpected relationship between religious experience, religious orientation, and secular activity. Clearly Allport's general conceptualization of the intrinsically oriented person is one of a truly devout person whose religion pervades his entire life and influences all his experiences and activities (Allport 1950, 1959, 1963, 1966; Allport and Ross 1967). Other investigations are beginning to offer additional empirical evidence consistent with this view. For instance Ludwig and Blank (1969) have demonstrated that persons most influenced by their religion have a perceptual set to respond religiously even in a nonreligious setting, while Wilson and Kawamura (1967) report a significant positive correlation between a measure of religiousness and a measure of social responsibility. Similarly, Schweiker (1969) has demonstrated that persons high on indicators of *both* religious belief and church participation are especially likely to be meaningfully involved in secular activities. If these authors' measures of religiosity can be demonstrated to coincide with Allport's intrinsic types, then the picture is indeed one of a devoutly religious person, actively involved in both secular and church activities and, in light of the present study, *reporting the occurrence of significant religious experiences.* Such a picture is clearly contrary to the evidently common assumption that persons who report having religious experiences are individualistically oriented and often at odds with their society, even to the extent of being "mavericks" (King 1968). It is possible that empirical facts will indicate that at least some persons who report religious experiences are both devoutly religious and deeply involved in secular activities.

## NOTES AND REFERENCES

[1]Copies of this booklet (REEM) are available upon request from the author. Now at the University of Tennessee at Chattanooga, Department of Psychology, Chattanooga, Tennessee, 37401.

[2]The extrinsic and intrinsic scales were scored so that for *both* scales higher scores indicate a greater degree of that particular orientation. This reverses the scoring procedure for the intrinsic scale used by Allport and Ross (1967). Intrinsic orientation is defined as a high score on the intrinsic scale and a low score on the extrinsic scale; extrinsic orientation is defined as a high score on the extrinsic scale and a low score on the intrinsic scale. "High" and "low" were based upon median splits for each scale.

[3]Based upon our scoring procedure indiscriminately anti-religious orientation is defined as a low score on both the extrinsic and the intrinsic scale; indiscriminately pro-religious is defined as a high score on both the extrinsic and intrinsic scale. Again, "high" and "low" were based upon median splits for each scale. This is a slight change from Allport and Ross (1967) but has the practical advantage of avoiding subject loss.

[4]The fact that the posteriori comparisons were made on the basis of an harmonic mean calculated from fairly widely discrepant sample sizes might have influenced these results (Winer 1962). However, a random procedure to equate all groups to the sample size of the smallest group ($N = 18$) was undertaken and both the analysis of variance and the a posteriori comparisons among these means were recalculated with identical results.

ALLPORT, G. W. 1950 *The individual and his religion.* New York: Macmillan. 1959 Religion and prejudice. *The Crane Review* 2:1-10. 1963 Behavioral science, religion, and mental health. *Journal of Religion and Health* 2:187-97. 1966 Religious context of prejudice. *Journal for the Scientific Study of Religion* 5:447-57.

————, AND J. M. ROSS 1967 Personal religious orientation and prejudice. *Journal of Personality and Social Psychology* 5:432-43.

FREUD, S. 1928 *The future of an illusion:* New York: Liveright Publishing Corporation.

FRIEDMAN, H. 1968 Magnitude of experimental effect and a table for its rapid estimation. *Psychological Bulletin* 70:245-51.

FROMM, E. 1959 *Psychoanalysis and religion.* New Haven: Yale University Press.

GLOCK, C. Y., AND R. STARK 1965 *Religion and society in tension.* Chicago: Rand McNally.

JAMES, W. 1958 *The varieties of religious experience.* New York: Mentor Books; first published in 1902.

JUNG, C. G. 1938 *Psychology and religion.* New Haven: Yale University Press.

# R. W. Hood, Jr.

KING, W. L. 1968 *Introduction to religion*. New York: Harper and Row.

LEUBA, J. H. 1925 *The psychology of religious mysticism*. New York: Harcourt, Brace, and Company.

LUDWIG, D. J., AND T. BLANK. 1969 Measurement of religion as perceptual set. *Journal for the Scientific Study of Religion* 8:119-21.

MASLOW, A. H. 1964 *Religions, values, and peak-experiences*. Columbus, Ohio: Ohio State University Press.

NUNNALLY, J. C., JR. 1970 *Introduction to psychological measurement*. New York: McGraw-Hill.

SCHWEIKER, W. 1968 Religion as a superordinate meaning system and socio-psychological integration. *Journal for the Scientific Study of Religion* 8:300-307.

STARBUCK, E. D. 1899 *The psychology of religion*. New York: Charles Scribner's Sons.

VAN KAAM, A. 1964 *Religion and personality*. New Jersey: Prentice Hall.

WILSON, W., AND W. KAWAMURA 1967 Rigidity, adjustment, and social responsibility as possible correlates of religiousness: A test of three points of view. *Journal for the Scientific Study of Religion* 6:279-80.

WINER, B. J. 1962 *Statistical principles in experimental design*. New York: McGraw-Hill.

# The Religious Association Scale: A Preliminary Validation Study

ROBERT A. EMBREE

Scientific study of religion continues to be hampered by the problem of measuring religious variables. The adequacy of available scales and such indices as church preference or frequency of church attendance has been questioned (Allen and Spilka, 1967). Employing the "abilities" approach to personality measurement (Wallace, 1966, 1967), the *Religious Association Scale* (RAS) was an attempt to confront the measurement issue. RAS has been shown to be objectively scorable. The scale has high reliability and appears to be relatively free of social desirability response bias (Embree, 1970). This report is a follow-up of an effort to develop a general measure of religiousness.

RAS was constructed from 80 consonant-vowel-consonants previously scaled for religious association value (Embree, 1970). "RAB", "MOS", and "ZEK" are typical of the trigram items. The testee's instructions were to make a religious association (a biblical character, place, idea, church, or church teaching) and to use the associated word in a brief sentence. In format RAS resembles *The Rotter Incomplete Sentences Blank* (Rotter and Rafferty, 1950). The basic assumption for RAS is that interest in religion or religious training will develop the verbal skills that the test requires. It is further assumed that those verbal skills can be used to tap general religiousness. Since the high scorer must be familiar with the Judeo-Christian tradition, the score is taken as an indicator of religiosity in that sense.

This report investigated the possibility that RAS might be contaminated by general verbal abilities and explored, in a preliminary way, its relationship with some simple criteria of religiousness.

Reprinted with permission of author and publisher from:

*Journal for the Scientific Study of Religion*, 1973, 12(2), 223-226, published by the SOCIETY FOR THE SCIENTIFIC STUDY OF RELIGION, University of Connecticut, Box U68A, Storrs, Connecticut 06268.

## METHOD

Data were obtained from students enrolled in an introductory psychology course at Westmar College. Excluding middle-aged subjects, the group tested consisted of 48 males and 73 females. The religious affiliation of the subjects was primarily United Methodist (46%), Lutheran (24%), or Roman Catholic (12%).

A RAS item was scored 1, 2, or 3 depending upon the degree of religious association. "*Liberty* can be found in Christ" illustrates a three-point response. "Our goal is to find *liberty*" is a two-point response. "I studied in the *library*" is clearly not a religious association. The scale score for RAS was an algebraic summation of items thus scored.

Campbell (1960) has argued that a new test should correlate better with the criterion variable than with intelligence. The *American College Testing Program Examination* (ACT) composite score was selected to evaluate RAS's possible relationship with scholastic aptitude (American College Testing Program, 1971).

Four single-item criterion instruments of unknown validity and reliability were employed. All scales utilized the Likert-type format. *Religious viewpoint, religious influence, self-rated religiosity,* and *importance of God* measures were as follows:

1) Check the one religious viewpoint that best describes you. (Conservative, liberal, non-religious.)

2) What influence has a church, synagogue, or similar religious group had on your understanding of religion? (None; very little; an average influence; more than is typical; a great deal of influence.)

3) Check the one statement that best describes you. (I am a very religious person; I am more religious than most persons; I am about as religious as the next person; I don't think about religious things very often and am not a very religious person; I do not consider myself to be a religious person.)

4) How important is God in your life? (I don't believe in God as a person; I think I believe in God, but he doesn't affect my life much; I think I would do certain things that I now don't because of my belief in God; God is the center of my life.)

The single-item criterion should be interpreted with caution; however, as a measure of general religiosity the single-item approach has potential value (Gorsuch and McFarland, 1972).

## RESULTS AND DISCUSSION

An odd-even estimate of scale reliability of .96 (Flanagan formula, Guilford, 1954) replicated the previous evidence. The mean of

143 (SD = 31.5) and the 166 average (SD = 35.5) for males and females respectively were consistent with previously reported data (Embree, 1970). The intercorrelations for all the variables are shown in Table 1. RAS was found to correlate positively with all the criterion variables. ACT composite also correlated positively with RAS. A factor analysis of the intercorrelations (see Table 2) produced two rotated factors. RAS was found to load on both the religious criterion factor and the aptitude factor. However, only about half of the RAS variance was accounted for by the two factors. Because of the high scale reliability it would appear that RAS is measuring a dimension not represented in this investigation or that the criteria used were of limited value.

The results of this study suggest that RAS has promise as an approach to religious measurement. However, the low but positive correlation with scholastic aptitude would indicate a need for a revision in the scale. Effort should be directed toward suppressing its relationship with intelligence. Also more research is needed to determine what dimension or dimensions of religiousness the scale is measuring.

TABLE 1

INTERCORRELATION OF RAS AND CRITERION VARIABLES (N = 121)

| Variables | 2 | 3 | 4 | 5 | 6 |
|---|---|---|---|---|---|
| 1-RAS Score | .20 | .20 | .25 | .17 | .33 |
| 2-Religious viewpoint | | .02 | .40 | .39 | .24 |
| 3-ACT composite | | | .08 | .00 | -.14 |
| 4-Religious influence | | | | .62 | .35 |
| 5-Self related religiosity | | | | | .42 |
| 6-Importance of God | | | | | |

TABLE 2

ROTATED FACTORS FOR RAS AND CRITERION VARIABLES (N = 121)

| Variables | Rotated Factors | | $h^2$ |
|---|---|---|---|
| | I | II | |
| 1-RAS Score | .38 | .58 | .48 |
| 2-Religious viewpoint | .63 | .12 | .41 |
| 3-ACT composite | -.15 | .90 | .83 |
| 4-Religious influence | .78 | .18 | .65 |
| 5-Self-rated religiosity | .81 | .03 | .66 |
| 6-Importance of God | .70 | -.10 | .50 |
| Eigenvalues | 2.34 | 1.20 | |
| Percent of variance accounted for | 38.9 | 20.1 | |

Note.—The factoring employed the method of principal components. Factoring was stopped when the eigenvalues dropped below 1. The resulting factors were rotated according to the Varimax solution (Harman, 1960).

# R. A. Embree

## REFERENCES

ALLEN, RUSSELL O., AND BERNARD SPILKA 1970 "Committed and consensual religion: A specification of religion-prejudice relationships." *Journal for the Scientific Study of Religion* 6:191-206.

AMERICAN COLLEGE TESTING PROGRAM, INC., 1971 *Using ACT on the Campus.* Iowa City, Iowa: ACT Publications.

CAMPBELL, DONALD T. 1967 "Recommendations for APA test standards regarding construct, trait or discriminant validity." Pp. 147-156 in D. N. Jackson and S. Messick (eds.), *Problems in Human Assessment.* New York: McGraw-Hill.

EMBREE, ROBERT A. 1970 "The Religious Association Scale as an 'abilities' measure of the religious factor in personality." *Journal for the Scientific Study of Religion* 9 (Winter): 299-302.

GORSUCH, RICHARD L. AND SAM G. MCFARLAND 1972 "Single vs. multiple-item scales for measuring religious commitment." *Journal for the Scientific Study of Religion* 11 (March): 53-64.

GUILFORD, J. P. 1954 *Psychometric Methods.* New York: McGraw-Hill.

HARMAN, H. H. 1960 *Modern Factor Analysis.* Chicago: University of Chicago Press.

ROTTER, J. G., AND JANET E. RAFFERTY. 1950 *Manual, The Rotter Incomplete Sentences Blank, College Form.* New York: Psychological Corporation.

WALLACE, J. 1966 "An abilities conception of personality: Some implications for personality measurement." *American Psychologist* 21:132-138. 1967 "What units shall we employ? Allport's question revisited." *Journal of Consulting Psychology* 31:56-64.

# Single vs. Multiple-Item Scales for Measuring Religious Values

## RICHARD L. GORSUCH AND SAM G. MCFARLAND

Each investigator faces a choice when designing a research study: should he measure religious values by single-item scales or should he use multiple-item scales? Several factors may be involved in reaching a decision but the most important one is validity. If the validities of the single-item and multiple-item scales differ widely, then there is no problem: the more valid measure is chosen. But when the scales have the same validity, then another factor is investigated: cost.[1] Here the choice goes to the single-item scales since they are invariably less expensive to prepare, administer and analyze. However, occasions arise when the differences in validity or cost are insufficient to decide the issue and there is a real question whether to use single or multiple-item measures of religious values.

In the present paper, we shall assume that the investigator is interested in a basic coverage of religious values. The criterion of validity then becomes the degree to which the single-item scales cover the area as compared to the multiple-item scales. This question can be pursued through factoring single and multiple-item scales jointly. Examining the factor loadings would lead to conclusions about which scales cover which areas best.

In addition to better factor loadings, the better measures of religiosity would be expected to form clearer patterns of relationships with variables from outside the area of religion. Since a current topic of investigation is the relationship of religious beliefs to prejudice and ethics (cf. Glock and Stark, 1966, Allport and Ross, 1967, Rokeach, 1969a, 1969b), the ability to predict ethical positions could be used as an indicator of each measure's research potential. It is expected that an

Reprinted with permission of authors and publisher from:

*Journal for the Scientific Study of Religion*, 1972, 11(1), 53–64, published by the Society for the Scientific Study of Religion, University of Connecticut, Box U68A, Storrs, Connecticut 06268.

item found useful in this one area may be more useful in other areas as well.

A further question can be asked: do most people interpret an item in the same way? If not, then the results gained from using the item would be ambiguous. This could be particularly dangerous if the different interpretations were associated with systematically different responses to that item. Multiple-item scales would not be likely to be affected by this problem since idiosyncratic interpretations tend to average out across the items, but it could be a major problem with a single-item scale.

With information on the above three questions, the interaction of costs and validity for single and multiple-item scales can be discussed.

## PROCEDURE

A "Background Questionnaire" presented the four single-item scales of religiousness and gathered miscellaneous information. The religious items asked the respondent to check his religious preference, to check his frequency of worship service attendance, to rate the importance of religion to his life, and to indicate the degree of his belief in Jesus as the Christ.[2] Two free response questions were asked at the end of this questionnaire: "What does this phrase 'Jesus is the Christ' mean?" and "What does the phrase 'Jesus is my Lord and Savior' mean?"

A multiple-item Christology scale was developed for the present study as a parallel to the single-item Christological scale. A pool of 20 items was initially developed to embody the various theological positions along the continuum of seeing Jesus as human to seeing Jesus as divine. Seven local ministers, representing a wide range of religious denominations, judged whether each item reflected belief in Jesus' deity or in his complete humanity. The thirteen items with the most consistent ratings were interspersed in a number of other items and administered to a test-development sample of 94 college students. The internal consistency reliability (i.e., alpha coefficient or generalized KR 20, see Cronbach, 1951) was .83 for a "short-form" of the scale consisting of those six items prejudged by the authors as best measuring belief in Jesus' deity, while the full-scale reliability was .89. On the basis of item-total correlations, two items in the six-item form were replaced by two items from the longer scale to yield the final six-item Christology scale.[3] Its reliability in the present study was .87.

Feagin's (1964) Intrinsic and Extrinsic religious orientation multiple-item scales were also administered. They were derived from Allport's (1959) theories separating people truly committed to their faith for its own sake from those who are committed for reasons external to the faith itself. These scales have been hypothesized to relate to the non-religious measures of the present study, particularly prejudice. Lee's (1965) 8-item Fundamentalism scale was selected as a good measure of the subjects' attitudes toward biblical infallibility, a dimension basic to the conservative-liberal distinction within Christianity. These scales thus represent theoretical religious distinctions.

In order to represent distinctions developed from more empirical approaches, the Religious Individualism Scale (Jeeves, 1957; Brown, 1962) was selected to represent a major factor confirmed by Spilka (personal communication), who, in turn, built upon the more detailed analyses of King (1967). Spilka found the Individualism scale to be generally uncorrelated with other measures of religious activity and attitudes and to load an independent factor. His other major factors were already represented by other scales.

All of the questions from the multiple-item scales were cyclically mixed and administered in the same questionnaire with Struening's (1963) measure of generalized prejudice. The subjects answered on a five-choice continuum from 1 ("Strongly Agree") to 5 ("Strongly Disagree"). While the presentation procedure departed from earlier methods of administering some of the scales, the internal consistency reliabilities of the scales obtained in the present study indicated that they were not adversely affected (cf. Table 1 for the alpha coefficients).

TABLE 1

CORRELATIONS WITH PROMAX FACTORS

|  | Intrinsically Pro-Religious | Christian Orthodoxy |
|---|---|---|
| A. *Single-Item Scales* | | |
| "Jesus is the Christ" | .69 | .77 |
| Rated Importance of Religion | .84 | .40 |
| Frequency of Religious Attendance | .61 | .56 |
| B. *Multiple-Item Scales*[a] | | |
| Christology Scale ($r_{xx} = .87$) | .62 | .90 |
| Extrinsic ($r_{xx} = .76$) | −.53 | −.25 |
| Intrinsic ($r_{xx} = .67$) | .78 | .49 |
| Religious Individualism ($r_{xx} = .59$) | .07 | −.20 |
| Fundamentalism ($r_{xx} = .78$) | .57 | .91 |

Correlation between factors = .6

[a]With alpha reliability.

A fifty-item moral judgment questionnaire (Crissman, 1942) was given in addition to the prejudice scale. Actions ranging from "forging a check" to "having sexual relations while unmarried" were rated from 1 ("not wrong at all") to 10 (" 'wrongest' possible"). Judgments on the entire scale formed one score.

Previous studies have suggested that Crissman's moral judgment questionnaire can be divided into subscales. The four factor analytic subscales used in the present study represent factors found in college students (Rettig & Pasamanick, 1959) and confirmed in at least one other nonstudent sample (Rettig & Pasamanick, 1960, 1961, 1962, 1963). These scales included Misrepresentation, Absence of Philanthropic Acts, Hedonistic Instrumentalism (which represents the tendency to perform a deviant act of minor social importance in order to obtain a personal benefit, e.g., "falsifying about a child's age to secure reduced fare"), and Non-Catholic Marriage Pattern (e.g., "married persons using birth-control devices"). Three nonfactoral subscales were selected by the authors in consultation with other researchers using the scale. These included Nontraditional Sex Behavior, Business Immorality and Interpersonal Crimes. Two single items, "a nation dealing unjustly with a weaker nation over which it has power" and "refusing to bear arms in a war one feels is unjust," were also scored separately. A high score represents condemnation of the behaviors. There were no overlapping items in any of the 10 subscales of moral judgment.

## SUBJECTS

Eighty-four introductory psychology students at two universities were administered the materials. All subjects were tested in class in a single one-hour session. All had previously participated in at least one hour of psychological research. The members of the classes were told that their participation was voluntary, but only one student declined to take part in the testing. They were asked not to place their names on the papers. Fifty-five of the 84 subjects were females. The freshman to senior classes were represented by 12, 27, 26, and 19 subjects respectively.

## FACTOR ANALYSIS OF SINGLE
## AND MULTIPLE-ITEM SCALES

The validity question asks the extent to which the single-item scales measure the same areas of religious values as do the multiple-item scales. Since the single items used in the present study are primarily oriented towards religion as broadly defined, the question is one of how the single and multiple-item scales compare when measuring general religiosity.

One approach to the problem is factor analysis. By extracting factors from the scales one can see how each scale related to the various aspects of general religiosity. Hence, principal axes with iterated communalities were extracted from the correlations among the measures for the two roots greater than 1.0, both of which were highly significant with p < .0005 (Bartlett, 1950, 1951). The factors were rotated to Varimax and Promax positions (Gorsuch, 1970). The Promax factors gave better simple structure.

The correlations of the single-item scales and the multiple-item scales with the Promax factors are given in Table 1 and indicate the extent to which each individual scale had variance in common with the other scales in the analysis. Note that several of these scales had a heavy Christological content and so the factors were somewhat more Christologically oriented than they would otherwise have been.

From an examination of the first factor's loadings, it appears that the single-item scales are the equal of the multiple-item scales in measuring that dimension. The first factor appears to be a general pro-religious attitude and its best measure is the single item of Rated Importance of Religion. The multiple-item Intrinsic Religiousness scale was also high but both of the other single-item scales correlated as well with the factor as the other multiple-item scales.

The second factor is best termed "Christian orthodoxy." The multiple-item measures of Christology and Fundamentalism correlated higher with this factor than even the best single-item scale. However, all the single-item scales were somewhat correlated with the factor and the Christologically oriented single-item measure was reasonably valid. The authors now wish they had requested the subjects to rate the single item "The Bible is the literal, infallible truth"; it might have loaded this factor quite highly. The factor would then have been named "Fundamentalism."

Note that Religious Individualism had unimpressive loadings on both factors and so was measuring something not included in any of the other scales.

The two factors correlated .6, which means that one could ignore the distinction between the factors and combine them into one general factor. While some information would be lost, the general factor approach would be useful in studies where religion was not the central focus. In that case, the investigators might be interested in only the gross relationships and would need a measure loading relatively high on both factors. The variables meeting such a criterion again include several of the single-item scales; the single item of belief that "Jesus is the Christ" is the best measure of this general religiosity. The multiple-item scales tend to be too specific.


## FORMING RELATIONSHIPS WITH ANOTHER DOMAIN

The efficacy of a measuring instrument can also be determined by examining its relationship to other variables of potential interest. If one measure shows more systematic relationships to external measures than do other similar variables, then it probably has greater potential usefulness.

Analyses of variance were calculated for each religious scale with each of the ethical scales serving as a dependent measure. This method of analysis was selected over correlation coefficients because of possible curvilinear relationships and because the Religious Preference item was only a nominal scale.

Analysis of variance required that the continuous religious scales be divided, so the subjects were grouped into four categories ranging from low to high on each scale. On the basis of the responses to the question of Jesus as the Christ, subjects were divided into the disbelievers ("definitely not" and "no"), the undecided ("no, I don't think so," "can't decide"), the believers ("yes, I think so") and the committed believers ("yes, definitely").

The subjects were similarly regrouped for analyses with the other religious scales. The only exception was Religious Preference where the major observed religious denominations and the "nones" served as categories. Analyses based on this variable had 16 nones, 9 Southern Baptists, 6 Catholics, 15 Methodists, 10 Presbyterians and 8 Jews. The 20 subjects who selected other denominations were excluded from this variable's analyses. To estimate the strength of relationships, correlation ratios (Guilford, 1965) were calculated from the analyses of variance. These are presented in Table 2. (This particular report is not, of course, interested in the interpretations of these relationships but only in the ability of the various measures to identify relationships).

## TABLE 2

### THE ABILITY OF RELIGIOUS MEASURES
### TO CORRELATE WITH ETHICAL VARIABLES[a]

Severity of Moral Judgments Concerning:

| | Prejudice | All Issues | Nontraditional Sex Behavior | Business Immorality | Interpersonal Crimes | Misrepresentation | Absence of Philanthropic Acts | Hedonistic Instrumentalism | Non-Catholic Marriage Pattern | Misuses of National Power | Refusing Induction |
|---|---|---|---|---|---|---|---|---|---|---|---|
| **A. Single-Item Scales** | | | | | | | | | | | |
| "Jesus is the Christ" | .15 | .29 | .37† | .13 | .17 | .24 | .18 | .24 | .16 | .10 | .34† |
| Frequency of Religious Attendance | .14 | .34† | .53† | .12 | .16 | .33† | .17 | .24 | .32 | .23 | .25 |
| Rated Importance of Religion | .22 | .43† | .53† | .26 | .14 | .31* | .26 | .37† | .19 | .33* | .31* |
| Religious Preference | .13 | .39 | .53† | .26 | .20 | .34 | .18 | .30 | .58† | .28 | .47† |
| **B. Multiple-Item Scales** | | | | | | | | | | | |
| Christology | .29 | .33* | .40† | .18 | .04 | .22 | .10 | .27 | .28 | .15 | .32* |
| Extrinsic | .25 | .16 | .27 | .14 | .19 | .15 | .11 | .19 | .13 | .21 | .18 |
| Intrinsic | .23 | .49† | .54† | .41† | .27 | .41† | .33* | .32* | .25 | .21 | .21 |
| Religious Individualism | .26 | .19 | .14 | .29 | .15 | .11 | .13 | .25 | .17 | .33* | .30 |
| Fundamentalism | .32* | .25 | .36† | .13 | .10 | .15 | .16 | .26 | .59† | .28 | .33* |

[a]Body of the table contains correlation ratios which summarize both non-linear and linear trends. Note that a correlation ratio cannot be negative; no information is given in the table as to direction of relationship. No $F_{max}$ was sufficiently great to invalidate the significance sets.
*$P_{F—ratio} < .05$.
†$P_{F—ratio} < .025$.

From examining the pattern of correlation ratios in Table 2, one can gain an impression of the extent to which the measures formed relationships. Despite the fact that the multiple-item scales should be better defined and have higher reliabilities—both of which should produce clearer relationships—the four single-item measures had the same number of significant relationships (14) as did the five multiple-item measures. Of course, any such global comparison is only an approximation. The multiple-item scales are not exact replicates of the single-item scales and contain one scale, Religious Individualism, that correlated only slightly with the other religious measures.

In the case of Christology, a more direct comparison is possible. One has data on both the single-item confession in Jesus as Christ and the multiple-item Christology scale. Here it appears that, as measurement theory would predict, the multiple-item scale has clearer relationships than the single-item scale but the improvement is not great. This conclusion is consistent with the previous data on the interrelationships of the variables.

The general conclusion from Table 2 is that the multiple-item scales do not necessarily form stronger relationships to another domain of current research interest. The best single-item scale, Rated Importance of Religion, and the best multiple-item scale, Extrinsic, formed the same number of significant relationships. The single-item indicators are generally the equal of the multiple-item scales.

## VARIATIONS IN THE MEANING OF A SINGLE ITEM

A single item should have a relatively unambiguous interpretation to be useful as a measurement tool. Scales such as denominational preference and frequency of worship service attendance appear to be unambiguous. But what of the confession in Jesus as Christ? To determine the extent to which the Christological item was interpreted in different ways, the answers to the free response questions of the meaning of belief in Jesus as Christ were examined.

A subjective reading of these answers indicated a variety of responses at any given level of commitment. For example, disbelievers replied to the open-ended questions with responses such as the following:

"Nothing."

"Jesus is capable of saving man from the troubles and anxieties of life through faith. He is the Lord of anyone who would attempt to live a good life."

"This means that within the Christian context Jesus was indeed the son of the Christian God—that he was a part of the Christian trinity—was more than mortal—necessarily had to die so that all mortals would be saved."

At the other end of the commitment scale, the subjects also showed a variety of responses:

"It means Jesus is the son of God. I believe in this, but I also believe that you cannot give a name to the entity which governs our lives, and that all people worship this entity each in their own way."

"Jesus was God's only begotten son, who came here to save the world and died for our sins."

"Jesus and Christ to me are one meaning, the same. Just different words."

"This phrase means that Jesus was and is at once God and the son of God."

Each author developed a categorical rating system of meanings ascribed to the confessional statement by a prior sample of 94 college students. The final categories were those agreed upon by both raters which could be reliably scored and which reflected the major dimensions of meaning assigned to Christological statements.

Responses to the open-ended questions by subjects in the present sample were then rated independently by the authors without knowledge of the subjects' theological position. A subject's failure to mention a particular category was scored as a zero; the subject received a one for referring to the concept in answering that particular question. The final score assigned to each subject in each category was the sum of the scores given by both authors to both open-ended questions. The proportion of inter-rater agreement or the inter-rater correlation coefficient (corrected by the Spearman-Brown formula) is given in Table 3 for each of the scoring categories.

Table 3 also presents the results of analyses on the ratings. These analyses test the frequency with which each of the categories of meaning was used across subjects with different responses to the confessional item. A simple analysis of variance was used to determine the significance of differences among the means.

It can be seen that there are a variety of meanings given of the confession in Jesus as Christ but that these do not vary systematically across the groups of differing commitment. The most common idea is that Jesus is divine, with the next most frequently mentioned concept being that he has enabled one's sins to be forgiven. The conclusion from Table 3 is that the variety in objective meanings given to Christological statements is basically unrelated to one's evaluation of Jesus. The question means the same thing to most subjects at all points on the scale. The validity does not appear to be reduced by different interpretations, a result which did not match the authors' expectations.

TABLE 3

FREQUENCIES OF MEANINGS GIVEN TO THE CONFESSION OF CHRIST

| Meaning Categories (with possible range) | Proportion of Rater Agreement | Mean Number of Times the Meaning Category Was Used | | | | Simple Analysis of Variance Probabilities |
|---|---|---|---|---|---|---|
| | | Disbelievers in Jesus as Christ (N=14) | Undecided (N=18) | Believers in Jesus as Christ (N=17) | Strong Believers in Jesus as Christ (N=35) | |
| Deity (0-4) | .86 | 1.4 | 1.3 | 1.7 | 2.0 | >.05 |
| Care, Protection, Comfort (0-4) | .93 | 0.5 | 0.4 | 0.9 | 0.4 | >.05 |
| Forgives Sins (0-4) | .80 | 1.1 | 0.6 | 1.6 | 1.4 | >.05 |
| Way to Eternal Life (0-4) | .98 | 0.1 | 0.7 | 0.7 | 1.0 | >.05 |
| Messiah (0-4) | .88 | 0.3 | 0.4 | 0.3 | 0.3 | >.05 |
| Guide (0-4) | .92 | 0.5 | 0.5 | 0.9 | 0.7 | >.05 |
| Number of Ideas (0-24) | .94[a] | 7.3 | 5.7 | 9.3 | 9.3 | >.05 |

[a]Correlational reliability for combined raters instead of proportion of rater agreement.

Considering the fact that the Christological confession is a stereotypic question with an institutionally defined answer, the results of the present analysis are encouraging. They suggest that a single item may be quite useful in measuring religious values, even when some would consider that item a trite cliché.

## COST VS. VALIDITY

The most important consideration in choosing a single or multiple-item scale is, of course, the relative validity. If the validity of a single-item measure is equal to or greater than the validity of a multiple-item scale, the single item is the obvious choice. However, the extent to which a multiple-item scale must be more valid than the single item in order to be selected can only be decided by considering the costs in the context of a particular study. At times, the use of a single item may answer the research question equally well but at less cost even though its validity is somewhat lower.

The increase in precision gained from using multiple-item scales instead of single-item scales generally arises from the increase in precision due to higher reliability. Increased precision in estimating statistics such as means can also be gained by using more subjects. This is particularly appropriate when one is interested in whether a relationship exists rather than in estimating the size of the relationship. Whether one chooses to increase his precision by increasing the number of items measuring the construct or by increasing the number of respondents depends upon the relative cost of each.

Fig 1. illustrates the effects of changes in the validity of an instrument relative to the number of respondents (N) necessary for the observed relationship to be statistically significant.[4] The curves represent three underlying relationships between an independent variable, e.g., a religious scale, and a dependent variable. These are: slight (a population correlation, $r_{xy}$, of .3), moderate ($r_{xy} = .5$) and moderately strong ($r_{xy} = .7$). These curves are plotted so that the expected observed correlation for that population coefficient can be read off the left side for scales of varying validity as indicated along the bottom. The N necessary for the observed correlation to be significant is presented on the right edge of the graph.

## FIGURE 1

### VALIDITY NECESSARY TO FIND A GIVEN RELATIONSHIP

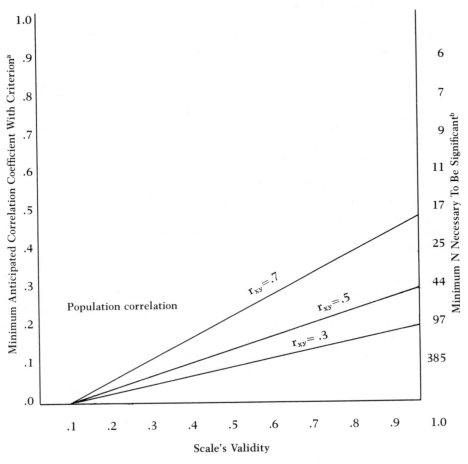

[a]Criterion is assumed to be unbiased and to have a reliability of .9. The minimum anticipated co-efficient is the one which would be significant in 90% of the samples of this size.

[b]Using $\sigma z = \dfrac{1}{\sqrt{N-3}}$ and $p < .05$ for a two-tailed test. In actual practice, student's $t$ should be used for $N < 30$.

For example, if one accepts the loadings on the second factor of Table 1 as the validity coefficients for a particular study, one can estimate the necessary increase in N to offset the use of the single-item

Christological confession as compared to the multiple-item Christology scale. The single item has a "validity" of .77 as compared to .90 for the six-item scale. If one expected a moderate relationship between this facet of religiosity and some independent variable—and were willing to ignore any smaller relationship—then one would need 55 to 65 observations with the multiple-item scale to have 90% chance of verifying the population relationship. Using the single-item scale would require 85 to 90 observations for the same probability of reaching a proper conclusion.

As the example shows, the possibilities of finding a significant relationship where one actually exists are quite good with only moderate validities and moderate size samples, assuming an excellent dependent variable. As Fig. 1 shows, it is only when one expects a small underlying relationship or has scales of poor validity that a very large N is needed to test a given correlation coefficient for significance.[5]

If the expense involved in testing each subject by the two scales and the cost of adding more subjects is known, one can logically choose between the scales. For example, assume that the cost of the one-item Christology scale is estimated to be X per subject. This includes the costs of preparing and administering the materials as well as preparing the results for data processing; it excludes the cost of gaining access to each subject. Assume the cost of the multiple-item scale (including the additional costs of preparing, administering and scoring the scale) to be 8X. Then the costs in the above example would be 85X to 90X for the single-item scale but 440X to 520X for the six-item scale. If obtaining subjects involves no cost, one could do considerably more research by using the lower validity, single-item measure. If data from each subject cost more than 5X to obtain—which would be true if, for example, a stratified block sampling procedure were used—then the multiple-item scale would allow one to do the most effective research.

## SUMMARY AND CONCLUSIONS

If one is interested in measuring general religiosity or an intrinsically proreligious attitude, the only major difference between the multiple-item and single-item scales is the greater costs of the former. Some people do interpret a single item such as the confession in Christ differently from others but these differences are unrelated to one's confessional position. In the case of Christian Orthodoxy (Fundamentalism?), the multiple-item scales functioned somewhat better than the single-item scales. In this case, the decision to use a single or multiple-item scale lies with cost-validity considerations.

The multiple and single-item scales both related to another domain at about the same level. The patterns of relationships to the other domain were not completely consistent, suggesting that different facets of religiosity related to different facets of that domain. Therefore, it may be wise to use several single-item indicators as opposed to one multiple-item scale if, for example, only a half-dozen items on religosity can be included in the study.

The above conclusions should not be generalized too widely. They are based on only one subset of scales. In addition, they result from one study of college students who varied widely in their religious commitments. Quite different results might occur with a more homogeneous sample, e.g., Jesuits, where exact separation between subtle differences of outlook would be at stake.

The experiences encountered in this study suggest that the various single-item scales may be useful in different situations. If one is interested in the impact of all variations of religious faith, then Religious Attendance or Rated Importance of Religion would be possible choices. The former would represent a more institutional emphasis than the latter but the general conclusions would tend to be similar in research on moral judgments. However, these measures could break down if the variations in faith extended much outside the Judeo-Christian tradition. The scales may have different meanings and different external relationships in other faiths.

Religious Preference is useful also. It appears to have somewhat stronger relationships to other domains than does the Christological confession, but this is to be expected. To belong to a Christian denomination provides the information that one accepts Jesus as the Christ but which denomination he joins provides additional information as to his beliefs and values. The utility of this item is generally limited to studies which assure a sufficient number of subjects from each denomination.

The confession that Jesus is the Christ is also helpful, but the range of appropriate application is distinct from the other measures. It is probably more useful than Religious Preference if the sample has a large number of denominations relative to the number of subjects. It could also be useful as a preselection device for examining variations within Christianity. After finding subjects high on Christology, one would use other measures to separate the confessors into the desired categories.

The Christological confession can also be used to identify a sample of relatively committed Christians from a total sample pool where different faiths are represented. These could then, for example, be compared with committed individuals from other faiths. As research progresses, one suspects that more attention will be given to the differential impact of various faiths and that, therefore, the Christological confession will become a more important measure of religious faith.

## NOTES AND REFERENCES

[1] Note that a variable with inadequate reliability cannot form relationships which would indicate a high validity. Any single-item measure showing better validity than a multiple-item scale is sufficiently reliable to replace that scale. Therefore a separate consideration of reliability is not necessary when validity information is available.

[2] The single-item indicators were worded as follows: Check religious preference: ___none, ___Baptist, American ___Baptist, National, ___Baptist, Southern, ___Catholic, Roman, ___Christian (Disciples of Christ), ___Churches of Christ, ___Eastern Orthodox, ___ Episcopal, ___Jewish, ___Latter Day Saints, ___Lutheran, ___Lutheran, Evangelical Synodical Conferences, ___Lutheran, National Council, ___Methodist, ___Presbyterian, ___United Church of Christ (Congregational, Evangelical & Reformed), ___Other (Specify).

Check how often you attend religious worship services: ___1. Less than several times a year, ___2. Several times a year to once a month. ___3. Several times a month. ___4. Once a week, ___5. More than once a week.

Circle the number which indicates how important your religion is to you: 1 (Not at all; have no religion); 2; 3; 4; 5; 6; 7; 8; 9 (Extremely important; my religious faith is the center of my entire life).

Do you believe that Jesus is the Christ, the Son of the Living God? 1. Definitely not; 2. No; 3. No, I don't think so; 4. Can't decide; 5. Yes, I think so; 6. Yes; 7. Yes, definitely.

[3] The items in the Christology scale are as follows: 1. Jesus was the Son of God even before he lived on the earth. 2. God personally came to earth in human form as Jesus. 3. Any man of exceptional ability and goodwill could have done as much as Jesus under similar circumstances (reversed in scoring). 4. No mere human could have done what Jesus did for mankind. 5. Jesus had a source of strength greater than any mortal man can ever have. 6. Jesus' powers were of a strictly human nature (reversed in scoring).

[4] Figure 1 was calculated by assuming that the criterion was unbiased and had a reliability of .9, and that the reliability of the predictor scale equaled the validity squared. Then, from the correction for attenuation, one has:

$$r'_{xy} = r_{xy} \, r_{xx} \, \sqrt{r_{yy}}$$

where $r'_{yy}$ is the expected correlation, $r_{xy}$ is the population correlation, $r_{xx}$ is the scale's validity and $r_{yy}$ is the criterion's reliability. The coefficient that one would find as significant in most samples and the minimum number of subjects necessary for that coefficient to be significant were then computed by iterating. First, the expected correlation was computed for a given population coefficient and given validity level. Then it was transformed to Fisher's Z and the minimum N necessary for such a coefficient to be significant ($p < .05$; two-tailed test) was calculated. Since that N would find the coefficient significant only 50% of the time, the standard error of the expected coefficient was calculated for this initial N. This was used to determine the minimum anticipated coefficient that could be expected in at least 90% of the samples, and the N necessary for that to be significant. With this new N, the iteration continued by computing the new standard error of the new minimum anticipated coefficient and another new N necessary for the latest minimum anticipated coefficient to be significant. Iteration continued until the minimum anticipated coefficients for validities of 1.0 changed less than .004. The authors would like to thank the Peabody and Vanderbilt Computer Centers for providing computer facilities for this study.

[5]While the figure is presented for simple tests of significance, the same principle holds for more complex tests and confidence interval estimation. But these results cannot be directly extrapolated to situations which allow capitalizing on chance, as is generally true of multivariate statistical procedures.

ALLPORT, G. W. 1959 Religion and prejudice. *Crane Review* 2, 1–10.

ALLPORT, G. W. AND ROSS, J. M. 1967 Personal religious orientation and prejudice. *Journal Personality and Social Psychology* 5, 432–443.

BARTLETT, M. S. 1950 Tests of significance in factor analysis. *British Journal Psychology, Statistical Section* 3, 77–85. 1951 A further note on tests of significance in factor analysis. *British Journal Psychology, Statistical Section* 4, 1–2.

BROWN, L. B. 1962 A study of religious belief. *British Journal Psychology* 53, 259-272.

CRISSMAN, PAUL 1942 Temporal change and sexual difference in moral judgments. *Journal Social Psychology* 16, 29–38.

CRONBACH, L. J. 1951 Coefficient alpha and the internal structure of tests. *Psychometrika* 16, 297–334.

FEAGIN, J. R. 1964 Prejudice and religious types: A focused study of southern fundamentalists. *Journal Scientific Study of Religion* 4, 3–13.

GLOCK, C. Y., AND STARK, R. 1966 *Christian Beliefs and Anti-Semitism*. New York: Harper & Row.

GORSUCH, R. L. 1970 A comparison of Biquartimin, Maxplane, Promax, and Varimax. *Educational and Psychological Measurement* 30, 861–872.

GUILFORD, J. P. 1965 *Fundamental Statistics in Psychology and Education*. New York: McGraw-Hill. (4th Ed.)

JEEVES, M. A. 1957 Contribution on prejudice and religion. *Proceedings of the XIth International Congress of Psychology,* Brussels, 508–510.

KING, M. 1967 Measuring the religious variable: nine proposed dimensions. *Journal Scientific Study of Religion* 6, 173–190.

LEE, R. R. 1965 Theological belief as a dimension of personality. Unpublished Ph. D. Dissertation, Northwestern University.

RETTIG, S., AND PASAMANICK, B. 1959 Changes in moral values among college students: a factorial study. *American Sociological Review* 24, 858–863. 1960 Differences in the structure of moral values of students and alumni. *American Sociological Review* 25, 550–555. 1961 Moral value structure and social class. *Sociometry* 24, 21–35. 1962 Invariance in factor structure of moral value judgments from American and Korean college students. *Sociometry* 25, 73–84. 1963 Some observations on the moral ideology of first and second generation collective and non-collective settlers in Israel. *Social Problems* 11, 165–178.

ROKEACH, M. 1969a Religious values and social compassion. *Review of Religious Research* 11, 3–23. 1969b Value systems and religion. *Review of Religious Research* 11, 24–39.

STRUENING, E. L. 1963 Anti-democratic attitudes in midwest university. In H. H. Remmers (Ed.), *Anti-Democratic Attitudes in American Schools*. Evanston, Ill.: Northwestern University Press.

**351**

# N=1 Methodology in the Psychology of Religion

## H. NEWTON MALONY

During the past decade much has been written about the use of single cases in research (cf. Davidson & Costello, 1969). Discussion of this design, termed N = 1, brings up the perennial question of whether knowledge is best derived from the study of single individuals or from groups. It has become more than respectable to gather information about the behavior of individuals. Data derived from the study of one person is considered as valid and reliable as that obtained from groups of persons. In fact one journal, *The Journal of Applied Behavioral Analysis,* is devoted entirely to the study of single cases.

Method in the psychology of religion has not been informed by the N = 1 dialogue. To be sure, the history of the field is replete with case studies, such as those reported by James (1902) and Freud (1925). James (1902) purposely chose single cases of exceptional religious persons to illustrate what he felt to be the essence of religious experience. He relied heavily on autobiographical accounts. For example, he reports an account by Mrs. Jonathan Edwards of the experience of the friendliness of Christ. He quotes her as writing, "Last night was the sweetest night I ever had in my life . . . all night I continued in a constant, clear, and lively sense of the heavenly sweetness of Christ's excellent love, of his nearness to me, and of my dearness to him, etc." (p. 219). Freud (1925) easily generalized from his dynamic analysis of individuals. For example, he interprets a fellow physician's return to religious faith after an unnerving experience in a dissecting room as a function of that physician's relationship with his mother. The fact of a "dear, sweet, old woman" evoked in him a longing for his mother, followed by indignation at his father, i.e., God, whom he desired to destroy. This anger, in turn, evoked quiet, which he reacted to by remorse and penitence. At this point he asked forgiveness and became faithful through the process of

Paper presented at the annual meeting of the Society for the Scientific Study of Religion, San Francisco, 1973.

identification with the aggressor. As Freud said, "He had a religious experience and had undergone a conversion" (p. 245). In both James and Freud, however, the extensive study of single cases, as defined by contemporary theorists, is not present.

Only with Stewart's study of religion in adolescents (1967) do we see anything approaching the N = 1 method in the psychology of religion. Making use of clinical interviews conducted over a period of several years, he studied the religious changes in a small group of adolescents in Topeka, Kansas. He reports commonalities in their experience derived primarily from intensive study of them as individuals rather than as a group.

Stewart's study is, however, the exception to the rule. Most contemporary psychology of religion is concerned with group comparisons and correlational statistics. The research of Maddock and Kenny (1972) is illustrative. They compared the philosophy of human nature among 200 subjects who were classified according to their relative intrinsic or extrinsic orientation toward religion. Using t-tests for statistical differences between the two groups, they found that there was a significant tendency for those interested in religion for its own sake (the intrinsically oriented) to have a more positive view of human nature than those who were interested in religion for social impressionistic reasons (the extrinsic). N = 1 methodologists would have several criticisms of this method—as will be discussed later in this essay.

There is thus room for informing the psychology of religion concerning the N = 1 method and for considering the applicability of this approach to future research. The remainder of this essay will deal with this issue. A survey of several N = 1 approaches will be reported, and possible research paradigms will be suggested. Finally, a summary report of a recent research project will be given.

## N = 1 APPROACHES

Much historical precedent exists for single-subject study in psychology. Dukes (1965) reports some of these. Ebbinghaus (1885) performed 163 memory experiments on himself. Bryan and Harters' (1889) data on the plateau in learning curves was obtained from one telegraph key operator. Prince's (1905) study of dissociation was done on a Miss Beauchamp. Anna O. provided Beuer and Freud (1895) the basis for a theory of neurosis. Evidence for residual memory was provided Burtt (1932) by quizzing his son 14 years after the fact. Most of Piaget's theorizing about mental development was based on observations of his own children—taken one at a time. Much of behaviorism began with Watson and Rayner's (1920) study of conditioned fear in a person named Albert; it continued with the deconditioning of a similar fear in one boy, Peter (Jones, 1924).

However, more of these researchers theorized about his design to the extent that Gordon Allport (1955, 1962) has done. He has called for study of the unique individual since his early work on personality in 1937. The naming of common traits based on similar behaviors one sees in many individuals tells us very little about the essence of individual persons. Nomothetic, or group research, is more or less naming for the convenience of the researcher. It gives the illusion of meaning. Real law, or meaning, is idiographic, i.e., exists in the inner organization of the single person. Better to look in each person for this unique pattern, according to Allport. This he calls the "Billian quality of Bill." Individual differences are the essence of reality rather than accidents to be overcome or rejected, as Wundt was apt to do.

Individuality is the prime fact, not a residual—as some researchers are prone to insist. Allport felt that prediction in the single instance was always based on the individual's unique organization and response to forces in his life. Morphogenic, or inner pattern study, is the preferred and, in the final analysis, the only meaningful approach.

Allport is closely paralleled by the emphasis of Lewin (1936) who reiterates the distinction made by Dilthey between "explanation" and "understanding." This viewpoint insists there is a qualitative difference between the physical and human sciences. Physical entities are inert and their behavior can therefore be understood and predicted by description of the outer forces acting upon them, but human entities are dynamic and their behavior can only be understood by appealing to the inner forces, i.e., mind, self-consciousness, will, etc., which determine their behavior. This places $N = 1$ issues squarely in the middle of mind-body problems in philosophy. The distinction made by Lewin and others is reminiscent of the observation made by Descartes that the fountains of Paris operated by natural, mechanistic law while persons functioned out of spirit or free will. Suffice it to say that Lewin observed, as did Allport, that accidents or inexplicable events were not exceptions to the norm—they were the norm. Commonality in behavior is only an apparition. Human behavior cannot be predicted by a description of outer forces acting upon persons. Explanation and prediction are impossible goals in the human sciences. Understanding, defined as intuitive attempts to appreciate the life space of another, is possible *after the fact*—never before the act. Man is always free and can only be understood, not explained. Thus, the proper objects of study are individuals, rather than groups.

Allport and Lewin were better theoreticians than practitioners. However, Murray (1963) reported research during his year as an American Psychological Association Distinguished Scientist that does get at some of these issues. In his classic manner he described his work as an antidote to those psychologists who were "dissociated from the nature and experiences of actual people by binding their energies to an enthralling intellectual game played with abstract counters of dubious importance and of spurious relevance to human life" (p. 28). Twenty-one subjects were intensely studied for their reactions in a debate of their philosophy of life, which each had taken a month to write. Heart and respiration rates during time segments plus ratings of anxiety, motility, verbal intensity, and task involvement on videotapes, typescripts, and audio tapes were obtained for each subject. Murray thus tried to get at the unique inner pattern of each individual, which Allport called for and Lewin espoused. Although he did not radically affirm individual uniqueness, he did show a strong bias toward the intensive study of single subjects and a concern for particularity. This project did not include detailed historical analysis of unique patterns, although Murray is well known for his concern with the dynamic study of individual personality. The methodology he demonstrates is highly suggestive for the field.

Cattell (1965) systematized Murray's concern for measuring many traits within one person over a number of situations. He contrasted this approach (termed P-technique) with the more typical group approach (termed R-technique). R-technique is the ordinary procedure in factor analysis whereby numbers of people are measured on a set of traits and their scores correlated. This is the typical design of most group research. It is cross-sectional, in that no provision is made for changes over time or chance scores at the time of measurement. It is a one-time event. The inference made is that persons are all alike and that they do not change. P-technique, in contrast, is the measurement of a set of traits in one individual over time, e.g., 100 days. Instead of correlating many persons' scores, one individual's scores at different times are related to each other. The resultant factors are indices of how traits fluctuate or remain the same within one individual. Uniqueness and change are assumed. As Cattell (1965) states:

> Whether we apply stimuli-stresses, tranquilizers, work and rest periods—or just leave an "awful week" to produce its own differences from "a delightful week"—is of no moment. Our interest is in the or-

ganism's natural dimensions of bounce under the impact of events (p. 154).

Thus, an understanding of a particular person, not people in general, is possible. Cattell has advanced $N = 1$ methodology greatly through this technique. As a model it provides the base for much current single-subject research.

Before turning to the contemporary scene, Skinner's somewhat left-handed concern for uniqueness should be mentioned. He is without question the unsung hero of modern $N = 1$ method. While Sidman in *Tactics of Scientific Research* (1960) acknowledges this, it is of interest that Dukes (1965), in an article entitled "$N = 1$," makes no reference to Skinner. Skinner (1956) appropriated Cannon's term serendipity—the finding of the unexpected—for the knowledge that could come to the experimenter by following the rat across the floor when he jumped out of the maze—just to see how he behaved under new conditions. Further, he suggested that a research equipment failure should never be repaired until the experimenter had fully observed what effect the new conditions were having on behavior. In both cases new knowledge was possible. Those who stuck to predetermined hypotheses and the analysis of group averages would miss these findings. In fact, Skinner anticipated the ecological psychologists by suggesting observations should be made without prior theoretical predictions (1950). To be "a-theoretical" meant, to him, to be free to see what was there in research. And, of course, the analysis of individuals was the method *par excellence!*

Prior to discussing such theorists as Dukes (1965) and Sidman (1960), who are pure $N = 1$ theorists, we should mention Barker (1951), an ecological psychologist. His work is a variation on the theme in the sense that he combines something of the P-technique (Cattell, 1965) and the a-theoretical approach (Skinner, 1950). In the unusual book *One Boy's Day* (1951), Barker reports the total behavior events in a day in the life of a boy in the Midwest. He notes the several behavior settings in which the boy finds himself and groups these into categories. It is a provocative attempt to study one individual and to demonstrate behavioral consistency. The question of whether or not the individual is the appropriate object of study is inconsequential. The data do not lend themselves to any other approach.

Sidman (1960) is representative of a number of researcher-theoreticians who explicitly affirm $N = 1$ methodology (cf. Davidson and Costello, 1969; Bijou, et al., 1969; Dukes, 1965). He refers to Porter's discovery of ulcers in monkeys who died while part of a project studying their reactions to varied conditions. What was considered an unavoidable bother became the prime finding of the study because Porter pursued research on individual monkeys who did not fit the paradigm. Sidman believes that data should take precedence over theory and suggests that science should return again and again to this exploratory base. He posits that there is no better ground to explore than individual behavior, which is a function of its own consequences. If these relationships are left unexamined, theories will mean little, and data based on groups will be meaningless. In contrast to Barker (1951), Sidman favors laboratory analysis of behavior because everyday observation tends to be unreliable and controlling variables impossible to define. Using an individual instead of a group is defended on the assumption that individuals are probably much more alike than has been assumed and that, on the other hand, uniqueness has a better chance of being understood if it is being sought, as in N = 1 research. Thus, the method allows for both generality and individuality.

Sidman's (1960) model should be considered in more detail because it provides the basis for my treatise on N = 1 in the psychology of religion. It is illustrated by a recent doctoral dissertation on the alleviation of thumbsucking among six children, each of whom was an experiment unto himself, i.e., N = 1. The issue centered around the location of treatment interventions and the generalization of treatment effects into other situations.

Treatment consisted of turning off the television on a variable interval schedule when the child sucked his thumb. The mother administered the treatment either at home or at a treatment center. When the relationship was established treatment ceased. This was done to see if the previous baseline of frequent thumbsucking would return. After observation, treatment was reinstated. The persistence and generalization of this behavior were then determined by ceasing all treatment and by observing the child watching television at home and at the treatment center. The experiments were replicated five times.

The elements of this design are noteworthy. A baseline of the behavior is reported; an intervention consequence is presented; thus, the situation changes. Subsequent change in the frequency, intensity, or duration of behavior is observed; the situation is returned to its original state. The behavior is observed again. If it returns to baseline, the assumption is made that a true behavior-consequence relationship is being manipulated. The intervention is reinstated and the behavior observed once more. Finally, the effect of the experience in other situations is observed. The experiment is replicated in other subjects, not to see whether the results on the first subject were real, but to see whether the researcher has, in fact, found a variable related to the behavior in which he is interested.

This last point is critical. Variations between subjects are pursued as real, not artifactual. It is assumed that human behavior is complex and overdetermined, i.e., is a function of more than one motivation. If a child desists from thumbsucking when the television is turned off, it is not assumed that is all he is doing. However, we can establish that he is *at least* doing that much. In those cases where he does not, the job then becomes one, not of forcing the child into our theory, i.e., he *should* stop thumbsucking when the television is turned off, but of finding out what *else* he is doing, i.e., what *does* determine *his* behavior.

## RESEARCH PARADIGMS IN THE PSYCHOLOGY OF RELIGION

I propose that $N = 1$ research has much to teach the psychology of religion. For one thing, it is experimental. Elsewhere (Malony, 1970) I called for an "experimental" psychology in which religion could be the well-controlled independent variable on the operationally defined dependent variable. The $N = 1$ method provides a framework for such an endeavor. It allows us to retain an appreciation for the uniqueness so essential to religious interpretation, while investigating the commonalities that do exist. Rokeach's (1969) investigation of values is a case which does not illustrate the point. He assessed the effect that short term input regarding value conflict had on the tendency to change values and to persist in that change over a year's period. Group measures of central tendency were used to analyze data, and the hypothesis was confirmed. Had the $N = 1$ approach been used, so much data would not have been lost and the nuances of each religious individual's responses over the year-long period could have been assessed. The data need not have been statistically analyzed. Commonalities among plotted curves could have been demonstrated while unique reactions could have been delineated.

Such an approach assumes that we can bring some agreement to the definition of "religion" itself. As has been pointed out by many, those definitions that are so broad as to define any passionate concern as religious, e.g., communism, use the term in a manner with which few would agree. On the other hand, those definitions which are so narrow that they confine religion only to cultural expressions, e.g., sect ethics or public worship, use the term in a way that is false to experience. From William James to the present the understanding of religion as that which man does in relation (or response) to that which he considers divine is a sufficient and functional definition. Note that this approach does not confuse theology and psychology. As Vander Leeuw (1969) has said:

> For religion, then, God is the active agent in relation to man, while the sciences in question can concern themselves only with the activity of man in his relation to God; of the acts of God Himself they can give no account whatever (p. 56).

This definition does, however, allow us to view religion as it is delimited by each person. Whatever a man says he does in response to God is admissible data. Two illustrations of this are in order. In an article concerned with relating faith to profession (Malony, 1973), I suggested that there were no signs, e.g., vocational placement, area of research interest, church participation, etc., which definitely indicated who were and who were not the psychologist-Christians. The psychologists who were Christians were those who *said* they were psychologist-Christians. It was up to them, I continued, to say how they related their faith to their professions. To a great extent, categories in the area of religion are personal. In principle, kite-flying is as admissible behavior as church membership.

An example of such an attempt to get at the personal dimension of religion is reported in an article on undergraduate research in religion (Malony, 1972). Students were polled as to whether they thought about God during a myriad of events within a typical day. Although the idea was to identify situations that evoked thoughts about God, the same approach could be used to determine those situations that were religious for a particular individual.

In his discussion of religion and the motor system, Pruyser (1968) includes a persuasive apology for understanding religious action. He notes that one of the distinctive aspects of all religious experience is the sense of new energy which must be expressed in acts. He catalogues a plethora of such behaviors, often considered religious. The variety is endless, ranging from rituals to service, from worship to crusades or freedom marches. That is always personally defined.

Thus, let it be said that N = 1 methodology is of the essence of the psychology of religion. Religion is that which an individual says he does in relation to the divine.

Turning next to some thoughts on how N = 1 research might be designed in the psychology of religion, Dittes (1969) offers a suggestive model in a table on "Identifying different designations of the functions of belief" (p. 643). The distinction between independent and depen-

dent variables is helpful in designating areas of investigation. The table
is reproduced here for purpose of discussion.

TABLE 1

IDENTIFYING DIFFERENT DESIGNATIONS OF THE FUNCTIONS OF BELIEF

| | Dependent variables | | |
|---|---|---|---|
| Independent variables | *Intensity of belief* (for example, open-mindedness, toler-ance of ambiguity, dogmatism) | *Content of belief* (for example, be-nignness of God) | *Protection of belief* (for example, evi-dence of the benign-ness of God) |
| Reinforcement from objective reality | 1. Disappointments are reduced by learning to read a train timetable (acquisition of elementary ego process of "reality map-ping"). | 4. Highly varied experiences of personal sup-port and satis-factions are generalized into a broader ex-pectation and optimism. | 7. Instances of benign experience are selectively recalled. |
| Social reinforcement | 2. Parents praise child's skills of naming objects, solving prob-lems; are less warm to "I don't know." | 5. Parents reward expressions of "God is good", frown on alter-natives. | 8. Membership in likeminded group is sought or others are proselytized to the view. |
| Intrapsychic reinforcement | 3. The pain of in-decision over internally con-flicting motives, or the anxiety of overwhelming raw emotion is reduced by labeling, de-cision, control. | 6. Oedipal anx-ieties are stilled by feeling as-surance of a loving father. | 9. Behavior and atti-tudes of gratitude and thanksgiving, e.g., benevolence, prayer, are fostered as a "con-firming response" to God's goodness. |

(Dittes, "Psychology of Religion," from *The Handbook of Social Psychology,* Vol. 5, 2nd
Ed., ed. by Lindzey-Aronson; Reading, Mass.: Addison-Wesley, 1969. Used by permission)

Several comments and corrections are necessary prior to actually
generating $N = 1$ research from this format. First, an additional column
for "Confession of belief" needs to be added. This would be a measure of
whether belief is explicitly expressed in a given instance and, if so, how
often. It is a frequency measure. Sidman (1960) notes, in standard
learning theory jargon, that dependent measures are best measured in
frequency, intensity and duration. Column 1 is an intensity criterion

and column 3, "Protection of belief," could be conceived as a duration measure. Thus, with the addition of column 4, "Confession of belief," we have all three, i.e., intensity, frequency and duration, with the addition of a qualitative measure, "Content of belief" (column 2).

Next, it should be noted that Dittes' independent and dependent measures are reversible in N = 1 research. For example, a given project could either compare individuals who differed initially on content of belief or on previous family and group religious experience. Again, this same project could make as the criteria measure the seeking of group or family support or the appropriation of certain religious beliefs within a given situation. In N = 1 research one is concerned with understanding the differences in behavior of a single person over several situations or at different times. And these differences can be a function of forces that are situational or are within the person. Thus, an individual could be chosen for study because of the number of events he recalled that had religious meaning to him, and his behavior could be studied in situations with little or much support for such religious interpretations. His responses could be understood as a function of either or both. This represents a subtle departure from Sidman's (1960) N = 1 approach, which primarily looks upon the method as an attempt to determine controlling independent, i.e., extrinsic, variables.

Finally, the basic "subjects by replications" approach of N = 1 methodology needs to be remembered when one generates research problems from the foregoing table. Herein, there is little interest in one-time measurement of relationships, e.g., between church membership and participation in Key-73 evangelistic visitation—cell 8. Instead, the emphasis is on repeated measures of the same individual in various controlled situations, e.g., how many hours a church member spends in evangelistic visitation: the first week after a Key-73 planning meeting, the third week, then back to the first week again, etc. It is a so-called A-B-A-B design in which situations are replicated over and over again. Variations in behavior are plotted on a graph and understood as a function of either the extrinsic situation or the inner state, e.g., salience of church membership, or both. As Sidman (1960) and others have noted, it is this baseline-intervention-return-to-baseline demonstration that illustrates the power of the N = 1 method.

## RECENT RESEARCH USES N = 1 METHODS

In this last selection a detailed illustration of the N = 1 approach will be given. It is based on a recent doctoral dissertation entitled "The physiological effects of Christians visualizing they are committing a sinful act and the function religious variables play in the intensity of such effects" (Forman, 1973).

In this study subjects were instructed to visualize themselves committing two sins—stealing and ignoring a cry for help. Subjects for whom the religious importance of acting righteously was high and low were exposed to these conditions in an A-B-A-B sequence. The A conditions were resting states, while the B conditions were the sinful visualizations. Physiological measures of heart rate, skin conductance, and respiration rate were taken. The problem was similar to Murray's (1963) research on challenges to philosophy of life, yet with two important differences. First, the issues were specifically religious ones in Forman's research, and second, the subjects were analyzed individually in addition to group analysis. Each was a subject-by-replications study unto itself, i.e., N = 1.

Figures of responses under the several conditions for a subject high and a subject low in the reported importance of righteousness are given on the following page.

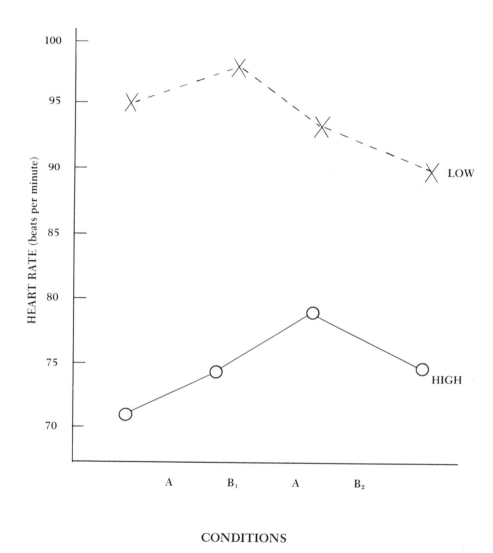

Fig. 1. Heart rate differences for Ss high and low in reported importance of righteousness.

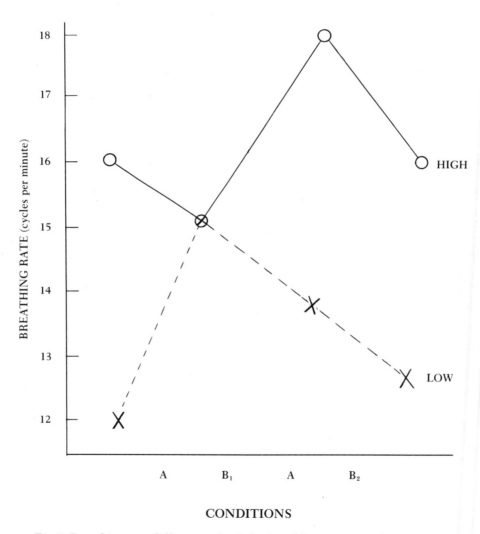

Fig. 2. Breathing rate differences for Ss high and low in reported importance of righteousness.

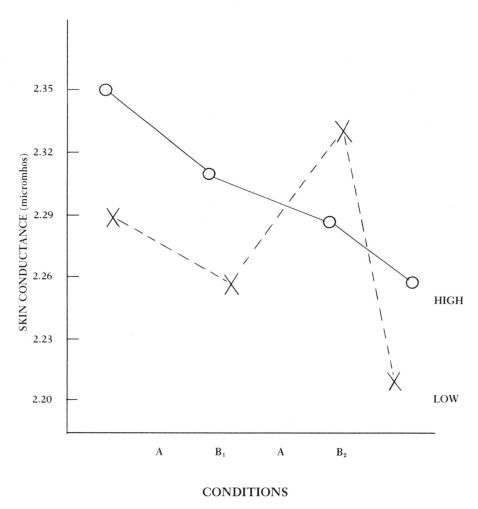

Fig. 3. Skin conductance differences for Ss high and low in reported importance of righteousness.

Table 2 gives the values included in Figure 3.

## TABLE 2

Psychophysiological Indices in Neutral and Sinful Conditions

| Righteousness rating | Conditions | Heart rate | Breathing rate | Skin conductance |
|---|---|---|---|---|
| | N | 95.8 | 12.0 | 2.30 |
| Low S | $S_1$ | 96.2 | 15.0 | 2.25 |
| | N | 95.8 | 14.0 | 2.34 |
| | $S_2$ | 93.2 | 13.3 | 2.21 |
| | N | 72.0 | 16.5 | 2.34 |
| High S | $S_1$ | 72.7 | 15.4 | 2.30 |
| | N | 77.4 | 17.5 | 2.29 |
| | $S_2$ | 74.9 | 17.8 | 2.25 |

The method is suggestive even if the above data are somewhat confusing. The only obvious datum that is consistent in both subjects is the decrease in stress indices under sinning conditions. This, in itself, is difficult to interpret. However, $N = 1$ methodology dictates that the parameter of such evidence be explored rather than ignored or explained away by group statistics. Anecdotal reports seemed to suggest that subjects either adapted to the visualization or refused to identify with the act. In the research, participants had been told they would be exposed to a situation which violated their conscience. Many reported that the actual situations were less threatening than they had anticipated. This would seem to account for the lower stress indices.

Again, let it be noted that the above research only illustrates the method. Its results are inconclusive. The approach is a suggestive one, however, and research problems could be gleaned from any one of the cells in Dittes' (1969) table or for any self-defined religious dimension.

In conclusion, this essay has suggested appropriating $N = 1$ methodology for use in the psychology of religion. Several of the theorists who have called for more intensive study of individuals were considered. Psychology of religion formats using $N = 1$ methodology were presented. Finally, a recent study relating stress to visualized sinning was presented as an example of the $N = 1$ approach. The model appears to be valid but remains to be demonstrated.

## REFERENCES

ALLPORT, G. W., The general and the unique in psychological science. *Journal of Personality*, 1962, 30, 405–422.

BARKER, R. G. AND WRIGHT, H. F., *One boy's day: a specimen record of behavior.* New York: Harper and Row, 1951.

BIJOU, S. W., PETERSON, R. F., HARRIS, F. R., ALLEN, E., AND JOHNSTON, M. S. Methodology for experimental studies of young children in natural settings. *Psychological Record*, 1969, 19, 177–210.

CANNON, W. B. *The way of an investigator.* New York: W. W. Norton, 1945.

CATTELL, R. B., *The scientific analysis of personality.* Baltimore, Maryland: Penguin Books, 1965.

DAVIDSON, P. O. AND COSTELLO, C. G. (Eds.). *N = 1: Experimental studies of single cases.* New York: D. Van Nostrand, 1969.

DITTES, J. E. Two issues in measuring religion. In M. P. Strommen. *Research on religious development.* New York: Hawthorn Books, Inc., 1971, 78–108.

DITTES, J. E. Psychology of religion. In G. Lindzey and E. Aronson (Eds.). *The handbook of social psychology, vol. 5.* Reading, Massachusetts: Addison-Wesley, 1969, 602–659.

DUKES, W. F. *N = 1. Psychological Bulletin,* 1965, 64, 74–79.

FORMAN, R. H. The physiological effects of Christians visualizing they are committing a sinful act and the function religious variables play in the intensity of such effects. Unpublished Ph.D. dissertation, Fuller Theological Seminary, Graduate School of Psychology, Pasadena, California, 1973.

FREUD, S. *Collected papers vol. 5.* London: Hogarth, 1925.

JAMES, W. *The varieties of religious experience.* New York: New American Library (1902), 1958.

LEWIN, K. A. *Principles of topological psychology.* New York: McGraw Hill, 1936.

MADDOCK, R. C. AND KENNY, C. T. Philosophies of human nature and personal religious orientation. *Journal for the Scientific Study of Religion,* 1972, 11, 277–281.

MALONY, H. N. New methods in the psychology of religion. Paper read at the annual meeting of the Society for the Scientific Study of Religion, New York, Oct. 1970.

MURRAY, H. A. Studies of stressful interpersonal disputations. *American Psychologist,* 1963, 18, 28–36.

PRUYSER, P. *A dynamic psychology of religion.* New York: Harper and Row, 1968.

ROKEACH, M. Religious values and social comparisons. *Review of Religious Research,* 1969, 11 (1), 24–39.

SIDMAN, M. *Tactics of scientific research.* New York: Abingdon, 1960.

SKINNER, B. F. A case history in scientific method. *American Psychologist,* 1956, 11, 221–233.

SPILKA, B. Research on religious beliefs: A critical review. In M. P. Strommen. *Research on religious development.* New York: Hawthorn Books, Inc., 1971, 485–520.

SIDMAN, M. *Tactics of scientific research.* New York: Abingdon, 1960.

STEWART, C. W. *Adolescent Religion.* New York: Abingdon, 1967.

VANDER LEEUW, G. Religion in essence and manifestation. In J. B. Bettis (Ed.). *Phenomenology of religion.* New York: Harper and Row, 1969, 53–84.

WALTERS, SISTER A. AND BRADLEY, SISTER R. Motivation and religious behavior. In M. P. Strommen. *Research on religious development.* New York: Hawthorn Books, Inc., 1971, 599–654.

# Measuring the Religious Variable: National Replication

MORTON B. KING AND RICHARD A. HUNT

Multidimensional definitions of religion have been widely accepted since proposals by Allport (1954) and Glock (1954). However, by 1965 little quantitative work had been done to test that view. Such research was needed because use of unidimensional definitions was failing (in general) to produce understanding of the correlates, causes, and consequences of religious behavior. In previous studies (King, 1967; King and Hunt, 1969, 1972a and 1972b), we attempted to identify dimensions of religious belief and activity within the setting of local congregational life. All the subjects have been white main-line Protestants. The data came from questionnaires containing a large number of diverse items. Factor analysis was used to look for sets of items which could be interpreted as different aspects of religious behavior. The highest loading items in each factor were subjected to item-scale analysis (Hunt, 1970). This analysis greatly aided the judgment whether, and which, items from a factor formed a cluster homogeneous enough to be potentially useful as a scale. (See King and Hunt, 1972b; Chapters III and VI.)

In 1965, 575 Methodists from six congregations in urban North Texas were studied. Eleven scales were developed (King, 1967; King and Hunt, 1969) which defined theoretically interesting religious dimensions. In 1968, items from those scales plus new items were used to obtain data from 1,356 members of the Disciples, Lutheran-Missouri Synod, Presbyterian-U.S., and United Methodist denominations in the same area (King and Hunt, 1972a).

Scales were developed for the following basic dimensions: Creedal Assent, Devotionalism, Church Attendance, Organizational

Reprinted with permission of authors and publisher from:

*Journal for the Scientific Study of Religion*, 1975, 14, 13–22, published by the SOCIETY FOR THE SCIENTIFIC STUDY OF RELIGION, University of Connecticut, Box U68A, Storrs, Connecticut 06268.

**368**

Activity, Financial Support, Religious Knowledge, Orientation to Growth and Striving, Extrinsic Orientation, Salience-Behavior, and Salience-Cognition (King and Hunt, 1972b: 103–106). The dimensions and scales developed for each denomination separately were highly similar to each other, and to those for all cases combined. The latter were very similar to those of the 1965 study. The religious dimensions thus defined were useful in predicting ethnic prejudice and in distinguishing between categories of subjects, such as those based on age and years of schooling. For example, persons with more years of schooling were "less religious" on all scales except that they scored higher in religious knowledge. Prejudice toward Negroes and other minorities had no significant relationship with Creedal Assent, Devotionalism, Financial Support, or Extrinsic Orientation. However, it was negatively associated with Church Attendance, Organizational Activity, Orientation to Growth and Striving, Knowledge, and both Salience scales (King and Hunt, 1972b: 37–39).

An important question persisted: Was the similarity of findings due to attitudes, beliefs, and practices shared by main-line Protestants? Or was it due to common features of life in urban North Texas? An opportunity came to answer that question through a nation-wide sample of the members of the United Presbyterian Church in the U.S.A. (UPCUSA).[1]

## METHODS

The questionnaire contained 98 items. Of these, 37 were prepared by Dean Hoge to measure priorities for one's congregation and several independent variables. The remaining 61 items represented 8 basic religious scales and 3 cognitive-style scales developed by our 1968 study (King and Hunt, 1972b: 103–115), plus Allport-Feagin "intrinsic" items which had not formed a homogeneous scale (Feagin, 1964). The scales included, by decision of UPCUSA staff, were: (1) Religious Dimensions: Creedal Assent, Devotionalism, Church Attendance, Organizational Activity, Financial Support, Orientation to Growth and Striving, Salience-Behavior, and Salience-Cognition; (2) Cognitive-style Variables: Intolerance of Ambiguity (Martin and Westie, 1959) and "Positive" and "Negative" forms of a Purpose in Life scale (Crumbaugh and Maholick, 1964; Crumbaugh, 1968). In addition, two composite scales of religious orientation developed in 1968 for Presbyterian-U.S. respondents were included: "Hope and Faith" and "Without Hope or Effort."

A Presbyterian Panel was used composed of 1990 lay persons, selected by stratified random procedures to be a representative sample of all UPCUSA communicant members. Usable returns were secured from 872. A study by Dean R. Hoge (Personal letters from Dr. Hoge dated 22 April and 27 September 1974) of 104 randomly selected non-respondents uncovered some response bias in the data: regular church-attenders, women and more educated persons were slightly over-represented among the respondents. A weighting formula was calculated to eliminate these sources of bias. It had little effect on interrelationships among the responses. Seventeen selected items were intercorrelated, separately, for weighted and unweighted data. Only about 10% of the correlations differed by as much as .03. Therefore, the analysis here reported was made using the raw, unweighted data.

TABLE 1

COMPARISON OF ROTATED FACTOR STRUCTURES: 1968 AND 1973

| North Texas Study: 1968 (118 items) | | National Study: 1973 |
|---|---|---|
| Presbyterian: U.S. (346 cases) | All Subjects (1356 cases) | 98 items;[1] 822 cases) |
| 27 factors with eigen values over 1.0 | 19 factors with eigen values over 1.0 | 21 factors with eigen values over 1.0 |
| 15 interpretable as dimensions | 15 interpretable as dimensions | 20 interpretable as dimensions |
| 1. General: Creedal assent strong (17)[2] | 1. General: Creedal assent strong (28)[2] | 1. General: Creedal assent strong (22)[2] |
| 2. "Intolerance of Ambiguity" (15) | 2. "Intolerance of Ambiguity" (11) | 2. "Intolerance of Ambiguity" (9) |
| 3. Organizational Involvement (21) | 3. Organizational Involvement (19) | 3. [Hoge items][3] |
| 4. "Purpose in Life: Positive" (8) | 4. "Purpose in Life: Positive" (8) | 4. Organizational Involvement (13) |
| 5. Devotionalism (23) | 5. Salience: Behavior (13) | 5. "Purpose in Life: Positive" (7) |
| 6. [Items not used in 1973][4] | 6. [Items not used in 1973][4] | 6. "Purpose in Life: Negative" (7) |
| 7. [Items not used in 1973] | 7. "Purpose in Life: Negative" (10) | 7. Salience: Behavior & Cognition (13) |
| 8. [Items not used in 1973] | 8. [Items not used in 1973] | 8. [Hoge items] |
| 9. Religious Despair (8) (Includes "Purpose in Life: Negative") | 9. Financial Support (6) | 9. [Hoge items] |
| 10. [Items not used in 1973] | 10. [Items not used in 1973] | 10. Devotionalism (5) |
| 11. (Not interpretable)[5] | 11. Growth and Striving (13) | 11. [Hoge items] |
| 12. Financial Support (4) | 12. (Not interpretable)[5] | 12. [Hoge items] |
| 13. [Items not used in 1973] | 13. Devotionalism (10) | 13. Growth and Striving (4) |
| 14. (Not interpretable) | 14. [Items not used in 1973] | 14. [Hoge items] |
| 15. [Items not used in 1973] | 15. [Items not used in 1973] | 15. [Hoge items] |
| 16–22. (Not interpretable) | 16. (Not interpretable) | 16. [Hoge items] |
| 23. Growth and Striving (7) | 17. (Not interpretable) | 17. Religious Despair (2) |
| 24–26. (Not interpretable) | 18. (Not interpretable) | 18. Financial Support (5) |
| 27. [Items not used in 1973] | 19. (Not interpretable) | 19. [Hoge items] |
| | | 20. [Hoge items] |
| | | 21. (Not interpretable)[5] |

[1]Of the 98 items factored in 1973, 61 were taken from the 1968 study.
[2]Number of items on the factor with loading of .30 and above.
[3]37 items (publication pending) were developed for the UPCUSA study by Dr. Dean Hoge, now at Catholic University of America.
[4]Some 1968 scales were not selected by UPCUSA staff for the 1973 study.
[5]These were later-appearing factors which explained little of the variance and usually had only 1 to 3 items with loadings of .30 or above.

**370**

The factor and item-scale analyses reported in the 1968 study (King and Hunt, 1972b: 16–19) were repeated. The factor analysis used principal components with varimax rotation for factors with eigenvalues of 1.0 and above.

## RESULTS

Twenty-one factors were found. A subjective analysis of item content was able to interpret all but one as religious dimensions or as one of the independent variables. Of these twenty, ten had only "Hoge" items with high loadings, while high-loading items on the other 10 factors came entirely from our 1968 study. The "Hoge" factors produced scales for several interesting and potentially useful variables. They are not discussed here since they do not involve replication of our previous work.

Table 1 compares the rotated factor structure obtained for UPCUSA members in 1973 with that for all 1356 cases and for the 346 Presbyterians-U.S. in 1968. Each factor is shown with a working label assigned to summarize its apparent content. Disregarding 1968 factors defined by items not included in the 1973 study and 1973 factors defined by Hoge items not in the 1968 study, the three structures are similar but not identical both in content and in the order in which factors appeared. The structure for United Presbyterians appears more like that for the total of all 1968 cases combined than either is like the (1968) Presbyterians-U.S. That fact probably results from the number of cases: 872, 1,356, and 346 respectively. However, both Presbyterian samples produced one interesting factor not found for the combined 1968 sample here labeled "Religious Despair" (in 1968, "Without Hope or Effort").

The Appendix displays the 1973 scales compared with those for all cases in 1968. Following the name of each scale, coefficients of homogeneity (Cronbach's alpha; see Hunt, 1970) are given first for 1973, then 1968. Item-scale correlations for each item are shown for both studies.

The scales developed for North Texans in 1968 are almost identical with those for the nation-wide sample in 1973. Table 2 gives the correlation coefficients between the ten religious and three cognitive-style scales developed on the two populations. Eight of the religious scales and all three of the cognitive style scales were identical, item for item. Therefore, their correlations were 1.00. The Creedal Assent scales differed by one item and intercorrelated .98. Two of the composite religious scales (Salience: Cognition and The Active Regulars) each differed by three items, but intercorrelated .95 and .90 respectively. The differences in items on these three scales were due to item-scale correlations falling above an arbitrary cut-off point in one year and below it in the other. In fact, for all but two scales (The Active Regulars and Intolerance of Ambiguity) differences for all individual items were .10 or less. One can probably conclude that these differences are due to sampling error, rather than to different patterns in the two populations.

TABLE 2

CORRELATIONS BETWEEN 1968 AND 1973 SCALES: 1973 DATA

| Scales | Correlation Coefficient |
|---|---|
| Religious Scales | |
| Basic | |
| Creedal Assent | .98 |
| Devotionalism | 1.00 |
| Church Attendance | 1.00 |
| Organizational Activity | 1.00 |
| Financial Support | 1.00 |
| Orientation: Growth & Striving | 1.00 |
| Orientation: Religious Despair[1] | 1.00 |
| Composite | |
| Salience: Behavior | 1.00 |
| Salience: Cognition | .95 |
| The Active Regulars | .90 |
| Cognitive Style Scales | |
| Intolerance of Ambiguity | 1.00 |
| Purpose in Life: Positive | 1.00 |
| Purpose in Life: Negative | 1.00 |

[1]In 1968 called 'Without Hope or Effort' and developed on Presbyterian-U.S. members, not four denominations combined.

Table 3 presents the intercorrelations of the thirteen 1973 scales with each other. The pattern of relationships is, in general, quite similar to that obtained for the 1968 data (King and Hunt, 1972b, IV-9, 119). Usefulness of the scales is further indicated by the fact that the correlations have some explanatory power. For example, there were higher correlations among scales of belief and attitude (e.g., scales 1, 2, 6, 9) and among those of participation (e.g., 3, 4, 5, 10) than between scales from those two sets. Also, participation scales tend to be less related to Intolerance of Ambiguity (shown in 1968 to be associated with racial prejudice) than the Creedal and Devotionalism scales.

## DISCUSSION

The findings from this national sample lead us to conclude that the similarities found in the 1965 and 1968 studies were not due to the urban North Texas culture. These dimensions seem to be features which main-line Protestants have in common. The scales should prove useful for research on members of similar groups in the United States, and probably in Canada. It remains to be seen whether the responses of Roman Catholics and other types of Protestants will contain the same elements.

Certain other limitations should be noted. For many purposes, no scale, these included, should be used routinely on new populations. For example, a set of items which are homogeneous for one population may or may not have adequate homogeneity when used on a different one. Therefore, the homogeneity and other characteristics of these scales should be tested for each new population. With that information, the researcher could decide whether the scale(s) are useful for the purposes of that study.

Three types of replication have now been made of our original findings. *Religious background:* Highly similar results have now been obtained for two samples of United Methodists and for four other denominations: Disciples, Lutherans-Missouri Synod, Presbyterians-U:S., and United Presbyterians. *Geographic area:* Equally similar findings were produced by residents of urban North Texas and by a composite rural-urban nation-wide sample of a denomination not included in the Texas study. *Universe of items:* Each study has involved a large number of items, using some of the same items but also some new and different ones. Each such matrix of items has given a similar set of factors, plus other factors containing the new items.

TABLE 3

SCALE INTERCORRELATIONS: 1973 SCALES AND DATA

| The Scales | | Correlation Coefficients | | | | | | | | | | | |
|---|---|---|---|---|---|---|---|---|---|---|---|---|---|
| | | 1 | 2 | 3 | 4 | 5 | 6 | 7 | 8 | 9 | 10 | 11 | 12 | 13 |
| Creedal Assent | 1 | .84 | | | | | | | | | | | | |
| Devotionalism | 2 | .03 | .84 | | | | | | | | | | | |
| Church Attendance | 3 | .34 | .36 | .82 | | | | | | | | | | |
| Organizational Activity | 4 | .33 | .34 | .63 | .81 | | | | | | | | | |
| Financial Support | 5 | .30 | .33 | .63 | .49 | .73 | | | | | | | | |
| Growth and Striving | 6 | .54 | .72 | .44 | .49 | .43 | .79 | | | | | | | |
| Religious Despair | 7 | -.45 | -.37 | -.19 | -.22 | -.16 | -.36 | .79 | | | | | | |
| Salience: Behavior | 8 | .39 | .58 | .44 | .54 | .42 | .76 | -.26 | .80 | | | | | |
| Salience: Cognition | 9 | .75 | .80 | .39 | .41 | .38 | .82 | -.49 | .59 | .84 | | | | |
| Active Regulars | 10 | .38 | .42 | .87 | .85 | .71 | .56 | -.22 | .62 | .48 | .86 | | | |
| Intolerance of Ambiguity | 11 | .22 | .21 | .15 | .06 | .14 | .19 | .07 | .16 | .23 | .16 | .86 | | |
| Purpose in Life: Positive | 12 | .23 | .26 | .05 | .16 | .13 | .31 | -.57 | .28 | .41 | .14 | .06 | .74 | |
| Purpose in Life: Negative | 13 | -.17 | -.15 | -.03 | -.11 | -.04 | -.18 | -.86 | -.12 | -.25 | -.06 | .17 | -.63 | .78 |

Note: Internal consistency reliabilities form the main diagonal.

Other questions remain unanswered, however. Is the similarity of findings an artifact of the particular techniques of observation (written reactions to these questionnaire statements) or of analysis (principal component factor analysis, varimax rotations, Hunt item-scale analysis)? Is the similarity related to cognitive or semantic relationships which respondents implicitly assign to these items? That is, do "religious structures" overlap with other structures, and thus reflect underlying *psycho-logic* characteristics of different kinds of persons? How are items in religious scales developed by other workers related to these factors, dimensions, and scales?

The question about statistical method is now being explored through additional, and different, analyses of the 1973 data. A principal axis (instead of principal components) factor analysis is being made, with both oblique (promax) and orthogonal (varimax) rotations. In addition, second and higher order analyses are being attempted (Gorsuch, 1974: chapters 6, 10, 11). Research on the other questions is needed.

## NOTES AND REFERENCES

[1]Our thanks are due to the Presbyterian Panel; to Dr. Everett L. Perry, Dr. Gerald L. Klever and their associates; and to Dr. Dean R. Hoge of Princeton Theological Seminary who acted as a consultant to the study. Dr. Samuel W. Blizzard and Dr. William E. Chapman were helpful in the organizational phase of the project.

ALLPORT, G. W. 1954 "Religion and prejudice." Chapter 28, pp. 444–459 in *The Nature of Prejudice*. Cambridge: Addison-Wesley.

CRONBACH, L. J. 1970 *Essentials of Psychological Testing* (3rd ed.). New York: Harper and Row.

CRUMBAUGH, J. C. 1968 "Cross-validation of Purpose-in-Life Test based on Frankl's concepts." *Journal of Individual Psychology* 24: 74–81.

CRUMBAUGH, J. C. AND L. J. MAHOLICK 1964 "An experimental study in existentialism." *Journal of Clinical Psychology* 20: 200–207.

FEAGIN, J. R. 1964 "Prejudice and religious types." *Journal for the Scientific Study of Religion* 4: 3–13.

GLOCK, C. Y. 1954 *Toward a Typology of Religious Orientation*. New York: Bureau of Applied Social Research, Columbia University.

GORSUCH, RICHARD 1974 *Factor Analysis*. Philadelphia: W. B. Saunders.

HUNT, R. A. 1970 "A computer procedure for item-scale analysis." *Educational and Psychological Measurement* 30: 133–135.

KING, M. B. 1967 "Measuring the religious variable: nine proposed dimensions." *Journal for the Scientific Study of Religion* 6: 173–190.

KING, M. B. AND R. A. HUNT 1969 "Measuring the religious variable: amended findings." *Journal for the Scientific Study of Religion* 8: 321–323. 1972a "Measuring the religious variable: replication." *Journal for the Scientific Study of Religion* 11: 240–251. 1972b *Measuring Religious Dimensions: Studies of Congregational Involvement*. Studies in Social Science, No. 1. Dallas: Southern Methodist University.

MARTIN, J. G. AND F. R. WESTIE 1959 "The tolerant personality." *American Sociological Review* 24: 521–528.

## APPENDIX: 1968 AND 1973 SCALES COMPARED
### BASIC RELIGIOUS SCALES

| Item-Scale[1] Correlations 1973 | 1968 | The Items |
|---|---|---|

*I. Creedal Assent* (.84; .83)[2]

| | | |
|---|---|---|
| .68 | .65 | I believe in God as a Heavenly Father who watches over me and to whom I am accountable.[3] |
| .66 | .70 | I believe that the Word of God is revealed in the Scriptures. |
| .65 | .58 | I believe that Christ is a living reality. |
| .63 | .58 | I believe that God revealed Himself to man in Jesus Christ. |
| .58 | .54 | I believe in salvation as release from sin and freedom for new life with God. |
| .55. | .58 | I believe in eternal life. |
| (.42)[4] | .53 | I believe honestly and wholeheartedly in the doctrines and teachings of the Church. |

*II. Devotionalism* (.84; .85)

| | | |
|---|---|---|
| .79 | .74 | How often do you pray privately in places other than at church?[5] |
| .70 | .73 | How often do you ask God to forgive your sin? |
| .63 | .63 | When you have decisions to make in your everyday life, how often do you try to find out what God wants you to do? |
| .59 | .65 | Private prayer is one of the most important and satisfying aspects of my religious experience. |
| .53 | .59 | I frequently feel very close to God in prayer, during public worship, or at important moments in my daily life. |

*III. Church Attendance* (.82; .82)

| | | |
|---|---|---|
| .71 | .64 | If not prevented by unavoidable circumstances, I attend church: (More than once a week—Twice a year or less) |
| .67 | .69 | During the last year, how many Sundays per month on the average have you gone to a worship service? (None/Three or more) |
| .65 | .71 | How often have you taken Holy Communion (The Lord's Supper, the Eucharist) during the past year? |

*IV. Organizational Activity* (.81; .83)

| | | |
|---|---|---|
| .71 | .69 | How would you rate your activity in your congregation? (Very active—Inactive) |
| .64 | .63 | How often do you spend evenings at church meetings or in church work? |
| .60 | .59 | Church activities (meetings, committee work, etc.) are a major source of satisfaction in my life. |
| .56 | .55 | List the church offices, committees, or jobs of any kind in which you served during the past twelve months (Coded: None—Four or more) |
| .50 | .57 | I keep pretty well informed about my congregation and have some influence on its decisions. |
| .49 | .59 | I enjoy working in the activities of the Church. |

*V. Financial Support* (.73; .73)

| | | |
|---|---|---|
| .61 | .56 | Last year, approximately what per cent of your income was contributed to the Church? (1% or less—10% or more) |
| .49 | .40 | During the last year, how often have you made contributions to the Church IN ADDITION TO the general budget and Sunday School? (Regularly—Never) |
| .47 | .51 | During the last year, what was the average MONTHLY contribution of your family to your local congregation? (Under $5—$50 or more) |

| .46 | .48 | In proportion to your income, do you consider that your contributions to the Church are: (Generous—Small) |
| .45 | .53 | I make financial contributions to the Church: (In regular, planned amounts —Seldom or never) |

VI. *Religious Despair* (.79; .77)[6]

| .62 | .56 | My personal existence often seems meaningless and without purpose. |
| .62 | .56 | My life is often empty, filled with despair. |
| .55 | .55 | I have about given up trying to understand "worship" or get much out of it. |
| .50 | .49 | I often wish I had never been born. |
| .47 | .47 | I find myself believing in God some of the time, but not at other times. |
| .47 | .38 | Most of the time my life seems to be out of my control. |
| .42 | .45 | The Communion Service (Lord's Supper, Eucharist) often has little meaning to me. |

VII. *Orientation to Growth and Striving* (.79; .81)

| .61 | .60 | How often do you read the Bible? |
| .60 | .61 | How often do you read literature about your faith (or church)? (Frequently —Never) [A-F][7] |
| .60 | .54 | The amount of time I spend trying to grow in understanding of my faith is: (Very much—Little or none) |
| .57 | .57 | When you have decisions to make in your everyday life, how often do you try to find out what God wants you to do?[8] (II) |
| .53 | .59 | I try hard to grow in understanding of what it means to live as a child of God. |
| .44 | .52 | I try hard to carry my religion over into all my other dealings in life. [A-F] |

## COMPOSITE RELIGIOUS SCALES

A. *Salience: Behavior* (.80; .83)

| .67 | .68 | How often in the past year have you shared with another church member the problems and joys of trying to live a life of faith in God? |
| ..58 | .59 | How often do you talk about religion with your friends, neighbors, or fellow workers? |
| .57 | .60 | How often have you personally tried to convert someone to faith in God? |
| .54 | .54 | How often do you read the Bible? (VII) |
| .49 | .57 | When faced with decisions regarding social problems how often do you seek guidance from statements and publications provided by the Church? |
| .49 | .53 | How often do you talk with the pastor (or other official) about some part of the worship service: for example, the sermon, scripture, choice of hymns, etc? |
| .43 | .49 | During the last year, how often have you visited someone in need, besides your own relatives? |

B. *Salience: Cognition* (.84; .81)

| .66 | .59 | Religion is especially important to me because it answers many questions about the meaning of life. [A-F] |
| .63 | .64 | I try hard to grow in understanding of what it means to live as a child of God. (VII) |
| .59. | .64 | My religious beliefs are what really lie behind my whole approach to life. [A-F] |
| .59 | .54 | I frequently feel very close to God in prayer, during public worship, or at important moments in my daily life. (II) |
| .56 | (*)[9] | I often experience the joy and peace which come from knowing I am a forgiven sinner. |
| .55 | (*) | When you have decisions to make in your everyday life, how often do you try to find out what God wants you to do? (II, VII) |

| | | |
|---|---|---|
| .53 | (*) | I believe in God as a Heavenly Father who watches over me and to whom I am accountable. (I) |
| .52 | .56 | I try hard to carry my religion over into all my other dealings in life. [A-F] (VII) |

C. *The Active Regulars* (.86; .84)
(In 1968, called Index of Attendance and Giving)

| | | |
|---|---|---|
| .77 | .60 | If not prevented by unavoidable circumstances, I attend church: (More than once a week—Twice a year or less). (III) |
| .68 | .57 | How would you rate your activity in your congregation? (Very active—Inactive) (VI) |
| .67 | .66 | How often have you taken Holy Communion (The Lord's Supper, The Eucharist) during the past year? (III) |
| .60 | .69 | During the last year, how many Sundays per month on the average have you gone to a worship service? (None—Three or more) (III) |
| .55 | (*) | How often do you spend evenings at church meetings or in church work? (IV) |
| .55 | (*) | Church activities (meetings, committee work, etc.) are a major source of satisfaction in my life. (IV) |
| .54 | (*) | During the last year, how often have you made contributions to the Church IN ADDITION TO the general budget and Sunday School? (Regularly—Never) (V) |
| .47 | .54 | I make financial contributions to the Church: (In regular, planned amounts—Seldom or never) (V) |
| .46 | .54 | Last year, approximately what percent of your income was contributed to the Church? (1% or less—10% or more) (V) |
| (.42) | .52 | During the last year, what was the average MONTHLY contribution of your family to your local congregation? (Under $5—$50 or more) (V) |

## COGNITIVE STYLE VARIABLES

A. *Intolerance of Ambiguity* (.82; .82)
(Martin and Westie items)

| | | |
|---|---|---|
| .69 | .62 | You can classify almost all people as either honest or crooked. |
| .64 | .66 | There are two kinds of women: the pure and the bad. |
| .62 | .60 | There are two kinds of people in the world: the weak and the strong. |
| .59 | .48 | A person is either a 100% American or he isn't. |
| .55 | .57 | A person either knows the answer to a question or he doesn't. |
| .50 | .52 | There is only one right way to do anything. |
| .44 | .48 | It doesn't take very long to find out if you can trust a person. |

B. *Purpose in Life: Positive* (.74; .78)
(Items adapted from Crumbaugh and Maholick)

| | | |
|---|---|---|
| .56 | .56 | Facing my daily tasks is usually a source of pleasure and satisfaction to me. |
| .55 | .60 | My life is full of joy and satisfaction. |
| .53 | .62 | I have discovered satisfying goals and a clear purpose in life. |
| .50 | .55 | I usually find life new and exciting. |
| .39 | .47 | If I should die today, I would feel that my life has been worthwhile. |

C. *Purpose in Life: Negative* (.78; .73)
(Items adapted from Crumbaugh and Maholick)

| | | |
|---|---|---|
| .65 | .61 | My life is often empty, filled with despair. (VI) |
| .64 | .57 | My personal existence often seems meaningless and without purpose. (VI) |
| .56 | .47 | I often wish I had never been born. (VI) |
| .48 | .45 | Most of the time my life seems to be out of my control. (VI) |

# M. B. King and R. A. Hunt

[1] The correlation coefficient of each item with the scale, the item itself having been dropped from the scale for that computation.

[2] The coefficient of homogeneity (Cronbach's alpha) obtained for the scale in 1973 and 1968, respectively.

[3] Unless otherwise indicated, the items were statements to which one responded with one of four degrees of assent: "Strongly agree," "Agree," "Disagree," "Strongly disagree."

[4] Values in parentheses indicate items in the matrix but below the cut-off point for that year. The correlation is given so that the reader may evaluate the decision not to include that item.

[5] A number of "how often" questions had as alternatives "Regularly," "Fairly frequently," "Occasionally," and "Seldom or never."

[6] The 1968 scale was developed only for Presbyterian-U.S. members. However, similar scales were developed for Methodists and Lutherans-M.S. All other 1968 scales are based on members of all four denominations.

[7] Items indicated by [A-F] appear in Feagin's (1964) scale of Gordon Allport's Intrinsic religion.

[8] Items which have appeared on a preceding scale are indicated by the number of that scale.

[9] An asterisk (*) indicates an item in the 1968 matrix, but not included in the maximally homogeneous scale for that year.

The items for two of the 1968 basic religious scales were not included in the 1973 study by decision of the sponsoring denomination: Religious Knowledge and Extrinsic Orientation. The Allport-Feagin "intrinsic" items were included in both studies. In neither did they form a single factor, but appeared on several factors: see "Growth and Striving" and "Salience: Cognition" above.

# THE RELIGION
# OF PSYCHOLOGISTS

# Introduction

H. NEWTON MALONY

This section goes behind the psychology of religion to the religion of psychologists. It asks and answers important questions about the personality and the faith of those psychologists who study religion.

Motivation and interest are two important bases for action. It has long been known that interests help people decide what they want to do, and motivation helps them to do it! How does being religious inspire the study of religion?

Beit-Hallahmi's article suggests that psychologists who study religion are, most often, religious themselves. Religion is still not in vogue as a topic of research among most psychologists, and personal religious faith seems to motivate many who do study it. Here, it often serves to justify rather than to investigate faith.

Malony's article describes various ways in which psychologists have related their profession to the Christian faith. He defines both Christianity and psychology and illustrates how psychologists have integrated the two in theory, practice, and research.

In his chapter, Pavelsky makes an explicit attempt to relate biblical teaching to the practice of clinical psychology. He attempts to delineate the meaning of "love" in the New Testament and to show how such love can be expressed in psychotherapy.

The last article, by Ellison, denotes the conflicts and complements that exist between Christianity and psychology and proposes ways in which the Christian relates faith to these issues.

This portion of the book will introduce the student to some of the interrelationships between psychologists' individual faith and their professions. It may serve to provoke introspection concerning ways in which basic assumptions influence scientific endeavor.

# Curiosity, Doubt, and Devotion: The Beliefs of Psychologists and the Psychology of Religion[1]

BENJAMIN BEIT-HALLAHMI

The history of the psychology of religion, as an area in American academic psychology, is one of ups and downs, rise and decline (Beit-Hallahmi, 1974). Especially when compared with the initiatives of James, Leuba and Starbuck around the turn of the century, contemporary American psychology seems to consider religion marginal, if not "taboo" (Farberow, 1963). Surveys of empirical research (Argyle & Beit-Hallahmi, 1975; Beit-Hallahmi, 1973; Dittes, 1969) indicate that psychologists have done some significant work on religious behavior, but for most psychologists religion is probably not an area of interest (i.e., research).

One way of measuring the impact and importance of the psychology of religion today is by looking at the treatment given this topic in introductory psychology texts. Such texts aim to reflect the state of knowledge and activity in the field as a whole; this is their survey function. They also perform an important gate-keeping role, since they present an authoritative view of the field to the newcomer, and are likely to channel his budding interests. Most introductory textbooks in psychology ignore religion completely, while some (e.g., Hilgard, Atkinson & Atkinson, 1971; Ruch & Zimbardo, 1971) mention it once or twice.

This chapter attempts to explain the current zeitgeist regarding the psychology of religion by exploring the attitudes of psychology, as a discipline, and psychologists, as individuals, toward religion. In addition to some "ecological" factors, which are part of the environment of psychology, the personal attitudes of psychologists towards religion are the focus of discussion. Our thesis is that there is a direct relationship between the religiosity of psychologists and the amount of interest which they display in the psychology of religion. This may explain the relative paucity of studies in this field.

[1]This is a revised version of a paper presented at the 1971 meeting of the Society for the Scientific Study of Religion.

## SECULARIZATION AS A FACTOR

There can be little doubt that the decline in the interest which psychologists have shown in religion as an area of study parallels the decline in the importance of religion as a social institution. The latter decline is a major fact of modern history and modern society (Luckmann, 1967; Wilson, 1966; Argyle & Beit-Hallahmi, 1975). Psychologists may be regarded as justified in neglecting religion to some extent, especially in connection with individual dynamics. In a secularized world, religion may be seen as a social label, helpful in predicting some group trends, but of minor significance in explaining individual motivation. However, despite the evidence for secularization, there are indications that the religious subidentity will remain significant because of specific features of modern society (Wilson, 1966).

## SCIENTISM AS A FACTOR

A major reason for the neglect of religion as a topic of research may be the dominant scientism (Chein, 1972) in the discipline of psychology. The triumph of positivism and operationalism and the insistence on the myth of "value free" social science (Gouldner, 1962) contributed to the desire to stay away from religion, on pain of contamination by "unscientific" attitudes. Religion reminds psychology of its "unscientific" past, with ideas of the soul, absolute judgments, and untestable beliefs. Some psychologists may wish that this embarrassing relic would disappear, since they believe that what they are engaged in signifies a triumph over the old, mistaken traditions.

## THE DEVELOPMENT OF PSYCHOLOGY AS A FACTOR

The development of academic psychology over the past several decades has been influenced by the rise of several areas of research and the rise of related research methodologies. Methodology has become the key factor in the development, acceptability, and respectability of areas in psychology. Social psychology, which could have been expected to take over initial efforts in the psychology of religion, has moved in other directions and over the past two decades has centered on laboratory methodologies.

There are certain inherent difficulties in religious behavior as a subject of study, and these have been a factor in influencing research activities. Both theoretically and empirically, religious beliefs and actions pose awesome problems for psychologists. Dittes (1969) has described the various measurement problems confronting the psychologists of religion in selecting units and variables for study. The formidable task facing the psychology of religion could be construed as a challenge, but it seems that psychologists preferred to face easier ones. The trend in psychological research has been more and more towards manipulative laboratory experiments, and religion does not lend itself easily to such experiments. Its behavioral data are produced naturally.

## THE ECOLOGY OF RESEARCH ON RELIGION

Empirical research in behavioral sciences does not exist in a social vacuum. It is supported, or hindered, by its social environment. Part of this environment is the academic community itself, but sources of pressure extend far beyond the universities. Most psychological research projects have been supported by outside sources, especially the U.S. government. Applicants for research grants have to defend the importance and relevance of the projects, and it is doubtful whether many psychologists have proposed projects dealing with religious behavior. From the government's side, it is also doubtful whether much encouragement would have been given those who had applied. Discussions during the uproar over invasion of privacy in psychological testing, in 1965, made it clear that members of the U.S. Congress (Gallagher, 1966) considered questions on religion in psychological research undesirable. These discussions also made it clear that government support would not be forthcoming for any research dealing specifically with questions of religious belief, beyond those concerned with nominal religious affiliation.

Though it may seem logical that religious organizations would be a natural source of support for psychologists interested in studying religion, only limited work has been sponsored by these. The relationship of religious organizations to research on religious behavior is ambivalent. As Glock and Stark (1965) have suggested, any serious systematic study of religion, which follows the canons of social science, must be a threat to religious institutions. Leuba (1916) wrote about the resistance to scientific studies of religious beliefs: "It is rather the old desire to protect 'Holy things' from too close scrutiny, and also the more or less unconscious antagonism of those interested in the maintenance of the *status quo* in religion that have stood in the way of those who might have been disposed to face the difficulties of a statistical investigation of religious convictions" (p. 175). Another problem, from the organization's viewpoint, arises with findings that correlate religiosity with negatively-valued attitudes or behaviors, e.g., prejudice. Glock and Stark

(1965) suggested that the solution to this dilemma is the encouragement of descriptive, rather than explanatory, research.

## RELIGIOUS BELIEFS AMONG SCIENTISTS AND ACADEMICIANS

The finding that scientists and academicians are less religious than the rest of the population has been amply documented (Argyle & Beit-Hallahmi, 1975; Anderson, 1968a, 1968b; Hajda, 1961; Lehman & Witty, 1931; Rogers, 1966; Thalheimer, 1965; Vaughan, Smith & Sjoberg, 1966). Even those who found that academicians were not totally divorced from religiosity described them as adhering to a most secularized kind of religious creed (Faulkner & DeJong, 1972).

Stark (1963) has provided a convincing illustration of the incompatibility of the scholarly ethos and religion, and also pointed to the lack of productivity on the part of religious scholars. What has been presumed to be incompatible with the religious stance has been designated by various authors as the "scientific," "scholarly" or "intellectual" viewpoint (Campbell & Magill, 1968; Knapp & Greenbaum, 1953; Lazarsfeld & Thielens, 1958; Stark, 1963; MacDonell & Campbell, 1971). The presumed incompatibility between the scientific orientation and the religious one is supported by the fact that sectarian schools generally rank lower with respect to the quality of their educational programs, student ability and faculty productivity (Trent, 1967; Pattillo & Mackenzie, 1966; Hassenger, 1967). The explanation for this is that religious commitment leads to a compromising of scholarly standards.

Since academic communities are, in general, less religious than most of the population, social scientists have the impression that religion is "neutralized." The "ivory tower effect" is part of what Anderson (1968a, 1969) has described as the intellectual subsociety. Steinberg (1973) reports that the religious composition of faculty members in higher education is markedly different from that of the general population. Catholics are underrepresented while Jews are overrepresented among faculty members. The fact that Jewish faculty members tend to be concentrated in a relatively small group of institutions, most often of high quality, tends to make their influence more pronounced, according to Steinberg. The intellectual subsociety studied by Anderson (1968a) appears to be transethnic and transreligious. It is not surprising that this subsociety will tend to minimize the importance of religious and ethnic factors. There may be a feeling that the long war between science and religion was won by science, and that little remains to be studied in religion.

## RELIGIOUS BELIEFS AMONG PSYCHOLOGISTS

While most studies agree on the fact that scientists and academicians tend to be less religious than the general population, more detailed investigations discovered differences in religiosity among academic disciplines. Lehman and Shriver (1968) introduced the concept of *scholarly distance from religion* as a predictor of religiosity among academicians. This concept refers to the extent to which an academic discipline considers religion a legitimate object of study. Thus, historians would be lower in scholarly distance than biologists because religion is an accepted subject for historians to study while for biologists it is not. Lehman and Shriver (1968) predicted that a greater degree of religious involvement would be found among academicians in the disciplines with high scholarly distance. Physicists and chemists were expected to be more religious than anthropologists, psychologists and sociologists, and the findings supported this prediction.

These findings are especially relevant to the discussion of religious beliefs among psychologists. Psychology is, at least in principle, a "low distance" discipline, and its practitioners are likely to explore religion as they explore other human behaviors. Psychology, as a discipline, would prescribe an analytical stance toward religion, and thus would make it less likely for psychologists to be religiously committed. An identical prediction regarding the religiosity of psychologists can be made from the point of view of occupational psychology (Bordin, Nachmann & Segal, 1962; Bordin, 1966). The choice of psychology as an occupation stems from an individual's strong need for the exploration of interpersonal and personal experiences. Scientific creativity requires skepticism and doubt (Bordin, 1966), which in psychology include skepticism about beliefs and mores. The "debunking" effect of psychology, as a science which often finds that widely held ideas are empirically invalid, should have a reinforcing influence on the initial skepticism of those who decide to become psychologists.

Together with other social scientists, psychologists are considered unconventional, and with some justification (Bereiter & Freedman, 1962; Roe, 1956). This lack of conventionality coupled with the attitude of skepticism that the scientist displays toward social norms should be reflected in lower religious involvement. As to differences among subdisciplines in psychology, the concept of *scholarly distance from religion* should help us predict the direction of difference.

**385**

On that basis, we would predict that in those subdisciplines of psychology which are less likely to be involved with the study of religion a higher degree of religious involvement will be found. Thus, we would expect that experimental psychologists, industrial psychologists and physiological psychologists will be more religious than social psychologists, personality psychologists and clinical psychologists. This prediction is contrary to the common sense split between the hard-nosed, more rigorous experimental psychologists and the "soft," less "scientific," clinicians. The relevant distinction here seems to be the one between person-oriented specialties in psychology and non-person-oriented specialties, suggested by Medvene (1970) and Little (1972). For that reason, we would also expect experimentalists to be more conventional and more religious. This prediction has not been tested empirically, and it is offered here only as a hypothesis.

Empirical studies of religious beliefs among psychologists tend to support the impression of relative irreligiosity. Leuba (1916) studied the religious beliefs of 50 "distinguished psychologists" and 57 "lesser psychologists" (p. 267). They were compared to scientists, sociologists and historians. He reported that the proportion of believers in "God" among the distinguished psychologists was the lowest of all the groups studied (13.2%). The percentage of believers among the "lesser" psychologists was 32.1 and within the whole group was 24.2. These results were consistent with Leuba's hypothesis that religious personalities are less likely to be found among social scientists than among physical scientists. Very similar findings regarding psychologists and other scientists were reported by Rogers (1965).

Roe (1952) studied a group of 64 eminent scientists, including 22 psychologists and anthropologists. Most of the scientists came from a Protestant background, and a small minority were Jews. Only three members of the group were active in any church, and the rest were "indifferent" to religion. One clear limitation of the Roe study is that only eminent scientists and psychologists were included. On the other hand, their eminence may have something to do with the embodiment of traits crucial to the fulfillment of the academic psychologist's role. A confirmation of Roe's (1953) and Anderson's (1968a) findings came from McClelland (1964), who stated: "I can hardly think of a psychologist, sociologist, or anthropologist of my generation who would admit publicly or privately to a religious commitment of any kind . . ." (p. 118).

Two groups of psychologists that would be expected to show less interest in religion are social psychologists and clinical psychologists. No systematic data are available on social psychologists, but at least one study provides data on religious attitudes of practicing clinical psychologists. Henry, Sims and Spray (1971) studied a large group of "mental health professionals"—psychologists, psychiatrists, clinical psychologists and social workers. Almost 50% of the clinical psychologists in this study described their "cultural affinity" as Jewish. In terms of religious affiliation, as differentiated from cultural affinity, 20% of the clinical psychologists identified themselves as Protestants, 8% as Catholic, and 30% as Jewish. The rest reported various shades of nonreligiosity. This picture is, of course, striking when compared with national figures for religious affiliation. Henry et al. (1971) see it as part of the "social marginality" of all mental health professions (Szasz & Nemiroff, 1963). This marginality is similar to that described by Anderson (1968a) for academicians in general; we have no reason to assume that nonpracticing clinical psychologists are different. Burtchaell (1970) stated that many of the most influential and capable social scientists have been Jews who felt antagonism towards religion and were reluctant to study it. This claim is especially significant in view of the findings by Steinberg (1973) quoted above.

## PSYCHOLOGISTS WHO STUDY RELIGION

Given the findings on the indifferent or negative attitudes of most social scientists and psychologists towards religion, combined with lack of professional interest in it, we would expect those psychologists who are interested in religion as a topic of study to present a totally different picture. The stereotype of the psychologist who is interested in religion, at least among his academic colleagues, embodies the notion of strong religious commitments or frustrated theological ambitions. This stereotype, strangely enough, seems to have much truth to it. A close, even superficial scrutiny of the personal histories, education and writings of most of the contributors to the psychology of religion shows that they come, in most cases, from religious backgrounds. Their commitment to religion is clear (Allport, 1950), and many of them see their main contribution in terms of helping religion become better and stronger (Dittes, 1967). Many of these psychologists have had some formal religious education and quite a few have been ordained as ministers or priests. Many of them are affiliated with divinity schools, theology schools or departments of religious studies. (This is also a reflection of the fact that divinity schools today are more hospitable to the psychology of religion than psychology departments. Department chairmen looking for experts on the psychology of religion are rare indeed.)

Two organizations that seek to promote psychological studies of religion are the Christian Association for Psychological Studies and Psychologists Interested in Religious Issues, Inc. The latter is the successor to the American Catholic Psychological Association, but is nondenominational. The Christian Association for Psychological Studies is clearly more religious than psychological. Its constitution states: "The basis of this organization is the belief in the Lordship of Jesus Christ and that through God's Word, the Bible, and through communion of Christians, the Holy Spirit guides us as members of the helping professions in achieving personal growth of self and others" (Christian Association for Psychological Studies, 1972). Psychologists Interested in Religious Issues, Inc. is consciously trying to overcome its denominational heritage and aims at becoming an APA division. (See PIRI, 1972.) The Society for the Scientific Study of Religion (SSSR), an interdisciplinary nonsectarian organization, includes a minority of psychologists among its members, the majority of whom are sociologists, theologians, historians and clergymen. Most of the well-known researchers in both the sociology and the psychology of religion are members of the SSSR. As suggested above, most SSSR members who are psychologists also have a background of religious education; some of these have even been ordained.

It seems that a personal religious commitment will motivate a psychologist to break the strong norm against studying religion. Most psychologists of religion are religious, and in their cases personal involvement overrides disciplinary norms. Religious psychologists who study the psychology of religion do not regard such psychological endeavors as a threat. For them the warfare between religion and science is over, both personally and collectively. Studying religion "objectively" may even be a way of working through conflicts and finding justification for their beliefs. This does not imply that most religious psychologists are actively involved in studying the psychology of religion. The situation is probably just the opposite. Most religious psychologists, as was suggested above, are in the subdisciplines of psychology that are unlikely to study molar, social, human behavior. Other religious psychologists are still reluctant to consider the application of systematic research methods to religious behavior. We may suspect that this kind of compartmentalization is prevalent among those in the experimental subdisciplines of psychology.

## CONCLUSION

The suggestion was made that there is a relationship between the religiosity of psychologists and their interest, or mostly lack of interest, in the psychology of religion. Findings by Leuba, Roe, Henry et al., Stark, and others suggest that psychologists, like most scientists, are a pretty irreligious bunch. They are mostly nonaffiliated and non-committed, and may tend to project this lack of interest onto the rest of the population. The assumption that there is not much left of religion is common among academic psychologists. At the same time, there is a clear tendency among psychologists who are interested and active in the psychology of religion to be religious themselves. A look at the personal history and education of most of the contributors to the area shows that they are, in many cases, from a religious background, which often included seminary education. This introduces another kind of personal involvement, and creates a situation today in which those who study religion are committed to it, while those who are not show little interest in the area, or sometimes even a slight disdain. This imbalance creates an obvious problem in terms of basic theoretical perspective. The dominant perspective appears to be based on an interest in the preservation of religion as a social institution. The belief that religion is a positive force in individual and social life is central to this approach. Although most psychologists are not committed to religion, either as a personal belief system or as a topic of study, there exists a minority who are, and they are the ones responsible for most of the activity in the psychology of religion. As a result, we may have today primarily a *religious* psychology of religion.

## REFERENCES

ALLPORT, G. W. *The Individual and His Religion.* New York: Macmillan, 1950.
ANDERSON, C. H. The intellectual subsociety hypothesis: An empirical test. *Sociological Quarterly,* 1968 a, *8,* 210–227.
ANDERSON, C. H. Religious communality among academics. *Journal for the Scientific Study of Religion,* 1968 b, *7,* 87–96.
ARGYLE, M. AND BEIT-HALLAHMI, B. *The Social Psychology of Religion.* London: Routledge & Kegan Paul, 1975.
BEIT-HALLAHMI, B. (Ed.) *Research in Religious Behavior: Selected Readings.* Belmont, Cal.: Brooks/Cole, 1973.
BEIT-HALLAHMI, B. Psychology of religion 1880–1930: The rise and fall of a psychological movement. *Journal of the History of the Behavioral Sciences,* 1974, *10,* 84–90.
BEREITER, C. AND FREEDMAN, M. B. Fields of study and the people in them. In N. Sanford (Ed.) *The American College.* New York: Wiley, 1962.
BORDIN, E. S. Curiosity, compassion and doubt: The dilemma of the psychologist. *American Psychologist,* 1966, *21,* 116–121.
BORDIN, E. S., NACHMANN, B. AND SEGAL, S. J. An articulated framework for vocational development. *Journal of Counseling Psychology,* 1963, *10,* 107–118.

# B. Beit-Hallahmi

BURTCHAELL, J. T. A response to "Christianity and symbolic realism." *Journal for the Scientific Study of Religion*, 1970, 9, 97–99.

CAMPBELL, D. F. AND MAGILL, D. W. Religious involvement and intellectuality among university students. *Sociological Analysis*, 1968, 29, 79–93.

CHEIN, I. *The Science of Behavior and the Image of Man*. New York: Basic Books, 1972.

Christian Association for Psychological Studies. Constitution and Bylaws adopted on April 6, 1972. Available from CAP, 6850 Division Avenue South, Grand Rapids, Mich. 49508.

DITTES, J. E. *The Church in the Way*. New York: Scribner's, 1967.

DITTES, J. E. Psychology of Religion, In Lindzey, G. and Aronson, E. (Eds.) *The Handbook of Social Psychology*. 2nd ed. Reading, Mass.: Addison-Wesley, 1969.

FARBEROW, N. L. (Ed.) *Taboo Topics*. New York: Atherton Press, 1963.

FAULKNER, J. E. AND DEJONG, G. Religion and intellectuals. *Review of Religious Research*, 1972, 14, 15–24.

GALLAGHER, C. E. In testimony before the House Special Subcommittee on Invasion of Privacy of the Committee on Government Operations. *American Psychologist*, 1966, 21, 404–422.

GLOCK, C. Y. AND STARK, R. *Religion and Society in Tension*. Chicago: Rand McNally, 1965.

GOULDNER, A. Anti-minotaur: The myth of a value-free sociology. *Social Problems*, 1962, 10, 199–213.

HAJDA, J. Alienation and integration of student intellectuals. *American Sociological Review*, 1961, 26, 758–777.

HASSENGER, R. (Ed.) *The Shape of Catholic Higher Education*. Chicago: University of Chicago Press, 1967.

HENRY, W. E., SIMS, J. H. AND SPRAY, S. L. *The Fifth Profession*. San Francisco: Jossey-Bass, 1971.

HILGARD, E. R., ATKINSON, R. C. AND ATKINSON, R. L. *Introduction to Psychology*. 5th ed. New York: Harcourt, Brace & World, 1971.

KNAPP, R. H. AND GREENBAUM, J. J. *The Younger American Scholar*. Chicago: The University of Chicago Press, 1953.

LAZARSFELD, P. AND THIELENS, W., JR. *The Academic Mind*. Glencoe: Free Press, 1958.

LEHMAN, E. C., JR. AND SHRIVER, D. W., JR. Academic discipline as predictive of faculty religiosity, *Social Forces*, 1968, 47, 171–182.

LEHMAN, H. C. AND WITTY, P. A. Scientific eminence and church membership. *Scientific Monthly*, 1931, 33, 544–549.

LEUBA, J. H. *The Belief in God and Immorality*. Boston: Sherman, French & Co., 1916.

LITTLE, B. R. Personal-Thing orientation. Unpublished manuscript. University of Oxford, 1972.

LUCKMANN, T. *The Invisible Religion*. New York: Macmillan, 1967.

MACDONELL, A. J. AND CAMPBELL, D. F. Permanence and change in the religious dimensions of an intellectual elite. *Social Compass*, 1971, 18, 609–619.

MCCLELLAND, D. C. *The Roots of Consciousness*. New York: Van Nostrand, 1964.

MEDVENE, A. M. Person-oriented and non-person-oriented occupations in psychology. *Journal of Counseling Psychology*, 1970, 17, 243-246.

PATTILLO, M. M. AND MACKENZIE, D. M. *Church-Sponsored Higher Education in the United States*. Washington, D. C.: American Council on Higher Education, 1966.

Psychologists Interested in Religious Issues. Program for the Second Annual Meeting, September 2, 1972, Honolulu, Hawaii.

ROE, A. *The Making of a Scientist*. New York: Dodd, Mead, 1952.

ROE, A. *The Psychology of Occupations*. New York: Wiley, 1956.

ROGERS, D. P. Some religious beliefs of scientists and the effect of the scientific method. *Review of Religious Research*, 1965, 7, 70–77.

RUCH, F. L. AND ZIMBARDO, P. G. *Psychology and Life*, 8th Ed. Glenview, Ill.: Scott, Foresman & Co., 1971.

STARK, R. On the incompatibility of religion and science. *Journal for the Study of Religion.* 1963, *3*, 3–20.

STEINBERG, S. The changing religious composition of American higher education. In C. Y. Glock (Ed.) *Religion in Sociological Perspective.* Belmont, Cal.: Wadsworth, 1973.

SZASZ, T. S. AND NEMIROFF, R. A. A questionnaire study of psychoanalytic practices and opinions. *Journal of Nervous and Mental Disease,* 1963, *137,* 209–221.

THALHEIMER, F. Continuity and change in religiosity: A study of academicians. *Pacific Sociological Review,* 1965, *7,* 101–108.

TRENT, J. W. *Catholics in College: Religious Commitment and the Intellectual Life.* Chicago: University of Chicago Press, 1967.

VAUGHAN, T. R., SMITH, D. H. AND SJOBERG, G. The religious orientation of American natural scientists. *Social Forces,* 1965, *44,* 519–526.

WILSON, B. R. *Religion in Secular Society.* London: Watts, 1966.

# The Psychologist-Christian

H. NEWTON MALONY

How does Christian belief relate to one's daily work? This question has been considered with regard to a number of jobs and professions: medicine (Stephens and Long, 1960), business (Johnson, 1964), education (LeFevre, 1958 and Pelikan, 1965), science (Barbour, 1963), farming (Wentz, 1967), real estate (Wentz, 1967), and architecture (Wentz, 1967). Others have considered the relationship of faith to the practice of counseling (e.g., Roberts, 1950; Hoffman, 1960; and Mowrer, 1961) and psychiatry (Knight, 1964). Little has been written about psychology. This essay intends to remedy this situation by considering the relevance that being Christian has for the psychologist and his work.

## WHO ARE THE PSYCHOLOGISTS?

Psychology is comparatively new, and, although Melanchthon coined the term "psychology" in the early 1500's (La Pointe, 1970), it was not recognized as a discipline separate from philosophy until the late 1800's. Wilhelm Wundt established the first psychological laboratory in 1879 at the University of Leipzig. By the end of the next decade James McKeen Cattell had been appointed the first Professor of Psychology in America and Joseph Jastrow had been awarded this country's first Ph.D. degree in Psychology. Before the turn of the century William James had written his popular *Principles of Psychology* (1890), the American Psychological Association (APA) had been organized, and the first psychological clinic had been opened.

Psychology has grown rapidly. The APA began with 31 persons and now includes over 25,000 members. The National Science Foundation reported in 1968 that approximately one in twelve scientists was a

Reprinted with permission of the author and publisher from:
*Journal of the American Scientific Affiliation*, 1972, 24(4), 135–144.

psychologist. Many students aspire to careers in psychology, as is evident by the more than 2000 doctoral and 5000 masters degrees in psychology awarded each year (APA, 1970).

There have been numerous attempts to define psychology. One widely agreed upon definition is that psychology is that ". . . scholarly discipline, . . . scientific field, and . . . professional activity which studies animal and human behavior" (APA, 1970, p. 3). Behavior is defined as the physiological reactions, feelings, thoughts, words and actions of people and animals. Normal, abnormal, individual and interpersonal behaviors are of interest to psychologists.

One need only point out that principles of behavior are a major field of study in colleges and universities, in order to show that psychology has become a respected discipline. It is a science that utilizes research methods to investigate behavior and draws conclusions on the basis of empirical results. Furthermore, psychology has attained professional stature by reason of the fact that it applies itself to resolving individual and social problems.

Clark (1957) notes some of the procedures psychologists have used to study behavior since the turn of the century.

> These years have seen both complete reliance on introspection and the complete abandonment of it; a rejection of thinking as a proper part of psychology, and the claim that it is critical to understanding behavior; a complete faith in tests and other objective measures, and a swing away from all measurement; a bandwagon for the conditioned reflex and a strong plea for putting purpose back into the animal; a stress on the use of large Ns (numbers), and a strong swing to studies of small group behavior; a strong antipathy to the idea of the unconscious, and development of projective tests, hypnosis, and other depth analytic methods; a one-time preference for laboratory work has shifted as psychologists now predict presidential elections and run daily columns on child development, obtain information on racial and religious differences, and conduct action research (p. 20).

The diversity has been, and still is, tremendous.

However, modern psychology is homogenous in that it possesses a vast literature on individual and social behavior, a broad understanding of human development from infancy to old age, many techniques for working with individuals and groups, considerable new knowledge about physiological functioning, refined mathematical and statistical techniques, and numerous methods for applying its knowledge to industry, society, and education (Clark, 1957).

While all psychologists obtain the M.A. or Ph.D. degree, they have varied interests and skills and work in many different types of locations. They can be found in schools, colleges and universities, clinics and hospitals, governmental and welfare agencies, industries and businesses, and in the public health service. Some are even self-employed. The wide variety of psychologists can be seen in the thirty-one divisions of APA. Among them are the divisions of clinical, counseling, experimental, educational, school, industrial, social, engineering, and physiological psychology.

The largest single group is composed of Clinical psychologists. They comprise twenty-nine percent of the total membership of the APA. The term "clinical" was coined in the early 1930's by Lightner Witmer to designate a type of psychologist who works with persons in the assessment and resolution of problems of emotion and adjustment. Thus, most Clinical psychologists are professionals in the sense that they apply principles of behavior. They are not psychiatrists, as some have presumed. They use nonmedical means, such as psychotherapy and behavior modification, to change behavior and to solve people's problems. Clinical psychologists often function as academicians and scientists; they teach and conduct research, and many have several part-time jobs in which they relate their professional, scientific and scholarly interests. They are most often found in schools, hospitals, mental health centers, colleges, and in private practice.

Another significant group of psychologists is made up of Experimental psychologists, who function most often as scientists or academicians. While it is true that all psychologists are experimental because they have been trained as scientists, the term is frequently reserved for those who conduct basic research in behavioral processes. Most often, this is done in laboratories connected with academic institutions. Nevertheless, many experimentalists are becoming, to some degree, professionals acting as consultants to businesses and industries. For example, the design of industrial machines to best fit the capabilities of their operators is known as the field of Engineering psychology. Most Engineering psychologists are Experimental psychologists functioning in a professional role.

Numerous other types of psychologists could be discussed. However, there is a growing opinion within the profession that there is, in reality, only one type of psychologist, not many. While their interest in various areas of behavior may differ, they are all in agreement that the empirical study of basic behavioral processes provides the foundation for applied efforts to change behavior. Further, while a given psychologist may spend more or less time in consultation or basic research, all are interested primarily in persons and their problems.

In summary, psychologists are academicians, scientists, and professionals who attempt to understand and influence behavior in all its manifestations. While men have always studied each other's actions, psychology has only recently been recognized as a separate discipline; thus, persons known as psychologists have been in existence only a little more than seventy-five years.

## WHO ARE THE CHRISTIANS?

Just as there have been numerous attempts to define psychology, so have there been many definitions of Christianity. Perhaps the simple assertion that a Christian is one who has faith in Jesus Christ would receive common approval even if there was disagreement over its implications. The early Christian word for "fish," *ichthus*, sums up this definition. The letters stand for the simple statement of faith that He is "Jesus Christ, Son of God, Saviour."

There would probably also be wide agreement with the statement that a person's Christian faith should affect his or her behavior. Supposedly, faith in Jesus Christ influences the actions and daily work of the Christian. This is as it should be, in spite of the fact that Wentz (1963) and others have reported that over half their samples indicate they felt no relationship between their faith and their business life. The Christian is one who *has* faith and *does* work. The rhythm of the Christian life moves back and forth between worship which renews faith and work which expresses faith. As Wentz (1963) states, "the Christian finds himself moving between his sources in Christ and his services in the world" (p. 66).

The emphasis is subsumed under the Christian doctrine of "vocation" or "calling." In times past, "calling" has been a term applied only to those who became ministers or pastors; this is a misunderstanding of the issue. It is the Christian conviction that all men are called to live by their faith in God, through Christ, which gives them the understanding that they are the children of God. As LeFevre (1958) suggests:

> Christian are "called". They are called to the Christian life, to a Christian vocation in a larger sense, at the same time that they may feel themselves to be called to some specialized vocation such as law, medicine, preaching or teaching. A particular profession can be a calling from God only because it is possible to exercise the more general calling, that of living the Christian life, within it (p. 14).

Thus the Christian vocation consists of living life as a child of God within one's chosen occupation.

Four biblical metaphors that have been used to describe the vocation of the Christian are: "servant," "light," "salt," and "soldier."

**395**

They are offered here as a possible model for our later discussion of the psychologist-Christian.

Jesus pictured himself as a servant and often encouraged his disciples to follow him in serving their fellow men (Mark 10:43–44). Thus, the first way of working out one's calling is to be a servant. Matthew 25:40 explicitly suggests that to meet the needs of a neighbor is to serve God. Philippians implies that the characteristics of such service should include a love for people, require sacrifice of oneself, be based on identifying with the needs of others, and result in direct help (Wentz, 1963).

The second metaphor for Christian action is "light." "You are the light of the world," Jesus told his followers (Matthew 5:14). The implication is that the Christian by his goodness is to lead others to faith in Christ. It suggests that the Christian will behave in such a manner that others will admire him and/or inquire as to his motives. In all things and experiences he will defer to faith and will attempt to live out the implications of his faith. As Wentz (1963) suggests, "the layman ministers by relating secular things to God....His actions try to show that Christ's death has somehow made these things look different" (p. 98).

"Salt" is the third term for Christian behavior. Jesus told his followers they were the "salt of the earth" (Matthew 5:13). It is a term that suggests seasoning—thus making food taste better by permeation. Like salt scattered over meat, Christians are dispersed over the activities of the modern world. In the daily events of home, work, and play the Christian will be found actively involved in witnessing to his faith, working to make things become as they should be.

The last metaphor for the Christian life is that of "soldier" (II Timothy 2:3–4). Soldiering involves one in active efforts to make Christ the Lord of activities and situations, regardless of the suffering that results when success does not come easily. This aspect of the work of the Christian implies that one is in tension with his environment and is engaged in a struggle to change things. The old hymn "Onward Christian Soldiers" speaks of many of these issues.

These are four qualities of the Christian's behavior. They are metaphors rather than concrete prescriptions, because the precise acts of Christians are impossible to predict. Similarly, it is difficult to describe the types of occupations in which Christians can be found. It is now agreed that all Christians are called to live the Christian life and that any occupation which allows a person to excercise his calling as a child of God is acceptable. This was certainly Martin Luther's intent in his doctrines of "vocation" and the "priesthood of all believers." Work is what Christians do to fulfill their calling.

This suggests the specific concern of this essay: What does it mean to be a psychologist-Christian?

## WHO ARE THE PSYCHOLOGIST-CHRISTIANS?

Commitment to Christian beliefs might be expected to influence one's choice of and specialization within a particular occupation. Clement (1969) proposed five ways in which the faith can be expressed in the life of a psychologist. He suggested that the psychologist can integrate faith: (1) intrapersonally; (2) professionally or scientifically; (3) experimentally; (4) theoretically; and (5) interprofessionally.

Intrapersonal integration refers to the influence of faith on vocational choice and on beliefs. As Christian, it is important for persons to feel that by becoming psychologists they can obey God's call to be his children. As LeFevre (1958) notes:

> Should we feel that we could no longer be Christians within our particular profession or that we could better exercise our responsibility as Christians within another calling, other things being equal, we would feel a strong inward pressure to relinquish our present work and to seek some other (p. 14).

Thus, we might expect to find persons who chose to become psychologists because that profession offered them a way to fulfill their Christian calling.

Another aspect of intrapersonal integration concerns the area of personal belief. One would expect to find, among psychologist-Christians, persons for whom faith continued to be a live option and persons whose faith was well integrated with their knowledge of psychology. While their faith would not be free from doubt, they would, nevertheless, have come to some basic resolution of the science-religion issues. Their faith would be "mature" in the sense that Allport (1960) indicated when he suggested that mature faith included a "unifying philosophy of life" which consciously integrated all of one's experience. Such would be the character of the faith of the psychologist-Christian who attempted intrapersonal integration.

The theological training of a particular psychologist might provide a rough indication of attempts at this sort of integration. Both the first and second presidents of APA, G. Stanley Hall and G. T. Ladd, studied for the ministry before becoming psychologists. Contemporary psychologists such as Adrian Van Kaam, Carl Rogers and Rollo May have also had theological training. In their survey, Vayhinger and Cox (1970) found 392 members in the 1963-1966 Directories of APA who had received theological degrees. This was just under two percent of the total membership. Table 1 assesses the degree to which these psychologists with theological training were represented in the various divisions of APA. It reports these results for a five percent random sample of seventeen of the divisions.

TABLE 1

INCIDENCE OF PSYCHOLOGISTS WITH PREVIOUS THEOLOGICAL TRAINING
AMONG MEMBERS OF SEVENTEEN APA DIVISIONS

| Division | N. in Division | N. in Sample | Psychologists with Previous Theological Training (%) |
|---|---|---|---|
| HIGHEST THIRD | | | |
| Teaching | 1773 | 115 | 5 (4.34) |
| Personality-Social | 3086 | 199 | 5 (2.51) |
| Clinical | 2905 | 143 | 6 (4.20) |
| Educational | 2107 | 106 | 7 (6.60) |
| Counseling | 1479 | 74 | 6 (8.12) |
| Sub Total | 11350 | 637 | 29 (5.15) |
| MIDDLE THIRD | | | |
| Evaluation-Measurement | 828 | 48 | 1 (2.08) |
| Physiological-Comparative | 510 | 27 | 1 (3.70) |
| Consulting | 510 | 25 | 1 (4.00) |
| Industrial | 834 | 40 | 1 (2.50) |
| School | 847 | 41 | 1 (2.44) |
| Psychotherapy | 1021 | 51 | 1 (1.96) |
| Sub Total | 4550 | 232 | 6 (2.78) |
| LOWEST THIRD | | | |
| Experimental | 1061 | 56 | 0 (0.00) |
| Developmental | 810 | 45 | 0 (0.00) |
| Psychological Study of Social Issues | 1405 | 72 | 0 (0.00) |
| Public Service | 497 | 25 | 0 (0.00) |
| Military | 334 | 17 | 0 (0.00) |
| Engineering | 360 | 27 | 0 (0.00) |
| Sub Total | 4467 | 242 | 0 (0.00) |
| Grand Total | 20307 | 1111 | 35 (2.49) |

It is to be noted that psychologists normally belong to more than one division and that the above data do not control this factor. Also, divisions were grouped into thirds according to the relative number of psychologists that had previous theological training. The respective percentages of psychologists having had such training in the highest, middle, and lowest groups of divisions were 5.00%, 2.78% and 0.04%. A Chi Square analysis of these differences indicated that the lowest group differed significantly from each other.

The division groupings are of interest. There is a tendency for more service-oriented psychologists to have had theological training. However, this inference is not entirely appropriate in view of the fact that among members of divisions such as Teaching, Personality-Social, and Evaluation-Measurement there was a higher incidence of theological training. Again, divisions such as the Psychological Study of Social Issues and Psychologists in Public Service are among those with the least incidence of such training.

The overall average of 2.4% is similar to the 2% figure of Vayhinger and Cox (1970).

Vayhinger and Cox (1970) found that the majority of the 246 who returned questionnaires sent to them considered themselves to be psychologists with theological training rather than vice versa. Thus, their primary role identification was with psychology. Yet their religious concern was indicated by the fact that over eighty percent of them continued to be interested in the relationship between psychology and theology. Sixty-two percent had retained membership in their denominations and ninety percent were active members of local churches. While these data are not conclusive, it does suggest that among these psychologists there was a continuing concern with faith and an interest in relating their faith to that which they had learned in psychology.

No doubt we would make a serious correlation-causation error if we assumed that we had selected all the psychologist-Christians merely by relying on previous theological training. By examining a person's background, we can, at most, say that at one time the issues of faith were important enough for that person to devote serious study to them. That there are others to whom faith was of equal importance and who did not pursue such study cannot be denied. At best, it could be assumed that, for many Christians, psychology becomes the culturally prescribed channel through which they dynamically resolve the conflicts of their development and express the tenets of their faith. This is Erikson's (1958) view of vocational choice and personal integration, wherein a person finds himself and his God through socially acceptable work. The autobiographical method, the collection and examination of diaries, letters, interviews and other personal documents, is best used to detect such people since the ways in which these issues are resolved and expressed are so unique.

Very little of a confessional nature has been written by psychologists. Meehl, et al. (1958) probably provides the closest thing there is to an affirmation of the faith of a psychologist, although, even here, the authors who are psychologists are not clearly distinguished from those who are theologians. Both Havens (1964) and Pruyser (1968) note that the psychologist must himself act as a participant in order to relate Christianity to psychology. He must at least admit the possibility that God exists, in order to conduct valid research in the psychology of religion. Thus, the psychologist who is also a Christian should have a distinct advantage over nonbelieving psychologists who also seek to understand religion. His efforts will be "faith seeking understanding" and will thus have a greater possibility of being valid. In the eighty percent of the psychologists from the Vayhinger and Cox (1970) survey who expressed continued interest in relating psychology and theology, we could expect to find sincere, ongoing efforts at this type of intrapersonal integration.

The metaphor that comes closest to expressing this type of integration is that of "light." Personal faith remains vital to the believer who chooses psychology as an avenue for expressing his calling to be a child of God. These motivations bring new insight, or light, to that person's life.

The second type of integration of faith and vocation suggested by Clement (1969) is in the practice of one's vocation. Since psychology has been designated a profession, a science and an academic discipline, this would mean integration of the Christian faith with professional tasks, scientific endeavors, and scholarly activities.

No doubt the classic metaphor for day-to-day activity within the Christian life is that of "servant." The Christian is to respond to others by being good to his neighbor, i.e., by loving mercy and doing justly (Micah 6:8). This is Christian service. The actual meaning of this on the job becomes the problem, for as Barbour (1963) said, "Being a Christian geologist does not mean finding oil on church property. It means serving God and man in the daily work of geology" (p. 11). Certainly the same is true for psychology.

At one level, working in a religious setting such as a church college, hospital, or seminary could be considered an example of this type of integration. In order to assess the incidence of such vocational placement among psychologists, a five percent random sample of the membership of seventeen of the divisions of APA was surveyed. Table 2 is a report of this survey.

TABLE 2

INCIDENCE OF PSYCHOLOGISTS WORKING IN
RELIGIOUS SETTING AMONG SEVENTEEN DIVISIONS
OF THE AMERICAN PSYCHOLOGICAL ASSOCIATION (1968)

| Division | N. in Division | N. in Sample | Working in Religious Setting (%) |
|---|---|---|---|
| Clinical | 2905 | 143 | 7  (4.89) |
| Consulting | 510 | 25 | 11  (4.00) |
| Counseling | 1479 | 74 | 0  (0.00) |
| Developmental | 810 | 45 | 5(11.11) |
| Educational | 2107 | 106 | 6  (5.66) |
| Engineering | 360 | 27 | 0  (0.00) |
| Evaluation-Measurement | 828 | 48 | 2  (4.16) |
| Experimental | 1061 | 56 | 0  (0.00) |
| Industrial | 834 | 40 | 0  (0.00) |
| Military | 334 | 17 | 2  (6.06) |
| Personality-Social | 3086 | 199 | 13  (6.53) |
| Physiological-Comparative | 510 | 27 | 2  (7.41) |
| Psychological Study of Social Issues | 1405 | 72 | 2  (2.77) |
| Psychotherapy | 1021 | 51 | 2  (3.92) |
| Public Service | 497 | 25 | 0  (0.00) |
| School | 847 | 41 | 0  (0.00) |
| Teaching | 1773 | 115 | 6  (5.21) |
| TOTAL | 20,307 | 1,111 | 48  (4.32) |

Again, the above results are confounded by the fact that a particular psychologist may appear on more than one membership list. Nevertheless, it seems safe to say that about one in twenty-five psychologists actually work in a setting which could be considered religious. These vary from veterans' social service organizations under the auspices of a religious body to church-related colleges and universities. As would be expected, there were no such placements among Engineering, Industrial, Military, or Public psychologists. However, it is puzzling that there were no "religious placements" among Counseling and School psychologists, especially in view of the fact that there is a vast network of parochial elementary and secondary schools in the United States, and there are numerous church-sponsored counseling centers.

In the Vayhinger and Cox (1970) survey, over twenty-seven percent of those with previous theological training were counselors or professors in religious settings. Thus, we can conclude that there is a much greater tendency to work in a religious setting if one has had theological training than if one has not. In the present survey it is of interest to note the various kinds of psychologists that work in religious settings. They range from Physiological-Comparative to Personality-

**401**

Social to Developmental psychologists. A cursory survey indicates that many of them were instructors in church-related colleges and universities.

Of course the content of a man's work is probably more important than the context. What the psychologist-Christian does is more crucial than where he does it. The integration of faith and profession refers to the teaching, consulting, and researching activities of psychologists as well as to the more obviously service-related tasks of counseling.

Clark (1957) reports that while many students enter graduate study in psychology with the thought of helping people, they often become interested in other roles such as research and teaching. Many psychologists combine clinical, research, and academic tasks. Within themselves these psychologists exemplify the tripartite nature of psychology as a profession, a science, and an academic discipline. The integration of faith with practice should apply to these teaching, researching, and consulting activities as well as the more obviously service-oriented tasks of counseling.

The day of valueless counseling is over, and, as London (1964) points out, all psychotherapy has its "morals." The psychologist-Christian will certainly be interested in helping people, but will also be concerned with the kinds of persons his patients become in the process. How the psychologist-Christian behaves with reference to problems that arise cannot be explicitly stated, but that he will relate his faith to his decisions is a foregone conclusion. This is true in spite of London's (1964) assertion that "psychotherapists must finally appeal to science to justify these activities, just as ministers appeal to revelation" (p. 130).

A further issue in this regard is the relationship between the search for self-understanding in counseling and the Christian view of life. Roberts (1950) and Tillich (1952) are theologians who have considered these issues. Tweedie (1961, 1963) is illustrative of psychologists who have written on these matters. He has explicitly related the thinking of Viktor Frankl's Logotherapy to the Christian faith and has indicated how he attempts to integrate a person's search for meaning with the communication of the gospel. Many psychologist-Christians are interested in relating faith to clinical procedures.

The teaching of psychology is usually done at the undergraduate level. While there is a great need for psychologists in church-related institutions of higher learning and while we have noted that many theologically trained psychologists work in such settings, most psychologist-Christians do not work in these situations. They teach instead in state-supported or nonreligious private schools. It is important to consider the ways in which personal faith influences teaching. LeFevre (1958) suggests that faith should affect the method and the assumptions with which the professor works. He notes Allport's concern for the "total person" and suggests that the Christian teacher will not reduce man to less than he is or imply that a full understanding of man can be had with stimulus-response, cause-effect principles. While LeFevre may oversimplify the issue, he is probably correct in suggesting that the psychologist-Christian teacher will present his material within a framework which views man as self-conscious, free, goal-directed, value-determined, and capable of response to God. Many of the humanistic psychologists make these assumptions even though they may not state them in theological terms (cf. Rogers, 1961; Jourard, 1963).

Concerning research, several points could be made. First, the traditional distinction between pure and applied science is no longer seen as a dichotomy but as a continuum. Basic research is now much more easily perceived as providing the foundation for later applications of psychological principles to human problems. Thus, the "servant" motivation of the psychologist-Christian could be implicit in experimentation that had no obvious connection with social or individual problems if that research could be conceived as providing knowledge for later use in solving these problems. A concern for service to persons would be implicit or explicit.

However, it could be that knowledge for knowledge's sake is itself a worthy goal for the psychologist-Christian. As Barbour (1963) asserts, "The Christian is called not only to serve human need but to seek truth" (p. 39). This is based on the faith that nature is God's creation and that man is to have dominion over all the things on earth. The search for truth, regardless of whether it has practical meaning, enhances this dominion by increasing understanding. Some psychologists may elect to work in a secular rather than religious setting because of their Christian conviction that in the secular setting they have more resources and equipment for discovering truth. This is often true because of the responsibility of the Christian intellectual to be more than adequate in his chosen field of study. Therefore, the Christian's task is to search for truth with the best tools available.

The metaphor of "soldier" probably best fits this activity of the psychologist-Christian in the sense that he is actively pursuing, through research and study, the God-given task of transcending the world through knowledge, which makes man less subject to finitude and better able to relate to the divine.

Finally, psychology must be concerned with the rights of persons who serve as subjects in research projects (APA, 1967). Issues such as manipulation, harmful results, secrecy, and deception are important. While ethics and values are not solely Christian virtues, the psychologist-Christian conceives of others as children of God and thus respects the dignity of persons in his investigation.

Overall, the integration of faith in professional, scientific, and academic practice could be understood through the metaphor of "salt." In a wide variety of tasks psychologist-Christians attempting this type of integration are indeed seasoning their environments with their faith.

Integration through research in the psychology of religious behavior is a third means by which the influence of faith can be expressed in the work of the psychologist. There is a long tradition of such interest, beginning with G. Stanley Hall's extensive surveys of religious conversions in adolescence (1891, 1904). With his 1902 Gifford lectures, William James stimulated enough interest in the field for a *Journal of Religious Psychology and Education* (Hall, 1905) to be published. Dittes (1969b) reports that almost one-fourth of APA's presidents have been concerned with the study of religion at some point in their careers. However, according to Strunk (1959), who wrote a historical survey of the field, interest in this area nearly disappeared in the period between 1920 and 1940, and religion became a taboo topic (cf. Douglas, 1966).

The survey reported in Table 3 seems to indicate that interest in the psychological study of religion is still at a low ebb. Herein, the seventeen APA divisions referred to before are examined in five percent random samples of their memberships for the listing of religion as an area of interest. About one and one-third psychologists in a hundred express interest in the psychology of religion. There appears to be a significantly greater percentage of psychologists in such divisions as Teaching, Personality-Social, Physiological-Comparative, and Public Service. These are combinations which do not seem to have logical relationships. Even here, expressed interest is rare and appears in less than one in twenty psychologists.

TABLE 3

INCIDENCE OF PSYCHOLOGISTS REPORTING
INTEREST IN RELIGION AMONG 17 APA DIVISIONS

| Division | N. in Division | N. in Sample | Psychologists reporting interest in religion |
|---|---|---|---|
| HIGHEST | | | |
| Teaching | 1773 | 115 | 5 (4.34) |
| Personality-Social | 3086 | 199 | 4 (2.01) |
| Clinical | 2905 | 143 | 1 (0.69) |
| Educational | 2107 | 106 | 2 (1.89) |
| Counseling | 1479 | 74 | 6 (8.12) |
| Sub Total | 11350 | 637 | 11 (1.79) |
| MIDDLE | | | |
| Evaluation-Measurement | 829 | 48 | 0 (0.00) |
| Physiological-Comparative | 510 | 27 | 1 (3.70) |
| Consulting | 510 | 25 | 0 (0.00) |
| Industrial | 834 | 40 | 0 (0.00) |
| School | 847 | 41 | 0 (2.44) |
| Psychotherapy | 1021 | 51 | 0 (1.96) |
| Sub Total | 4550 | 232 | 1 (0.62) |
| LOWEST | | | |
| Experimental | 1061 | 56 | 0 (0.00) |
| Developmental | 810 | 45 | 0 (0.00) |
| Psychological Study of Social Issues | 1405 | 72 | 1 (1.38) |
| Public Service | 497 | 25 | 1 (4.00) |
| Military | 334 | 17 | 0 (0.00) |
| Engineering | 360 | 27 | 0 (0.00) |
| Sub Total | 4467 | 242 | 2 (0.90) |
| GRAND TOTAL | 20307 | 1111 | 14 (1.10) |

A possible explanation for the dearth of listed interests among psychologists is that these interests might be subsumed under other areas. Hiltner (1959) and Gregory (1959) noted that interest in the psychology of religion, in the early part of the century, became divided into the religious education and pastoral counseling movements. Thus, we might find concern for the psychological study of religion subsumed under Educational psychology, Counseling or Developmental psychology, or it may be under Personality or Social psychology. This last division was one in which a high percentage of psychologists were interested. Finally, Philosophical psychology or Cognitive processes could be other listed areas under which an interest in psychology and religion might be subsumed. Pruyser (1968) illustrates the latter point in his discussion of basic processes, e.g., cognition and emotion, in the religious experience.

Yet there is evidence that there has been a renewed concern in the 1960's. Some of the organizations which are stimulating research and writing within this area are The Society for the Scientific Study of Religion, The Catholic Psychological Association, The *Lumen Vitae* International Commission of Religious Psychology, and The Christian Association for Psychological Studies. A symposium on religious psychology was reintroduced into the program of the Fifteenth International Congress of Psychology in Brussels (1957) after an absence of 30 years. In 1961 the *Journal for the Scientific Study of Religion* began publication.

Some contemporary researchers in this area are Strunk (1958), Clark (1969), Allport and Ross (1967), Gorsuch (1968), King (1967), and Spilka, Armatas, and Nussbaum (1965). Strunk (1958) investigated motivations in the choice of a religious vocation; Clark (1969) studied the relationship of drug experiences to religious experience; Allport and Ross (1967) compared prejudice with the type of value a person placed on religion; Gorsuch (1968) analyzed adjective descriptions of God; King (1967) attempted to measure the religious dimension; Spilka, Armatas, and Nussbaum (1965) factor-analyzed the concept of God; Godin (1965) gathered together several studies on religious development; and Argyle (1958) summarized research on the differences among people who participate in religious activities. These efforts could be conceived as "faith seeking understanding," in the words of Augustine. The behavior of these psychologist-Christians could be understood by the metaphor of "light" in the sense that it illuminates religious experience.

A type of integration closely related to research in the psychology of religion is conceptual, theoretical integration. Theologians such as Tillich (1952) and Outler (1954) addressed themselves to this, but few psychologists have done so. Among those who did were early writers such as William James (*The Varieties of Religious Experience,* 1902) and G. Stanley Hall (*Jesus the Christ in the Light of Psychology,* 1917). Through the years others have written on these issues (e.g., Leuba, 1912; Thouless, 1923; McDougall, 1934; and Clark, 1958). More recently Finch (1967) has attempted an explication of psychoanalytic theory according to the Christian view of man, and Mowrer (1961) has analyzed the distortion of theology by psychological theory. Other writers have considered religious myths and guilt (Pruyser, 1964, 1965), religion and existentialism (Royce, 1962), mental health and salvation (Rogers, 1968), and the relations between psychological and theological methods (Havens, 1968). Oakland (1969) and Van Kaam (1964) have related personality development to religion. These are indices of how a psychologist might express his faith through conceptual or theoretical efforts to integrate his faith and his science. Theorizing, like research, requires interest as a motivating factor. As has also been said in regard to research, the metaphor of "light" is appropriate as an indication of the type of Christian action involved. This is also "faith seeking understanding."

The last mode of integration is that of interprofessional relationships. This refers to relationships psychologists have with religious institutions and religious professionals. It is exemplified by a willingness to consult with churches and to confer with pastors. Many ministers refer persons to psychologists for counseling. There are numerous instances where the psychotherapy of the psychologist complements ·the pastoral counseling of the minister. Cooperative endeavors in church counseling centers are also typical. The Church Federation of Greater Chicago Counseling Center is one example. Psychologists are frequently asked to consult with the boards and agencies of denominations as well.

I have described several ways in which psychologists might consult with and be of service to pastors and churches (Malony, 1970a). In a subsequent article, I have proposed a model for interprofessional relationships between the psychologist and the church (Malony, 1970b). In brief, psychologists can consult or collaborate with the church either in educational efforts or in attempts to ameliorate problems of persons within the church. No doubt, many of the problems of church life can benefit from interprofessional cooperation between a sympathetic psychologist and an open-minded pastor or religious leader.

Some psychologists have tried to analyze church behavior through psychological categories. Dittes (1967) has provided a psychodynamic understanding of the ebb and flow of administering the program of the church while Hites (1965) has summarized the principles of behaviorism as they apply to the tasks of church workers. Barkman (1969) analyzed motivations for missionary service among college students. These are forms of indirect, interprofessional integration of psychology and religion.

Further, many psychologists have been involved in direct vocational counseling for the ministry (e.g., Hunt, 1966). Webb (1968) has constructed an inventory designed to guide students into areas of interest within the ministry. Many studies have been done on ministerial effectiveness and the personality dynamics of ministerial leadership (cf. Menges and Dittes, 1965; Malony, 1964). Dittes (1964) and others have expended a good deal of effort on the construction of the Theological School Inventory (1962), widely used as a guidance tool in theological seminaries.

The metaphor that best fits this type of integration is that of "servant" because, herein, the psychologist uses his skills in service to his faith. In summary, there are many ways in which the faith of the psychologist can influence his behavior. Five possible modes of relating faith to science and the scholarly discipline of psychology have been discussed: intrapersonal, professional, experimental, conceptual, and interprofessional.

## CONCLUSION

Some final comments are in order. This essay has dealt with the problem of relating faith to vocation. The vocation of psychology should be an expression of faith for the Christian who chooses this vocation. Thus, the title of this essay, "The Psychologist-Christian," was selected to emphasize the primacy of faith. The four metaphors of "salt," "soldier," "servant," and "light" were offered as types of expressions of faith. A number of possible behavioral indices of these metaphors were suggested. The critical question is: has this essay fully enumerated these behaviors or determined that even one of the listed behaviors is essential for the life of the psychologist-Christian? In the final analysis, I think the answer to the above question must be "No"—for three reasons.

First, the ideas of Bonhoeffer (1955), among others, regarding "religionless Christianity" have influenced many persons. Many intellectuals, psychologists among them, have become impatient with organized religion. Thus, they may have intentionally chosen to be overtly nonreligious out of Christian conviction. This is paradoxical. Dittes (1969a) wrote about these "religious Nones" and indicated they would assume increasing importance in the decade to come. Persons who express their faith in nonreligious ways would not evidence integration of the types referred to in this essay but might at the same time be psychologist-Christians. They might not be churchmen, work in religious settings, or show interest in the psychology of religion. They might be functioning in positions far removed from organized religion but be believers nevertheless.

Second, there always remains the problem between behavior and motivation. Jesus himself spoke of foolish generations which seek after or look for signs. Smith (1966) represents some modern theologians who suggest that ". . . the manifestation of faith is not simple, but dialectical" (p. 55). By "dialectical" they mean that the inference from behavior to motive is not simple and may, in fact, be absolutely false. For example, human intentions always fall prey to the capriciousness of human life. Therefore, it may be impossible for a man to express his faith in the ways this essay has mentioned. More importantly, the Christian faith is itself an affirmation of hope in the face of meaninglessness. Therefore, faith may be present more in weakness than in strength and more in the absence of a manifestation than its presence. Christian theology has noted that the forgiveness of sin is a greater reality than the power to express one's faith. This does not mean that believers should resign themselves to antinomianism or libertarianism. Nevertheless, it is a recognition that the absence of an overt sign of relationship between the Christian faith and the life of the psychologist may not indicate a lack of faith at all. If this is so, our overt indices would be insensitive to these dialectical distinctions. We might find psychologist-Christians witnessing to their faith in the way they handled failure or suffering, in their persistence at humdrum tasks and meaningless duties, and in their humane solutions for administrative and research problems.

Finally, Allport (1942), among others, insisted on the importance of "personal documents" in understanding the vital issues of personality. These methods include a heavy reliance on autobiographical reports as opposed to inferences based on objective behaviors. Instead of judging overt indices of faith one would need to question a given psychologist concerning his unique expression. The implication is that, ultimately, a man's behavior makes sense to himself irrespective of its consistency in the eyes of others. As Allport insisted, true laws are idiosyncratic, i.e., personal. Comparison of a man to others or to standards is far less important than assessing the degree to which he believes that he has integrated himself around his values. The psychologist-Christian, therefore, may best be understood from within or by listening to him reflect on the relationship of faith and vocation in his own terms. This is not to reject observable criteria for the relationship. It is simply to confess our methodological inadequacies and to allow ample room for unique interpretations. No doubt, autobiographies are the best method for accomplishing this goal and such gross measures as have been discussed herein must pale in importance when compared to such data.

In conclusion, there is a need to reaffirm confidence in the effect of faith on daily work. As has been suggested earlier, in the Christian faith:

"Calling" or "vocation" means primarily the call to acknowledge a relationship to God, and to live in responsible obedience to him wherever one is. Hence it also means a call to a particular task, and response to God in one's daily work (Barbour, 1963, p. 13).

The Christian lives his life as a response. If he happens to be a psychologist, that aspect of his life will be no different; the activities he engages in will be influenced by his faith. As Argyle (1958) states, "The beliefs of the psychologist cannot affect his findings unless he actually cheats, so that there is no special kind of psychologist known as a 'Christian Psychologist'—that would simply be a psychologist who happens to hold certain beliefs" (p. 1).

While by no means suggesting that cheating could characterize the psychologist-Christian, this essay takes issue with Argyle and asserts that the "simple holding of certain beliefs" about Jesus Christ will have distinguishable influences on one's behavior.

## REFERENCES

ALLPORT, G. W. *Becoming: Basic considerations for a science of personality.* New Haven, Connecticut: Yale University Press, 1955.

ALLPORT, G. W. *The Use of Documents in Psychological Science.* New York: Social Science Research Council, 1942, Bulletin 49.

ALLPORT, G. AND ROSS, J. M. Personal religious orientation and prejudice. *Journal of Personality and Social Psychology,* 1967, 5, 432–43.

AMERICAN PSYCHOLOGICAL ASSOCIATION. A *Career in Psychology.* Washington, D.C.: American Psychological Association, 1970 A.

AMERICAN PSYCHOLOGICAL ASSOCIATION. *Casebook on Ethical Standards of Psychologists.* Washington, D. C.: American Psychological Association, 1967.

AMERICAN PSYCHOLOGICAL ASSOCIATION. *1968 Directory.* Washington, D. C.: American Psychological Association, 1968.

ARGYLE, M. *Religious Behaviour.* Glencoe, Illinois: The Free Press, 1958.

BARBOUR, I. C. *Christianity and the Scientist.* New York: Association Press, 1963.

BARKMAN, P. F. *Christian Collegians and Foreign Missions, an Analysis of Relationships.* Monrovia, California: Missions Advanced Research and Communication Center, 1969.

BONHOEFFER, D. *Ethics.* New York: The Macmillan Co., 1955.

BRAUN, J. R., *Clinical Psychology in Transition.* Cleveland, Ohio: Howard Allen, Inc., 1961.

CALHOUN, R. *God and the Day's Work.* New York: Association Press, 1957.

CLARK, K. E. *America's Psychologists.* Washington, D. C.: American Psychological Association, 1957.

CLARK, W. H. *Chemical Ecstasy.* New York: Sheed and Ward, 1969.

CLARK, W. H. *The Psychology of Religion.* New York: Macmillan, 1958.

CLEMENT, P. Integration of psychology and therapy in theory, research and practice. *Newsletter, Corresponding Committee of Fifty, Division 12, APA.* 1969, 6 (11), 12–19.

DITTES, J. E. *Vocational Guidance of Theological Students.* Washington, D. C.: Ministry Studies Board, 1964.

DITTES, J. E. *The Church in the Way.* New York: Scribners, 1967.

DITTES, J. E. Secular religion: Dilemma of churches and researches. *Journal of Religion and Health,* 1969 A, 19 (2), 65–81.

DITTES, J. E. Psychology of Religion. In G. Lindzey and E. Aronson, *The Handbook of Social Psychology,* 2nd edition. Reading, Massachusetts: Addison Wesley, 1969 B, 602–659.

DOUGLAS, W. Religion. In N. L. Farberow (Ed.) *Taboo Topics.* New York: Atherton Press, 1966, 80–95.

ERIKSON, E. H. *Young Man Luther.* New York: W. W. Norton, 1958.

FINCH, J. Some evaluations of Freud's view of man from psychoanalytical perspectives and some implications for a Christian anthropology. Unpublished Ph.D. dissertation, Drew University, 1958.

FINCH, J. Toward a Christian psychology. *Insight: Interdisciplinary studies of man.* 1967, 6 (1), 42–48.

GODIN, A. *Child and Adult Before God.* Chicago: Loyola University Press, 1965.

GORSUCH, R. L. The conceptualization of God as seen in adjective ratings. *Journal for the Scientific Study of Religion,* 1968, 7 (1), 56–64.

GREGORY, W. E. Research and the psychology of religion. In O. Strunk, Jr. *Readings in the Psychology of Religion.* New York: Abingdon Press, 1959, 261–265.

GUILFORD, J. P. *Fields of Psychology* (3rd ed.). N.Y.: D. Van Nostrand Co., Inc., 1966.

HALL, G. S. The moral and religious training of children and adolescents. *The Pedagogical Seminary,* 1891, *1,* 199–210.

HALL, G. S. *Adolescence* (Vol. I and II). New York: D. Appleton, 1904.

HALL, G. S. (Ed.) Editorial. *Journal of Religious Psychology and Education,* 1905, *1,* 1–7.

HALL, G. S. *Jesus, the Christ, in the Light of Psychology* (Vol. I and II). New York: Doubleday, 1917.

HAVENS, J. The participant's vs. the observer's frame of reference in the psychological study of religion. *Journal for the Scientific Study of Religion,* 1964, *3,* 216–226.

HAVENS, J. (Ed.) *Psychology and Religion: a contemporary dialogue.* Princeton, New Jersey: D. Van Nostrand, 1968.

HILTNER, S. The psychological understanding of religion. In O. Strunk, Jr. *Readings in the Psychology of Religion.* New York: Abingdon Press, 1959, 74–104.

HITES, R. W. *The Act of Becoming.* New York: Abingdon Press, 1965.

HOFFMAN, H. (Ed.) *The Ministry and Mental Health.* New York: Association Press, 1960.

HOLLAND, J. L. *The Psychology of Vocational Choice.* Waltham, Massachusetts: Blaisdell Publishing Co., 1966.

HUNT, R. A. A Counseling and Guidance Program Based on Psychological Evaluation of Ministerial Candidates. Unpublished manuscript, Southern Methodist University, 1966.

JAMES, W. *Principles of Psychology.* New York: Holt, 1890.

JAMES, W. *The Varieties of Religious Experience.* New York: The New American Library, 1961.

JOHNSON, H. L. *The Christian as a Businessman.* New York: Association Press, 1964.

JOURARD, S. *Personal Adjustment: An Approach Through the Study of Healthy Personality,* 2nd Edition. New York: The Macmillan Company, 1963.

KING, M. Measuring the religious variable: nine proposed dimensions. *Journal for the Scientific Study of Religion,* 1967, 6 (2), 173–185.

LA POINTE, F. H. Origin and evaluation of the term "psychology." *American Psychologist,* 1970, 25 (7), 640–646.

LeFEVRE, P. D. *The Christian Teacher.* New York: Abingdon Press, 1968.

LEUBA, J. H. *A Psychological Study of Religion.* New York: Macmillan, 1912.

LONDON, P. *The Modes and Morals of Psychotherapy.* New York: Holt, Rinehart and Winston, 1964.

MAITLAND, D. J. "Vocation." In M. Halverson and A. Cohen, *A Handbook of Christian Theology.* New York: Meridian Books, 1958, 371–72.

MALONY, H. N. Human nature, religious beliefs and pastoral care. Unpublished Ph.D. dissertation, George Peabody College, 1964.

# H. N. Malony

MALONY, H. N. When pastor and psychologist meet: a case study in church-community relations. *Theology News and Notes,* 1970 A, *16* (2), 7–9.

MALONY, H. N. Psychology and the church: toward a model for relating. Unpublished manuscript, Fuller Theological Seminary, 1970 B.

McDOUGALL, W. *Religion and the Sciences of Life.* Durham, North Carolina: Duke University Press, 1934.

MEEHL, P., KLANN, R., SCHMEIDING, A., BREIMEIER, K. AND SCHROEDER-SLOMANN, S. *What, Then, Is Man?* St. Louis, Missouri: Concordia Publishing House, 1958.

MENGES, R. J. AND DITTES, J. E. *Psychological Studies of Clergymen.* New York: Thomas Nelson & Sons, 1965.

MOWRER, O. H. *The Crisis in Psychiatry and Religion.* New York: Van Nostrand, 1961.

NATIONAL SCIENCE FOUNDATION. Summary of American Science Manpower, 1968. Washington, D. C.: U.S. Government Printing Office, 1970.

NELSON, J. O. *Work and Vocation.* New York: Harper & Bros., 1954.

OAKLAND, J. A. Symposium: The relation between the Bible and science. *Journal of the American Scientific Affiliation,* 1969, *21* (4), 122.

OUTLER, A. *Psychology and the Christian Message.* New York: Harper & Row, 1954.

PELIKAN, J. J. *The Christian Intellectual.* New York: Harper & Row, 1965.

PRUYSER, P. W. *A Dynamic Psychology of Religion.* New York: Harper & Row, 1968.

PRUYSER, P. Anxiety, guilt and shame in the atonement. *Theology Today,* 1964, *21,* 15–33.

PRUYSER, P. Life and death of a symbol: a history of the Holy Ghost concept and its emblems. In "Myth and Modern Man," special supplement, *McCormick Quarterly,* 1965, *18,* 5–22.

REISMAN, J. M. *The Development of Clinical Psychology.* New York: Appleton-Century-Crofts, 1966.

ROBERTS, D. Psychotherapy and a Christian View of Man. New York: Scribner, 1950.

ROE, A. *The Psychology of Occupations.* New York: John Wiley & Sons, Inc., 1956.

ROGERS, C. *On Becoming a Person.* Cambridge, Massachusetts: The Riverside Press, 1961.

ROGERS, W. R. Order and class in psychopathology and ontology: a challenge to traditional correlations of order to mental health and ultimate reality, and of chaos to mental health and alienation. In P. Homan's (Ed.) *The Dialogue Between Theology and Psychology.* Chicago: University of Chicago Press, 1968, 249–262.

ROYCE, J. R. Psychology, existentialism and religion. *Journal of General Psychology,* 1962, *55,* 8–16.

SHAPLEY, H. (Ed.) *Science Ponders Religion.* New York: Appleton-Century-Crofts, Inc., 1960.

SLOCUM, W. L. *Occupational Careers.* Chicago: Aldine Publishing Co., 1966.

SMITH, R. G. *Secular Christianity.* New York: Harper and Row, 1966.

SPILKA, B., ARMATAS, P. AND NUSSBAUM, J. The concept of God: a factor analytic approach. *Review of Religious Research,* 1956, 6 (1), 28–36.

STEPHENS, J. T. AND LONG, E. R. *The Christian as a Doctor.* New York: Association Press, 1960.

STRUNK, O., JR. Theological students: a study in perceived motives. *Personnel and Guidance Journal,* 1958, 36, 320–322.

STRUNK, O., JR. *Readings in the Psychology of Religion.* New York: Abingdon Press, 1959.

THEOLOGICAL SCHOOL INVENTORY. Washington, D.C.: Ministry Studies Board, 1962.

THOULESS, R. N. *Introduction to the Psychology of Religion.* New York: The Macmillan Co., 1923.

TILLICH, P. *The Courage to Be.* New Haven, Conn.: Yale University Press, 1952.

TWEEDIE, D. F., JR. *Logotherapy and the Christian Faith.* Grand Rapids, Michigan: Baker Book House, 1961.

TWEEDIE, D. F., JR. *The Christian and the Couch.* Grand Rapids, Michigan: Baker Book House, 1963.

VAN KAAM, A. *Religion and Personality.* Englewood Cliffs, New Jersey: Prentice Hall, Inc., 1964.

VAYHINGER, J. M. AND COX, R. H. Study of psychologists holding theological degrees. Unpublished manuscript, Anderson College, 1970.

WEBB, S. *Inventory of Religious Activities and Interests*. Princeton, New Jersey: Educational Testing Service, 1968.

WENTZ, F. K. *The Layman's Role Today*. New York: Abingdon Press, 1963.

WENTZ, F. K. *My Job and My Faith*. New York: Abingdon Press, 1967.

# The Commandment of Love and the Christian Clinical Psychologist

## ROBERT L. PAVELSKY

In recent years there has developed a renewed interest in the dialogue between psychology and theology. This interest is expressing itself in two ways. One way is the psychological investigation of religious phenomena. The other, which is the concern of this study, is the integration of psychology and theology. More particularly, this paper is concerned with integrating Christian theology and clinical psychology, using the concept of love as a basis. It is appropriate to begin with an investigation of the biblical commandment of love recorded in Mark 12:30–31 and to show how this commandment is further developed in other parts of the New Testament. Following biblical investigation of the concept of love, this paper will concern itself with the parallel ideas of love in psychology and psychotherapy. Lastly, this essay will attempt to integrate the coordinate ideas of love in psychology and theology in order to illuminate the potential ministry that exists for the Christian clinical psychologist.

### EXEGESIS OF MARK 12:30-31

Working from the biblical perspective establishes a certain exegetical method to determine the author's intended meaning. In accord with that method the first section of this paper deals with the exegesis of the biblical data dealing with love.

Jesus' commandment of love is recorded in Mark 12:30–31: *kai agapēseis kurion ton theon sou ex holēs tēs kardias sou kai ex holēs tēs psuchēs sou kai ex holēs tēs dianoias sou kai ex holēs tēs ischuos sou. Deutera hautē, agapēseis ton plēsion sou hōs seauton.* This passage is part of Jesus' answer to the scribe's question, "Which commandment is first of all?" In his

Reprinted with permission of author and publisher from:
*Studia Biblica et Theologica*, 1973, 3, 57–65.

answer Jesus reaffirms monotheism, and then issues the commandment to love God and neighbor. The following exegesis is an investigation of this data to determine its intended meaning.

*Agapaō* means "to love, cherish." Here it refers to the love or cherishing of God. Although *agapaō* and *phileō* seem to be used synonymously on occasion (John 18:27; 21:15–17), the force of *phileō* is generally taken to indicate liking—where there is some return for the one liking—while *agapaō* generally indicates a state where there is not necessarily a return to the one loving (Arndt & Gingrich, 1956, pp. 4, 866). Lenski (1946, p. 538) points out that the usage of *agapaō* expresses the love of intelligence and purpose and is far above *phileō*, which would be the love of mere liking or affection. *Agapaō* indicates one's knowledge of the true God and turning to him with one's being.

Because the future indicative *(agapēseis)* is used, some, notably Joseph Fletcher (1966, pp. 69–75), hold that this is not a command, but simply a statement of fact. This overlooks the use of the future tense in legal phraseology. It can substitute for the imperative and express the lawgiver's will (Lenski, 1946, p. 358). The force, then, would be imperative, a command.

In the first part of this verse the recipient is *kurion ton theon sou,* the Lord your God. The following phrases are not condensed, but spread out so that each one would receive separate emphasis. *Ex* is used instead of *en* and the force indicated is "out of," a source, rather than "in," a sphere (Arndt & Gingrich, 1956, p. 257). The four sources of love are *kardia, psuchē, dianoia,* and *ischus.* Each of these four phrases includes *holos*, which means "whole, complete," thus giving the force of being a totality (Arndt & Gingrich, 1956, p. 567).

*Kardia:* This word is not commonly used in secular writings of the Greek Bible period, but is common in the LXX. It can be used to indicate the center and source of the physical life. In this case, however, it indicates the center and source of the whole inner life, with its thinking, feeling, and volition in the natural man as well as the redeemed man. Here too, it is especially used as a source of love (Arndt & Gingrich, 1956, pp. 404–405).

*Psuchē:* Usually this word is used to indicate soul or life. Although it is often difficult to draw distinct lines between the meanings of this many-sided word, here it refers to the "soul" as the seat and center of the inner life of man in its many and varied aspects, especially of the feelings and emotions (Arndt & Gingrich, 1956, p. 90).

*Dianoia:* Here it indicates the source of understanding or intelligence, the mind as the organ of *noein* (Arndt & Gingrich, p. 186), rational reflection or inner contemplation (Arndt & Gingrich, p. 542).

*Ischus:* Here, this word specifically means one's strength rather than power or might (Arndt & Gingrich, p. 384).

This first section might well be simplified as, "You shall love the Lord your God with all that comes out of the center of your whole inner life, which is the source of your thinking and volition, including all that comes out of the center of your inner life, which is the source of your feelings and emotions; with all that comes out of the source of your understanding or intelligence; and with all of the power that comes out of the source of your strength."

In the second part of that section the key words for consideration are *seauton* and *plēsion. Seauton* means "yourself." A person is to measure his love for his neighbor by his love for himself. "Every man naturally loves himself, and all he needs to do is to measure his love for his neighbor by that love for himself" (Lenski, 1946, p. 539). *Plēsion* here means "the one who is near." Our neighbor is the one whom we know and with whom we come into contact, no matter who he may be. This command does not demand love toward those of whose existence one knows nothing (Lenski, 1946, p. 539).

This whole commandment is in answer to an ethical question that one of the scribes asked Jesus. Jesus' answer states the characteristic of the law, namely love. The way that love is to be manifested to God is by one's heart, soul, mind, and strength, which are all varied ways of saying to the "uttermost degree, with all that is within" (Nicoll, 1967, I, p. 424). The love of one's neighbor is to be equal to the love of oneself, and it is added as an application of the first part of the commandment, thereby underlining the truth of the first part (Alford, 1958, I, p. 402). This is especially true if one's neighbor shares his faith.

Indeed, one cannot love God without also loving his brother: "If anyone says, 'I love God,' and hates his brother he is a liar; for he who does not love his brother whom he has seen, cannot love God whom he has not seen. And this commandment we have from him, that he who loves God should love his brother also" (I John 4:20–21). In this passage the brother is the one who also believes that Jesus is the Christ. "Only the believer is the believer's brother; only the reborn is brother to the reborn" (Lenski, 1945, p. 517). Thus, the command takes on particular strength when applied to a neighbor who also happens to be a Christian.

The basic concept of love developed from this commandment is further amplified in the other New Testament writings where it is restated and behaviorally defined.

## LOVE IN THE NEW TESTAMENT

The concept of love in the New Testament is developed out of the sayings of Jesus and the writings of the apostles. In dealing with the sayings of Jesus, one finds that he stands in the moral tradition of the Jewish people. He does, however, demand "love with an exclusiveness which means that all other commands lead up to it and all righteousness finds in it its norm" (Stauffer, 1967, I, p. 44). Jesus indicates that to love God is to be a slave for him (Luke 17:7–10), to base one's whole being on God; conversely, it is to hate and despise all that does not serve God nor come from Him (Matthew 5:29). The great and basic demand of Jesus is to love God and neighbor, but he frees the love of one's neighbor from its previous restriction to compatriots (cf. the Parable of the Good Samaritan, Luke 10:29–37). Jesus even goes so far as to demand love for one's enemies. The emphasis in this love for one's enemies is not "stupidity," but *agapē*. The person is to love "without expecting it to be returned" (Stauffer, 1967, p. 46).

In the writings of the apostles, Paul is representative of the apostolic idea of love. For Paul the loving action of God is revealed in Christ (Romans 5:8). "The eternal love of God becomes in the love of Christ a world changing event of which Paul usually speaks in verbal forms and then always in the aorist" (Stauffer, 1967, p. 49).

Paul takes up the love of neighbors as in Jesus, but emphasizes brotherly love (Galatians 6:10). For him "beloved" (*agapētos*) and "brethen" (*adelphos*) become synonymous terms (I Thessalonias 2:8; Philemon 16). "Decisive definition is given to brotherly love, however, by the cosmic, historical *kairos* (cf. Galatians 6:10; Romans 13:11) which demands it. Brotherly love is the only relevant and forward-looking attitude in this time of decision between the cross and the *telos*....Love builds up (I Corinthians 8:1). It builds the work of the future. *Agapē* stands under the sign of the *telos*. This is the great truth of I Corinthians 13. For this reason love is a heavenly gift surpassing all others..." (Stauffer, 1967, p. 51).

I Corinthians 13 points to love in the *telos*. But Paul also speaks of love for the "now." His guide for Christian conduct is found in Romans 12:9–21, where he speaks of genuine love (*agapē*):

> Let love be genuine; hate what is evil, hold fast to what is good; love one another with brotherly affection; outdo one another in showing honor. Never flag in zeal, be aglow with the Spirit, serve the Lord. Rejoice in your hope, be patient in tribulation, be constant in prayer. Contribute to the needs of the saints, practice hospitality.
>
> Bless those who persecute you; bless and do not curse them. Rejoice with those who rejoice, weep with those who weep. Live in harmony

with one another; do not be haughty, but associate with the lowly; never be conceited. Repay no one evil for evil, but take thought for what is noble in the sight of all. If possible, so far as it depends upon you, live peaceably with all. Beloved, never avenge yourselves, but leave it to the wrath of God; for it is written, "Vengeance is mine, I will repay, says the Lord." No, "if your enemy is hungry, feed him; if he is thirsty, give him drink; for by so doing you will heap burning coals upon his head." Do not be overcome by evil, but overcome evil with good.

Among the other New Testament writers there is no lack of consensus with Paul with the exception perhaps of James. James and Paul have often been placed at opposite ends of a continuum. This probably need not be so, as far as James' concept of love is concerned. He seems to be in perfect accord with Paul. For James the living force of faith is dependent on its activity in love. Love implies:

> primarily fulfilling immediate duties to our neighbors and not with-holding rights from laborers (James 5:1ff). It means taking seriously the basic affirmation that all who love God are my brothers and are not to be put in the background even though they come shabbily dressed (James 2:14), since God has thought them good enough to be called into his *basileia* (James 2:8). This love is the work of faith, demanded by it, made possible by it, and counted for righteousness on account of it (James 2:14ff). The love for God which stands behind all brotherly love is also a work of faith. It holds fast to God, to His commands in the warfare against passions and to His promises in the long periods of tribulation and affliction. It is strong in *hupomonē* (James 1:2ff).

New Testament love, then, is an outgoing response to God and neighbor. The horizontal relationship, person to person, expresses the vertical relationship, person to God. The love of neighbor includes certain behavior that can indicate the existence of love for God. This New Testament evidence, then, points to a love of God which manifests itself by love of neighbor. One does not exist without the other. Also, in order to love one's neighbor one must love oneself. So the New Testament data on love points to love of self, love of neighbor, and love of God.

## THE CONCEPT OF LOVE IN PSYCHOLOGY

The science of psychology also concerns itself with the concept of love, even though the psychologist seldom, if ever, calls it love. Having delved into some of the facets of love, psychology is faced with many descriptions and definitions of this phenomenon. The following four writers represent trends within the varied descriptions and defini-tions. Harry Stack Sullivan states that, "when the satisfaction or the security of another person becomes as significant to one as one's own security, then the state of love exists" (Shonle, 1969, p. 227). According to Erich Fromm love is expressed within five relationships: (1) Brotherly love, oriented toward all mankind; (2) Parental love, oriented toward growth and well being of one's child; (3) Erotic love, investment of self in happiness of another and self; (4) Self love, which is equivalent to self-acceptance and self-esteem, and (5) Love of God, which arises from a man's need and is not a response to God's love (Goldenson, 1970, I, p. 708). Unfortunately, psychologists have focused their attention on parental love and erotic love to the exclusion of the three other categories that Fromm mentions. William Glasser has written about two basic psychological needs: "The need to love and be loved and the need to feel that we are worthwhile to ourselves and to others" (Glasser, 1965, p. 9). And Freud stated that the goals of the healthy personality were to love and to work.

Goldenson has extrapolated from the various theories of love the following basic ingredients: "(a) feelings of empathy, the ability to enter into the feelings and share the experiences of the loved one; (b) profound concern for the welfare, happiness and growth of the loved one; (c) pleasure in actively devoting thought, energy, time, and all other resources to the loved one; and (d) full acceptance of the uniqueness and the individuality of the loved one and his right to be himself" (Goldenson, p. 708).

Although Rogers does not label it love, he also has outlined three central ingredients of a therapeutic relationship that correspond with some of the things already noted. The first of these is accurate empathy or sensitivity to current feelings of another and verbal facility to communicate this understanding. This accurate empathy corresponds to Goldenson's first point as well as Paul's statement of true Christian love in Romans 12:15, "Rejoice with those who rejoice, weep with those who weep." Second is non-possessive warmth or the acceptance of another without imposing conditions. This corresponds to Goldenson's fourth point as well as to Paul in Romans 12:10, "Love one another with brotherly affection" or in I Corinthians 13:5, "Love does not insist on its own way." The last ingredient is genuineness or knowledge of self at any given moment—a prerequisite for neighbor-love in the second part of the commandment of love. If these three elements—accurate empathy, non-possessive warmth, and genuineness—are present in a relationship, then the persons experiencing them will grow toward realizing their potential.

The research on these three characteristics proves that they are of therapeutic value in healing damaged psyches or repairing human relationships (Truax & Carkhuff, 1967). The point is that these three characteristics, which have been defined and extensively researched by Rogers and others (although they are not labeled as love by Rogers, et al.), are essentially the same elements that Goldenson writes about, and are included in the biblical concept of love. Therefore, the three characteristics can be used as a measure or indication of love. This is not an attempt to use psychology to validate the Bible, but is simply to point out that psychology has come to a point where certain characteristics of psychological theories correspond to the biblical concept of love and therefore may be used as indicators, not validators, of biblical love.

Truax and Carkhuff (1967, pp. 31–33) are careful to note that these three characteristics are not restricted only to the client-centered approach of counseling and psychotherapy, but are present in all major forms of counseling and psychotherapy. In fact Fiedler (Truax & Carkhuff, p. 28) has shown that, "skilled or experienced therapists of divergent schools of psychotherapy agreed on the elements of an ideal therapeutic relationship, which they characterized as being warm, accepting and understanding."

From the information so far, several summary statements may be made: (1) The Bible commands love of God with all that one is capable of giving; (2) The love of God is manifested by neighborly love; (3) Neither 1 nor 2 can be accomplished apart from the other; (4) The Bible defines love as specific behavior; (5) There are corresponding concepts of love in the field of psychology which are: accurate empathy, non-possessive warmth, and genuineness; (6) That which I have called love in psychology is a central ingredient in the healing of persons; (7) That which I have called love in psychology lays the foundation for neighbor-love.

## THE POTENTIAL MINISTRY OF THE CHRISTIAN CLINICAL PSYCHOLOGIST

Although research has shown that psychologists in clinical practice employ the characteristics that correspond to the biblical notion of love, these same psychologists rarely say that they are loving or teaching others to love. This is also true for the Christian clinical psychologist. In fact, "if psychologists are personally religious, they tend to keep this fact aseptically separate from their professional work" (Havens, 1968, p. 1). It seems to me that the Christian clinical psychologist needs an understanding of behavior that includes a therapeutic model which actively considers God and his command of love in its approach. Therein lies the potential of love in Christian psychology: acceptance of the fact that it is the employment of God's tools that creates healing.

The basis of this potential starts with the fall of man. As recorded in Genesis, it resulted in four major separations. First, man was separated from God—the spiritual division. Second, ever since the fall man is separated from himself—the psychological division, which is the basic psychosis. Third, man is separated from nature (Schaeffer, 1970, p. 67). Fourth, man is separated from members of his own species. These are the divisions which form the predicament of man. These are the areas where healing must occur. Complete healing will come only at the Parousia, but since the Kingdom of God is present here and now (Ladd, 1964), we may expect substantial healing as a reality here and now (Schaeffer, p. 67).

The Christian clinical psychologist already practices in the spheres of the psychological and sociological dimensions, already promotes substantial healing of the divisions between man and himself and between man and other men. It seems, then, that the Christian practitioner ought to consider seriously Oden's concept of the incognito Christ: "The last parable of Jesus before his crucifixion (Matthew 25:31–46) impinges powerfully upon our thoughts on the presence of Christ amid the therapeutic process. For it focuses upon the inconspicuous service to a troubled neighbor as a ministry in which Christ himself is a hidden participant" (Oden, 1967, p. 98).

It seems to me that Oden is correct in the inference that the Christian clinical psychologist is actually serving in an active ministry, in which Christ is present, and bringing others into a closer relationship to God. I also believe that Oden is correct when he says,

> Psychotherapy is a process of "welcoming" the stranger—he who is estranged from himself, away from home, wandering in an alien land—into a relationship of trust, care, and mutual respect. Psychotherapy is a process of "visiting" the imprisoned, those chained to their own compulsions, shackled by self-deception, pacing the narrow cells of guilt and anxiety, and talking with them about their prospects for freedom. Psychotherapy is a process of "clothing" the nakedness of those who have been stripped by illness of all pretense and self-respect, whose emptiness and failure have been laid bare to the world, who have been deprived of all protective devices, masks, barriers, and hiding places. Psychotherapy is a special way of "calling" upon and sojourning within the inner frame of reference of those who wait under the conditions of helpless sickness, yearning daily for the day of deliverance (Oden, 1967, pp. 101–102).

The Christian clinical psychologist is actively ministering in the horizontal relationship, thus enabling a person to love himself, and thus producing substantial healing of the psychological division. This, then, provides a basis to fulfill the self-love portion of the commandment of love, "You shall love your neighbor *as yourself.*" The Christian psychologist enables a person to love others, thus producing substantial healing of the sociological division. This, then, provides a basis to fulfill the neighbor-love portion of the commandment of love, "You shall *love your neighbor* as yourself." It brings a person halfway to the self-actualization of his humanity. Full self-actualization would be fulfilling the whole of the commandment of love: love of self, love of others, and love of God.

On the human level one may bring another person into the Kingdom of God by one of two approaches. First, one might present the knowledge of God to another, thus establishing a vertical relationship (Turnbull, 1967, p. 148), and then might use that relationship to establish a horizontal one. This is the option generally employed in the pastoral ministry. Secondly, one might enable another person to love himself and others, thus establishing a horizontal relationship, and then using this newly established horizontal relationship as a foundation to develop a vertical one (Oden, 1967, pp. 98–99). The second option provides potential for the Christian practitioner, who can promote substantial healing of the psychological and sociological divisions which make up part of the predicament of man. Through psychotherapy the Christian clinical psychologist can enable persons to attain greater awareness of themselves (genuineness), and to react to others with greater empathy and warmth. Genuineness, empathy, and warmth are those psychological definitions that correspond to the biblical concept of love. So the Christian can actually minister to others through the commandment of love. By employing love, God's tool for healing, the Christian psychologist can promote substantial healing of the spiritual division and enhance the person's capacity for establishing communion with God.

Thus, the application of love by the Christian can result in the building of supports upon which the divisions of the fall may encounter substantial healing and mankind might achieve true humanity—community with God and neighbor.

## REFERENCES

ALFORD, H. *The Greek Testament.* Chicago: Moody Press, 1958.
ARNDT, W. F. AND GINGRICH, F. W., trans. and eds. *A Greek English Lexicon of the New Testament.* Chicago: University of Chicago, 1956.
FLETCHER, J. *Situation Ethics.* Philadelphia: Westminster Press, 1966.
GLASSER, W. *Reality Therapy.* New York: Harper and Row, 1965.
GOLDENSON, R. M. *The Encyclopedia of Human Behavior.* New York: Doubleday, 1970.
HAVENS, J., ed. *Psychology and Religion.* San Francisco: Van Nostrand, 1968.

LADD, G. E. *Jesus and the Kingdom*. New York: Harper and Row, 1964.

LENSKI, R. C. H. *Interpretation of the Epistles of St. Peter, St. John, and St. Jude*. Minneapolis: Augsburg, 1945.

LENSKI, R. C. H. *The Interpretation of St. Mark's Gospel*. Minneapolis: Augsburg, 1946.

NICOLL, W. R. *The Expositor's Greek Testament*. Grand Rapids: Eerdmans, 1967.

ODEN, T. C. *Contemporary Theology and Psychotherapy*. Philadelphia: Westminster Press, 1967.

SCHAEFFER, F. A. *Pollution and the Death of Man*. Wheaton: Tyndale, 1970.

SHONLE, R. C., ed. *Marriage and Family in the Modern World*. New York: Crowell, 1969.

STAUFFER, E. *"agapaō." Theological Dictionary of the New Testament*. Gerhard Kittel, ed. G. W. Bromiley, trans. Grand Rapids: Wm. B. Eerdmans Publishing Co., 1967.

SULLIVAN, H. S. In Ruth C. Shonle, ed. *Marriage and Family in the Modern World*. New York: Crowell, 1969.

TRUAX, C. B. AND CARKHUFF, R. R. *Toward Effective Counseling and Psychotherapy*. Chicago: Aldine, 1967.

TURNBULL, R. G. In *Baker's Dictionary of Practical Theology*. Grand Rapids: Baker Book House, 1967.

# Christianity and Psychology: Contradictory or Complementary?

## CRAIG W. ELLISON

Psychology has grown into a giant during the 20th century. No other age has witnessed such intense concentration upon the nature and functioning of *homo sapiens*. Psychological terminology has become an integral part of the common vernacular and psychological concepts strongly influence contemporary thought.

Both psychology and Christianity deal intimately with the phenomenon of man. Psychology attempts to gather data inductively, formulate theories, and arrive at a probabilistic and naturalistically based understanding of the human being. Christianity, as revealed in the coherent whole of the Scriptures, proceeds deductively from the supernatural *a priori* of special creation in God's image. The psychologist generally concentrates upon man's attitudes and behavior as they relate to each other as empirical phenomena, while Christianity roots these behaviors and attitudes in the framework of man's inherent relationship and responsibility to God.

Psychology has challenged contemporary Christianity to a more involved understanding of men as human beings, while debunking or ignoring much of the basic Christian system in the process. Complementarity between psychology and Christianity is implicit in an honest investigation of the common subject matter, man, while conflict is implied in the necessary embrace of (antithetical) philosophical positions prior to the accumulation of data and during interpretation of those data.

We would like to consider briefly some of these areas of conflict as well as some dimensions of potential complementarity.

Reprinted with permission of author and publisher from:
*Journal of the American Scientific Affiliation*, 1972, 24(4), 130–134.

## AREAS OF CONFLICT

### Content Domain

Although the root word for psychology, *psuchē*, originally meant "soul," modern psychology generally rejects consideration of any dimension except the scientifically verifiable. This is particularly true for the American psychological tradition. Strict adherence to the scientific methodology of the physical sciences has characterized the approaches of bio-chemical reductionists and behaviorists like John Watson and B. F. Skinner.[1] While the full impact of bio-chemical reductionism is yet to be felt, the behavioristic approach has widely influenced contemporary theory and therapy.

The basic behavioristic assumption is that man is the product of environmental reinforcement patterns. Consequently, there is no need to talk about internal psychic or spiritual realities except as a convenient intermediate construct which is to be considered only as a temporary equation. An increasing number of therapists, such as J. Wolpe,[2] are using behavior therapy which is based primarily upon conditioning techniques and ignores the consideration of internal dynamics as valid data *per se*. One has only to consider derogatory attitudes toward the parapsychological (ESP, telepathy, etc.) to realize that even psychologists who are not strict behaviorists are firm adherents to naturalistic explanation of the solely empirical domain.

Adoption of this system can be criticized as potentially inadequate because it is a closed system which precludes information from human experience that may be metaphysically real and psychically meaningful but not empirically testable. A further problem is that the atmosphere created is one of despair. Man becomes hollow, the fated victim of impersonal environmental forces. His values, hopes, concept of responsibility and purpose, self-awareness, and wishes become debunked and are treated as irrelevant except as they are the product of environmental input. Man, as we have known him historically, and as we still experience awareness of ourselves, disappears in dutiful compliance to the method.

The essential conflict with Christianity, then, stems from an over-emphasis on empirically-oriented methodology which may result in the rejection of valid content because it doesn't fit the method. Such naturalistic disregard for man's spiritual dimension, if it really is an integral part of man's nature, produces a truncated understanding of man's nature. Such an approach might be expected to be long on analysis and short on solutions.

**425**

On the other hand, Christianity contributes unnecessarily to the conflict over acceptable data if valid factual information, which complementarily fills in the Scriptural framework, is rejected. Ignorance of man's basic psychic and biological character presents us with an unrealistic picture of ourselves, which does not quite match our experience of daily living. Such data need to be retained in a more harmonious interpretative framework, and not be rejected because they aren't strictly spiritual. For example, the Christian must basically accept the fact of sin as the cause of personal and interpersonal disruption. Given man's fallen state, one of imperfection even after redemption, he must seek to employ all truths at his disposal in the correction of his condition. To suggest that everything would be corrected if the whole world were simply saved overlooks our need for sanctification. Consequently, we must bring spiritual truth to bear on the personal and social conditions we face as fallen men, while at the same time helping to meet those very real needs of incarnated humanity. Failure to acknowledge the interrelated needs of the whole man leaves us bewildered and frustrated as we try to understand and help ourselves and others as parts of God's creation.

The Christian simply suggests that when all of truth is known, that is, when and if all information about man (including the non-empirical) is validly gathered, accurately interpreted and integrated, man will be seen as a creature fundamentally related to God the Creator. Incorporated in that complete perspective is an interrelationship of psychological and spiritual realities which makes man so unique. The burden of the proof, at this point, is upon psychological theories and hypotheses being presented as part of an incomplete, inductive system. Attempts to discredit the "open" Christian system (one which incorporates both empirical and non-empirical dimensions in the understanding of man) must be based on *a priori* philosophical differences because such conclusive attacks cannot be made purely on the basis of probabilistic, incomplete evidence.

## Philosophical Assumptions

Twentieth-century man must stand in awe at the physical and technological achievements produced through the application of scientific methodology. For many, however, this awe has been extended into worship of scientific objectivity. The result has been the debunking of any "non-objective" experience as non-valid, irrational or irrelevant.

This decision to admit only the objective, or empirically obtained, data as meaningful and valid knowledge is a philosophical choice which reflects a naturalistic value system. All psychological conclusions, particularly those about man's essential nature, are drawn on the basis of subjective presuppositions. Even the choice of areas and techniques for experimentation reflect subjective preferences, "non-scientific" value judgments, and philosophical assumptions of the experimenter. The point is that science cannot be totally objective as long as man is in the picture, and should not be represented as such. It *is* more objective than any other system man has devised, and should be used with an awareness of initial assumptions.

To begin one's investigation of man with acceptance of his spiritually-rooted origins becomes, then, an equally valid starting point. The test of these initial value preferences is in their ability to describe adequately the essential expriences of men, and to prescribe effective avenues for enduring personal and interpersonal growth.

One basic assumption which permeates contemporary social science and conflicts with the Scriptural view of man is that man is a passive, environmentally determined being.[3] While there is strong evidence which supports the *influence* of genetic and environmental input upon our development as persons, complete acceptance of this viewpoint, within the naturalistic system, forces us into despairing fatalism. Without the reality of the choosing self and its correlate of personal responsibility, we might just as well authenticate ourselves by committing suicide because it conceivably is the only act of freedom available (cf. Jaspers). In effect, decisionless man is man without responsibility, Hollow Man.

Popularization of the deterministic motif has led to increasing personal and social irresponsibility. Indeed, William Glasser[4] suggests that the basic pathology *is* a failure to take responsibility; that psychological health and interpersonal relatedness can only come as we choose and accept our momentary responsibilities. Viktor Frankl[5] argues that meaning in life is gained only as one fulfills his unique tasks in life. The Christian position adds that those tasks stem from our fundamental relationship of creature to Creator.

Failure to accept our positions as active agents capable of producing changes as we act responsibly has resulted in increased feelings of despair and alienation, in which the main effort becomes an attempt to blame others for our condition. Such projective defenses breed conflict, and the pathology of chronic bitterness. Certainly other people and conditions are to blame some of the time, but we are responsible for how we accept and creatively utilize those conditions.

The hope of man is in the possibility of making decisions, and in the supreme decision of establishing and maintaining a relationship with God. Indeed, the very act of salvation necessitates complementary responses and responsbilities on the part of both God and man. Living the Christian life necessitates a responsible, active process of "living life with a due sense of purpose, understanding what the will of the Lord is" (Eph. 5:15–17). In this view, cause and effect relationships—including prior choices—influence man but do not irrevocably and impersonally determine him. Irresponsibility becomes a choice, not a necessary condition.

In this conception of man as an active, determining, responsible and whole being, we find complementarity between the Scriptures and psychology. This is particularly so with more humanistically-oriented schools of psychology represented by such figures as Gordon Allport,[6] Viktor Frankl,[7] Rollo May,[8] Erich Fromm[9] and Abraham Maslow.[10] Complementarity, of course, does not imply complete agreement.

## AREAS OF COMPLEMENTARITY

Three areas in which psychology and Christianity are potentially complementary are the necessity of transparency for personal and inter-personal growth, the necessity to transcend a mechanical existence through the experience of Love in I-Thou relatedness, and the necessity for a sense of significance or positive self-esteem. These concepts, while distinct, are so interrelated that they will be treated as a whole.

The recent rise of encounter or T-groups indicates a growing concern for honest and genuine relationships with one's self and with others. Although such groups have been criticized as to their long-range effects outside of the encounter groups, their positive emphasis has been upon the establishment of transparent relationships. Such transparency represents the peak of psychological growth. It necessitates painful honesty with one's self and the courage to brave the potential pain of non-defensive interpersonal relationships.[11]

Christianity both adheres to and supplements this basic concept, differing to some extent in the method of achievement. The foundation of transparency, according to Christianity, is the willingness to open ourselves to God, in all of our personhood, and to maintain that genuine relatedness through daily response to God's Spirit and precepts in the written Word. Openness to God leads in turn to transparent, caring relationships with others. If such interpersonal relationships do not exist we have decided ourselves as to our being open to and knowing God (I John 4:7–12).

These relationships of transparency are primarily maintainable as we replace inadequate and debilitating emotional defenses by self-acceptance rooted in God's unconditional love and acceptance of us as persons (though perhaps still unregenerate), because we are made in His image (Ps. 139:13–16). Use of these ego-defenses leads only to self-deception, hence sin, and disrupts our relationships with both God and our fellow man. According to God's Word we are to root our self-significance in the Love and Relationships which God has directed to man as His special Creation.

One of the ego-defensive tactics which modern man seems to employ frequently and which also seems to be a reflection of responsibility-relieving determinism, is the attempt to deny the responsibility for negative (moral) actions by blaming the guilt on others or on one's background. Such techniques of repression and projection rob men of the opportunity to grow, and are ultimately psychically and societally destructive.

Any notion of responsibility must grapple with the experience of guilt. It seems that man was not made to live with guilt. It causes disintegration and alienation. Blaming others or denying its existence does not remove real guilt, but simply prevents an honest acceptance of one's self with resultant transparency. Guilt, therefore, should be a signal for confession and restitution. It should not be lugged around unresolved . . . indeed it cannot be if one is to experience the freedom of transparency.

Some psychologists have severely criticized Christianity for the concept of sin and guilt.[12] They state that these notions are psychologically disintegrative—which they are—while ignoring the complementary concept of the restorative power of horizontal and vertical confession. It might be nice if we could abolish guilt, and act as we please, but if man is a moral creature, as Christianity states and history seems to support, we might better deal with the abolition of guilt through appropriate prevention and restitution.

Clearly, there is imagined guilt, as Freud suggested, which is the product of manipulative and narrow subcultural interests. This guilt is definitely destructive and unnecessarily binds persons. There is also real guilt, with real moral culpability, which is the product of the destructive transgression of God's commandments, according to Christianity. Thus, there *should* be the experience of guilt, it seems, if one murders another or commits adultery. These actions are basically disintegrative, egocentric, and destructive breaches of God's lawful and harmonious relationships. Indeed, persons who have no such moral sensitivity and do not experience the feeling of guilt for obviously destructive actions are designated as sociopaths by the psychologist.

Guilt, of course, does not refer solely to some heinous act of murder, but seems to apply to any intentional act which would alienate us from God and from one another. If we try to embezzle or cattily criticize another, or don't engage in an act of compassion when given the opportunity, we are choosing actions which in their egocentricity alienate us from loving, caring, growth relationships with God and fellow men. God calls such actions sin, and the experience of anyone indicates the kinds of interpersonal barriers and personal callouses which form if proper responsibility is not assumed.

God has provided us with a remarkable set of restorative tools in the respective acts of forgiving and confessing sin (guilt). In our increasingly mechanical world where man can seemingly escape becoming a hollow machine only by his loving and transparent embrace of personal I-Thou relationships, these acts are essential. The Illinois psychologist, O. Hobart Mowrer, has written extensively about the need for confession between human beings as the way to intra and inter-personal wholeness.[13]

In the Sermon on the Mount, we read that we are not to offer gifts of worship to God if we remember that we have wronged our brother, until we ask his forgiveness. By this cathartic act of humanity we restore both our horizontal and vertical relationships. By removing the barrier of pride we become transparent and whole again.

The other side of the coin, given in Matthew 6, is that God will "forgive our trespasses [breaches of our relationship to God] as we forgive those who trespass against us." Such forgiveness is granted with the awareness that we are not better than our brother (Phil. 2:3). Such an attitude and action again prevents the establishment of disintegrative barriers which rob us of our wholeness and ability to be open. According to this verse, the implication is that if we don't voluntarily forgive those who have sinned against us we become as morally guilty as they are, because we prevent continued growth between ourselves as persons and God.

The refusal to ask for or to grant forgiveness also underlies a basically unhealthy ego-defense of a person who is not willing to see himself as he is, or must use manipulation to relate to others. In order to defend himself from exposure this nontransparent person usually engages in chronic criticism of others, verbally "murdering" them. The irony, of course, is that the faults he sees in others are his own in disguise. The result is a person constantly in internal and external conflict who is unable to relate in a positively intimate, growth-producing manner to either other human beings or God. Such a person is indeed isolated, and even a profession of belief in God becomes questionable as to its reality (1 John 4:7–8).

The tragedy of this defensive posture is that such self-deception and non-transparency is an attempt to preserve one's integrity and establish himself as a significant, worthwhile human being . . . something which God has already assured us of unconditionally by his willingness to love us through the personal relationship of Christ.

This search for a base of self-significance or esteem, so critical to each individual and recognized as such by both Christianity and psychology,[14] becomes increasingly crucial in an impersonal and mechanistic world. Material accumulation and the ability to exercise power through manipulation or productivity have become major secular indices of personal worthwhileness. The result is an ever-spiralling pressure for the individual to produce and obtain material goods. The standard of self-significance has increasingly become *what* one has or does, rather than *who* one is as a person, apart from power and position.

When modern man's reference point becomes the mechanical, material world, and he is also told by naturalistic philosophy that he is simply a chance product of impersonal forces, he begins to lose the capacity to relate to other human beings in a growth-giving manner.[15] Indeed, through such object fixation, as divorce statistics seem to corroborate, other people are transformed into objects, satisfiers of immediate need which can be thrown away or traded in. The endurance needed to develop accepting and meaningful relationships with others seems archaic in a society devoted to the economy of planned obsolescence and object satisfaction.

Some men, however, have begun to sense that their fixation on superficial I-It relations is an embrace of death, leading only to alienation and loss of personhood. They have begun to suspect such a foundation can be neither satisfying nor enduring because it is an attempt to gain significance by not facing one's human dilemma honestly. It is understandable that apart from a significant relationship to God, unable to find a reason for significance in a mechanical world, men begin to identify subtly with that which seems most significant and powerful. In the psychic frenzy of the search for some reassurance that he is, in fact, alive and worthwhile, modern man proceeds to destroy himself in object relationships or in reaction to I-It relationships through equally non-growth-oriented alternatives, such as the apparently autistic use of drugs, which ironically are also impersonal forces. Both of these instances are attempts to escape the psychic boredom and spiritual hollowness of secular man isolated from significance in God.

If, indeed, man's significance is foundationally related to an honest appraisal of his identity stemming from the context of being made in the image of God, these alternatives will not provide lasting worth. Nor will other reactive attempts at affirming Life, the natural response to recognition of the slow death inherent in the embrace of materialism. The natural response to the recognition that one is inwardly dying in this mechanical world is to affirm his aliveness through intense passion, demonstrated in acts of violence or in sexual preoccupation. Both acts seem to confer personal meaning, but each precludes the formation of intimate and enduring relatedness due to their manipulative and autistic character. They further alienate searching secular man from his only permanent source of Life and significance, because they are not founded upon the acceptance of an unconditional Love and personal relatedness. To many modern men, God seems dead, but it is only because they have embraced alternatives of death in their separation from God and alienation from men.

Into this desperate search of modern man for significance, wholeness, and Life must come Christians as *persons* (not statistic counters), who are willing to accept and relate to their unsaved counterparts as *persons*, in a manner which is reflective of God's caring love. According to Christianity the base of each person's significance is rooted in the purpose and relationship engendered in each person's special creaturehood and released in the Personal Encounter of Salvation through the person of Christ. Each Christian must function, then, as a bridge, as an involved friend introducing an even more Involved Friend.

The contemporary Christian then must be aware of some of the psychic needs and motivations of his secular counterpart. He must try to understand others as persons and relate Christ to their whole person, through his own involvement as a transparent individual. Evangelism from a distance will not meet the desperate cry of modern man for his personhood.

## REFERENCES

[1]B. F. Skinner, *Beyond Freedom and Dignity,* New York: Alfred Knopf, 1972.
[2]J. Wolpe, *The Conditioning Therapies,* New York: Holt, Rinehart, and Winston, 1964.
[3]For a sophisticated treatment of the determinism controversy and perspectives which suggest that at two levels there is no necessary conflict with Scripture, the reader is referred to *What, Then, Is Man?* by Paul Meehl, *et. al* (Concordia Publishing Co., 1958), especially ch. 3, 7, and 8, and to *The Clockwork Image,* by Donald M. MacKay (Inter-Varsity Press, 1974).
[4]William Glasser, *Reality Therapy,* New York: Harper and Row, 1965.
[5]Viktor Frankl, *The Doctor and the Soul,* New York: Bantam Books, 1969.
[6]Gordon Allport, *The Individual and His Religion,* New York: MacMillan Co., 1960.
[7]Victor Frankl, *Man's Search For Meaning,* New York: Washington Square Press, 1963.

⁸Rollo May, *Love and Will*, New York: W. W. Norton & Co., 1969.
⁹Erich Fromm, *The Revolution of Hope*, New York: Bantam Books, 1968.
¹⁰Abraham Maslow, *The Psychology of Science*, Chicago: Regnery Co., 1969.
¹¹Sidney Jourard, *The Transparent Self*, Princeton: Van Nostrand Co., 1964.
¹²Albert Ellis, "There is No Place for the Concept of Sin in Psychotherapy", *J. Counsel. Psych.*, 1960, 7, 188–192.
¹³O. H. Mowrer, *The New Group Therapy*, Princeton: Van Nostrand 1964.
¹⁴Nathaniel Branden, *The Psychology of Self-Esteem*, New York: Bantam Books, 1971 and Craig W. Ellison (Ed.), *Christian Perspectives on Self-Esteem*, Christian Association for Psychological Studies, 1976.
¹⁵Erich Fromm, *The Art of Loving*, New York: Harper and Row, 1962.
¹⁶C. G. Jung, *The Undiscovered Self*, Boston: Little, Brown & Co., 1958.

# Supplementary Reading

This book of contemporary readings can be combined profitably with three other kinds of material: (1) classics in the psychology of religion; (2) surveys written by single authors; and (3) other books of readings. A select, but not exhaustive, list of such recommended sources is given below.

*Classics:*

James, W. *The varieties of religious experience.* (Gifford Lectures, 1901 - 1902). New York: The New American Library, 1958.

> The best-known early effort in the field, this seminal volume calls for both phenomenological and descriptive studies of religious experience. Its numerous case studies distinguish between once-born (healthy-minded) and twice-born (sick-minded) persons. Considerable attention was focussed on the psychological study of religion as a result of this work. It is an indispensable basis for all contemporary study in the field.

Freud, S. *The future of an illusion.* Garden City, New York: Doubleday and Co., 1964.

> In this volume Freud applied his reductionistic hypothesis to religious phenomena. Religion was for him wish fulfillment directed toward a projected father figure. Instead of illusory thinking Freud emphasized need for responsibility and social ethics. He proposed a thesis that continues in force today.

Glock, C. Y. and Hammond, P. E. *Beyond the classics: Essays in the scientific study of religion.* New York: Harper and Row, 1973.

> This volume provides current views concerning the contributions of a number of behavioral and social scientists who have written about religion. Among the articles are essays on the work of William James and Sigmund Freud. Others discuss the work of Durkheim, Weber, Parsons, Niebuhr and Marx. This is an important survey of the historical trends and current applications that resulted from these early theoreticians.

*Surveys:*

Argyle, M. *Religious behavior.* London: Routledge and Kegan Paul, 1958.

In this text Argyle surveys objective indices of religiousness in Britain and the USA. He makes no mention of religion as experienced from within or as contained in self-reports. He is a contemporary example of those who have emphasized behavioral manifestations. Age, sex, personality, and environmental factors are considered.

Clark, W. H. *The psychology of religion.* New York: The Macmillan Co., 1958.

Clark's book indicated in the late 1950's a rebirth of interest in the psychology of religion. It is a comprehensive text in the tradition of William James. However, unlike James, Clark shows an appreciation for objective group research in addition to case studies. A valuable historical survey and suggestive study aids are included.

Johnson, P. E. *Psychology of religion.* New York: Abingdon Press, 1945.

This is one of the earliest systematic attempts to incorporate the findings of developmental and social psychology into an understanding of religion. Johnson was part of the "interpersonalism" of Boston University in the 1940's and 1950's. His contribution was to ground religious experience in the valuing, social person.

Oates, W. E. *The psychology of religion.* Waco, Texas: Word Books, Publishers, 1973.

An encyclopedic treatise on religious experience, this is written from the viewpoint of a practicing churchman. Thus, a number of theological categories (such as sin and revelation) are discussed. Oates also provides a provocative psychological analysis of faith.

Pruyser, P. W. *A dynamic psychology of religion.* New York: Harper and Row, 1968.

Writing from the distinctive thematic orientation of psychoanalytic ego psychology, Pruyser focusses uniquely on the way in which religious persons relate to themselves, things and ideas, and to other persons, within the context of "objective relationships." He considers basic mental processes, such as sensation, perception, mentation, emotion, and their relationships to religious experience.

Yinger, J. M. *The scientific study of religion.* New York: Macmillan Co., 1970.

This cross-disciplinary approach to the study of religions places emphasis on a field theory of religion. The thesis is especially influenced by sociology, although Yinger attends to individual needs and other psychological roots of religion. This volume provides a helpful overview of religious phenomena.

Thouless, R. H. *An introduction to the psychology of religion.* Third edition. London: Cambridge University Press, 1971.

In this revised edition of a book first published in 1923, Thouless attempts to incorporate much of the research which utilized quantitative methods. He nevertheless remains convinced of the value of rational and phenomenological approaches to religion. Like James he includes anecdotal material that enhances the readability of the volume.

*Readings:*

Brown, L. B. (Ed.) *Psychology and religion: Selected readings.* Baltimore: Penguin Books, Inc., 1973.

This collection of articles emphasizes objective research of religious behavior, belief, experience, involvement, and consequential effects. It covers the 1950's and 1960's and is a reliable survey of the studies of psychologists during this period.

Strunk, O., Jr. (Ed.) *Readings in the psychology of religion.* New York: Abingdon Press, 1955.

A comprehensive collection of early writings, this book also contains selections dating up to the late 1940's. Freud, Pratt, Starbuck, Leuba, and Hall are included. This is probably the best one-volume historical introduction to the field of the psychology of religion.

Strunk, O., Jr. (Ed.) *The psychology of religion: Historical and interpretive readings.* New York: Abingdon Press, 1971.

This is a reprint of several of the major articles in Strunk's earlier work. Newer articles by Pruyser, Spilka, and Strunk are included. Spilka's article "Toward an empirical psychology of religion" is not reprinted elsewhere, although the other two are included in the present volume.

Beit-Hallahmi, B. *Research in religious behavior: Selected readings.* Monterey, California: Brooks-Cole, 1973.

This volume includes seventeen empirical studies by psychologists and sociologists since 1962. These investigations pertain to religious socialization, attitudes, beliefs, personal adjustment and religion, religious experience, and political behavior. While not a comprehensive volume, it typifies current research.

Capps, Donald, Rambo, Lewis and Ranoshoff, Paul (Eds.) *The psychology of religion: a guide to information services.* Detroit: Gale Research Co., 1976.

A guide to articles and books dating primarily from 1950, this is organized around six dimensions of religion—mythological, ritual, experiential, dispositional, social, and directional. It includes a separate section on general work. This valuable annotated bibliography covers the activity of the last three decades.

One final volume that does not fit any of the above categories is:

Havens, J. (Ed.) *Psychology and religion: A contemporary dialogue.* Princeton, New Jersey: D. Van Nostrand and Company, 1968.

This is the transcript of conversations between a number of the leading theorists in the field.

# Author Index

# Author Index

# Author Index

# Author Index

**444**

# Author Index

# Subject Index

# Subject Index

Fall of man, 420, 426; healing, 421-422; psychological division, 421; separation from nature, 421; separation of man from man, 421; spiritual division, 421
Forgiveness, 430
Freudian psychology, 36; methods of research in, 41-48; theoretical constructions of, 36-40
Fuller Theological Seminary Graduate School of Psychology, 89
*Future of an Illusion,* 43, 57, 231

Gestalt approach to the psychology of religion, 80
God-image: development of, 222; locus of control, 209-224; and self-esteem, 209-224; and social action, 222
Guilt, 429-430

Harding-Schuman Scale, 131
Healthy-minded religion, 234, 239
Heston Personal Adjustment Inventory, 175
Historical religion, 164-168
Holiness, 164
Hospital chaplain, 63-64
Hospital psychiatry, 62-68
Hostility and obedience to authority, 191
Humanistic psychology: creativity, 315; description of, 30-34; holistic approach to personality, 307-309; individual freedom, 309-311; and psychotherapy, 315-316; and self-actualization, 313, 315, 317; and self-realization, 315; and values, 311-315; view of man, 403
Humanistic psychology of religion, 316-319; peak-experience, 317; search for meaning, 317
Humanitarianism and religiousness, 184-186
Hysteria and conversion, 241, 243-244, 247

*Idea of the Holy,* 69, 80, 235
Identity crisis and conversion, 260
Ideological dimension of religion, 94
Ideographic approach to research, 41-44, 48
Illusion and religious belief, 59
Indiscriminate type, 128-135, 155; religious experience of, 330
Indiscriminately antireligious or non-religious type, 127, 128, 135, 155, 157
Indiscriminately proreligious type, 127-128, 133, 135, 148, 150, 153, 155, 157, 182
*Individual and His Religion,* 139, 232, 236

Industrial psychologists, religiosity of, 386
Infancy and the search for conservation, 271-272
Institutionalized orientation, 180
Integrity crisis and conversion, 260
Intellectual dimension of religion, 94
Intelligence and conversion, 241, 243-244
Interiorized orientation, 180
Intolerance. *See* Prejudice and religion
Intrinsic-extrinsic orientation. *See* Extrinsic-intrinsic orientation
Intrinsic motivation, 94-95
Intrinsic orientation to religion, definition of, 121, 140-144
Inventory of Religious Belief, 193
*Ischus,* 416
Ivory tower effect, 384

Jamesian psychology, 36, 54-56; methods of research in, 41-48; theoretical constructions of, 36-40
*Jesus the Christ in the Light of Psychology,* 406
Jewish academicians and religious commitment, 384
*Journal for the Scientific Study of Religion,* 32, 89, 406
*Journal of Applied Behavioral Analysis,* 352
*Journal of Pastoral Counseling,* 173
*Journal of Religious Psychology and Education,* 404
*Journal of Religious Psychology, Including Its Anthropological and Social Aspects,* 19, 78

*Kairos,* 417
*Kardia,* 415
Knowledge: descriptive, 109-111; unitive, 109-111

Liberalism and social ethics, 185
Locus of control: external, 210, 214; and God-images, 209-224; internal, 215
Logotherapy, 313-314, 402
Love, 414-423, 432; and behavior, 420; biblical concept of, 414-418; and healing, 420; need for, 419; New Testament view of, 417-418; of God, 416, 418-420, 422; of neighbor, 418-422; of self, 416, 418-419, 421
Love Oriented—Other Centered Scale, 151, 155
*Lumen Vitae* International Commission of Religious Psychology, 406
Lutheran Church and personality modes, 205, 207

# Subject Index

# Subject Index